Feminism in Islam

Feminism in Islam

Secular and Religious Convergences

MARGOT BADRAN

ONEWORLD

OXFORD

A Oneworld Book

Published by Oneworld Publications 2009
Reprinted 2011

Copyright © Margot Badran 2009

ISBN 978–1–85168–556–1

Typeset by Jayvee, Trivandrum, India
Cover design by Lyn Davies
Printed and bound in the USA by Thomson Shore Inc.

Oneworld Publications
185 Banbury Road
Oxford OX2 7AR
England

CONTENTS

Part II: Muslim World – Late Twentieth to Twenty-First
Centuries: Widening Circles, New Directions

PREFACE

A few years ago it was suggested that I bring together some of my scattered work for publication in a single volume. With the expanding interest in feminism in Muslim societies, both from within the academy and the broader public, I decided to heed the suggestion. Here I present a selection of articles on feminism in Egypt and in other Muslim societies that I have written over the past two decades. Many chapters originated as articles that grew out of public lectures and conference papers presented in different parts of the world, with many subsequently published in scholarly journals and books. A few chapters originated as essays appearing in the popular press and specialized bulletins. Several of the recent pieces have also appeared on the web in various e-publications. One article is published here for the first time, and another appears for the first time in English. I draw attention in endnotes to some of my work which I would like to have included here but could not for lack of space.

Placing works such as these, which were composed at different moments, in juxtaposition, can provoke new readings of the feminist past and present. The works gathered are "of their time," giving windows into the building of women's history, and as such can, in part, be read historiographically. I have indicated dates of prior publication or original presentation of works at the end of each chapter. I would also like to note that in a collection of pieces that were composed over a long span of time and that were meant to stand on their own, a certain repetition and overlap is to be expected. I have gathered this material together in a single book in the hope that it will be of interest to students, scholars, and a wider readership.

Assembling this collection has brought back memories stretching back over a long time, evoking moments of enthusiasm and hope, of anxiety and despair, as I proceeded from enthusiastic graduate student along the bumpy road forward at a moment when some of us were trying to create the new discipline of women's studies and the new related field of women's history. By now women's studies is a well-established discipline, or "inter-disciplinary discipline" that has secured its place within Middle East studies and Islamic studies in the United States, parts of the Middle East, and the broader Muslim world. New questions continue to be asked and new methodologies to be devised as the field is constantly expanding and is being taken into exciting new directions by both established scholars and newer generations entering the field. It is a rich and dynamic time.

It is a happy moment when bringing a book to close to thank people for their contributions on many fronts. Because the list is too long and the line goes back so far, I issue a most sincere general thanks to colleagues who have been an important part of this broad venture and to friends and family who have sustained me along the way. I would, however, like remember and thank those who helped me early on. I mention with gratitude three mentors – all male, it will be noted, in the days when women were scarce in the academy – who played a role in facilitating the rise of women's studies by encouraging their persistent students: Carl Brown, who taught me at Harvard; Yehia Hashim, who taught me at al-Azhar University; and Albert Hourani, who taught me much as he supervised my D.Phil. thesis at Oxford University. While at Oxford I joined the Women's Social Anthropology Group which Shirley Ardener organized, and would like to register my appreciation to her and to the other women who provided a special atmosphere in which to share our work. I also express gratitude to the many women I met and worked with through the Berkshire Women's History Conference (revived as an organization in the 1960s) for creating vibrant triennial conferences where we shared work at a moment when the academy at large, including area studies, was wary of the new venture of women's history and women's studies, and which still continues to be at the cutting-edge of women's studies. While doing research on first-wave feminism in Egypt countless women helped me in so many ways and were living, remembering repositories of precious knowledge of the feminist past. In particular here I point to Saiza Nabarawi and Hawa Idriss (a long list of others is recounted in my book *Feminists, Islam, and Nation: Gender and the*

Making of Modern Egypt). Over the years in Egypt and elsewhere in the Muslim world, colleagues who form part of the large *silsila* (chain) of women's studies scholars and feminist activists are too numerous to even begin to name in this preface. I have, however, acknowledged many in chapter endnotes.

I have received numerous fellowships and grants for which I remain grateful and am pleased to acknowledge. These include awards from the American Research Center in Egypt, the American Institute for Yemeni Studies, the Research Institute in Turkey, the Fulbright Foundation (for several fellowships, the most recent being the New Century Scholars award), the Annenberg Research Institute, the Ford Foundation, the Institute for the Study of Islam in the Modern World (ISIM), the Rockefeller Center at Bellagio, the Social Science Research Council, and the United States Institute of Peace. The support of these organizations has greatly facilitated my research in numerous locations and provided me with extended opportunities to engage in the give and take of exchange and debate that has been invaluable to me and for which I thank all who were most generous with their time and ideas.

I have put the finishing touches on this book while a senior fellow at the Prince Alwaleed Center for Muslim–Christian Understanding at Georgetown University and would like to thank John Esposito, the founding director, and other colleagues for their welcome and the staff for their help. At Georgetown University Library I thank Brenda Bickett, bibliographer for Islamic & Middle Eastern studies, for her swift and generous assistance, as well as the many reference librarians who steered me in the right direction. In bringing this book to a close it gives me special pleasure to thank those at Oneworld Publications who have made this book a reality: Novin Doostdar, founder and director of Oneworld, for his enthusiasm for this project and more broadly for playing a key role in supporting the development of Islamic studies, and within this field, women's and gender studies; Omid Safi, supportive scholar and energetic series editor at Oneworld; Mike Harpley, commissioning editor, Kate Smith, production manager, and Mary Starkey, the sensitive copy-editor of this volume. Finally, I thank Ali Badran, who has been there from the very beginning of my engagement with feminism.

INTRODUCTION

Feminism in Islam has become the focus of intensified academic interest as well as a topic of public concern on an unprecedented scale in recent years. Concurrently, it remains the subject of confusion and contention, and of considerable ignorance, both within and beyond Muslim communities in the East and West. Feminism in Islam has long been presumed non-existent by most in the West, who have insisted that "feminism and Islam" is an oxymoron. In their view Muslims were incapable of producing feminism, and "Islam" itself would not allow it. In "the East," a term still commonly used in the early twentieth century to refer to Islamic and other societies in Africa and Asia, most Muslims have pronounced feminism produced by women in their midst an anathema. Feminism to such opponents served, so they insisted, as another form of Western assault upon their culture, and constituted a blasphemy to religion. Many in the West, on the other hand, have used the trope of the "oppressed Muslim woman," a set piece in Orientalist discourse, displaying a feigned concern for "her" plight, in order to justify colonial and neo-colonial incursions into Muslim societies, or simply to make a show of arrogant superiority.

When Muslim reactionaries, whether in the East or West, sustain repressive patriarchal versions of Islam to maintain control of women and to perpetuate the conventional hierarchical order – and with this their own power and privilege – they concurrently solidify Western stereotypes. Thus, we note that Westerners attack Muslims by belittling the very notion that they could generate a feminism of their own, and in so doing denigrate Islam as inherently gender-unjust, while many Muslims (playing into their hands) attack the West for foisting feminism upon their hapless coreligionists, wantonly discrediting Muslim women's feminisms. The two opposing forces – the one disparaging of and the other hostile to Muslim women's feminisms – have tenaciously persisted from early last century into the twenty-first century. Muslim women's feminisms meanwhile have resolutely stayed the course. It is this story that *Feminism in Islam* aims to tell.

At the outset it should be made clear – as history and empirical research attest – that the feminisms Muslim women have created are feminisms of their own. They were not "Western;" they are not derivative. Religion from the very start has been integral to the feminisms that Muslim women have constructed, both explicitly and implicitly, whether they have been called "secular feminism" or "Islamic feminism." This is in contrast to feminisms in the West, which have been largely secular enterprises in the sense of being typically articulated outside religious frameworks. Yet those Westerners who believe secularism – in the sense of moving beyond religion, or even assuming an anti-religious stance – to be a *sine qua non* of feminism forget the role religion has played in their own feminisms. To cite American experience, they ignore their forebears who produced the Woman's Bible in the mid-nineteenth century and the Jewish and Christian religious studies scholars who created women's liberation theology in the late twentieth century. In the main, however, feminism in the West has been cast within a secular framework and has neither explicitly invoked religious principles nor looked to religion for support or legitimacy. In chapter 9, I point to the basic differences between feminisms produced in Muslim societies, where religion saturates the broader culture, and those in contemporary Western societies, where religion has been experienced differently and is often more compartmentalized. I note that Islamic feminism speaks, actually or potentially, to society at large, while Christian and Jewish liberation theology is a form of feminism that for the most part speaks to the concerns of the few.

Historically, Muslim women have generated two major feminist paradigms, which they have referred to as "secular feminism" and "Islamic feminism." It is important to immediately observe, however, that these two feminisms have never been hermetic entities. Nor, concomitantly, have those known as "secular feminists" and "Islamic feminists" operated strictly within the separate frameworks that the designations of the two feminisms might suggest.

Muslims' secular feminisms first arose on the soil of various emergent nation-states in Africa and Asia from the late nineteenth century through the first half of the twentieth, during processes of modernization, nationalist anti-colonial struggle, dynastic decline, and independent state building. Islamic feminism emerged in the global *umma* (Muslim community) simultaneously in the East and West, in the late twentieth century during the late postcolonial moment. Islamic feminism appeared, as well, at the time of an accelerating Islamist movement, or movement of political Islam – and, in the case of Iran or, later, Sudan, following the installation of an Islamic regime – as well as during widespread Islamic religious cultural revival in many Muslim-majority secular states and minority societies. Concomitant with these phenomena have been new waves of modernization experienced by more modest economic segments of urban and rural populations. Secular feminism emerged as a composite of intersecting secular nationalist, Islamic modernist, and humanitarian (later human rights) discourses. Secular feminism signified a model of feminism located within the context of a secular territorial nation-state composed of equal citizens, irrespective of religious affiliation and a state protective of religion while not officially organized around religion. From the beginning, secular feminism has been action-oriented, engaging in social and political militancy. Indeed, it emerged as a social movement – or, more precisely, social movements within national contexts, although, as evident in the Middle East, they were also transnational, notably in a regional sense.[1]

Islamic feminism, by contrast, burst on the global scene as a new discourse or interpretation of Islam and gender grounded in *ijtihad*, or independent intellectual investigation of the Qur'an and other religious texts. The Islamic, or religious, framing of this new feminism did not mean that "the secular" in the sense of worldliness was absent. This new critical thinking was understood by its shapers from the outset as linked, of necessity, to paving the way for gender liberation and social change in particular contexts. Its concern has not been simply a religious and societal reform but a fundamental transformation reflecting the practice of an egalitarian Islam, as I discuss in chapter 14.

The two feminisms, secular feminism and Islamic feminism, have approached gender equality differently. Emergent secular feminism insisted upon the implementation of gender equality in the public sphere while acquiescing in the notion of gender complementarity in the private sphere or the domain of the family. This was in keeping with the late nineteenth- and early twentieth-century Islamic modernist discourse first promoted by the Egyptian Shaikh Muhammad 'Abduh that pioneering secular feminists accessed.[2] Women who were incipient feminists did not have access to the education and training that would enable them to engage directly in systematic re-readings of religious texts themselves; the exception only proved the rule.[3] Secular feminists used Islamic modernist arguments to demand equal access for women to the public sphere in the domains of secular education and work, and political rights, as well as to call for women's ability to participate in congregational worship in the mosque. Secular feminists' Islamic modernist understanding equipped them to demand revisions of Muslim personal status codes, or family law, and to call for the optimalization of the practice of complementary roles and responsibilities in the family, insisting especially that men honor their duties. Their Islamic modernist understanding, however, did not enable them to go beyond a patriarchal construction of the family in arguing for a fundamental recasting of Muslim personal status or family law on an egalitarian model.

Islamic feminists, on the other hand, have through their own *ijtihad* made compelling arguments that the patriarchal model of the family does not conform to the Qur'anic principles of human equality and gender justice. Islamic feminists promote gender equality along a more fluid public–private continuum, promoting an egalitarian model of both family and society. They thus do not conceptualize a public–private division, as was typical of secular feminists. Moreover, Islamic feminists insist upon gender equality within the religious part of the public sphere – that is, in the religious professions and mosque ritual. It was women exegetes' direct scrutiny of the Qur'an and other religious texts that brought them into the universe of holistic egalitarian Islam encompassing the intersection of family and society that constitutes the *umma*.

In recognition of the diverse secular feminist movements that arose in different national locations I often pluralize the term secular feminism. Secular feminism, as noted, has been primarily "movement feminism," exploding upon the scene as social movements – clearly suffused, however, with fresh gender ideas. The secular feminist movements that arose in various Muslim-majority countries were organized within a national rather than a religious framework, but were decidedly imbued with religious principles; secular, in this sense, signified national. Such secular/national feminist movements were called Egyptian feminist movements, Syrian feminist movements, etc. Speaking of secular feminism in the plural captures its expression in the form of these multiple movements situated in diverse locations.

On the other hand, in speaking of Islamic feminism mainly in the singular I seek to maintain a focus on what is, *au fond*, an intellectual endeavor or *ijtihadic* project of articulating a coherent model of an egalitarian Islam, and one that can serve as a template for religious and socio-cultural transformation. By referring to Islamic feminism in the singular I do not wish to suggest the absence of intellectual differences within the Islamic feminist framework or a lack of different activist priorities in various places.

Until now the historical trajectories of secular and Islamic feminism have not been examined together in a single volume. I have titled my book *Feminism in Islam* to underscore that feminism exists within Islam – that is, within Islamic discourse and among Muslims. I chose the subtitle *Secular and Religious Convergences* to draw attention to the presence of what is conventionally understood as both "the religious" and "the secular" within the feminisms that Muslim women have created. The juxtaposition of these two feminisms illustrates how "the religious" constitutes a vertical thread in the history of Muslims' feminisms, as does "the secular" in the worldly or quotidian sense, and reveals the multiple valences of the terms "secular" and "religious" and how their meanings, and our grasp of them, change over time. Indeed, there is significant recent interrogation and debate about how "the secular" and "the religious" are constituted as seen in the work of Talal Asad, Saba Mahmood, and others.[4] Terms such as secular feminism or Islamic feminism, which are necessary for purposes of identification and analysis, can be, and indeed sometimes have been, understood in ways that are rigid, reductive, or misleading, and frequently have been deliberately manipulated for political ends. Feminism *per se*, "secular feminism," and "Islamic feminism" have for a variety of reasons all been highly contested terms, even for protagonists of their projects, as I discuss in various chapters.

Scrutinizing secular feminism and Islamic feminism side by side brings to light the confluences between these two feminist paradigms, and not simply the divergences that many presume. Examination of concrete experience indicates how Muslim women as feminists employ multiple discourses and possess multiple identities, and how secular feminists and Islamic feminists have worked together, and do so increasingly, to achieve shared goals.[5] At the same time it shows the different work that the two feminisms do. Muslims' secular and Islamic feminisms should not be seen as oppositional forces, as some are inclined to do, seemingly influenced by the hostility between Islamist and secular forces in societies at large from the final decades of the twentieth century with the spread of political Islam, and which Islamists indeed frequently take pains to promote. Islamic feminists who articulate an egalitarian mode of Islam should not be confused with Islamist women who promote political Islam and its patriarchal version of the religion.[6] Indeed, we must be wary of Islamist women's specious renditions of feminism which, as just noted, Islamists are typically wont to deprecate. During my research and interactions in diverse parts of the Muslim *umma* since the1990s, I have observed how secular and Islamic feminisms have been in constructive conversation, and how secular and Islamic feminists have joined forces in activist campaigns, as we see in part II of this book.

BUILDING A NEW HISTORIOGRAPHY

In my four decades of work I have been concerned with the theory and practice of feminisms within Muslim societies. I began my exploration of feminism in the 1960s within the context of Middle East studies with a focus on the late nineteenth century to the middle of the twentieth. In the 1990s I turned my attention to the contemporary moment, and also opened my lens to include the Muslim world at large – and in so doing became part of what was gradually coalescing as the new Islamic studies. It is worth noting that Middle East studies was formed in a "patriarchal moment" and came under its influence. It took considerable effort, as it did in other area studies and "mainstream" disciplines, to introduce women's studies into Middle East studies curricula and scholarly vehicles in the United States and elsewhere.[7] In order to support and accelerate this process, a group of women scholars from a variety of disciplines created the Association of Middle East Women's Studies (AMEWS) in 1985, and twenty years later the *Journal of Middle East Women's Studies* (*JMEWS*) was created under the aegis of AMWES.[8] The new Islamic studies, on the other hand, was consolidated after feminist thought had already made a deep impact on the academy and was well reflected in scholarly production.[9] The new Islamic studies in the main moved beyond the patriarchal thought that had for so long influenced area studies.

When I embarked upon my investigation of the feminism that pioneering Muslim and Christian women in Egypt created together in the early twentieth century, I did so as a historian belonging to the founding generation of women's studies. When I set out to explore the rise of women's "feminist consciousness" and evolution of the organized feminist movement in Egypt I was moving in largely uncharted territory. In the 1960s and 1970s feminist experience was virtually unrecorded in mainstream histories in Egypt, apart from the occasional fleeting mention in the nationalist narrative. The beginnings of feminist history were evident, however, in a few theses and books produced by young women scholars in Egypt, with such exceptions proving the rule.[10] In Middle East studies in the United States the absence of work on women and on feminism was as glaring as it was in other area and disciplinary studies.

Like other emergent historians of women and feminism, my first task was to search for imagined sources and to work out new methodologies appropriate to the retrieval and analysis of a forgotten past.[11] When I began my research the few remaining first-wave feminists and early witnesses of feminist activism were of indispensable help to me in conveying the *esprit*, along with illuminating details of the pioneering feminist movement. They spent countless hours recalling this past, serving as living repositories of precious information and insightful stories. They shared their personal papers and photographic collections, and led me to what were then little-known writings of women by opening their private libraries to me.[12] The lack of a historiography of women and feminism in Egypt at the time, as elsewhere in the Middle East and Muslim societies, presented numerous challenges, starting with the most basic: how to frame and contextualize the feminist narrative. In confronting conventional periodization and analytical apparatus, one had to ask: what were the seminal moments and turning points in women's pasts? How was women's experience inflected by class, region, and communal affiliation? Such were the concerns of all who were striking out then to research, narrate, and analyze women's unexplored histories. For those of us starting out in the 1960s, it would be two decades before the construct "gender" would be devised as an analytical tool. In chapter 8 I explore the travels of "gender" into the Arabophone world.

Between the 1960s and 1980s, the heyday of second-wave feminism in many parts of the world, I continued to research the history of secular feminism/s, often called simply feminism, maintaining a primary focus on Egyptian feminism in the first half of the twentieth century while I also explored feminist history elsewhere in the Middle East, as seen in chapters 1 through 5. Taking a deep historical look at Muslim women's feminism/s and providing thick detail reveals the textures and fine-tuning of women's feminism/s and the minutiae of their moves forward, as seen for example in chapter 4. The history of women's feminist thinking and activism, as I mentioned at the start, gives lie to the assertion that Muslims and others from beyond the West borrowed their feminism from the West. Such insistence imposes upon Muslim women's feminism/s an illegitimate birth and tainted past. Women's own experiences tell a very different story.

In the late 1980s I turned my attention from the feminist past in Egypt to the feminist present. In my previous research I had talked exclusively with women who recollected the feminist past. Now, instead of working with memory, I wanted to see how Egyptian women, in the midst of the vibrant second wave, understood contemporary feminism. It was then that I found that some socialist women who earlier had adamantly eschewed feminism as superfluous to and detracting from the socialist project were now, following the demise of state socialism (at the beginning of the 1970s), gravitating toward feminism while the second wave was well underway. Nawal al-Saadawi, pioneering second-wave feminist, stood out from the beginning for combining socialism and feminism, while Inji Aflatun, a first-wave precursor, connected Marxism and feminism. Both women claimed a dual identity: Aflatun as a communist and a feminist; and al-Saadawi as a socialist and a feminist. Among the new generation of women I had presumed to be feminists – "daughters," heirs, and beneficiaries of feminist predecessors – I unexpectedly encountered a troubled ambivalence toward feminism. These younger women questioned contemporary feminism's methods and politics which did not suit their needs. Women of the rising generation, whom I called "gender activists" – along with others who eschewed a feminist identity – wanted to distance themselves from the high-profile and high-gear second-wave feminists.

Meanwhile, I sought out women who were part of the new religious, cultural and political resurgence, and were presumably critical of feminism, to share with me their understandings of feminism. The handful of "religious women" (referred to as *mutadayyinat*, a neologism that appeared in the 1980s) I was able to meet, to my surprise revealed that they were gesturing toward a new "feminism" by posing their own questions about women and Islam and looking to the Qur'an for answers. They were impelled to critique the resurgence of a gender-reactionary Islam that threatened the gains women had made but recoiled from the word "feminism" because of the associations it held for them, seeing it as "Western"; yet they had difficulty in coming up with an alternative term. I soon learned that similar moves on the part of religiously identified women were underway in other societies. I discuss these new gesturings on the part of the "religious" women I met, the reluctance of young secular progressives to align themselves with feminism, and the new gender sensitivity of their some of their socialist elders in chapter 6.

In various parts of the *umma* most producers of the new women-friendly and gender-sensitive Islamic discourse did not regard their intellectual work as part of a "feminist" project. A striking early exception were the new religious intellectuals – women and men – scholars, writers, and journalists in Iran who were explicit about the feminist dimension of their work, and indeed played a seminal role in the development of the new Islamic feminism as their ideas circulated globally. It was Muslim secular feminists as writers and scholars in various locations who recognized, in the new *ijtihad*, the emergence among coreligionists of a "feminism in a new voice" and coined the term "Islamic feminism," as I note in chapter 9.

By the time Islamic feminism surfaced as a named phenomenon in the 1990s there was a significant and rapidly-growing literature in women's studies focusing on Muslim women and an expanding literature on Muslims' feminisms. Indeed, the work of "secular" women who were scholars in these fields helped bring to wider notice the emergent discourse of Islamic feminism generated by "religious women" or those who explicitly identified themselves with religion. Interestingly, Fatima Mernissi, a Moroccan sociologist and secular feminist scholar, produced in 1987 what would be hailed as the first major work of Islamic feminism.[13]

My eagerness to investigate the emergent Islamic feminism took me far beyond the borders of Middle East studies, catapulting me into research in South Africa,[14] West Africa,[15] South Asia,[16] Southeast Asia,[17] and Muslim communities in America[18] and Europe.[19] Most recently (June 2008), I visited Indonesia, where I met with a large range of scholars and activists, and members of communities in different parts of the country, and was deeply struck by how ideals and practices of Islamic feminism were widely in evidence – and especially remarkable were manifestations of this at the level of local communities.

Since the rise and spread of Islamic feminism I have also maintained my interest in Muslim women's secular feminisms, and indeed I am especially interested in the intersections of the "two feminisms" and the interactions of their protagonists. These intersections might be obscured by the separate terms "secular feminism" and "Islamic feminism," yet they remain discernible strands of what constitutes "feminism in Islam."

ORGANIZATION OF THE BOOK

I have divided the book into two parts. Part I is devoted to my work on Egypt. It deals with the history of secular feminism from the late nineteenth century to the end of the twentieth.[20] Chapters 1 and 5 analyze the longer historical trajectory of feminism in Egypt. Chapters 2, 3, and 4 offer a fine-grained treatment of women's feminist thinking and experience in the first half of the twentieth century.[21] Connections between women's feminism and their own self- and society-enabling nationalism, and how feminists did not privilege their nationalism above their feminism but linked the two, are analyzed through an autobiographical reading in chapter 4.[22] Feminist regrouping in the final years of the twentieth century is examined in chapter 6 at the moment of an incipient move toward a paradigm shift in feminism. Chapter 7 unravels the political battles around women's bodies and sexuality, with a focus on FGM, and analyzes secular feminist and Islamic feminist interpolations. Chapter 8 explores the entry of "gender" into the analytical lexicon in Arabic, which would become a key tool for secular feminist theoreticians and activist strategists and for scholars engaged in the new *ijtihad* that was shaping the incipient Islamic feminist discourse, and for the state was a welcomed mechanism in attracting development funds. In chapter 3, I address memory, history, and gender in the politics and practice of commemorating feminist history at the end of the twentieth century.[23]

Part II examines the rise and spread of Islamic feminism in the late twentieth and early twenty-first centuries in the broader Muslim world or *umma*. Chapter 9 discusses how disaffection with political Islam pushed some women in Turkey, late last century, to quit

Islamist ranks and to move into their own independent activism on behalf of women's rights and liberation within an Islamic framework of their own making, and draws a comparison with how secular feminists' disappointments with male secular nationalists in Egypt earlier that century had spurred them into independent feminist organizing. Chapter 10 grew out of a talk at the American Research Center in Egypt in 2002, aiming to draw the contours of Islamic feminism and to contextualize it at a moment when Islamic feminism was still a largely unfamiliar phenomenon. Chapters 11 and 12 demonstrate how women draw at once upon both secular and Islamic feminist discourses in struggles for gender justice within the realm of *shari'a*-based laws. Chapter 11 discusses how women as secular and religious activists moved successfully to stave off the imposition of a more conservative family law in Yemen. Chapter 12 analyzes how Muslim women as secular feminists and religious activists, joined by Christian supporters, triumphed in their efforts to realize justice for women accused of *zina* (adultery) under *hudud* laws in northern Nigeria through meticulous readings of *fiqh* and demands for responsible application. Chapter 13 describes imbrications of secular feminism and Islamic feminism over time and space, looking at the secular roots of Islamic feminism and the Islamic future of secular feminism. Chapter 14, as its title indicates, regards "Islamic Feminism on the Move." The chapter, a reflection and overview, originated as a talk at a well-attended conference on Islamic feminism in Paris in 2006, sponsored by the NGO Islam & Laïcité and UNESCO, where presenters and participants representing a wide ideological spectrum engaged in lively debate on women and gender.[24]

Together parts I and II provide a window onto trajectories of Muslims' feminisms in diverse places in the global *umma*. The appearance of the new Islamic feminist paradigm did not spell the disappearance of secular feminisms. The "two feminisms" continue to exist side by side, and are increasingly mutually interactive. Secular feminists have a long historical memory of women's gender struggles and a repertoire of organizational practices and skills highly honed over time. Islamic feminists have built upon and extended the Islamic modernist thinking that has been an integral component of Muslims' secular feminism and moved it into a whole new space. Islamic feminists are providing the new intellectual fuel necessary to push forward feminist goals in Muslim societies in Africa and Asia, and in Muslim communities in the West, in an effort to move closer to achieving a transformed *umma*. Secular and Islamic feminists now work side by side in productive synergy more than ever, in a highly volatile environment; one which is full of more peril and of more promise.

NOTES

1. See chapter 12, "Arab Feminism," in my book *Feminists, Islam, and Nation: Gender and the Making of Modern Egypt* (Princeton: Princeton University Press, 1995), pp. 223–250, where I delineate the Arab (secular) national and the Islamic threads or dimensions of the feminism(s) Muslim and Christian women collaborated in creating.

2. On Muhammad 'Abduh, see Albert Hourani, *Arabic Thought in the Liberal Age 1798–1939* (Cambridge: Cambridge University Press, 1962), pp. 130–160.

3. Nazira Zain al-Din, a Lebanese who was educated by her father, who was a prominent member of the 'ulama, engaged in examination of religious texts, especially the Qur'an. See her *al-Sufur wa al-hijab* (Beirut: Matabi' Quzma, 1928) and *al-Fatah wa al-shuykh: nazirat wa munazarat fi al-sufur wa al-hijbab* (Beirut: al-Matba'a al-Amirkaniya, 1929). Her work was praised by contemporary Egyptian secular feminists.

4. See Talal Assad, *Formations of the Secular: Christianity, Islam, Modernity* (Stanford: Stanford University Press, 2003); and Saba Mahmood, "Rethinking Secularism. Is Critique Secular?," posted on *Immanent Frame*, edited by Jonathan Van Antwerpen, www.ssrc.org/blogs/immanent frame, a blog on secularism, religion, and the public sphere.

5. I write about this in "Locating Feminisms: The Collapse of Secular and Religious Discourses in the Muslim Mashriq," *Agenda* (South African feminist journal), special 50th issue on African Feminisms, 59 (2001), pp. 41–57; "Zur Verortung von Feminismen: Die Vermischung von Sakularen und Religiosen Diskursen im Mashriq, der Turkei und dem Iran," in Barbara Pusch (ed.), *Die neue muslimische Frau* (Istanbul: Orient Institute, 2001), pp. 213–22; and "Locating Feminisms: Secular and Religious Discourses, A Selective Look at the Middle East," in Fatima Sadiqi et al. (eds.), al-Harakat al-nisa'iyyat: *al-'asl wa al-tawjihat/Mouvements feministes: origines et orientations Feminist Movements/ Origins and Orientations* (Fes: Centre d'Etudes et de Recherches sur la Femme, Universite Sidi Mohamed ben Abdallah, 2000), pp. 73–88.

6. See my essay "Understanding Islam, Islamism, and Islamic Feminism," Journal of Women's History, 13, 1 (Spring 2001), pp. 47–52.

7. I wrote about this early process in "The Institutionalization of Middle East Women's Studies in the United States," MESA Bulletin, 22, 1 (July 1988), pp. 25–28.

8. On the growth of women's studies in the context of Middle East studies and the founding of JMEWS see "Editors' Introduction" by Marcia C. Inhorn and Mary N. Layoun, in the inaugural issue JMEWS, 1, 1 (Winter 2005), pp. 1–5.

9. I speak of Islamic studies as a still-new interdisciplinary field organized as independent departments or centers as distinct from the classic study of Islamic

theology in departments of religion or seminaries, although presently these are often sites of the new Islamic studies. This is not to overlook that new trends have been underway for as long as two decades or more in some divinity schools such as Harvard Divinity School where the Women's Studies Program in Religion, which has been an important site of the study of women and gender in Islam, goes back to the 1980s.

10. For example, Ibrahim 'Abduh and Duriyya Shafiq, al-Mar'a al-misriyya min al-fara'ina ila al-yaum (Cairo: Matba'at al-Misr, 1955); Ijlal Khalifa, al-Haraka al-nisa'iyya al-haditha (Cairo: al-Matba'a al-'Arabiyya al-Haditha, 1974); and Ijlal Khalifa, "al-Sihafa al-nisa'iyya fi misr min 1919 ila 1939," M.A. thesis, Cairo University, 1966.

11. I discussed the process of retrieval of women's feminist past in "The Origins of Feminism in Egypt," in Arina Angerman et al. (eds.), *Current Issues in Women's History* (London: Routledge, 1989); published in Arabic in *al-Mar'a al-Jadida* (Cairo: December 1990) and in Nun (Algiers: December 1990).

12. I remembered two women who were key in helping me in my research in "Defiance on her Brow: Remembering Suffragist Activist Duriyya Shafiq Forty Years after Women Obtained the Vote," al-Ahram Weekly, 1996 and on Saiza Nabarawi in "An Alternative Vision of Gender," al-Ahram Weekly, 1997.

13. *Le harem politique* (Paris: Albin Michel, 1987), trans. Mary Jo Lakeland as *Women and Islam: An Historical and Theological Enquiry* (Oxford: Basil Blackwell, 1991). A young Moroccan scholar, Raja Rhouni, has done an incisive study of Mernissi in her forthcoming book entitled *Secular and Islamic Feminist Critiques in the Work of Fatima Mernissi: Thinking a Post-Foundationalist Islamic Feminism.* See also her "Deconstructing Islamic Feminism: A Look at Fatima Mernissi," in Margot Badran (ed.), *Islam and Gender in Africa*, forthcoming.

14. I taught a course on Islamic feminism in the Centre for Contemporary Islamic Studies at the University of Cape Town in 2002 and wrote on this experience in "Reflections on Teaching Islamic Feminism/s at the Center for Contemporary Islam [University of Cape Town]," ARISA: Annual Review of Islam in South Africa (Fall 2002).

15. In Abuja in July 2004 I participated in the International Conference on the Implementation of Shari'ah in a Democracy: The Nigerian Experience, organized by the Center for the Study of Islam and Democracy, where I gave a paper entitled "Ongoing Tafsir on Men and Women in Islam: Constructions and Practices of Democracy and Social Justice." It subsequently appeared in the online CSID Bulletin. In the spring of 2005 I traveled extensively in northern Nigeria engaging in interviews, group discussions, and collecting materials as a Fulbright New Century Scholar. This research informed chapter 12 of this book.

16. In December 2003 I met with feminists in India and gave talks on Muslims' secular and Islamic feminisms in New Delhi, Pune, Kolkata, Bhopal, Mumbai, Chennai, Hyderabad, and Kozikhodi.

17. In June 2008, I met with activists and scholars, and engaged in discussions and gave talks in Jakarta, East Java, Central Java, and West Sumatra. Four years earlier, in September 2004, I participated in an international meeting on Sexuality and Human Rights in Muslim Societies in South/Southeast Asia organized by Women for Women's Human Rights in Istanbul. It was an important event in the drive for human rights for all irrespective of gender and sexualities.

18. See my entries on "Feminism," "Patriarchy," and "Women," in Jocelyne Cesari (ed.), *Encyclopedia of Islam in the United States*, 2 vols., Center for Middle Eastern Studies, Harvard, a sponsor of the encyclopedia (Westport, Conn. and London: Greenwood Press, 2007), vol. 1, pp. 487–489, 633–637, and 244–249 respectively.

19. See my chapter "Il femminismo islamico e la nuova cultura mediterranea," in Danilo Zolo (ed.), *L'alternativa mediterranea. Un dialogo fra le due sponde* (Milan: Feltrinelli, 2007).

20. Chapters 1, 2, 4, and 5 were published before in my book *Feminists, Islam, and Nation*, trans. Ali Badran as *Raidat al-harakat al-niswiyya al-misriyya wa al-islam wa al-watan* (Cairo: Supreme Council of Culture, 2000), drawing upon my D.Phil. thesis entitled "Huda Sha'rawi and the Liberation of the Egyptian Woman," Oxford University, 1977, which circulated not long afterwards when the Bodleian Library in Oxford made D Phil. theses available for purchase.

21. I also do this in "The Feminist Vision in the Writings of Three Turn-of-the-Century Egyptian Women," British Journal for Middle Eastern Studies Bulletin, 14, 1–2 (1988), pp. 15–34.

22. Which first, feminism or nationalism, has been a question for women during times of anti-colonial struggle and early nation-state building. I discuss this in "Dual Liberation: Feminism and Nationalism in Egypt from the 1870's to 1925," Feminist Issues (Spring 1988), pp. 15–24. This also appeared in Dutch as "Dubble bevridjing: feminism en nationalisme in Egypte," Socialisties-Feministiese Teksten (Amsterdam: Fall 1987), and in Arabic as "al-Haraka al-nisa'iyya wa al-wataniyya fi misr min 1870s illi 1925," Nun (Cairo, 1989) and Nun (Algiers, 1990).

23. I wrote two articles for a broad audience on feminism in Egypt during the nineteenth century: the first occasioned by the UN Conference in Beijing is entitled "Half a Nation: A Century of Feminism," al-Ahram Weekly, 20–26 July 1995, which also appeared in Arabic in al-Ahram, 20 July 1995; the second, appearing in a special edition of al-Ahram Weekly looking back over the twentieth century, is entitled "Feminism in a Nationalist Century," al-Ahram Weekly, 20 July 1995.

24. A selection of papers presented at this conference appears in Islam & Laïcité (ed.), *Existe-t-il un feminism musulman?* (Paris: L'Harmattan, 2007). Another important venue for the presentation and debate of work on Islamic feminism were the landmark first and second international conferences on Islamic Feminism held in Barcelona in 2006 and 2007, with a third happening in the fall of 2008.

Part I

Egypt – Late Nineteenth to End of
the Twentieth Centuries:
First Century of Feminism

1

COMPETING AGENDA: FEMINISTS, ISLAM, AND THE STATE IN NINETEENTH- AND TWENTIETH-CENTURY EGYPT

In Egypt the "woman question" has been a contested domain involving feminists, Islamists, and the state. This chapter explores their competing discourses and agendas in nineteenth- and twentieth-century Egypt and how they have shifted over time.[1] Divergent discourses arose in the context of modern state and class formation, and economic and political confrontation with the West. These multiple discourses have been sustained in strikingly different political and economic cultures as state and society continually negotiate changing realities.

From the second quarter of the nineteenth century, the state in Egypt tried to draw women into the economic and technological transformations under way. As a consequence it began to wrest women away from the exclusive control of the family, threatening the authority and domination of men over their women. Earlier in the century, after freeing Egypt from direct Ottoman rule, the new ruler, Muhammad 'Ali, while consolidating his power, had placed the Islamic establishment centered at al-Azhar under the control of the state. The formerly broad purview of the religious establishment was eroded piecemeal in the drive toward secularization of education and law. The only exception to this was the sphere of personal status laws.[2] For women this created an awkward dichotomy between their role as citizens of the nation-state (*watan*) and members of the religious community (*umma*). In a division that was never precise, the state increasingly came to influence their public roles, leaving to religion the regulation of their private or family roles. The structural contradictions and tensions this created have, to this day, not been fully resolved.[3]

While promoting new social roles for women, the state could not afford unduly to alienate patriarchal interests, and has therefore made various accommodations and alliances. Whatever their competing interests, the state and religious forces have retained patriarchal forms of control over women. It is this patriarchal dimension that feminists have identified and confronted, for which they have been variously attacked, contained, or suppressed by state authorities and Islamists alike. However, in Egypt, there has been sufficient space – albeit more frequently taken than granted – within state and society for women to speak out as feminists and activists. Moreover, the authorities have at times deliberately encouraged women's initiatives for their own purposes.

The earliest articulation of women's feminist consciousness, first discernible in occasional published writings – poetry, essays, and tales – by the 1860s and 1870s, preceded colonial occupation and the rise of nationalism.[4] It was more widely expressed from the 1890s, in the rise of women's journalism and salon debates. This new awareness (not yet called feminist; in fact, the term "feminism" was not used in Egypt until the early 1920s) was based on an increased sensitivity to the everyday constraints imposed upon women by a patriarchal society. Muslims, Christians, and Jews alike shared this sensitivity, and they projected an understanding, implicit or explicit, that these constraints were not solely religiously based, as they had been made to believe. Furthermore, from the rise of feminism in Egypt to the present, its advocates across the spectrum from left to right have consistently used Islam, as well as nationalism, as legitimizing discourses. In this chapter, feminism is broadly construed to include an understanding that women have suffered forms of subordination or oppression because of their sex, and an advocacy of ways to overcome them to achieve better lives for women, and for men, within the family and society. I am using a definition of feminism broad enough to be all-inclusive without intending to suggest a monolithic feminism. I indicate divergences within this larger framework while keeping the primary focus on the interplay among three major discourses: those of feminists, Islamists, and the state.[5]

Feminist, nationalist, and Islamist positions on the "woman question" have seldom been considered together in the literature.[6] Here, I pay particular attention to the agendas of women who are feminists across the political spectrum, and of women Islamists. Focusing on what women have to say makes it possible to discern their departures from, and agreements with, their male counterparts, as well as their own internal differences.

The exploration of the competing agendas and discourses on women is organized within the following historical framework: (1) the modern state-building and colonial periods; (2) the period of the liberal experiment; (3) the period of the revolution, Arabism, and socialism; and (4) the era of *infitah* capitalism and populist Islamist ascendancy.

THE MODERN STATE-BUILDING AND COLONIAL PERIODS: NINETEENTH CENTURY TO 1922

During the nineteenth century, especially in the later decades, new contenders appeared in the shaping and control of discourse in general and, more particularly, discourses on women. With the broadening of opportunities for education and the rise of women's feminist consciousness, women who had previously been the objects of prescriptive pronouncements began to challenge patriarchal domination.

The expanding modern state promoted new educational and work opportunities for women, especially in health and teaching, but incurred resistance from families. In the early nineteenth century, for example, Egyptians did not initially allow their daughters to attend the new state school for *hakima*s (Ethopian slaves were recruited as the first students).[7] In 1836, Muhammad 'Ali appointed a Council for Public Education to look into creating a state system of education for girls, but it was found impossible to implement. Later, however, during the rule of Isma'il, one of his wives sponsored the first state school for girls, which opened in 1873, serving the daughters of high officials and white slaves from elite households. Meanwhile, encouraged by the state, Shaikh Ahmad Rifa'i al-Tahtawi and 'Ali Pasha Mubarak published books in 1869 and 1875 advocating education for women, using Islamic justifications from the Qur'an and Hadith.[8] It was not easy, however, to draw women out of the realm controlled by the family.

Feminist discourse first emerged in the writings of women of privilege and education who lived in the secluded world of the urban

harem.[9] Women gained new exposure through expanded education
and widening contacts within the female world. They made comparisons between their own lives and those of women and men of other
social and national backgrounds. Through their new education
women also gained deeper knowledge of their religion. Some urban
middle- and upper-class women began to contest the Islamic justification for their seclusion, *hijab* (then meaning the veiling of both face
and body), and related controls over their lives.[10] In 1892, Zainab al-
Fawwaz protested in *al-Nil* magazine, "We have not seen any of the
divinely ordered systems of law, or any law from among the corpus of
[Islamic] religious law ruling that woman is to be prohibited from
involvement in the occupations of men."[11] When Hind Naufal
founded the journal *al-Fatah* (The young woman) in the same year,
inaugurating a women's press in Egypt, women found a new forum
for discussing and spreading their nascent feminism.[12]

This emergent feminism was grounded, and legitimized, in the
framework of Islamic modernism expounded towards the end of the
century by Shaikh Muhammad 'Abduh, a distinguished teacher and
scholar from al-Azhar. 'Abduh turned a revolutionary corner when
he proposed that believers could go straight to the sources of religion,
principally the Qur'an and the Hadith, for guidance in the conduct of
everyday life.[13] Through *ijtihad* (independent inquiry into the sources
of religion), 'Abduh demonstrated that one could be both Muslim
and modern, and that many traditional practices violated the principles of Islam. In dealing with gender issues, 'Abduh confronted the
problem of patriarchal excesses committed in the name of Islam. He
especially decried male abuse of the institutions of divorce and
polygamy.[14]

The opening-out encouraged by *ijtihad* had a number of consequences. While Muslim women's earliest feminist writing may not
have been immediately inspired by Islamic modernism, it was not
long before it developed within this framework. The gender-progressive discourse of Muslim secular men, on the other hand, was initially
situated within Islamic modernist discourse as articulated by 'Abduh.
However, 'Abduh's successors did not expand or perpetuate his
Islamic modernist discourse on women, while soon the new secular
intellectuals turned to secular nationalist and humanist discourse to
argue for women's rights and advancement.[15]

After women had been producing their own feminist writing
for some time, Murqus Fahmi, a young Coptic lawyer, published

al-Mar'a fi al-sharq (The woman in the East) in 1894, criticizing patriarchal tyranny over women in the home, which he claimed no religion sanctioned. Five years later, a Muslim judge, Qasim Amin, published his famous book, *Tahrir al-mar'a* (The liberation of woman, 1899), attacking the practice of female seclusion and the *hijab* – by which he meant face veiling, as the term *hijab* signified at that stage, rather than the modest covering of the head and body, which he did not oppose. Amin argued that women in Egypt were backward because they had been deprived of the legitimate rights accorded to them by Islam. He insisted that for the nation to advance and become modern, women must regain these rights. This pro-feminist discourse – or, some might say, feminist discourse – generated from within the establishment, by a Muslim lawyer and judge, drew wide criticism, especially from religious conservatives and members of the lower-middle class.[16] While it was perceived as more dangerous than women's feminist writing, which was less widely visible at the time, in the long run women's feminism would be more sustained and more threatening.[17]

Early in the twentieth century, women's feminist writing became more visible, and reached a wider mainstream audience, when Malak Hifni Nasif, known by her pen name, Bahithat al-Badiya (Searcher in the desert), began publishing essays in *al-Jarida*, the paper of the progressive nationalist party, al-Umma. These essays and her speeches were published by the party press in 1910 in a book called *al-Nisa'iyyat* (which can be translated as either Women's or Feminist pieces, in the absence of a specific term for "feminist" in Arabic). Women's feminism was becoming more explicit, and was increasingly expressed within a nationalist idiom, reflecting and fuelling the growing nationalist movement in Egypt.

Another principal producer of feminist ideas at this period was Nabawiyya Musa, who later published her essays in a book entitled *al-Mar'a wa al-'amal* (Woman and work, 1920). These two women were both from the middle class: Bahithat al-Badiya was from the upper-middle class, and Nabawiyya Musa from a more modest stratum. They were among the first graduates of the Saniyya Teachers' School, established in 1889, and both became teachers. In 1907, Musa became the first Egyptian woman to sit for the baccalaureate examination – and the last until after independence: the colonial authorities, with their policy of training men for practical administration, were not prepared to subsidize women's secondary education. Meanwhile, these two young women carried on consciousness-raising, through their public lectures to strictly female audiences composed mainly of upper-class women, and at special classes for women at the new Egyptian University (which soon were stopped and the money saved used to send three men on study missions abroad).[18]

In 1911, Bahithat al-Badiya became a pioneer in feminist activism when she sent demands to the Egyptian National Congress for women's education and rights to employment and to participate in congregational worship in mosques.[19] While they were claiming women's rights to public space, feminists such as Bahithat al-Badiya and Huda Sha'rawi, early in the century, actually opposed the unveiling of the face, which pro-feminist men advocated. They wanted women to gain more education and to reclaim public space before they unveiled, as a tactical move. While for progressive men unveiling had a key ideological and symbolic value, for women it was a practical matter that they themselves would have to undertake, with the attendant risks of taunts and assaults on their reputations.[20]

The nationalists of the Umma Party, led by Ahmad Lutfy al-Sayyid and other men of the upper class, supported feminism, while those of the Watani Party, mainly men of more modest middle-class origins, headed by Mustafa Kamil, were antagonistic toward women's emancipation, which they claimed was a result of Western influence and would undermine Egyptian society. Unlike the Umma Party, which advocated a more secular society, the Watani Party favoured an Islamic society, and supported the notion of a caliphate. It was within these frameworks that nationalist men constructed their views on the status and role of women, and developed their own attitudes toward feminism.[21]

During the national revolution (1919–1922), the first priority for both Egyptian feminists and for nationalists, men and women alike, was the independence of Egypt, causing them to unite temporarily in pursuit of this common goal. Upper-class women, mobilized by feminist and nationalist leaders among them, left the seclusion of their harems to demonstrate, while poor women also filled the streets in more spontaneous protest. Members of the Wafdist Women's Central Committee (WWCC), created in 1920 as the women's section of the nationalist party, the Wafd, refused to be confined to auxiliary activities, and insisted on full participation in decision-making within the party. In the midst of the revolution, these women at times took public feminist stands. In 1920, for example, when the male nationalist leadership did not consult the WWCC on the independence proposal they were circulating, the women publicly announced their objections.[22] Nevertheless, during colonial occupation a feminism that called for greater female participation in society was upheld by progressive male nationalists, and generally tolerated by others. Moreover, during the ferment of revolution, male nationalists enthusiastically welcomed women's militancy.

In the early modern state-building and colonial period, during which Islamic modernism, liberal nationalism, and the feminism of progressive men were prevalent, women's causes found a positive and supportive environment. The attacks of conservative *'ulama'* during this period focused on Qasim Amin's books, while the opposition to feminist ideas by nationalists such as Mustafa Kamil and Talat Harb did not create the broader conservative ground-swell that expressions of anti-feminism would produce later in the century. During colonial occupation (from 1882 to 1922, when a quasi-independence was declared), women's feminism was not connected with a public, organised, movement; it was rather the articulation of a broad, new philosophy. Men's pro-feminism likewise expressed a philosophical position, and at the time was seemingly more socially radical than women's – for example, in calling for an end to face-veiling. Men's feminist rhetoric, however, reached a climax during occupation. The following period saw the more radical development of women's liberal feminism, while men's earlier expression of liberal feminism faded, for reasons that will become apparent later in our discussion.

In the late nineteenth and early twentieth centuries, polemics were started that have plagued feminist and Islamist positions ever since, and have had political reverberations in official discourse. These concern definitions of culture, authenticity, identity, and modernity – and their implications for women's roles, around which a battle of legitimacy has raged. The debate continued right up to the final decade of the twentieth century, as did the state's efforts to control competing discourses and to appropriate elements useful to itself.

THE LIBERAL EXPERIMENT: 1923–1952

Early in this period, the feminist positions of progressive men and women, which had drawn closest during colonial occupation and in the pre-independence nationalist movement, started to diverge.

Women had a rude awakening when it became clear that liberal men were not prepared to implement their promise to integrate women into public life after nominal political independence in 1922. Feminists became openly militant, while most men who had been pro-feminist nationalists, in the forefront of whom was Sa'd Zaghlul, grew silent as their attention turned towards their new political careers. A few others responded with concrete positive actions, such as Ahmad Lutfy al-Sayyid, whose championship of university education for women will be noted later.[23] There were moments, moreover, when feminists would be beleaguered, especially in the early 1930s during the government of Isma'il Sidqi, a political and social reactionary. During the same period, a rising activist, Zainab al-Ghazali, would move from feminism to Islamic fundamentalism, beginning a conservative women's religious and political movement.[24] In the 1950s, the new, more radical, communist feminists would be openly harassed.

With the declaration of formal independence in 1922 (British troops remained on Egyptian soil until 1956), nationalist men become part of the new state. At first the official discourse articulated in the new constitution of 1923 seemed to fulfill the promises nationalist men had made to women when it declared: "All Egyptians are equal before the law. They enjoy equally civil and political rights and equally have public responsibilities without distinction of race, language, or religion." However, the principle of gender equality was soon flouted when an electoral law restricted suffrage to males only. The following year women were barred from attending the opening of the new parliament, except as wives of ministers and other high state officials. The idealism of nationalist men gave way to political pragmatism in the new independent, "liberal" era.

At this point, women's feminist stance became explicit, and their feminism became tied to an organized political movement led by al-Ittihad al-Nisa'i al-Misri (officially called l'Union féministe égyptienne or the Egyptian Feminist Union, EFU), created in 1923 and headed by Huda Sha'rawi. The first unequivocal use of the term feminism occurred in 1923, when EFU feminists employed the word *feministe*, in French, the everyday language of most members. From 1923, Egyptian women's feminism crystallized around a set of demands, a broad agenda of claims for political, social, economic, and legal rights. However, initial priority was given to women's education, followed by new work opportunities and the reform of the personal status law. Some demands were granted relatively easily, such as equal secondary school education for girls and raising the minimum marriage age for both sexes (achieved in 1923 and 1924 respectively). The entry of women into the state university was achieved in 1929, not without difficulty, with the support of the rector himself, Ahmad Lutfy al-Sayyid, one of the few nationalists who continued, post-1922, to actively strive to implement his progressive ideas. Gains in the sphere of employment were mainly achieved in those areas that were most congruent with the immediate priorities of the state, such as education and medicine. These were fields in which women professionals typically served the needs of other women; thus their new work also perpetuated gender segregation in public space. However, greater numbers of women were also drawn into employment in the expanding textile factories, where they worked more closely with men.

During the early 1930s, when the reactionary Isma'il Sidqi was at the head of government, feminists encountered some setbacks, such as a conservative education policy opposing higher education for women. With the change of government in 1933, however, the more characteristic liberal atmosphere was restored. Although feminists were able to conduct public activities, they would also encounter disappointments. Most importantly, no headway was made in formal political rights for women, or in the reform of personal status law. In addition, state-legalised prostitution, which the feminists opposed, was not abolished during the lifetime of Huda Sha'rawi.[25]

During this period religious officials and feminists shared some common social concerns. When the feminists called for the prohibition of alcohol and the ending of state-licensed prostitution, the Shaikh al-Azhar, Muhammad Abu al-Fadl, wrote to the president of the EFU, saying: "We appreciate the value of your honorable association and its diligent efforts to spread virtue and combat vice. There are now in Egypt distinguished women whose impact on society is no less important than that of honorable men."[26] However, when it came to demands for political rights for women, the same Islamic authorities pronounced them to be un-Islamic, both officially through *fatwas* (religious pronouncements) and through unofficial utterances.[27]

Official Islam was not the only Islamic platform during this period. A conservative popular Islamic movement emerged with the creation of the Muslim Brothers (al-Ikhwan al-Muslimin) by Hasan al-Banna in 1928. This movement drew on a wide base of support from the modest and lower strata of the middle class, strongly opposed to the continued British military presence and economic imperialism. The Muslim Brothers, connecting Egypt's ills with a deviation from the practice of true Islam, went to the sources of their religion for fresh inspiration. They emphasized individual reform as the first step toward improving society, but their ultimate, more radical, goal was the creation of an Islamic state. The ideology of the Muslim Brothers, laying stress on the moral foundations of society, articulated a conservative discourse privileging the patriarchal family, with male authority over women, and clear-cut differentiation of gender roles.[28]

During the militancy of the 1919 revolution and its immediate aftermath, class differences between women as feminists and nationalists were of little importance in the face of larger common causes. However, in time, differences in class and culture produced cleavages between women and raised questions of cultural authenticity. The upper class had adopted elements of Western manners, expressed in dress, in everyday life, and in the use of the French language. Indeed, the EFU journal (*l'Egyptienne*), founded in 1925, appeared in French, the language of its upper-class leadership. With the EFU's feminist ideas mainly expressed in French, particularly in the early years (the EFU founded an Arabic-language journal, *al-Misriyya* [The Egyptian woman], in 1937), feminism came to be considered, especially by its detractors, as foreign. The nationalism of Egyptian men who also spoke French and wore Western dress, was not, however, denigrated in the same way.[29] The importance assigned to cultural symbols was different for the two sexes. Men could change without losing their cultural authenticity (the *tarbush* or fez, the Ottoman head-dress, was even forbidden to men by the state following the 1952 revolution), while the burdens of maintaining cultural and social continuity were placed on women.

The tension between feminism and cultural authenticity is well illustrated in the case of Zainab al-Ghazali. The daughter of a prosperous cotton merchant with an al-Azhar education, she joined the EFU as a young woman in 1935. Around that time, al-Azhar initiated seminars for women at the Kulliyya Shar'iyya (the Islamic law college) under the direction of Shaikh Ma'mun Shinawi (later Shaikh al-Azhar), which al-Ghazali joined. Within the year, al-Ghazali left the EFU and formed the Muslim Women's Society (MWS). Shinawi was present at the MWS inauguration. In an interview, al-Ghazali said

"The Egyptian Feminist Union wanted to establish the civilization of the Western woman in Egypt and the rest of the Arab and Islamic worlds." She also remarked that when she quit the feminist organization Huda Sha'rawi told her, "You are separating yourself from me intellectually," adding: "I ask you not to fight the Egyptian Feminist Union." And, al-Ghazali confessed, "I never fought it."[30] In fact, there was occasional cooperation between the two organizations, mainly around nationalist causes, as Hawa Idris, the head of the EFU's youth group, the Shaqiqat (established in 1935) recalled.[31]

The division between feminist and fundamentalist women that originated in the late 1930s was to persist, and their divergent orientations, perceptions, beliefs, and agenda would be articulated in competing discourses. While the EFU women found their feminist ideology and program compatible with Islam, and sought its legitimizing force, their overall ideological framework was secular rather than religious. For al-Ghazali and the MWS, on the other hand, since the *shari'a* regulates all aspects of life, a separate ideology of feminism was at best redundant and at worst constituted a corrosive Western ideology. Al-Ghazali, extolling "the absolute equality" (*musawa mutlaqa*) between women and men in Islam, finds women's liberation within the framework of religion.[32] Yet she and fundamentalist men and women typically speak of complementarity in the private sphere, rather than equality, and stress male authority over women. The EFU championed greater access for women to public roles, while the MWS lauded women's family duties and obligations.

As a secular Egyptian organization the EFU included under its aegis Muslims and Christians alike, while the MWS, as a strictly Muslim religious organization, did not cater to all Egyptians. The issue of "secularism" (*al-'almaniyya*) has been contentious. Fundamentalist women called Egyptian feminism "secular," implying that it was outside the bounds of Islam. However, Egyptian Muslim women distinguished their feminism, which they based on Islamic principles, from the "secular" basis of Turkish feminism. An article in the EFU's journal, *al-Misriyya*, in 1937 said, for example, that "while the Turkish woman has attained her freedom by virtue of foreign laws [alluding to the 1926 Turkish civil code, based not on the Islamic *shari'a* but on a Swiss model] the Egyptian woman will never ask for her rights except by basing her requests on the Islamic *shari'a*."[33] The EFU and most other feminists later shied away from a secularism that severed all links with religion. This would later be called al-ʿ*almaniyya la dini* (literally, "secularism without religion") by some of today's [published in 1990] fundamentalists. Women's fundamentalist leadership under al-Ghazali favoured an Islamic state with a theocratic ruler, while the EFU feminists accepted the notion of a secular state whose legitimacy was grounded in the basic principles of Islam.

Around the time of the creation of the MWS, Egyptian feminist activism broadened in response to the 1937 Arab revolt in Palestine and calls for support from Palestinian women to Egyptian feminists. Both Arab and religious, Muslim and Christian, identities were invoked in the drive to save Palestine. The EFU hosted the Conference for the Defence of Palestine in 1938, which religious and state authorities applauded equally. It was yet another instance when militant nationalism blurred divergent gender ideologies. The feminists' collective nationalist action in 1938 led to the first Pan-Arab Feminist Conference in 1944. Waving the banner of Arab unity, the conference again won the praise of governments and the Islamic establishment for their nationalist actions. While the conference resulted in the creation of *al-Ittihad al-Nisa'i al-ʿArabi* (the Arab Feminist Union) headquartered in Cairo, it would be some time before many of the more than fifty resolutions covering virtually all aspects of women's lives would be realized. Like Egypt, other Arab states were slow to reform the personal status laws and to give women equal political rights, but they welcomed and needed women's political support. Arab regimes were not politically strong enough to change family laws significantly, and in so doing challenge patriarchal authority in the family as well as threaten the last legal bastion of the religious establishment. The earliest and most drastic change in family law occurred in Tunisia in 1957 under Bourguiba, who, because of his own political power base and the particular political culture of Tunisia, was able to promote significant change and survive. Almost two decades later, in 1974, the People's Democratic Republic of Yemen also instituted a more secular law within a Marxist–Leninist framework.[34]

Towards the end of the 1930s, and in the 1940s, feminism in Egypt broadened its reach and new organizations proliferated. The EFU began its Arabic-language journal, *al-Misriyya*, in 1937, aiming to "elevate the intellectual and moral level of the masses and to create lines of solidarity between the different classes of the nation."[35] The Arabic periodical aimed at a wider audience than *l'Egyptienne*, and projected a self-consciously Islamic tone heralded in the journal's motto: "Take half your religion from 'Aisha." It was to be "the minbar [pulpit] for feminist demands" as well as "the tongue of the most noble nationalist hopes." However, while EFU leaders Huda Sha'rawi and Saiza Nabarawi tried to serve the needs of a broader constituency, the rank and file of the EFU resisted opening up the organization's membership to women of more modest class background. In two separate encounters with this author in the late 1960s and early 1970s, Duriyya Shafiq, from a middle-class family in Tanta in the Delta, contrasted Huda Sha'rawi's welcoming encouragement to her when she returned from France in 1939 with her doctorate with the grudging reception of the EFU membership.[36]

EFU resistance to broadening its constituency and the political and economic changes following World War II in Egypt encouraged a proliferation of more populist feminist organizations headed by middle-class women. Wishing to accelerate the struggle for political rights for women, former EFU members Fatma Ni'mat Rashid and Duriyya Shafiq founded respectively the Hizb al-Nisa'i al-Watani (National Feminist Party, NFP) in 1944 and al-Ittihad Bint al-Nil (Daughter of the Nile Union, DNU) in 1948. Along with the advocacy of political rights for women, both the NFP and DNU mounted literacy and hygiene campaigns among the poor. They also sustained the concern for family law reform, and education and work rights for women. Duriyya Shafiq, a protégée of Sha'rawi, was the more dynamic leader of the two new activists. Her DNU was larger, longer-lived, and more effective, with branches throughout the country. Rashid's NFP was a strictly Cairene organization with limited outreach. The social projects of these two feminist organizations, unlike their political goals, could scarcely have antagonized the Muslim Brothers or the MWS.[37]

Despite the widening class base of the feminist movement through new organizations led by women who had come of age during the first phase of feminist activism, this new strand remained essentially within the liberal framework evolved by the EFU. In the middle 1940s some women from the younger generation, university students and graduates, moved issues of gender and nation in a new direction as socialists and communists. For them the liberation of women was tied to the liberation of the masses, and both necessitated the end of imperialism and class oppression in Egypt. A young leader of the new leftist feminists, Inji Aflatun, a landowner's daughter, discovered

Marxism at the French Lycée in Cairo. After graduating from Fuad I University (later Cairo University) in 1945, she helped found the Rabitat Fatayat al-Jami'a wa al-Ma'ahid (the League of University and Institutes' Young Women) which Latifa Zayyat, a student leader, soon joined. The League sent Aflatun and others to the first conference of the International Democratic Federation of Women, but it was closed down the following year in the drive to suppress communists. The leftist feminists went on to form other associations, including the Jamiyya al-Nisa'iyya al-Wataniyya al-Mu'aqata (the Provisional National Feminist Association). Within the mainstream communist movement there was no room to address women's liberation, which was subordinated to the struggle against imperialist military occupation and class oppression. Aflatun linked class and gender oppression, connecting both to imperialist exploitation, and at the same time was careful to argue in her books *Thamanun milyun imra'a ma'na* (Eighty million women with us, 1948) and *Nahnu al-nisa' al-misriyyat* (We Egyptian women, 1949) that women's liberation was compatible with Islam.[38]

Meanwhile, not only were secular leftist groups coming under siege, but the Muslim Brothers also experienced the heavy hand of the state. In 1948, the formal organization of the Muslim Brothers was dissolved. At that time Zainab al-Ghazali, who a decade earlier had resisted the overtures of the Muslim Brothers' founder, Hasan al-Banna, to include her new MWS under the umbrella of his organization, immediately joined forces with the Brothers. From then on she became, in her word, "a soldier" in the common struggle for the creation of an Islamic state, and the MWS changed their name to the Muslim Sisters.[39]

Not only did the MWS, now the Muslim Sisters, side with the Muslim Brothers, but the growing nationalist determination to expel British troops from Egypt led to coalitions among feminist and fundamentalist women. In 1950, the Harakat Ansar al-Salam (Movement of the Friends of Peace) brought together EFU feminist and then president, Saiza Nabarawi (Sha'rawi had died in 1947), and the young communist Inji Aflatun. The same year, Nabarawi created the Lajna al-Shabbat (Youth Committee), attracting women like Aflatun, who went to poor quarters of Cairo to politicize women. In 1952, when violence broke out in the Canal Zone, the Lajna al-Nisa'iyya lil-Muqawama al-Sha'biyya (Women's Committee for Popular Resistance) brought together women from the left and right, including the communist and feminist Aflatun and the fundamentalist al-Ghazali. Once again, women joined ranks with male nationalists in common cause, and again men welcomed their support.

In addition to various moves to clamp down on leftist feminists from the mid-1940s, out of fear of a communist threat, governments were not always tolerant of the political criticism of liberal feminists either. This was clear in 1942 when Nabawiyya Musa, a staunch nationalist for more than two decades, attacked the Prime Minister, Nahhas Pasha, for accommodating British wartime needs. An order was thereupon issued closing her schools for girls and sending her to prison, where she was thrown in with prostitutes. Musa went to the pro-feminist lawyer Murqus Fahmi (whose book on women's rights was mentioned earlier), who took up her case. He pointed out that the Prime Minister's wife had been one of her students.[40]

During this period, as we have noted, the religious establishment at times supported women's demands and at other times opposed them. While fundamentalists did not support any of the feminists' demands, neither were they overtly anti-feminist. This changed, however, on the eve of the 1952 revolution, when religious scholars held a conference to examine all aspects of women's status within the context of Islamic law. They now openly attacked the feminist movement, claiming that it was influenced and supported by British imperialists, and saying that "colonialism had encouraged women to go out in order to destroy Islamic society."[41] The conference condemned the Egyptian feminist movement for its disruptive effects on society, and held Sha'rawi and Shafiq responsible. Evaluating the past, it attacked Murqus Fahmi and Qasim Amin, and praised the (anti-feminist) stance of Mustafa Kamil.

The reactionary conclusions of the conference seemed to be, in part, a response to the growing numbers of women in the workforce. By the early 1950s, women were found in shops, factories, the professions, and the social services in sufficient numbers to alarm the patriarchal sensibilities of male fundamentalists. The conference, wishing to turn the tide, or at least to stem it, scorned women's forays into public life, lamenting that women "wished to be degraded by going out to work and being seen by everyone."[42] The conference reiterated the reactionary refrain "a woman's natural place is her home," insisting that "her entry into public life is unnatural." The crux of the problem for these men was revealed in their declaration, "The most serious threat facing our society is the oriental woman's refusal to obey men."

Although fundamentalist men raised the alarm in March 1952, it was not until 1978 that the conference proceedings would be published under the title *Harakat nisa'iyya wa silatuha ma' al-isti'mar* (Feminist movements and their connections with colonialism, edited by Muhammad 'Atiya Khamis). This occurred six years after Sadat had come to power, by which time religious fundamentalism in Egypt had won considerable public prominence. (In another book, *Mu'amarat did al-usra al-muslima* [Conspiracies against the Muslim family, n.d.], Khamis charged that unveiling was a weapon of communism.) But during the period of Arab socialism under Nasser, these sentiments were not overtly expressed.

The period of the liberal experiment was a time in Egypt when a capitalist economy with ties of dependency to a dominant Europe still operated largely within a neo-imperialistic framework. The feminist or pro-feminist ideology that had served the nationalist cause during colonial occupation was no longer seen by most men to be useful or desirable during this new period of independence (albeit incomplete). Thus feminists achieved limited gains. Their successes did not threaten the ruling class. In fact, these limited gains could be said to have helped construct a more viable, modern society by harnessing women to the development goals of the state. Feminist discourse was for the most part allowed public expression by the state, except in its most radical leftist form, but even this managed to survive surreptitiously. When this period ended, women still lacked formal political rights, a symbol of their secondary status as citizens, while the stalemate on the reform of personal status laws affirmed their unequal position within the family.

REVOLUTION, ARABISM, AND SOCIALISM: 1952 TO THE EARLY 1970s

This was a time when independent feminist voices would be silenced. Islamists were also suppressed, although the Islam of the establishment and the apolitical discourse of religious scholars would be tolerated. In short, it was a time when the state heavy-handedly silenced all political competitors, and did so publicly. Those muzzled included rank-and-file fundamentalists from the among masses, whose liberation the state championed. Women, whose cause the state also claimed to support – for example, in granting female suffrage – were likewise suppressed by the state as independent political actors. However, the feminism of the leaders who had come of age in the previous period remained alive behind the scenes, while a rising generation of future feminists was nurtured as women took advantage of new state-sponsored opportunities in education and work. In this atmosphere of repression, feminists sharpened survival skills that would be useful in the battles they would encounter in the 1970s and 1980s.

The revolution of 1952, led by young military officers of the lower-middle class supported in their struggle for power by members of the same class among the Muslim Brothers, promised to usher in a new era. Soon, however, the Muslim Brothers were suppressed as dangerous to the state, and the leader of the Muslim Sisters, Zainab al-Ghazali, was imprisoned. From the early 1960s Arab socialism, with its new economic measures such as land reform and industrialization, dismantled the old class system. It was an era of hope for the majority, including the leader of the next generation of feminists, Nawal al-Saadawi, a 1955 graduate of the medical faculty at Cairo University, who in an interview recalled the early enthusiasm and optimism of her generation.[43]

The Arab socialism of the state in the 1960s called for social equality and justice for all citizens, and aimed at pan-Arab unity and wider Afro-Asian solidarity. The 1962 charter delineating the Arab socialist project announced itself as an amalgam of Islam, Arabism, and socialism. It declared: "The essence of religious messages does not conflict with the facts of our life ... All religions contain a message of progress ... The essence of all religions is to assert man's right to life and to freedom." The constitution of 1964 stated, in article 1: "The United Arab Republic is a democratic, socialist state based on the alliance of the working powers of the people. The Egyptian people are part of the Arab nation." Article 5 declared Islam the religion of the state. The new state suppressed Islam as a political force, but did not tamper with the Muslim identity of the society.

The state's stifling of competing discourses did not occur instantly. Feminist organizations continued their activism after the revolution of 1952. At this juncture, they made a final push for women's political rights, in which Duriyya Shafiq of the DNU led the way. In 1953, when a proposed revision of the Electoral Law was under review, she published *al-Kitab al-abiyad lil-huquq al-mar'a al-misriyya* (The white paper on the rights of the Egyptian woman), a

compendium of pro-suffrage arguments by sympathetic secular liberals and politicians as well as pro and con views from within the
Islamic establishment. For example, it included a piece by the constitutional lawyer Sayyid Sabri, arging that laws must change as the conditions and needs of society change. Since women were now part of
the public opinion of society (*al-ra'i al-'amm*), he insisted that they
should be able to participate in the formal political system. He
stressed that the electoral law contradicted the constitution, which
declared Egyptians equal in civil and political rights. However, the
state and official Islam came down firmly against political rights for
women. The Constitutional Affairs Committee of the Senate rejected
women's suffrage, and the Fatwa Committee of al-Azhar issued a
decree saying that Islam did not condone it. The Mufti of Egypt,
Shaikh Hasanayn Makhluf, contended that Islam opposed political
rights for women. However, Shaikh Allam Nassar, who was then a
former mufti, made the opposite claim. The day after the Fatwa
Committee made its announcement, Islamic organizations held a
conference in the office of the Muslim Brothers. Included in their
lengthy statement was the demand that the government close once
and for all "the door to this *fitna*" (chaos), claiming that it had been
proven that political rights for women were contrary to religion, the
constitution, and the public interest. Meanwhile, Shafiq intensified
her militancy in this heated battle through a sit-in at the parliament
and a hunger strike. Finally, in 1956, thirty-three years after EFU feminists had first demanded suffrage, the revolutionary government, in
its fifth year, granted women the right to vote.[44]

The intentions of the state, however, were made clearer in its
actions than in its official discourse. When feminist leaders tried to
continue their political struggle, the state put a final stop to their public activity. In 1956, the same year that the state granted women the
right to vote, it paradoxically started to ban feminist organizations
and to suppress public expression of feminist views, completing its
task by 1959. The EFU, under pressure from the government,
expelled Saiza Nabarawi, accusing her of being a communist. The
state dismantled the old EFU in 1956, but allowed a truncated
version to continue as a social welfare society under the name of the
Huda Sha'rawi Association. Meanwhile, after suffrage had been
achieved, feminists formed al-Lajna al Nisa'iyya li'l-Wa'i al-Intikhabi
(Women's Committee for Electoral Awareness) to make poor
women aware of their rights, but the authorities closed it down within

a year. Around the same time, a coalition of women of different political tendencies came together in *al-Ittihad al-Nisa'i al-Qawmi*
(National Feminist Union, NFU). The authorities, however, blocked
their project by withholding a permit for the NFU, and finally shut it
down in 1959. Aflatun was sent to prison in the same year. By then,
Shafiq was under house arrest. Nabarawi and Rashid were also
silenced. The clampdown on feminists occurred within the wider
context of political repression. The state apparently perceived feminists as more dangerous than fundamentalists, since the Muslim
Sisters did not suffer the same fate until 1964, when they were banned.
The following year their leader, al-Ghazali, was jailed. The same year,
new laws forbad the formation of women's political organizations.

With the official suppression of its organizations and the silencing
of its spokeswomen, feminism went underground; but it did not disappear. In 1967 I made contact with some of the older generation of
feminist leaders, including Saiza Nabarawi, Inji Aflatun (released
from jail in 1963), and Duriyya Shafiq, and found that feminism was
still alive behind the scenes. Nabarawi kept a low profile in Egypt but
was active internationally through the leftist Democratic Federation
of Women. The exception to the public censoring of feminists was
Amina Sa'id, a former schoolgirl protégée of Huda Sha'rawi and a
member of the EFU's youth group. Although her support for education and work for women coincided with the state's agenda to extend
opportunities to all citizens across class and gender lines, and she was
therefore conveniently accorded a public voice, Sa'id was not merely
the regime's "token woman," as we shall see.

The ideology of the new regime was set out in the 1962 charter.
The official discourse shifted from the more formal rhetoric of parliamentary democracy of the previous period to a fervent championing
of the rights of the masses and socio-economic development. The
grip of the old feudal class system was to be broken, and the final ves-
tiges of imperialist domination were to be eradicated. The charter
heralded Arabism expressed in language, culture, and pan-Arab
political links. Now, also for the first time, the official state ideology
confronted patriarchal supremacy. The charter stated: "Woman
must be regarded as equal to man and must therefore shed the
remaining shackles that impede her free movement so that she might
take a constructive and profound part in shaping life." This was situated in the context of the development needs of the country. The constitution promulgated two years later declared in article 8: "The State

guarantees equality of opportunity to all Egyptians." This was translated into free university education and a guaranteed job for every graduate. State support for fuller participation of women in public life would before long, however, trigger conservative reactions.

Meanwhile, official educational and employment policies opened up new opportunities for women. Women's literacy rates increased, and greater numbers of women graduated from university and entered the labor force. A corollary of this was a rise in the percentage of single women in the 1960s and 1970s, and a decline in fertility. (Lower fertility rates, however, were also connected with birth-control programs which the state supported.) Because of the state's interest in increasing its scientific and technical capacities, it enforced policies to encourage greater enrolment in the applied sciences at university. Larger numbers of women were accordingly attracted to these subjects, and subsequently into the professions. Nearly all women medical students graduating in the mid-1960s were reported to be practicing their profession.[45] The marked increase of women with training in applied subjects and in the scientific and medical professions during this period should be noted – for, as we shall discuss later, it was women university students specializing in these areas who were at the center of the new wave of young fundamentalists in the 1970s and early 1980s.

At a time when the state had suppressed the Muslim Brothers and contained the "dangerous" Islamist populist discourse, Muslim religious scholars were highly vocal in keeping alive a "safer" discourse on gender issues. The national charter calling for the removal of impediments to women's "free movement" and state policies to grant women free university education and guaranteed jobs constituted a direct challenge to traditional gender ideology and patterns of behavior based on male authority over women. As the 1960s and 1970s unfolded, the numbers of women university graduates continued to increase, as did their entry into various sectors of the labor force.

As often happens historically, when objective conditions change there is a burst of idealist and prescriptive literature extolling the very roles that are being altered in the process. Historian Yvonne Haddad, reviewing the publications of male conservative thinkers and *'ulama* in the decade following the proclamation of the national charter of 1962, found attempts to circumscribe the public roles of women through a reaffirmation of the doctrine of divinely sanctioned biological differences between men and women, and the renewed exaltation of wifely and maternal roles. There was also a call for different education for the two sexes corresponding to their different "natures" and roles. Conservatives recognized that women's economic independence would reduce their need and desire to remain dependent upon men.[46]

This period also witnessed the rare entry of a woman into the domain of scholarly religious discourse. 'Aisha 'Abd al-Rahman, known as Bint al-Shati' ("daughter of the shore," a name purportedly taken as a pseudonym to hide her life of scholarship and writing from her *fallah* [peasant] relatives), became a professor of Islamic thought at Cairo University and a prolific writer of articles and books, including a series on the lives of the wives and female relatives of the Prophet Muhammad, held up as paragons for the modern woman. Neither feminists nor fundamentalists would consider her radical enough; but widely differing regimes through the years have considered her both safe and useful. In the words of Hasan Hanafi, a founder of the Islamic left in the late 1970s, she belongs to the *fuqaha al-sultan* (the sultan's men of jurisprudence). Nasser, Sadat, and Mubarak all decorated her.[47]

While Nasser gave Bint al-Shati' space and awards, the fundamentalist Zainab al-Ghazali was imprisoned in 1965, and was only released after Nasser's death. Her brand of Islamist discourse, envisioning an Islamic state and insisting on the implementation of social justice for all, rather than remaining at the level of rhetoric, could not be tolerated during the Nasser period. She would only be allowed back on the scene from 1971 under the Sadat regime, when competing discourses would once again surface.

We have already noted that under Nasser, Amina Sa'id was the exception to the suppression of feminists. Two years after the 1952 revolution she founded *Hawwa'* (Eve), a popular magazine for women, issued by the large publishing complex Dar al-Hilal. In 1956 she became a member of the board of the Press Syndicate, and three years later its vice-president. Sa'id wedded the message of liberal feminism to the socialist state's "gender-neutral" agenda for the mobilization of its citizens. She used her pen to promote women's causes within the framework of the Arab socialist revolution. Speaking to a Beirut audience in 1966 she said: "[Women] as a group form the greatest obstacle to national progress to be found in our country today," echoing the same notion differently phrased by male progressives at the end of the nineteenth century. While noting that recent declarations concerning sexual equality in Egypt and other progressive Arab states had provoked public hostility, she assured her Arab sisters that the Egyptian state had "assumed responsibility for the emancipation of women."[48] Three years after this speech, on 13 September 1969, the influential semi-official daily *al-Ahram* recalled its mention seventy-five years earlier of Murqus Fahmi's then new book, *al-Mar'a fi al-sharq*. In reiterating the book's argument that lack of progress in the East had been caused by women's lack of education, and that women's lives must change so that the entire society might change, the article aptly reflected the message of the present regime.

Although her brand of feminism coincided in large measure with the agenda of the state, Sa'id was not simply its spokesperson, but a feminist who candidly criticized the failure of the state, then and later, to remedy inequities embedded in the personal status laws. She also decried women's new double burden, which accompanied their expanding economic roles, and which the state did little to alleviate.[49] It was feminists with a social mission, such as Hawa Idris, who devoted her life to providing childcare for mothers working in the state system, and women belonging to social service societies, who attempted to alleviate the double burden of poor working women.[50]

The education and work opportunities created after 1952 brought large numbers of women from middle- and lower-class families into the ranks of the educated and employed. However, while the new policies altered class and employment structures, gender inequalities persisted. The legacy of this partial change is apparent in the lives of two women born in the 1930s and educated at university in the 1950s, who in the 1960s and 1970s emerged as new feminist and Islamist activists.

Nawal al-Saadawi, after graduating as a medical doctor in 1955, found a mission among the rural poor. She was faced with physical and psychological health problems afflicting women, relating to such matters as the practice of circumcision [later referred to as female genital mutilation] and the obsession with female virginity. The connections she made between patriarchy, class, and religion (as commonly understood and enforced) in structuring the oppression of women led her to publish *al-Mar'a wa al-jins* (Woman and sex) in 1971, the first year of the Sadat regime. With al-Saadawi feminist discourse took a new turn: she broke a cultural taboo by introducing the issue of sexual oppression of women connected with everyday customs, as well as the prevalence of deviant behaviors such as incest, that victimized women inside the family. The following year she lost her job. Silenced in Egypt; her books and writings blacklisted and censored by the state, she went into self-imposed exile.[51]

Safinaz Kazim studied journalism at Cairo University, graduating in 1959. From 1960 to 1966 she studied in the United States, where she received an M.A. from New York University while living and working in Greenwich Village as a theater critic. It was in the United States that Kazim began to move from the political left to the right. The problem of identity nagged her. Around the same time she was inspired by the book *al-'Adala al-ijtima'iyya fi al-islam* (Social justice in Islam), by the Muslim Brother Sayyid Qutb, who had himself become disenchanted with the West and looked to Islam as a force of revolutionary revival. This mentor, whom she never met, was killed not long after her return from the United States in 1966. Six years later, after a pilgrimage to Mecca, Kazim took up Islamic dress, signaling her total commitment to Islam. In the 1970s she met Zainab al-Ghazali, with whom she shared the view of Islam as *din wa dawla* (religion and state) and the desire to see an Islamic state in Egypt.[52]

Between 1952 and the early 1970s, feminist voices – with the exception of Amina Sa 'id, whom the state found useful and safe – were muted. However, the state also created structures and conditions within which a new feminism incubated. The conservative pronouncements of Islamist scholars and thinkers were tolerated, even though they championed women's domestic roles at the very juncture when the state was encouraging women to join the workforce. However, radical Islam, which aimed at a more drastic overhaul of state and society, was quashed. Yet, as we have seen, although these plural discourses were suppressed, they were by no means eradicated.

INFITAH CAPITALISM AND POPULIST ISLAMIST ASCENDANCY: THE 1970S AND 1980S

This period, which spans the rule of Sadat and the ongoing regime of Mubarak, witnessed a resurgence of competing discourses. Women's feminism became public once more, while Islamic fundamentalists also found scope for new expression. In fact, the state itself became an agent in the promotion of forms of feminist and Islamist discourse to further its own objectives. At the same time, controls were imposed on the more independent or radical expressions of these two positions.

Under Sadat there was a fundamental shift from socialism and anti-Western imperialist rhetoric to *infitah* (open-door) capitalism and strong pro-Western rhetoric. This was accompanied by a shift from pan-Arabism to an inward focus on Egypt, which was sealed when Sadat made a separate peace with Israel in 1979 and Egypt was expelled from the Arab League.

When Sadat came to power in 1970, the country was in a condition people wearily called "no war, no peace," and still traumatized by the defeat of 1967 in the war with Israel. Sadat capitalized on the popular religious resurgence that followed the war, and encouraged it – in part as a counterpoise to Nasser's Arab socialism with its more "secular" cast.[53] After the war of 1973 and the acclaimed victory, there was a noticeable upsurge in the Islamic fundamentalist movement. It was popularly believed that victory had come because Muslims had returned to the correct practice of religion. The state encouraged the new emphasis on religion, fueling the spread of a fundamentalism which it subsequently needed to contain. Later, toward the end of the Sadat regime, the government's pro-Islamic positions were meant to appease fundamentalists, though it was hardly successful in containing the more radical among them.[54]

Meanwhile, the advocacy of women's causes espoused by Jihan Sadat and inspired by the UN decade of women (1975–1985) was encouraged by the state. However, the more independent and radical feminism promoted by Nawal al-Saadawi and others was contained. This has been interpreted in part as a result of Jihan Sadat's drive, and her ability as the president's wife to style herself the supreme advocate of women's causes in Egypt and so keep competing feminists out of the limelight.[55] However, on another front, the government could not tolerate independent feminist activism because of its need to appease conservative Islamist forces.

At the beginning of the Sadat period, for the first time since independence in 1922, the state promulgated a constitution spelling out a dichotomy between women as (public) citizens and as (private) family members governed by the *shari'a*. Thus women's right to the prerogatives of full citizenship became subject to male control. The new constitution of 1971 stated, in article 40: "Citizens are equal before the law; they are equal in public rights and duties, with no discrimination made on the basis of race, sex, language, ideology, or belief."

The unprecedented explicit declaration of no discrimination on the basis of sex would seem at first glance to represent a step forward. However, we must note the 1971 wording, "equal in public rights and duties," as opposed to the 1923 text, "They enjoy equally civil and political rights and equally have public responsibilities." Moreover, the 1971 constitution declared: "The state guarantees a balance and accord between a woman's duties towards her family on the one hand and towards her work in society and her equality with man in the political, social, and cultural spheres on the other without violating the laws of the Islamic shari'ah."[56]

Meanwhile, Islamic fundamentalism continued to gain new adherents among women, evidenced by the growing numbers of women wearing the *hijab*. Islamic groups became increasingly active on university campuses, spreading their message and actively recruiting. They were successful in appealing to large numbers of women, especially of the lower and more modest middle class. Many of the new recruits were women studying medicine and the sciences, who, moreover, tended to stay out of the workforce after graduation.[57] At the beginning of the movement to adopt Islamic dress, a young woman, Ni'mat Sidqi, published an account of her conversion to Islamic dress and an apology for the veil [which formerly covered the face] in Egypt, resurrected in the form of the *hijbab*, involving covering the head and wearing loose, enveloping clothing, in a book entitled *al-Tabarraj* (Flashy display, 1971), which became a cult book among young women in the early 1970s.

Around the same time, Amina Sa'id mounted an attack in the press, mainly in her magazine *Hawwa'*, on the return of veiling (in any form).[58] The new trend persisted, and by the mid-1980s women wearing *hijab* included some from the wealthier strata of society. Among these was Keriman Hamza, the first television announcer to wear Islamic dress, who recounted her conversion in her book *Rihlati min al-sufur hal-hijab* (My journey from unveiling to veiling). Veteran feminist Sa'id had been the main opponent of re-veiling until a young leftist, Sana al-Masri, attacked the practice and its wider implications in her book, *Khalf al-hijab* (Behind the veil, 1989).

Released from jail in 1971, the veteran fundamentalist leader Zainab al-Ghazali could return to discreet activism. Her prison memoirs, now [1990] in their tenth edition, attracted new generations to her cause.[59] As previously mentioned, the year after al-Ghazali's release, Safinaz Kazim took up Islamic dress, becoming active as a "committed Muslim" which she calls herself, rejecting the term "fundamentalist." An author of several books and drama critic for the weekly magazine *al-Musawwar*, she assumed the role of a crusading intellectual with a special concern for issues of culture, identity, and authenticity, while al-Ghazali has remained active as an organizer, along with writing, and mentoring young women disciples.

Both women favored an Islamic state in Egypt, and both have experienced state surveillance and incarceration. Kazim was imprisoned three times under Sadat, in 1973, 1975, and 1981. Each time, she was accused of being a communist. This kind of accusation was a useful way to discredit a fundamentalist leader and demoralize the movement without being seen to challenge Islam.[60]

The contradictory pressures on women under Sadat were enormous. The reversal of socialist policies became clear in the 1974 proclamation of the policy of *infitah*, when the door was opened to foreign investment, and the private sector was encouraged once again in Egypt. The state no longer promoted full employment of women but, on the contrary, propagated an ideology that curtailed women's public roles, encouraging a retreat into the home. This was attempted in different ways, many of them illegal. Lawyers and other women prominent in public life exposed this trend in a booklet, *al-Huquq al-qanuniyya lil-mar'a al-'arabiyya bain al-nadhariyyat wa al-tatbiq* (The legal rights of the Egyptian woman: theory and practice, 1988) writing: "We have observed a retreat from the principle of equality regarding the woman at work ... This has become clear in certain practices that are contrary to the Constitution and Egyptian law such as advertising in the newspapers for jobs specifying that applicants must be males."[61] Meanwhile, rising inflation and the migration of men to neighboring oil-rich countries, leaving women behind to cope, have pushed more women into the workforce.[62] The continued spread of the veil was connected in part with women's need to work and their wish to protect themselves from exposure to male harassment. This kind of personal security was sought at the price of engaging in passive rather than active resistance to male intimidation.[63] On a different front, in yet another of its contradictory moves, in 1979 the government unexpectedly enacted a law guaranteeing women thirty seats in parliament, which led to an immediate increase of women in the legislature.[64]

However, the most dramatic and politically sensitive move was the presidential decree making fundamental changes in the personal status laws for the first time in fifty years. Some of the excesses of patriarchal privilege were curtailed in an unprecedented manner with the expansion of women's ability to initiate divorce, added protection for women in divorce, and controls placed on polygamy. The president's wife had pushed hard for the 1979 decree, issued when parliament was in recess and which, indeed, became known as "Jihan's law." Many men, not only fundamentalists, were outraged, but for feminists the gains constituted an important, if still inadequate, step forward.[65]

The year 1979 was highly charged for Egypt, abroad as well as at home. Egypt ratified the Camp David accord with Israel, isolating itself from the Arab world and alienating both leftists and conservatives at home. The decrees favorable to women within the family and in parliament provoked Muslim conservatives. Meanwhile, the revolution in Iran brought Khomeini to power, ushering in a new Islamic state and heartening fundamentalists in Egypt. As Islamist forces gathered momentum, the Egyptian state made an important placatory move to Islamists and religious conservative in 1980 when it amended the constitution to read: "Islamic jurisprudence is the principal source of legislation," replacing the 1971 formulation that "the shari'ah is a principal source of law."[66]

Egypt entered a period of new and dangerous tensions, which the state could not control. In the fall of 1981, massive arrests were made across the political spectrum, including both feminists and fundamentalists. Among those arrested were Nawal al-Saadawi and Safinaz Kazim.[67] Not long afterward, Sadat was assassinated by a Muslim fundamentalist, and the two women were released, along with others, by the new president, Mubarak.

The early 1980s witnessed the renewed visibility and organization of independent feminism. Al-Saadawi, who had by then gained both a local following and international repute, was active in feminist organizing and politics. There was a significant number of highly educated women espousing feminism practicing law and medicine, teaching in university, working in business, and engaging as writers and journalists. A number of these women, under the leadership of al-Saadawi, struggled to establish the Arab Women's Solidarity Association (AWSA). In AWSA's own words: "We knew that the liberation of the people as a whole could not take place without the liberation of women and this could not take place without the liberation of the land, economy, culture, and information."[68] The process of becoming an official organization was not easy. The Ministry of Social Affairs refused AWSA a permit in 1983. It relented, however, at the beginning of 1985, and AWSA registered with the United Nations the same year as a non-governmental organization.

In 1985, in the face of growing opposition, the government canceled the 1979 decree revising the personal status law.[69] This galvanized feminists into collective political action. Within two months a new law was enacted, restoring most, but not all, of the benefits to women provided by the 1979 law. This occurred just before a large delegation of Egyptian feminists departed for the United Nations Forum in Nairobi that marked the end of the Decade for Women. It would have been impolitic for the Egyptian delegation to attend with such a major grievance.

There was marked concern among feminists at the growing conservatism in Egypt, evidenced in efforts we have already mentioned to curtail women's public roles and push them back into the home. In 1986, AWSA held its first conference under the banner of "unveiling the mind." The conference theme was "Challenges Facing the Arab Woman at the End of the Twentieth Century." The proceedings issued by the Association's publishing house declared: "It has become clear that the traditional stance towards women and their rights undercuts progress in Arab societies. The present situation demands a deeper, more modern look at women's roles in society as well as in the family."[70]

Meanwhile, the authors of *al-Huquq al-qanuniyya lil-mar'a al-'arabiyya bain al-nadhariyyat wa al-tatbiq*, calling themselves A Group of Women Concerned with Affairs Relating to the Egyptian Woman, pooled their professional talents to advance the cause of women, reminding them of their constitutional and legal rights as well as their rights under international treaties and conventions ratified by the Egyptian state. They published an open letter warning against the retrograde trends threatening to curtail women's rights and calling for the establishment of a women's platform to counteract these trends articulated in mass publications.[71]

The proliferating popular conservative Islamist literature of the 1980s echoed writings from the 1960s. According to the Egyptian historian Huda Lutfy, since the early 1980s an increasing number of Egyptian publishing houses had specialized in cheap editions of popular religious tracts. These tracts extol the domestic roles of women, held up as the cornerstones of a new virtuous society, and stress the need for male authority over women to guide them along the correct path.[72]

An important author of popular books with wide appeal is Shaikh Muhammad Mitwalli al-Sha'rawi, a former minister of *awqaf* (religious endowments), who has spoken to Muslims since the 1970s through state television, which accords him prime time. In the quietist tradition he praises the virtues of obedience and patience for men and women alike, while he preaches specifically to women about their family and domestic duties. In a reactionary vein, Shaikh Sha'rawi calls the woman who works while she has a father, brother, or husband to support her a sinful woman.[73] His tone supports the official line. In addition to enjoying continued television time, he received a state decoration in March 1988.

There is a different emphasis in the discourse of fundamentalist women leaders such as al-Ghazali and Kazim, who both play active public roles. Kazim finds no contradiction between women's public and private lives. Al-Ghazali left a husband because he interfered in her Islamic activism. She told me: "Woman companions [of the Prophet] have given as much to Islam as men, even more. The woman companion sacrificed herself, her husband, and her children while the male companion sacrificed [only] himself." Yet, although al-Ghazali has carved out a public role for herself and has attracted working women to her cause, she continues to commend women's primary roles as wives and mothers.[74] In 1979, in an article in *al-Da'wa*, al-Ghazali blamed feminists for encouraging women's public roles despite the dangers that await them in the public arena.[75] Muhammad Yahia, a fundamentalist intellectual and professor of English at Cairo University, told me: "The Islamic movement is seen as marginalising women but the Islamic movement itself sees attracting women to the movement [as public activists] to be its problem."[76] It seems that the mixed messages delivered by the movement contribute toward keeping women out of the public struggle.

Meanwhile, toward the end of the 1970s, there appeared what might be called a neo-Islamic modernism articulated by al-Ghazali Harb, a graduate of the languages section at al-Azhar and a former journalist, in his book, *Istiqlal al-mara'a fi al-Islam* (Independence of the woman in Islam). Harb, like 'Abduh a century before him, called for a return to the sources of religion for a correct understanding of Islam.[77] Asserting that women should consider themselves equal to men, he extolled the employment of women, not only to meet economic needs but as a guarantee of their independence. In this he attacked patriarchal supremacy in the family and opposed the expulsion of women from public space. Harb took on the fundamentalists when he declared that there is no such thing as Islamic dress, saying that Islam does not require *hijab*, either in the form of veiling the face, or simply the head and body. He asserted that only a correct upbringing, not veiling, can protect women. Harb was sternly criticized for these views by Muhammad Yahia, who saw the ideas of Harb (whom he claimed was far from the caliber and stature of 'Abduh) as useful to the state as a counterpoise to fundamentalism.[78] Some feminists have welcomed this position on women's liberation, argued in Islamic terms, because it suits them personally (that is, it resonates with their beliefs), while others simply acknowledged its wider political utility.

The state, trying to contain the spreading Islamic fundamentalist challenge, however, tries not to antagonize fundamentalist forces, alternating between tough and conciliatory attitudes, with the result that it generally displays a conservative stance regarding gender issues. It also favors more moderate religious conservatives such as Bint al-Shati', who advocate an Islamic society but not an Islamic state: the government bestowed a decoration on her in 1988. However, both women such as Zainab al-Ghazali and Safinaz Kazim, who call for an Islamic state, and Nawal al-Saadawi, who advocates an end to patriarchal and class oppression, make the state wary.

CONCLUSION

The "woman question" around which competing discourses have flourished in Egypt has been, as we have seen, about more than women. It has been about gender relations and sexual hegemony, and broader issues of power. It has been a means through which the state, the religious establishment, and Islamic movements have projected other designs. Women themselves helped to formulate the question on their own terms, both as feminists and as actors in Islamist movements. While as feminists they generated their own terms of debate and as Islamists they mainly reproduced male discourses, as actors in everyday life both assumed new roles, and in so doing gave further definition to the question. While there has always been room in Egypt for alternative positions on the "woman question," with the state,

Islamists, and feminists all keeping it alive, only feminists, for whom it is central, have meaningfully attacked patriarchal interests and opposed male supremacy.

The state has, in different phases, generated contradictory discourses and policies. It characteristically imposed its own agenda, and in so doing attempted to define the "woman question" to suit its own political ends. Thus we have seen that while the state has promoted new roles for women for pragmatic and ideological purposes, it has also upheld unequal gender relations and male authority out of political expediency. There have been shifts in rhetoric and emphasis between the state-building, liberal, socialist, and *infitah* capitalist periods. But while the terms of discourse shift, a substratum of basic gender inequality is retained, which ultimately challenges neither patriarchal relations nor the state's own power bases. Because of the state's own ambiguities, official discourses on the "woman question" have often been discourses of deception.

Islam, in modern Egypt, has been controlled by the state. The Islamic establishment has had to negotiate with and accommodate itself to the secular state. The last bastion of official Islam has been the regulation of family life. This is precisely the area where the state has allowed patriarchal control over women a free hand, and where gender relations have been most unequal. Populist, fundamentalist Islam confronted the state but upheld conservative codes of gender relations and endorsed male supremacy. Its uncompromisingly radical stance has elicited a defensive reaction from the state, which takes the form of a show of "Islamic toughness" in the area of gender relations, most notably demonstrated in conservative family laws. Women, normally excluded from the Islamic establishment, have joined the ranks of more radical, populist fundamentalist movements. The women leaders in such movements have taken on daring social and political roles while acquiescing in an ideology that contradicts their own conduct as activists.

Secular feminists have created the only discourse that insists upon radical changes in gender relations. Feminists have held their own, despite repression by the state, and feminist ideology in Egypt has always managed to survive. In more liberal political climates, feminism can be absorbed in what appears to be a more supportive environment, as we have seen in the period of struggle for national independence. In more contentious contexts, when the agendas of the state and Islamists promote extreme conservatism, such as that of contemporary Egypt [1990s and immediately preceding years], feminism emerges as an oppositional discourse.

This chapter on competing agendas on the "woman question" in Egypt has attempted to give a sense of the complex choreography of these discourses, how space is given and taken, and how for all but feminists the "woman question" in the end is a matter of political expediency.

*   *   *

Originally published in Deniz Kandiyoti (ed.), *Women, Islam, and the State* (London: Macmillan and Philadelphia: Temple University Press, 1991). This paper was first presented in the Workshop on Women, Islam, and the State that Deniz Kandiyoti organized at Richmond College in 1987.

NOTES

For their comments and suggestions regarding this paper I would like to thank Deniz Kandiyoti, the editor of the volume in which it was originally published, Yesim Arat, John Esposito, Sarah Graham-Brown, Enid Hill, and Albert Hourani.

1. For general definitions of feminism (women's rights, women's emancipation, women's liberation) see Karen Offen, "Defining Feminism: A Comparative Historical Approach," *Signs*, 14 (Autumn 1988), pp. 119–147; and Gerda Lerner, *The Creation of Patriarchy* (Oxford: Oxford University Press, 1986), appendix. For definitions of feminism in the Egyptian historical context see Margot Badran, "The Origins of Feminism in Egypt," in Arina Angerman et al. (eds.), *Current Issues in Women's History* (London: Routledge, 1989). In this chapter the various meanings of feminism should be gleaned from context and Margot Badran, "Independent Women: More Than a Century of Feminism in Egypt," in Judith Tucker (ed.), *Arab Women: Old Boundaries, New Frontiers*, (Bloomington: Indiana University Press, 1993); Margot Badran, "Dual Liberation: Feminism and Nationalism in Egypt, 1970s–1985," *Feminist Issues* (Spring 1988).

2. See Margot Badran, "Huda Sha'rawi and the Liberation of the Egyptian Woman," D.Phil. thesis, Oxford University, 1977: Badran, 'The Origins of Feminism in Egypt"; and Judith Tucker, *Women in Nineteenth Century Egypt* (Cambridge: Cambridge University Press, 1985).

3. On this dichotomy see Nawal El Saadawi, "The Political Challenges Facing Arab Women at the End of the 20th Century," ed. Nahid Toubia, in Margot Badran and miriam cooke (eds.), *Opening the Gates: A Century of Arab Feminist Writing* (Bloomington: University of Indiana Press, 2004), pp. 366–371; and Fatima Mernissi, "Democracy as Moral Disintegration: The Contradiction between Religious Belief and Citizenship as a Manifestation of the Ahistoricity of the Arab

Identity," in Nahid Toubia (ed.), *Women of the Arab World* (London: Zed, 1988), pp. 36–43.

4. See Margot Badran and Miriam Cooke (eds.), *Opening the Gates: A Century of Arab Feminist Writing* (London: Virago and Bloomington & Indianapolis: University of Indiana Press, 1990).

5. Badran, "Over a Century of Feminism in Egypt," pp. 15–34.

6. See Deniz Kandiyoti, "End of Empire: Islam, Nationalism and Women in Turkey," and Afsaneh Najmabadi, "Hazards of Modernity and Morality: Women, State and Ideology in Contemporary Iran," in Kandiyoti (ed.), *Women, Islam, and the State*; and Margot Badran and Eliz Sanasarian, "Feminist Goals in Iran and Egypt in the 1920s and 1930s," paper presented at the Middle East Studies Association Meetings, San Francisco, 1984.

7. See Laverne Kuhnke, "The 'Doctoress' on a Donkey: Women Health Officers in Nineteenth Century Egypt," *Clio Medica*, 9, 3 (1974, pp. 193–205.

8. The books are respectively: *Tariq al-hija wa al-tamrin 'ala qawa'id al-lugha al-'arabiyya* (The way to spell and practice the rules of the Arabic language, 1869); and *al-Murshid al-amin li'l-banat wa al-banin* (The faithful guide for girls and boys, 1875).

9. See, for example, selections by Warda al-Yaziji, Aisha Taimuriyya, and Zainab Fawwaz in Badran and Cooke (eds.), *Opening the Gates*.

10. On the *hijab* in nineteenth-century Egypt see Qasim Amin, *Tahrir al-mar'a* (The liberation of woman, Cairo: Maktaba al-Taraggi, 1899). Bahithat al-Badiya has written on the changing modes of *hijab* in early twentieth-century Egypt. She generally favored retaining the face veil for the time being for pragmatic reasons, but was aware this was not required by Islam. On the subject see, for example, her "Mabadi al-Nisa'i," in Majd al-Din Hifni Nasif (ed.), *Tahrir Bahithat al-Badiya Malak Hifni Nasif 1886–1918* (The heritage of Bahithat al-Badiya Malak Hifni Nasif, (Cairo: Matba'at al-Jarida, 1962), pp. 318–320. On the historical and contemporary context of *hijab*, see Valerie J. Hoffman-Ladd, "Polemics on the Modesty and Segregation of Women in Contemporary Egypt," *International Journal of Middle East Studies*, 19 (1978), pp. 23–50. For various interpretations in general of *hijab* see Mostafa Hashem Sherif, "What is Hijab?," *The Muslim World*, 3–4 (July–October 1978), pp. 151–163.

11. Zainab al-Fawwaz, "Fair and Equal Treatment," *al-Nil*, 151 (18 Dhu al-Hujja 1892), trans. Marilyn Booth in Badran and Cooke (eds.), *Opening the Gates*.

12. The early years of the women's Arabic press in Egypt are the subject of a dissertation by Beth Baron: "The Rise of a New Literary Culture: The Women's Press of Egypt, 1892–1919," Ph.D. thesis, University of California at Los Angeles, 1988.

13. See Albert Hourani, *Arabic Thought in the Liberal Age* (Cambridge: Cambridge University Press, 1983) pp. 130–163.

14. See 'Ali 'Abd al-Razek, "L'Influence de la femme dans la vie de Chiekh Mohamed Abdue," *L'Egyptienne* (August 1928), pp. 2–7. 'Abudh's writings include "Hajjat al-insan li'l-zawaj," "Fatwa fi ta'adud al-zaujat," and "Hukum ta'adud al-zaujat": see Muhammad 'Imara (ed.), *al-Imam Muhammad 'Abduh: siratahu, akarahu, a'malahu* ([The complete works of Muhammad 'Abduh,] Beirut: Dar al-Quds, 1978), pp. 49–54, 111–118, and 127–135.

15. See Hourani, *Arabic Thought*, pp. 164–182; Juan Ricardo Cole, "Feminism, Class, and Islam in Turn-of-the-Century Egypt," *International Journal of Middle East Studies*, 13 (1981), pp. 397–407; and Thomas Philipp, "Feminism and

Nationalist Politics in Egypt," in L. Beck and N. Keddie (eds.), *Women in the Muslim World* (Cambridge, Mass.: Harvard University Press, 1978).

16. On Qasim Amin see Hourani, *Arabic Thought*, pp. 164–170.

17. On women's feminist discourse from the 1860s to the present see Badran and Cooke (eds.), *Opening the Gates.*

18. On the public lectures see Huda Shaarawi, *Harem Years: The Memoirs of an Egyptian Feminist*, trans. Margot Badran (London: Virago, 1986) pp. 92–93. Writings and speeches of Bahithat al-Badiya and Nabawiyya Musa are found, among other places, in their respective books: *al-Nisa'iyyat* (Women's pieces/Feminist pieces, Cairo: al-Jarida Press, 1910) and *al-Mar'a wa al-'amal* (Woman and work, Alexandria: Matba'a al-Qawmi, 1920). Donald Reid communicated to me the information related here concerning the closing of the women's section and the new use of the funds saved.

19. See Majd al-Din Hifni Nasif (ed.), *Tahrir.*

20. See Margot Badran, "From Consciousness to Activism: Feminist Politics in Early Twentieth Century Egypt," in John Spagnolo (ed.), *Problems of the Middle East in Historical Perspective*, St. Antony's College, Oxford monograph series (London: Ithaca Press, 1992), and chapter 3 in this volume.

21. See Philipp, "Feminism and Nationalist Politics in Egypt"; and Cole, "Feminism, Class, and Islam in Turn-of-the-Century Egypt."

22. Badran, "Dual Liberation."

23. Progressive men, including Lutfy al-Sayyid, for example, acted as advisers to the EFU in their various professional capacities.

24. "Fundamentalist," like "feminist," is a term that needs to be understood in historical context, but broadly it signifies a person who returns to the fundamentals of Islam, especially the Qur'an and Hadith, and is associated with a conservative reading of Islam. Many persons generally referred to as fundamentalists reject the term, preferring to call themselves committed Muslims. In this chapter I use the term "fundamentalist" in a broad way, aware of the inherent difficulties, hoping the contexts in which it appears add clarification.

25. See Badran, "Huda Sha'rawi and the Liberation of the Egyptian Woman," pp. 299–308.

26. *Mudhakirrat ra'ida al-'arabiyya al-haditha Huda Sha'rawi* (Memoirs of the modern Arab pioneer Huda Sha'rawi, Cairo: Dar al-Hilal, 1981).

27. See Duriyya Shafiq, *al-Kitab al-abiyad lil-huquq al-mar'a al-misriyya* (The white paper on the rights of the Egyptian woman) (Cairo: n. p., 1953).

28. The most complete study of the Muslim Brothers remains Richard Mitchell, *The Society of the Muslim Brothers* (London: Oxford University Press, 1969).

29. On language, feminism, and cultural authenticity see Irene Fenoglio-Abd El Aal, *Défense et illustration de l'Egyptienne: aux débuts d'une expression féminine* (Cairo: Centre d'Etudes et de Documentation Economique, Juridique et Sociale, 1989).

30. Interview with Zainab al-Ghazali, Cairo, February 1989. On Zainab al-Ghazali see Valerie J. Hoffman, "An Islamic Activist: Zaynab al-Ghazali," in E. Fernea (ed.), *Women and the Family in the Middle East: New Voices of Change* (Austin: University of Texas Press, 1985).

31. Interview with Hawa Idris, Cairo, April 1988.

32. Interview with Zainab al-Ghazali, Cairo, February 1989.

33. Fatma Ni'mat Rashid, "Muqarana bain al-mar'a al-misriyya wa al-mar'a al-turkiyya," *al-Misriyya* (1 May 1937), pp. 10–13.

34. See Norma Salem, "Islam and the Status of Women in Tunisia," in Freida Hussain (ed.), *Muslim Women* (London: Croom Helm, 1984), pp. 141–168; John Esposito, *Women in Muslim Family Law* (Syracuse: Syracuse University Press, 1982), p. 92; and Maxine Molyneux, "The Law, the State and Socialist Policies with Regard to Women: The Case of the People's Democratic Republic of Yemen," in Kandiyoti (ed.), *Women, Islam, and the State*, pp. 237–271.

35. Huda Sha'rawi, "Tajdimat al-misriyya" (editorial), *al-Misriyya* (15 February 1937), p. 2.

36. Interviews with Duriyya Shafiq, Cairo, 1968 and 1974.

37. See Badran, "Huda Sha'rawi and the Liberation of the Egyptian Woman" and "Independent Women: A Century of Feminism in Egypt"; and Akram Khater and Cynthia Nelson, "al-Harakah al-Nissa'iyah: The Women's Movement and Political Participation in Modern Egypt," *Women's Studies International Forum*, 2, 5 (1988), pp. 465–483.

38. Interviews with Saiza Nabarawi, 1968 and 1973, and with Inji Aflatun, 1975. On socialist feminism see Khater and Nelson, "al-Harakah al-Nissa'iyya," pp. 473–477; Michelle Raccagni, "Inji Efflatoun, Author, Artist and Militant: A Brief Analysis of Her Life and Works," unpublished paper, n.d.; Selma Botman, "The Experience of Women in the Egyptian Communist Movement, 1939–1954," *Women's Studies International Forum*, 2, 2 (1988), pp. 117–126; Guiseppe Contu, "Le donne communiste e il movimento democratico feminile in Egitto al 1965," Oriente Moderno (May–June 1975), pp. 236–248.

39. Interview with Zainab al-Ghazali, Cairo, February 1989.

40. Information on the legal case came from Andree Fahmy, the daughter of Murqus Fahmi, and from papers in her possession relating to the case. See also Safinaz Kazim, "al-Ra'ida Nabawiyya Musa wa in'ash dhakkira al-'umma'" (The pioneer Nabawiyya Musa and the reviving of the nation's memory), *Majallat al-hilal* (January 1984).

41. Muhammad 'Atiya Khamis (ed.), *al-Harakat al-nisa'iyya wa silatuha ma' al-ist'mar* (Feminist movements and their relations with imperialism, Cairo: Dar al-Ansar, 1978).

42. This and the following quotations in this paragraph are from ibid.

43. Interview with Nawal al-Saadawi, Cairo, February 1989.

44. Shafiq, *al-Kitab al-abiyad.*

45. Kathleen Howard-Merriam, "Woman, Education, and the Professions in Egypt," *Comparative Education Review*, 23, 2 (June 1979, pp. 256–271.

46. Yvonne Haddad, "The Case of the Feminist Movement," in *Contemporary Islam and the Challenge of History* (Albany: State University of New York Press, 1982), pp. 54–70; and Yvonne Haddad, "Traditional Affirmations Concerning the Role of Women as Found in Contemporary Arab Islamic Literature," in Jane Smith (ed.), *Women in Contemporary Muslim Societies* (Lewisburgh, Pa.: Bucknell University Press, 1980). For a broader look at Islamic discourse on women see her "Islam, Women and Revolution in Twentieth Century Arab Thought," *The Muslim World*, 124, 3–1 (July–October 1984), pp. 137–160.

47. Bint al-Shati' wrote two autobiographies: *Sirr al-Shati'* (lit. Secret of the shore, which is a play on her pseudonym, Bint al-Shati', or daughter of the shore, is an autobiography, Cairo: Matba'a Ruz al-Yusif, 1952; now in the series al-Kitab al-Dhahabi, no. 6); and *'Ala jisr: ustur al-zaman* (On a bridge: a myth of time, Cairo Dar al-Hilal, 1967). See also C. Kooij, "Bint al-Shati': A Suitable Case for

Biography?' in Ibrahim A. El-Sheikh, C. Aart van de Koppel, and Rudolf Peters (eds.), *The Challenge of the Middle East: Middle East Studies at the University of Amsterdam* (Amsterdam: Institute for Modern Near Eastern Studies, University of Amsterdam, 1982), pp. 67–72. Hasan Hanafi's epithet was taken from Valerie Hoffman Ladd, "Polemics."

48. "Amina Said," in E. Fernea and B. Bezirgan, *Middle East Muslim Women Speak* (Austin: University of Texas Press, 1978).

49. On the double burden see Mona Hammam, "Women and Industrial Work in Egypt: The Chubra El-Kheima Case," *Arab Studies Quarterly*, 2 (1980), pp. 50–69.

50. Interviews with Hawa Idris, 1968 and 1972.

51. Interview with Nawal al-Saadawi, Cairo, February 1989.

52. Interview with Safinaz Kazim, Cairo, February 1989.

53. Interview in Cairo, January 1989 with Sa'id Ashmawi, judge in the High Court of Cairo, the High Court for State Security, and the High Court of Assize. He is the author of numerous books, including *Usul al-shari'a al-islamiyya* (Origins of the *shari'a*, Cairo: Maktabat Madbuli, 1983) and *Islam al-siyasi* (Political Islam, Cairo: Sina, 1987) who spoke of Sadat's stress on Islam as a means to distance his regime from Nasser's.

54. General analyses of what is called the Islamic resurgence include: Hamied N. Ansari, "The Islamic Militants in Egyptian Politics," *International Journal of Middle East Studies*, 16, 1 (1984), pp. 123–144; Said Arjomand (ed.), *From Nationalism to Revolutionary Islam* (Albany: State University of New York Press, 1984); Alexander Cudsi and Ali Dessouki (eds.), *Islam and Power in the Contemporary Arab World* (Baltimore: Johns Hopkins University Press, 1981), esp. Ali Dessouki, "The Resurgence of Islamic Organizations in Egypt: An Interpretation," pp. 107–119; R. H. Dekmejian, *Islam in Revolution: Fundamentalism in the Arab World* (Syracuse: Syracuse University Press, 1985); Ali Dessouki (ed.), *Islamic Resurgence in the Arab World* (New York: Praeger, 1982), esp. Saad Eddin Ibrahim, "Islamic Militancy as a Social Movement: The Case of Two Groups in Egypt"; John Esposito (ed.), *Voices of Resurgent Islam* (Oxford: Oxford University Press, 1983); Nazith Ayubi, "The Political Revival of Islam: The Case of Egypt," *International Journal of Middle East Studies* (December 1981), pp. 81–99; Fadwa El Guindi, "The Emerging Islamic Order: The Case of Egypt's Contemporary Movement," *Journal of Arab Affairs*, 1 (1981), pp. 245–261; Haddad, *Contemporary Islam and the Challenge of History*; Hassan Hanafi, "The Relevance of the Islamic Alternative in Egypt," *Arab Studies Quarterly*, 4 (1982), pp. 54–74; Saad Eddin Ibrahim, "Anatomy of Egypt's Militant Islamic Groups," *International Journal of Middle East Studies*, 12 (1980), pp. 481–499; Gabriel Warburg and Uri Kupferschmidt (eds.), *Islam, Nationalism and Radicalism in Egypt and the Sudan* (New York: Praeger, 1983); and Fouad Zakaria, "The Standpoint of Contemporary Muslim Fundamentalists," in Toubia (ed.), *Women of the Arab World*.

55. Nawal al-Saadawi mentioned this in her February 1989 interview. The need of Jihan Sadat to be the supreme woman – not just feminist – was mentioned by Safinaz Kazim in an interview in Cairo in February 1989.

56. On the 1971 constitution and gender see al-Saadawi, "The Political Challenges Facing Arab Women."

57. The literature on women's turn to fundamentalism and veiling includes: Fadwa El Guindi, "Veiling Infitah with Muslim Ethic: Egypt's Contemporary Islamic Movement," *Social Problems*, 28, 4 (1981), pp. 465–485; Fatima Mernissi, "Women and Fundamentalism," *Middle East Reports* (July–August 1988), pp. 8–11; Zainab Radwan, *Bahth zahirat al-hijab bain al-jam'iyyat* (A study of the phenomenon of the veil among university women, Cairo: National Centre for Sociological and Criminological Research, 1982); and John Alden Williams, "A Return to the Veil in Egypt," *Middle East Review*, 11, 3 (1979), pp. 49–54.

58. See Amina Sa'id, "Hadhihi idhahira ma'naha" (This phenomenon, what does it mean?), *Hawwa'* (18 November 1972); "Awdatu ila hadith al-ziyy hadhihi al-dajja al-mufta'ala ma'naha?" (Back to the story of the dress, this odd fuss, what does it mean?), *Hawwa'* (2 December 1972); and "'Id al-sufur 'id al nahada" (Feast of unveiling, feast of renaissance), *Hawwa'* (24 March 1973). In the latter article, written to commemorate the fiftieth anniversary of the founding of the EFU and the public unveiling of Huda Sha'rawi and Saiza Nabarawi, she attacks the current return to the veil, which she describes as "the greatest enemy of civilization."

59. Zainab al-Ghazali, *Ayyam min hayati* (Days of my life, Cairo: Dar al-Shuruq, 8th printing 1986).

60. Interview with Safinaz Kazim, Cairo, February 1989.

61. A Group of Women Concerned with Affairs Relating to the Egyptian Woman ('Aziza Husain, Inji Rushdi, Saniyya Salih, Awatif Wali, Mervat Ittalawi, Muna Zulficar, Magda al-Mufti), *al-Huquq al-qanuniyya lil-mar'a al-'arabiyya bain al-nadthariyya wa al-tatbiq* (The legal rights of the Egyptian woman: theory and practice, Cairo: n.p., 1988).

62. On elite women in the workforce in the early 1980s see Earl Sullivan, *Women in Egyptian Public Life* (Syracuse: Syracuse University Press, 1986); and for a general survey see Ann Mosely Lesch and Earl Sullivan, "Women in Egypt: New Roles and Realities," *USFI Reports*, 22, Africa (1986).

63. See El Guindi, "Veiling Infitah"; and Williams, "A Return to the Veil."

64. For an analysis of this see Kathleen Howard-Merriam, "Guaranteed Seats for Political Representation of Women: The Egyptian Example," *Women and Politics*, 10, 1 (31 March 1990). See also Sullivan, *Women in Egyptian Public Life*, on women in parliament.

65. See Aziza Hussein, "Recent Amendments to Egypt's Personal Status Law," in Fernea (ed.), *Women and the Family in the Middle East*, pp. 231–232; and Kathleen Howard-Merriam, "Egyptian Islamic Fundamentalism and the Law: Connecting the 'Private' and the 'Public'," *International Journal of Islamic and Arab Studies*, forthcoming.

66. For more on this see Enid Hill, *al-Sanhuri and Islamic Law*, Cairo Papers in Social Science 10, monograph 1 (Spring 1987), pp. 125–129.

67. For an account of her experience in prison see Nawal al-Saadawi, *Mudhakkirati fi sijn al-nisa* (Cairo: Dar al-Mustaqbal al-'Arabi, 1985), trans. Marilyn Booth as *Memoirs from the Women's Prison* (London: Women's Press, 1986); and for her reflections inspired by prison see Safinaz Kazim, *'An al-sijn wa al-hurriyya* (On prison and freedom, Cairo: al-Zahra' li'l-A'lam al-'Arabi, 1986). On women's prison experience and writings see Marilyn Booth, "Prison, Gender, Praxis: Women's Prison Memoirs in Egypt and Elsewhere," *MERIP* (November–December 1987), pp. 35–41.

68. AWSA, ed. Nadia Toubia, "Challenges Facing the Arab Woman," in Badran and Cooke (eds.), *Opening the Gates.*

69. See Nadia Hijab, *Womanpower: The Arab Debate on Women at Work* (Cambridge: Cambridge University Press, 1988), pp. 29–35; Howard-Merriam, "Egyptian Islamic Fundamentalism and the Law"; and Sarah Graham-Brown, "After Jihan's Law: A New Battle Over Women's Rights," *The Middle East* (June 1985), pp. 17–20.

70. AWSA, "Challenges Facing the Arab Woman," pp. 366–367.

71. *al-Huquq al-qanuniyya*, pp. 5–6. The introduction, translated into English by Ali Badran and Margot Badran, appears in Badran and Cooke (eds.), *Opening the Gates*, pp. 373–374.

72. On this phenomenon see "A Study of Muslim Popular Literature on the Role of Women in Contemporary Egyptian Society," presented at the Conference of the Middle East Studies Group, London, 1988, by Huda Lutfy, who has studied the recent literature; and Valerie Hoffman-Ladd, "Polemics," for an analysis of the historical debate up to the early 1980s on women in conservative Islamic literature, and the works by Yvonne Haddad cited in note 45.

73. See Mahmud Saif al-Nasr, "Shaikh Sha'rawi wa imra'a al-khati'a" (Shaikh Sha'rawi and the sinful woman), *al-Ahali* (3 July 1985), p. 8. A popular book written by Sha'rawi is *al-Mar'a kama araduha allah* (Woman as God wanted her to be, Cairo: Maktabat al-Qur'an, 1980). On Sha'rawi see Barbara Freyer Stowasser, *The Islamic Impulse* (London: Croom Helm, 1987).

74. Interview with Zainab al-Ghazali, Cairo, February 1989.

75. Zainab al-Ghazali, "al-Jamiyyat al nisa'iyya" (Feminist organizations), *al-Da'wa*, 42 (November 1979).

76. Interview with Muhammad Yahia, Cairo, March 1989.

77. al-Ghazali Harb, *Istiqlal al-mar'a fi al-islam* (The independence of the woman in Islam, Cairo: Dar al-Mustaqbal al-'Arab, n.d.). This book includes articles the author published in the Cairo daily *al-Akhbar* in the late 1970s.

78. Interview with Muhammad Yahia, Cairo, March 1989.

2

WOMEN, QASIM AMIN, AND THE RISE OF A FEMINIST DISCOURSE

On the occasion of our gathering together under the auspices of the Supreme Council of Culture to celebrate the centenary of the publication of Qasim Amin's *Tahrir al-mar'a* (The liberation of woman), I would like briefly to revisit Egyptian feminist history as I reflect upon women and Qasim Amin.[1]

Qasim Amin's *Tahrir al-mar'a*, published one hundred years ago, taking up the "woman question," evoked more impassioned outcry than any other book of its day and, as evidenced at this conference, continues to provoke heated passions in our own day. The "woman question" was and remains explosive for the cluster of issues treated and for the broader implications, and for what it has been made to symbolize. Historically, and especially today, where do we situate the "woman question"? Within a secular or religious discourse? Or within a more inclusive discourse that renders such categories simplistic and misleading?

By the time Amin wrote *Tahrir al-mar'a* Egyptians had been experiencing several decades of encounters with modernity. The country, and especially Cairo, had undergone vast changes in economic, political, and social institutions. New technologies increased possibilities for movement and communication among people within the capital and the country on an unprecedented scale. Education had been moving away from the more exclusive control of the religious establishment, fanning out from al-Azhar to that of secular authorities (of both the state and civil society). Since the early decades of the century, tuition for girls at the hands of private tutors in the home had been gaining momentum in the more privileged sectors of society. The beginnings of Egyptian formal school education for girls, beyond the previous limit of access to *kuttab*s for girls of modest backgrounds, had begun with the opening of the state school for elite girls in 1873. A decade later, British colonial occupation of Egypt made both more fraught and more urgent the need to educate all citizens, women and men alike, for national self-empowerment.

I start by setting out my broad claims and arguments concerning Qasim Amin's production of a feminist discourse in *Tahrir al-mar'a* and women's articulation of feminism. First, women in Egypt had begun to articulate a feminist discourse before Qasim Amin, widely acclaimed as the "father of Egyptian feminism," published *Tahrir al-mar'a*. Second, women's nascent feminist consciousness and evolving feminist discourse emerged directly out of their own experience. Women were "the mothers of (their own) feminism." The starting point of women's feminism was their own lives and the rights they were claiming for themselves. The starting point of Amin's feminism was the good of the family and the nation. Third, women's nascent feminist discourse emerged out of their encounters with modernity and of the awareness that they were being held back in comparison with men of similar circumstances. Amin was concerned with the skewed gender benefits of modernity and their implications for national welfare. Fourth, the evolving feminist discourse of women and of Amin emerged in the context of Islamic reform and secular nationalism.

The pioneering women's feminist discourse was a dispersed or scattered discourse. (I speak here of women's production before Amin published *Tahrir al-mar'a*.) Its site was their various books and essays in journals – often, but not exclusively, women's journals.[2] It was also an oral feminist discourse, as we know from memoirs.[3] Women initially wrote mainly to and for each other, as we see from their texts and their venues of publication. Yet they also wrote for a wider public and for men, to whose journals and papers they sometimes submitted their work. Qasim Amin, in *Tahrir al-mar'a* (and in his second major feminist work, *al-Mar'a al-jadida* [The new woman]), spoke to men about women.

I would like to focus for a moment on the disparate styles and discursive strategies of the women and Amin. In speaking to each other, women were gentle and compassionate. They had an agenda for change which they expressed in a forceful and confident voice. They also articulated what may be called a discourse of suffering – or long-suffering – to let other women know that they were not alone and to let men understand the profound effects of their neglect of or negative acts toward women.[4] Amin in his narrative style and modes of argumentation appeals to men, to what they – and the family and nation – will gain if women achieve their liberation. He describes women – women's condition and practices – in often offensive and crude ways, as women would not do, and as some later took offense to. I think Amin employed the strategy of overstatement – of exaggerating women's "backwardness" – as a goad to push men to act. This, however, does not make more palatable some of his deprecating depictions of women. Women, on the other hand, were often understated. While women spoke to each other with gentility and affection, Amin, on "the woman question," could be crude, sententious, and haranguing.

I would like to give examples of women who were writing, or expressing their ideas among themselves orally, before Amin published *Tahrir al-mar'a*. They published books of poetry and prose, and biographical compendia. They submitted essays to the (male-owned and run) press in the 1870s and 1880s, and to journals women themselves founded from the early 1890s. These include Maryam al-Nahhas, who published *Ma'rid al-hasna' fi tarajim mashahir al-nisa'* (Dictionary of the exemplary in the lives of famous women) in 1879; 'Aisha Taimuriyya, who published *Nata'ij al-ahwal fi al-aqwal wa al-af'al* (The results of circumstances in words and deeds) in 1887 *Hilyat al-tiraz* (Embroidered ornaments) in 1885; Zainab Fawwaz, who published *al-Durr al-manthur fi tabaqat al-khudur* (Pearls strewn in the women's quarters) in 1894 and *al-Rasa'il Zainabiyya* (Zainab's writings) in 1897; Hind Naufal, who founded and edited *al-Fatah*, the first women's journal in Egypt, in 1892; and Huda Sha'rawi, whose *Mudhakirrat* (Memoirs), published much later in the twentieth century, recall "feminist" discussions in a women's salon in Cairo in the 1890s.

There were significant differences between both the education and social status of these women and Amin. Amin had trained at the French School of Law and Administration in Cairo, and went on to study law in Montpellier for four years. Taimuriyya, Fawwaz, Naufal, and Sha'rawi were all schooled by private tutors at home. Amin was a judge when he wrote *Tahrir al-mar'a*, and as such an important public figure of the establishment, while the women were all leading discreetly secluded lives. Taimuriyya, who acted for a time in the 1870s as a translator for the khedive's court, and Sha'rawi, were from wealthy upper-class families; Naufal, from the professional middle class, published her journal from her home; while Fawwaz, of modest origins, was in the domestic employ of a middle-class family.

Qasim Amin and the women mentioned here all had foreign ancestry: Amin came from a Kurdish family originating from Iraq; Taimuriyya was of Turco-Circassian lineage; Fawwaz and Naufal originated from Lebanon; Sha'rawi, the only one with an Egyptian parent (her father), had a Circassian mother. Their non-Egyptian origins and connections did not place them on the margins, but rather conferred status, while also providing more than one optic on life. Later, the activists in the organized feminist movement would mainly be of Egyptian ancestry.

The writings of the women mentioned are from diverse genres. The biographical dictionaries of al-Nahhas and Fawwaz, *Ma'rid al-hasna' fi tarajim mashahir al-nisa'* and *al-Durr al-manthur fi tabaqat al-khudur*, respectively, were acts of retrieving women's past public accomplishments, restoring their names, and writing women's history. Such history-recording endeavors by women about women demonstrated that women had been important in the lives of their societies, and by implication could once again play significant public roles. Such writings become part of the new feminist canon.

In 1889, ten years before Amin published *Tahrir al-mar'a*, 'Aisha Taimuriyya wrote in *al-Adab*: "O you [men] who control our affairs, why have you left women behind?"[5] In his treatise Amin acknowledges that "the responsibility for this state of affairs [women's 'backwardness' or being left behind] lies with men rather than women."[6] The need to redress this situation – and how to do it – became the focus of attention of the women I mention and of Amin.

In the final decades of the nineteenth century, women employed their literacy both to decry and to transcend the intolerability of domestic seclusion, which Taimuriyya labeled "incarceration." In *Nata'ij al-ahwal fi al-aqwal wa al-af'al* she reaches out to other women in similar conditions: "I have suffered in this cave of isolation [the harem]. Compassion for all people [women] who have encountered what I have encountered and who have been struck by the same blows has led me to fashion a tale which would distract them from their cares when thoughts crowd in and would entertain them, drawing them far from the grief they feel in the exile of solitude which is harder to bear than exile from one's homeland."[7] The "women's world" was both enabling and restricting. It has been observed that women inhabiting a "women's world" have bonded in special ways and enjoyed certain freedoms from male interference in their lives. Yet, homosocial worlds of women, in particular the world of the harem, have distinct boundaries. It was far from uncommon in the earlier decades of the nineteenth century for women of the upper strata in Egypt to be restricted to the company of women of their extended family.

With the introduction of modern means of communication and transportation in the second half of the nineteenth century there was, for some women, an eroding of female domestic confinement. Sha'rawi, for example, speaks of traveling to Alexandria in the summer and wintering in Helwan as innovations that diminished the claustrophobia of women's routine seclusion. Women, from the position of experience, spoke of the constrictions, discomfort, and frustrations of domestic cloistering.[8] They yearned for less controlled lives and desired more freedom of movement and opportunity. While women speak of experiencing seclusion and delineate their frustrations, Amin, in condemning the practice, focuses on the societal consequences of seclusion, linking it to women's backwardness and, by extension, to the nation's backwardness. Amin catalogues gains to be had for men, the family, and the nation with the ending of female domestic seclusion. However, he does not call for its immediate dismantling. Both women and Amin point out that women's seclusion is not ordained by religion. Fawwaz says simply that there is nothing in the religion requiring such a practice, while Amin cites the Qur'an and other religious texts to back his argument.[9] Amin addresses the issue of "women's purity" (a much-used term in his day), making a strong argument that the seclusion of women is not the guarantee of their purity that men believe it to be, and he points out that the practice is, moreover, in decline. Rather, a proper upbringing and solid education "will be an impenetrable veil and a fortress protecting women."[10]

Women deployed their new-found literacy and education to promote their spread among other women. In an article entitled "'Asr al-ma'arif" (The age of education), first published in 1889 in *al-Adab* and later anthologized under a new title, "La tuslahu al-a'ilat illa bi tarbiyya al-banat" (Families only prosper through girls' education), Taimuriyya's piece, in Zainab Fawwaz's *al-Durr al-manthur*, makes a solid case for female education and the benefits that would accrue to daughters and their families. She mentions how education would enhance women's abilities to manage the home. Men would be able to "lean upon" such educated women. Neither Taimuriyya nor the other women of her day speak of how women's education would promote the creation of companionate marriages, a matter not considered at that moment. It was a subject that women would write about with the rise of the women's press in the early 1890s. In the 1930s, activists in the movement led by the Egyptian Feminist Union (EFU) would take up the matter.[11]

Subsequently, Amin took up this issue, claiming that the education of women would promote companionate marriages, and repeatedly stated his argument in different ways. He seems to do this, in part, as a strategy to persuade men to support women's education because it would benefit men by providing them with compatible mates, and out of a desire to promote a modern nuclear bourgeois family based on mutual understanding, love, and shared interests. Abu-Lughod sees the latter as the primary function of his treatise.[12]

Women combated the widespread notion – a "truism" in its day – that literacy and education would lead to women's loss of morality. In the inaugural issue of *al-Fatah*, the first journal for and by women, its founder, Hind Naufal, takes care to reassure her women readers of the respectability of writing. In her introductory editorial welcoming contributions from women she says: "Don't imagine that a woman who writes in a journal is compromised in modesty or violates her purity and good behavior."[13] Amin also undertook to dispel the notion of the moral dangers of female education: "The idea is deeply rooted in men's minds that an educated woman and a chaste woman cannot be one and the same." He insists: "We must deny that education will destroy a woman's character."[14]

Before the appearance of *Tahrir al-mar'a* women discussed the issue of *hijab*, which, as practiced at the time, included covering the face. In her memoirs Sha'rawi recalls the women's salon in the 1890s where the issue of veiling the face was debated. Women argued that covering the face was not ordained by Islam, revealing a familiarity with the Islamic reformist discourse of Shaikh Muhammad 'Abduh. In the final years of the nineteenth century, some women of the minorities in Egypt had quietly begun to unveil their faces, but the pioneering feminists did not call for unveiling in their writings, either before or after Amin advocated this in his book. Unveiling was something that women would not so much discuss – and thereby draw undue attention to – as simply proceed to do. Sha'rawi cautioned against premature unveiling, as did Malak Hifni Nasif (who was fourteen years old when *Tahrir al-mar'a* was published). At the start of their organized feminist movement in 1923, Sha'rawi, together with Saiza Nabarawi, unveiled in a highly public political act, uncovering-ing their faces at the Cairo railway station upon their return from an international feminist conference. After this, the newly public feminists would speak of the ills of face veiling and how it stood as an obstacle between women and a public life, but even then they were careful not to directly exhort women to uncover their faces.

What appeared most inflammatory in *Tahrir al-mar'a* was the chapter on women and the veil. This was also the chapter supported by the most stringent Islamic arguments. It has been widely alleged, on persuasive grounds, that Muhammad 'Abduh had a heavy hand in writing this chapter. The Islamic arguments against covering the face and critical of the extremes of female domestic seclusion were impeccably laid out. It was not so much religion as the force of tradition and the challenge to the prevailing structures of male power and privilege that interpretations of religion were enlisted to uphold that occasioned the fierce criticism of the book.

In 1891 Zainab Fawwaz made a strong case for work for women outside the domestic domain in what she called "men's occupations." There was nothing in religious law, she insisted, prohibiting women from working outside the home. She cited examples from history of eminent public women including Cleopatra, Zenobia, and other eastern queens. Fawwaz argued in favor of work for women as a basic right – one that the later EFU-led movement would strongly support.[15] Amin was not interested in promoting work as a woman's right, but simply conceded that work outside the home for women was acceptable for women of the poor class and others who might find themselves in need. He did not link his arguments for ending seclusion and promoting female education to public employment for women.

To recapitulate, Amin brought together a set of arguments, and anchored his plea for women's liberation within a larger argument for national liberation and a reconstructed modern family. Women were claiming rights and seeking freedoms from constraints, using instrumental and sometimes religious arguments, but they did not dwell on the notion of "women's backwardness." After the turn of the century, feminist women would increasingly ground their claims to their rights in a more highly articulated nationalist discourse, and would elaborate Islamic reformist arguments in demanding the return of what they called their lost rights, and particularly when arguing for the reform of the Muslim personal status code.

Finally, I would like to turn attention to the practice and politics of commemoration. Why do we celebrate the centenary of Qasim Amin's *Tahrir al-mar'a* when we have not celebrated the works of the women who wrote about women's liberation before Amin brought out his book? Is it because women's discourse was largely a "hidden discourse," or one that did not circulate widely in the "larger world"? Is it because, although the "woman question" was important, women were not important in their own right, and were not public figures? Qasim Amin was deemed important. He was a member of the male establishment and a respected judge. *Tahrir al-mar'a* was translated into many languages, both in its day and later, and has continued to be reprinted ever since it first appeared a century ago. It has found a secure place in the national canon, and so we celebrate it and the man who wrote it. We also continue to argue about it passionately one hundred years later.

The practice and politics of commemoration and canonization are related to the practice of writing history and processes of collectively remembering. While the names of some women in Egypt's past are known, often they are recognized merely in passing. It has only been with the still-recent rise of women's history that we know more about women's contributions and about Egyptian women's feminist history. It has been through research undertaken in the 1960s and 1970s and accelerating in the 1980s and 1990s that we have a fuller picture of women's experience, and that finally women's lives and stories have become part of national historiography. But the practice of national commemoration has not caught up with this. While we are gathered here together in Cairo to celebrate one hundred years of Qasim Amin's *Tahrir al-mar'a*, as far as I know we have not feted milestones in women's earlier feminism, nor their later feminist achievements, in a major national event such as this one. This seems to speak to a continuing practice of reading, remembering, and honoring our national history as men's history, of remembering men's names and men's works, even when it comes to the subject of women. I am pleased, however, to have been invited by the Supreme Council of Culture to celebrate Qasim Amin and through this event to play a small part in trying to bring women's history out of seclusion. What would Qasim Bey have liked better? He surely would have argued that this would contribute to national empowerment. He might even have called upon us to honor his feminist forebears and feminist women who followed their progenitors.

Addendum: A year later the Supreme Council of Culture organized the Conference on Women and Creativity, celebrating the writing of Egyptian and other Arab women.

* * *

Originally published in *Mi'at 'am 'ala Tahrir al-mar'a* (Cairo: Supreme Council of Culture, 2001) 2 vols., vol. 1, pp. 91–101.

NOTES

1. I would like to thank Gabr Asfour for inviting me to participate in the Conference on the Centenary of Qasim Amin's *Tahrir al-mar'a* and for selecting my book *Feminists, Islam, and Nation: Gender and the Making of Modern Egypt* to be translated into Arabic on the occasion of the centenary. I would also like to thank Ali Badran for translating the book.
2. On the discourse in the new women's Arabic press see Beth Baron, *The Woman's Awakening in Egypt* (New Haven: Yale University Press, 1994).
3. Huda Sha'rawi wrote about feminist debates in a women's salon in Cairo in the 1890s in her *Mudhakkirat ra'ida al-'arabiyya al-haditha* (Cairo: Dar al-Hilal, 1981); Margot Badran translated an unpublished copy of Sha'rawi's memoirs as *Harem Years: The Memoirs of an Egyptian Feminist, Huda Shaarawi* (London: Virago, 1986 and New York: Feminist Press, 1987).
4. Women's communications with each other through the texts (poetry, tales, letters) they sent each other letting other women know they were not alone in their frustrations and sufferings and to encourage and praise each other is reminiscent of the functions of the consciousness-raising groups in the United States in the 1960s and 1970s.
5. 'Aisha Taimuriyya, "Family Reform Comes Only Through the Education of Girls," trans. Marilyn Booth, in Margot Badran and Miriam Cooke (eds.), *Opening the Gates: A Century of Arab Feminist Writing* (Bloomington: Indiana University Press, 1990).
6. Qasim Amin, *The Liberation of Women: A Document in the History of Egyptian Feminism*, trans. Samiha Sidhom Peterson (Cairo: American University in Cairo Press, 1992), p. 16.
7. 'Aisha Taimuriyya, "Introduction to the Results of Circumstances in Words and Deeds," trans. Marilyn Booth, in Badran and Cooke (eds.), *Opening the Gates*, p. 128.
8. See Shaarawi, *Harem Years*, p. 53 and pp. 66–69.
9. Zainab Fawwaz, "Fair and Equal Treatment," trans. Marilyn Booth, in Badran and Cooke (eds.), *Opening the Gates*, pp. 223–224.

10. Amin, *The Liberation of Women*, p. 56.
11. On the 1930s see Margot Badran, *Feminists, Islam, and Nation: Gender and the Making of Modern Egypt* (Princeton: Princeton University Press, 1995), chapter 6, "Recasting the Family," pp. 136–40.
12. Lila Abu Lughod, "The Marriage of Feminism and Islamism in Egypt: Selective Repudiation as a Dynamic of Postcolonial Cultural Politics," in Lila Abu Lughod (ed.), *Remaking Women: Feminism and Modernity in the Middle East* (Princeton: Princeton University Press, 1998), p. 256.
13. Hind Naufal, "The Dawn of the Women's Press," trans. Beth Baron, in Badran and Cooke (eds.), *Opening the Gates*, p. 218.
14. Amin, *The Liberation of Women*, p. 31.
15. See Badran, *Feminists, Islam, and Nation*, chapter 9, "Women Have Always Worked," pp. 165–191.

3

FROM CONSCIOUSNESS TO ACTIVISM: FEMINIST POLITICS IN EARLY TWENTIETH-CENTURY EGYPT

To declare openly that this shadowy figure [woman] has a social existence, possesses a unity, a personality, has ceased to be an amorphous
member of an anonymous collectivity, oh!

Saiza Nabarawi[1]

The early twentieth century was a critical time in the history of feminism in Egypt.[2] From a little after the turn of the century to the beginning of the 1920s, a few women with a feminist vision moved more
fully, if discreetly, into public space, paving the way to expand the
lives of other women. This period followed the rise of a feminist
consciousness within the secluded middle- and upper-class female
world of the last decades of the nineteenth century and the first years
of the twentieth century.[3] It preceded that moment in 1923 when
women started using the word "feminism" and began to conduct an
organized political movement.[4]

I want to show how three pioneering middle- and upper-class
feminists set out to claim roles in the public sphere within the context
of everyday life. The three women, Huda Sha'rawi (1879–1947),
Nabawiyya Musa (1890–1951), and Malak Hifni Nasif (1986–1918),
the last better known by her pseudonym, Bahithat al-Badiya
(Searcher in the desert), manipulated some inherently restrictive
mechanisms, while tolerating others, in a piecemeal drive to realize
their vision through a politics of process. They eroded the institution
of female seclusion as they entered into life beyond the household,
encouraging other women to follow. Innovations, legitimized on

educational, humanitarian, or nationalist grounds, served their feminist purposes.

I also want to show how their assumption of new roles intersected with their efforts to reconstruct gender ideology. The life experience of these women furnished the substance of a new awareness, nurturing the formation of their feminist ideology – which was itself, I argue, a political act. Drawing on this ideology to guide everyday actions and to interpret ordinary experience was also political.[5] The struggle of these women as feminists was not removed from their everyday existence in the way it was from the personal experience of the men who were engaged in their cause. Moreover, the social construction of sexuality and gender both hindered and inhibited women in a fundamental and pervasive manner.[6] Feminist women dealt with these obstacles to their development in political ways – though not through party politics, and not always, especially early in the century, through the politics of explicit expression.

In the debates over the definitions and origins of feminism, historians argue that we can only discover and refine meanings in a historical context. Sharon Sievers, a historian of feminism in Japan, believes that "only by developing the history of feminism will we be able to confront problems of definition, links to theory, and the politics of feminism and its processes."[7] Karen Offen, a historian of feminism in France, writes how "in order to fully comprehend the historical range and possibilities of feminism, we must locate the origins and growth of these ideas within a variety of cultural traditions."[8] Indeed, this was what the Sri Lankan political scientist Kumari Jayawardena set out to do in her analysis of feminist experience in the Middle East and Asia.[9] In a historical context, it is to be observed that the phenomenon of feminism has often appeared before the term. The word, for example, was unknown to the American feminist pioneers Elizabeth Cady Stanton and Susan B. Anthony; according to Nancy Cott, it only became current in the United States in 1913.[10] Similarly, women in Egypt began to use the term "feminist" at the start of their organized movement in 1923, some time after a few women in late nineteenth-century Egypt had displayed a nascent feminist consciousness imbued with a sense of connection, commonality, and collectivity.[11] Some women deepened their awareness sufficiently to provide the impetus for a more dramatic transformation of their own lives and for the improvement of the lot of other women. They combined ideological and political perspectives to question the positions "assigned" to them by religion, nature, and culture. The feminist politics of these women developed from a base of what Linda Alcoff calls positionality, "a place from where meaning is constructed rather than simply the place where a meaning can be discovered (the meaning of femaleness)."[12] In this way, they evolved a more nuanced, profound, and committed combination of feminist theory and politics, with different priorities and timetables from the feminism (or pro-feminism) of men occupying dominant positions in the gender hierarchy.

Although the earliest stirrings of a new gender awareness had already surfaced, a more fully-articulated feminist consciousness expressed itself in the form of a discreet activism during the period of colonial occupation and the movement for national independence. This was a time when Egyptians, irrespective of gender, witnessed considerable social and economic repression as part of colonial political domination. The feminist consciousness of women, therefore, was soon bound up with their intensifying nationalist consciousness. However, while pro-feminist men used feminist arguments as part of their discourse of national liberation, the adversaries of feminism used their different brand of nationalism to discredit a feminism which they depicted as opening the way for the alien sabotage of an indigenous culture and its institutions. Consequently, the feminist project was caught up in a contradiction, being seen both as a source of indigenous liberation and as a means of colonial subversion of local culture and society. For the three women who are the subject of this chapter, nationalism was bound up with societal transformation and empowerment through new gender roles. For many, however, nationalism involved the preservation of traditional practices – many of which were on the wane – as a weapon of cultural defense.[13] Both in the early days of public feminism, and again when it resurfaced in the 1970s and 1980s (having been proscribed from 1956 until the end of the Nasser regime), the problem of the indigenous and the authentic continued to haunt the feminist enterprise and its projects.

It is important to note that Huda Sha'rawi, Bahithat al-Badiya, and Nabawiyya Musa, three pioneers of feminism, now with a firm place in Egyptian history, were Muslim and Egyptian.[14] Because most of the first generation of women (born in the middle of the nineteenth century) who had led the way in breaking out of domestic confinement to take on new roles were Christians of Syrian origin, the Muslim and national identities of of this second generation of feminists was of crucial symbolic value, especially as arguments drawn from the discourses of Islamic reform and Egyptian nationalism were mobilized to legitimize and further feminist projects in the country.[15] It was important for Muslims to establish that Islam did not ordain the domestic seclusion of women, or the segregation of the sexes. These practices were underpinned by an ideology of sexuality circulating in the culture that was seen to be bound up with Islam, giving it added force. Included in such thinking, for example, was the conviction that the honor of the family was dependent on the sexual purity of its women.[16]

Strongly-held beliefs about sexuality and codes of honor posed immediate practical problems for early feminist activists. Choosing to protect themselves by resorting to some of the same controls from which they were trying to work free won them, as we shall see, a degree of maneuverability, but it also sustained a repressive social framework. Historians are now analyzing connections between social constructions of sexuality and the patriarchal control and oppression of women, including how they were cunningly grounded in religious systems.[17] In Egypt, however, neither the feminists nor the pro-feminist men who had disengaged Islam from its association with extreme forms of control over women directly confronted how the social construction of sexuality was oppressive to women.

If it was women born in the middle decades of the nineteenth century who first voiced a rising feminist consciousness, it fell to those born in the concluding decades of the century to maneuver the final transition from consciousness-raising to open, organized activism. They embarked on a journey that took them from domestic seclusion, described by poet and writer 'Aisha al-Taimuriyya (1840–1902) as "a cave of isolation"[18] to what another poet and writer, Mayy Ziyada (1886–1941) called "the threshold of unknown territories."[19]

THE THREE FEMINISTS

Of the three feminists, Huda Sha'rawi and Nabawiyya Musa were publicly active until the middle of the twentieth century. Premature death in 1918 removed Bahithat al-Badiya from the scene at the age of thirty-two. Looked at in the order of their birth, Huda Sha'rawi, whose mother was a young Circassian woman, was born in Minya on the estate of her elderly father, Sultan Pasha, a vastly wealthy Upper Egyptian landowner, administrator, and politician who had taught himself to read and write as an adult. Following the death of her father when she was four, Huda was raised with her younger brother in an élite household in Cairo by her mother and her mother's co-wife. She was educated by tutors in the harem and, at thirteen, was married to an older cousin who was her legal guardian. At fourteen she separated from him, only returning in 1900, when she was twenty-one. In the interim she resumed lessons with her tutors. She also frequented the women's salon of Eugénie Le Brun Rushdi, where she took part in debates that sharpened a feminist awareness already ignited by early comparisons she had made between the treatment of her brother and herself. Huda Sha'rawi was to lead an organized and public feminist movement from 1923 until her death.[20]

Bahithat al-Badiya was born in 1886, the eldest of seven children, into a middle-class Cairo family. Her father, Hifni Nasif, was educated at al-Azhar and Dar al-'Ulum. A well-known scholar, he taught at the School of Law and later at the new Egyptian University established in 1908. Her brother, who encouraged her education and wrote a brief biography of her, noted that her father "was not saddened by her birth."[21] In 1900 she was in the first class of a specially created section for girls in the 'Abbasiyya School to be awarded primary school certificates. Three years later she passed the examination for a first diploma at the Saniyya Teachers' School. After the regulation two years teaching, she obtained her final diploma in 1905. However, two years later, when she married, she stopped teaching, as she was obliged to do by discriminatory government regulations, and also because she went to live with her husband in his desert home near the Fayyum oasis. The expression of her feminist consciousness was facilitated by her father's insistence that she be able to continue writing and giving talks. Her letters to Mayy Ziyada indicate that helping to fuel the intensity of her feminism was her misery in her marriage – she had been unaware when she married that her husband already had a wife, and a daughter whose upbringing she was expected to supervise. Bahithat al-Badiya maintained a public presence through her pen as well as occasional speeches and lectures.

Nabawiyya Musa, also from the middle class, was born in 1886, the year her father, who was an army captain serving in the Sudan, died. Her mother raised Nabawiyya and her brother, ten years her senior, on the military pension of her late husband. Nabawiyya entered the women's section at the 'Abbasiyya School two years after Bahithat al-Badiya, and followed in her footsteps through the Saniyya School and into teaching. Her struggle to obtain the baccalaureate degree in 1907, which we shall discuss more fully below, was surely a major force in her feminist evolution. She remained single, a rebellious or deviant act in a society where women and men alike were pressed into marriage. Making a decision not required of men because of the regulation forbidding married women from teaching, she dedicated herself to the profession of education, which became her lifelong cause and the arena for her activism.[22]

In addition to the fruits of their activism, all three women left a rich written legacy. Huda Sha'rawi's editorials appeared regularly in *l'Egyptienne*, the feminist journal she founded in 1925, and her speeches and writings also appeared in the press. At the end of her life she dictated memoirs which were published in Arabic in 1981, in English in 1986 in London and 1987 in New York, and in Dutch in 1987. Bahithat al-Badiya's articles for the liberal national paper *al-Jarida*, along with her speeches, were published under the title *al-Nisa'iyyat* (Women's pieces or Feminist pieces) in 1909, and republished in 1920 with some additions. A compendium of her articles, speeches, poetry, and essays was published posthumously by her brother. She was said to have started a book on the rights of Muslim women for which she had completed chapters on economic rights, on rights to administer public bequests, and on voting rights. Nabawiyya Musa published *al-Ayat al-bayyinat fi tarbiyyat al-banat* (The clear model in the education of girls) at an uncertain date, and *al-Mar'a wa al-'amal* (Woman and work), in 1920, as well as a *diwan* (collection) of poetry. She also edited a woman's page for the weekly *al-Balagh al-usbu'i* and founded a magazine for young women, *Majallat al-fatah* (1937 to 1943) in which she published her memoirs (*Dhikriyyati*).

CLAIMING PUBLIC SPACE

Innovative action becomes most telling when a feminist vision is articulated both in word and deed. Breaking out of confinement, Huda Sha'rawi, Bahithat al-Badiya, and Nabawiyya Musa matched their actions to their words and moved into public space early in the twentieth century, albeit circumspectly.[23] By then, it had become axiomatic in progressive male circles that national liberation required women's progress,[24] and it had also become axiomatic for feminists that their own liberation was to be fought for in and of itself, as well as for the good of the nation.[25] However, with the options available to them at the time, Bahithat al-Badiya and Nabawiyya Musa, as middle-class women, and Huda Sha'rawi from the the upper class, entered a life beyond domesticity in different ways. For example, while schooling had by then become acceptable for middle-class women, most upper-class daughters had to wait at least a generation before their tuition would shift from the household to the classroom.[26] Yet as we shall see below, other possible avenues out of household-centered activity existed for both classes in women's associations, usually organized by women of a similar background. Self-improvement activities organized by women's associations, however, brought middle- and upper-class women together.

School made it possible for middle-class women to develop new ways of thinking and conducting their lives under the tutelage of professional women, and offered them some respite from the strict control of the patriarchal family. Colonial education policy focused on training limited numbers of men for government service, and accordingly state education for women was extremely limited.

At the beginning of the twentieth century there was not a single state secondary school for girls (a section was opened for girls in a boys' primary school), and only three for boys. The administrators and the majority of the teachers, moreover, were British, promoting a foreign dimension to the educational formation of girls.[27] Nabawiyya Musa had to battle British colonial education politics and practices to obtain a baccalaureate degree. Following the completion of her teacher training course in the Saniyya School she wanted to sit for the baccalaureate examination. In the absence of a government secondary school for girls she was forced to prepare for the examination privately. Only with difficulty did she obtain permission from the Ministry of Education to take the examination, and then under the strict control of the British Adviser, Douglas Dunlop. She passed, and received her diploma in 1907, but no woman was allowed to sit for this examination again for twenty-one years.[28]

By not granting higher degrees to women the state also hindered their entry into new jobs, thereby siding against the progressive element in Egyptian society and supporting the conservative forces. Nevertheless, some middle- and upper-class women took their education into their own hands, thereby opening up a different avenue to the public realm. In 1909, this activity brought together the three women who form the subject of this chapter. Huda Sha'rawi and other upper-class women helped organize special lectures that were given by newly-educated middle-class women, including Bahithat al-Badiya and Nabawiyya Musa.[29] The lectures were held at the new Egyptian University and at the club of the progressive Umma Party, which had been established in 1907. The women's lectures were stopped in 1912. Two years later Huda Sha'rawi helped found the Jam'iyyat al-Raqi al-'Adabiyya li al-Sayyidat al-Misriyyat, referred to in English as the Women's Intellectual Association, which carried on the enterprise. Around this time Bahithat al-Badiya founded al-Ittihad al-Nisa'i al-Tahdhibi (Women's Refinement Union) for self-improvement and the expansion of education. While we do not have information on any of the talks sponsored by this last association, we do know that in 1914 Huda Sha'rawi collaborated with a Frenchwoman, Marguerite Clément, on the opening lecture for the Women's Intellectual Association, delivered by Clément under the title "Quel peut et doit être le rôle de la femme egyptienne dans l'activité sociale et nationale?"[30] They argued that women would find their way out of seclusion through participation in social welfare activities, from which they would gain new skills, widened horizons, and the legitimization of their public presence.

The talk described a process already underway, for both middle- and upper-class women had already formed various societies to help themselves and others. In 1908, for example, Fatma Rashid helped establish the Jam'iyyat Tarqiyyat al-Mar'a (Society for the Progress of the Woman) to further moral formation and assist in the expansion of women's knowledge. In 1909, Huda Sha'rawi, after refusing to join the Lady Cromer Society, and insisting instead on working within an Egyptian organization, had helped create the Mabarrat Muhammad 'Ali, which operated a medical dispensary for the poor. While this well-endowed organization was long-lived, most women's societies were not, although women perservered in creating new associations.[31] Bahithat al-Badiya founded a society which engaged in relief work during the Italian invasion of Libya in 1911. She also set up a school on her property in the Munira district of Cairo to teach women nursing.[32] The way in which women's organizations constituted an "invasion" of public space may be seen in Huda Sha'rawi's recollection of looking for premises for the new Women's Intellectual Association in 1914 when "it was still not acceptable for women to have a place [outside the harem] to congregate."[33]

So far we have noted that the forays of women into the public sphere occurred among women themselves or in women-only contexts. In 1911, however, Bahithat al-Badiya ventured further, making the presence of women felt at the Egyptian Congress when she sent a set of feminist demands to this gathering of Muslim men. Her comprehensive program, laying claim to a process already underway, charted a fuller course for the extension of the rights of women. For Huda Sha'rawi, and other upper-class women, the first opportunity to engage in overt political work came when the nationalist movement entered the militant stage during the 1919 revolution. In that year Sha'rawi helped organize a large women's demonstration. She founded the Wafdist Women's Central Committee, and remained at the head of women's nationalist activism, helping organize economic boycotts, supporting strikes, collecting funds, and raising morale, until independence. While this political militancy was undertaken for a nationalist cause, women at the same time insisted that gender equality was as important as citizenship rights and took feminist stands when necessary.[34]

VEILING AS FEMINIST STRATEGY

When the three feminists first moved into the public sphere they remained veiled (that is, they covered their faces and wore all-enveloping outer garments) so that, while they were in public, they were not fully seen to be there. However much this discretion served them in the short run, women would eventually find it important to assert full and open rights to be part of public life, unencumbered by the distancing mechanism of the face veil. Bahithat al-Badiya aptly noted both the strategic importance and complexity of the problem of *hijab* (at that time this term connoted the veiling of the face).[35] She argued: "If you want to destroy an edifice [face veiling] wouldn't you destroy it little by little and build a better one on its ruins?" She went on to observe: "This difficult issue [face veiling] has caused a violent war of the pen for years ... neither the conservatives nor the liberals have won."[36] Though face veiling smoothed the way for the entry of Muslim women into the public sphere, it not only signaled adherence to a system of female seclusion and separateness, it also implicitly upheld the prevailing sexual ideology, even after the link of face veiling with Islam was broken for women.

For complex reasons, there was a lag in Egypt between Muslim women's discovery that the face veil was not required by Islam and their discarding of it. Even if covering the face was not ordained by Islam, the association of the practice with religion was compelling, and was bound up with intersecting issues of identity, security, and respectability. Moreover, the decision to discard the face veil was by no means the woman's alone, but a matter involving the family. Around the end of the first decade of the twentieth century, the discourse on face veiling among feminist women and their adversaries shifted to issues of female morality and women's safety. The feminists and their adversaries approached the question in different ways and for different ends.

For Muslims, beyond the problem of the face veil's "Islamic symbolism" – that is, the identity it projected apart from any question of Islamic requirement – there existed an obstacle to its removal in a popular ideology of sexuality linked to family honor that was bound up in people's minds both with Islam and with broader social convictions. Popular belief construed women as essentially sexual beings – unlike men, who were only partly understood in terms of their sexuality. A woman was thought to possess greater sexual instincts than a man, and therefore threatened to ignite chaos, or *fitna*, with which she was equated. It was necessary to control the potentially disruptive force of a woman's sexuality for its own sake, and also because the honor of the family was tied to her sexual purity. Another popular notion held that the proximity of a man and a woman implicitly spelled danger.[37] Controlling devices were constructed out of these beliefs. In the city, among those classes where women were not required to engage in labor outside the house, they were cloistered. When city women of any class went outside the domestic enclosure they veiled their faces and bodies as a distancing device. Among the urban lower class and the peasants, for whom veiling was incompatible with their lives as laborers or cultivators, the community imposed mechanisms for the regulation and surveillance of women's behavior, and any interaction between women and men.[38]

Thus, middle- and upper-class women moving into the public sphere raised the specter of sexual danger. Sha'rawi, Bahithat al-Badiya, and Musa used the veil as a feminist tool to deflect attention from this "danger." During this transitional period, as women broke new paths, the veil could offer protection from sexual taunts or assault and attacks upon honor. When 'Abd al-Hamid Afandi, who founded the journal *al-Sufur* (Unveiling) in 1915, told women to unveil, Bahithat al-Badiya asked how this could be done when they were subjected to "rude stares and remarks" in the streets. The veil would only be discarded later, when it seemed expedient to do so.[39] Meanwhile, the feminists advocated gradual unveiling while they tried to prepare the younger generation of women for this step, and to enlist men in its support. Bahithat al-Badiya remarked of her generation of feminists, "If we had been raised from childhood to go out unveiled and if our men were ready for it, I would approve of unveiling for those who want it."[40] She told the men: "Reform yourselves and your morals because your corruption is the major cause for our veiling."[41]

Women themselves were seen to be complicating the issue. While retaining the veil, many modified it – and the rest of their dress – in a way that was seen as provocative rather than modest. The term *mutabarrija*, connoting a seductive, showy woman – who, nevertheless, was usually veiled – came into circulation.[42] The appearance of the veiled *mutabarrija* reemphasized the notion of woman as a sexual being, posing a problem for the feminists and supplying fuel to the conservatives. It added a new element to the debate on *hijab*. One way the feminists dealt with the problem was to call attention to it. Bahithat al-Badiya, who found the middle class the "most correct in morals," accused upper-class women, possessing wealth and leisure, of "letting themselves loose in amusements" displaying *tabarruj*. Pointing to moral corruption in society, she advocated more circumspection on the part of these women, urging them to move about with a seriousness of purpose.[43] She suggested to women that they take up the lighter veil worn by Turkish women in place of the thick veil typical of the older generation in Egypt. When speaking of women who had gone too far in modifying their *izar* (outer wrap), she acknowledged that "it would be acceptable if these women would only uncover their faces but keep their hair and figures concealed."[44] While this may appear contradictory to her stand in favor of the veil, she was clearly saying to those who insisted upon uncovering their faces that it would be better if they kept within the bounds of modest dress understood to be prescribed by Islam.

Huda Sha'rawi also favored gradualism. She prodded Saiza Nabarawi, returning to Egypt around 1910 after a girlhood in Paris, to put on the veil – with the promise, as the latter recalled, that it would be a temporary measure.[45] Nabawiyya Musa, in the introduction to her book *al-Mar'a wa al-'amal* (Woman and Work), published in 1921, declared that she would not discuss *hijab* and *sufur* (unveiling) because she found the terms meaningless. City women who covered their faces but were otherwise "in a state of immodesty" attracted passers-by with their seductive dress, while peasant women, who did not veil, deported themselves modestly. Women, in her opinion, should adopt a manner of dress and walk that would "blunt the desires of men." "That's what I call veiling," she declared. Musa shifted the focus of the debate to modesty, as Bahithat al-Badiya had, when she said, "Unveiling and veiling are the same for me as long as chastity [*iffa*] and modesty [*hishma*] are not violated."[46]

Although veiling the face was a practical expedient in the short run, as long as feminists condoned this they also implicitly condoned the social construction of women as essentially sexual. In the early years of the twentieth century the feminists' vision was concerned with a longer process of liberation which they did not wish to threaten. Feminists did not want women to lay themselves open to assaults on themselves and their honor. They wanted to avoid undue attention and outspoken opposition. They insisted upon their own agenda and timetable. Bahithat al-Badiya, who had written, "We know that veiling will not last forever," remarked that when man ordered women to veil, they veiled, and "now if he asks us to unveil we unveil."[47] What she wanted was that "man should let us reflect upon his ideas and decide what is most reasonable. He should not be a tyrant in our liberation as he was in our enslavement."[48]

EXPOSING THE SOCIAL CONSTRUCTION OF GENDER

It was commonplace in the world of the urban middle and upper classes, institutionally and ideologically bifurcated by gender, to consider women part of a different and inferior natural order. In 1905, for example, Talat Harb, in his *Tarbiyya al-mar'a wa al-hijab* (The education of the woman and veiling), repeated the popular doctrine of the essential differences between the sexes and of women's intellectual inferiority. Such reiterations elicited the mordant observation from Nabawiyya Musa that "men have spoken so much of the differences between the man and woman that they would seem to be two separate species."

Interrogating the supposed differences between males and females, therefore, became part of the formation of a feminist consciousness. Huda Sha'rawi reveals, in her memoirs, how she questioned the preferential treatment given to her brother. She also recalls observing how an itinerant female poet, who sat with the men and talked like them, was not like other women, but more like men. It is clear from her memoirs that the consequences of such "differences" rankled.[49] Bahithat al-Badiya and Nabawiyya Musa, as young women, also addressed the subject of differences in their lectures and essays. They rejected notions of inherent differences between women and men,[50] exposing them as products of social construction, not of nature. Nabawiyya Musa declared "that, like animals, woman and man are alike as scientists confirm ... [men] forget that is it only when people use their gifts that they develop."[51] However, she also explained that because domestic confinement stunted their development, middle- and upper-class women in the city might appear to be of a different order from men.

> It is unfair to compare the mind of an urban man with that of his wife. How can one compare the mind of a man of education and experience, who has developed himself, with that of his wife, which has been neglected since infancy? Her mind became rusty through lack of use ... Her abilities were stifled and she was sheltered from life's experiences before her mind could develop naturally.

Musa further reinforced her argument by remarking that peasant women and men appeared to be the same because their life experiences were similar.[52]

The essentialists stressed women's procreative functions as a determinant of difference. Muhammad Farid Wajdi, author of *al-Mar'a al-muslima* (The Muslim woman). published in 1912, asserted that "the woman is a noble being created to increase the species and in this man cannot compete with her."[53] Nabawiyya Musa retorted, "Is the woman able to procreate alone? Since the man participates with the woman in the creation of human life wouldn't it be more accurate to say that human beings are noble beings created for the purpose of multiplying the species like all other animals? Are men simply trying to create differences between the sexes?"[54]

In addressing the argument of fundamental differences between women and men, used to assign women to the home and deny them wider social roles, Bahithat al-Badiya rejected the premise, arguing that "men say to us categorically, 'You [women] have been created for the house and we have been created to be bread-winners.' Is this a God-given dictate? How are we to know since no holy book has spelled it out ... the division of labour is merely a human creation."[55] For her part, Nabawiyya Musa contended that "people can decide on this [work] themselves; nature has nothing to do with it."[56] Bahithat al-Badiya, in a speech entitled "The Woman in Society,"[57] further explained that maternal duties did not demand women's imprisonment in the house, nor did they conflict with women's roles in society. The feminists noted that women of the working class and peasant majority of Egypt worked both inside and outside the house.

THE FEMINIST SOCIAL AND ECONOMIC RECONSTRUCTION OF GENDER

The feminist assertion that women and men were inherently the same – that one sex was not superior to the other – set the stage for a challenge to male control over women. By articulating gender similarity the feminists began to undermine patriarchal hierarchy grounded in gender difference, and paved the way for women's equal access to social, economic, and political opportunity. Furthermore, if the apparent differences and oppression of women, particularly of urban women, were not nature's doing, but the result of formation, function, and environment, then it followed that changes in upbringing and roles were necessary if women's lives were to improve. Nabawiyya Musa insisted: 'We would not be misled about men's and women's innate abilities if we remembered how differently they have been brought up. We must educate both the same way."[58]

Education became an instrument for reconstruction of gender. State schooling in the nineteenth and early twentieth centuries had begun to shape the new male citizen in what remained a male society. By not providing the same schooling for women, the state prevented their formation as citizens. Bahithat al-Badiya and Nabawiyya Musa, as teachers, writers, and speakers, and Huda Sha'rawi, as an organizer and promoter of women's lectures and later as a speaker, set about the task of reconstruction. In the immediate sense, schooling and public lectures drew these women and others out of domestic confinement into the public realm, while the substance of the new education helped further shape their new lives. Whether the feminists campaigned for the expansion of education or the extension of employment opportunities, they aroused concerns and fears over three issues: motherhood, female morality, and female competition. It seems important to look at these problems both as reflections of real fears and as symptomatic of broader patriarchal concerns about the reduction of the family's control over the lives of women. By not advocating unveiling and by upholding gender segregation, the feminists had tried not to raise fears concerning morality. Yet, because of the popular notion of women as primarily sexual beings, virtually any advance was bound to give rise to a "moral" outcry. The very idea of literacy itself was called a threat to the morality of women, although Nabawiyya Musa turned this around, arguing that literacy would better arm women to protect themselves. Literacy, as the conservative patriarchal forces well understood, would give women entrée into the public sphere, enabling them to transcend physical barriers, as they were already doing in a disembodied way through their books and their magazines.[59]

When the new formal (school) education was blamed for the ruination of girls, Bahithat al-Badiya was ready to argue that it was "unfair to put the blame on the schools. The problem lies with the family."[60] The situation, however, became confused. Formerly (before the advent of modern schools), *tarbiyya* (education in the sense of formation of manners and morals) and *ta'lim* (education in the sense of imparting formal learning) were closely interconnected and under the supervision of the family. As middle-class girls started going to school, *ta'lim* became the task of the school, while *tarbiyya* remained the responsibility of the family. With the advent of modern education, the concepts came to have a different inflection with respect to females and males.[61] In the case of females, education, both *tarbiyya* and *ta'lim*, retained the sense of upbringing linked with the acquisition of general knowledge.[62] Males' education was associated primarily with *ta'lim*, connected with the new, disciplined, and public system of imparting learning and training, or education.[63] There was not the same concern about *tarbiyya*, or upbringing and moral formation, of men as there was about that of women.

As the site of education for girls shifted to the public sphere, the question of *tarbiyya* and related issues of authority and responsibility became more complicated.[64] New authorities, in the form of teachers, often British women, ushered girls into the public world, concomitantly trying, in addition to families, to assist in shaping the practical and moral formation of young schoolgirls. Egyptian primary school teacher Zainab Mursi, for example, published a book in 1912 called *al-Ayal al-bayinat fi tarbiyyat al-banat* (Clear rules for the upbringing of girls). For reasons such as these, Bahithat al-Badiya would not allow school to take the blame for the "ruin" of girls, real or imagined.

In smoothing the way for the education of girls, the feminists found it necessary to reaffirm the importance of motherhood, and to provide repeated assurances that neither education nor work was in conflict with mothering. Bahithat al-Badiya, in one of her talks on new roles for women, for example, felt obliged to point out that she was "not urging women to neglect their home and children."[65] The feminists argued further that the new education would enhance women's roles as mothers. At a time when the issue of single motherhood was all but ignored, Nabawiyya Musa stressed the importance of education for mothers left on their own with children to raise.[66]

Bahithat al-Badiya, in a lecture to women in 1909, affirmed her support for primary and secondary education for girls, while also asserting that training in home management should not be neglected. She also advocated training for women in medicine and other professional fields. These proposals became part of her demands to the Egyptian Congress of 1911.[67] Huda Sha'rawi in 1909 proposed providing classes in health, hygiene, and childcare for needy girls under the ægis of the Mabarrat Muhammad 'Ali.[68] Bahithat al-Badiya, as already noted, created a school to teach nursing skills to women in Cairo, and had made plans for a similar school in Fayyum, but she died before it was completed.[69]

Under colonialism, the feminist advocacy of education also had strong nationalist motivations. The feminists wanted to give female education a more national stamp, and to take state education out of the predominant control of the British. Musa insisted in 1920, in the midst of nationalist demonstrations and strikes, that "the best way to serve this country we are ready to die for is to direct attention of women to education and work."[70] In calling upon wealthy women to finance schools for girls, Musa was eager to have an Egyptian-run private secondary school for girls. Such a school, she argued, should include practical instruction in income-generating skills for poor girls.[71]

In promoting employment for women the feminists were giving direction to changes that had already begun to occur. Some women from the middle and lower classes had begun to enter the labor force.

Many lower-class women were pushed into the public workplace when the locus of artisanal production shifted away from the household. When men's fear of competition from newly-educated women began to surface, Bahithat al-Badiya retorted: "Men say that the day we are educated we shall push them out of work and abandon the role for which God created us. But, isn't it rather men have pushed women out of work?" She recited a list of jobs that men had taken over from women.[72] Nabawiyya Musa made strong arguments for work for women in need, pleading from the real-life experience of the many women who found themselves without the support of husbands through divorce, death, or desertion and were forced to work to support themselves and their children. Instead of being made the dependent recipients of charity, as some suggested, it was more fitting and more realistic that they earn their livelihood in decent jobs.[73]

Once again the problem of moral danger to women was raised when feminists promoted improved employment opportunities for females. Musa faced the issue head on by pointing out that many needy women in the cities were forced into menial jobs as household servants and street vendors, exposing them to sexual exploitation. Such women should be trained to assume better jobs. She also argued that middle-class women were likewise vulnerable when placed, as they usually were, in jobs subordinate to men. She argued that women who worked as doctors alongside male doctors would be less prone to sexual exploitation than women working as nurses under the authority of male doctors. Bahithat al-Badiya advocated creating a parallel workforce, especially in education and medicine, to protect women.

Opening the doors for the equitable employment of Egyptian women was a fundamental component of the nationalism of the feminists. From the middle of the nineteenth century to the start of the twentieth, the number of Europeans, both women and men, had increased over tenfold from about ten thousand to over one hundred and twelve thousand. Around 1900, about half of the eight thousand professionals in the labor force were European. European women took up jobs in families and in the public arena. The feminists argued for nationalizing the workforce by giving jobs to Egyptian women. However, patriarchal concerns appeared to override broader national interests.[74] Frustrated, Nabawiyya Musa wrote:

We neglect the education of women who thus remain ill-equipped to work. We look down on them, slam the door of work in their face, and welcome foreign women into our homes entrusting them with our basic needs ... Egyptian capital is lost to these foreign women who are found perfect while our own women, found wanting. If we had spent money on educating Egyptian women they would have been able to perform these jobs and we, Egyptians, would be keeping Egyptian money in Egyptian hands. At a time when we make a great effort to win our political independence why do we lag behind in fighting for our economic independence when the means is in our hands?[75]

EPILOGUE

The path from consciousness to activism – from the private sphere to the public world – exposed the problem of translating feminist theory into practice. While both women and men could, and did, evolve feminist theories, it was the women who had to make the move into the public realm. Society, however, made it difficult for them to translate the imperatives of feminism into practice. Nevertheless, if the social construction of sexuality was not addressed as such, feminist women and men did expose the so-called Islamic prescription of face veiling and female seclusion, thus paving the way for the public education of women and their gainful employment and the articulation of a nationalist dimension of women's liberation.

The feminists we have discussed wanted to protect both themselves and the emerging generation of women making their way into the public sphere to claim new roles. Consequently, during the period under study, they preferred to keep the face veil. This proved to be a double-edged weapon, facilitating their public presence and expanded roles, while reinforcing common perceptions of women as primarily sexual beings, or as Fatima Mernissi put it, as omnisexual beings. Men as feminists, by ignoring moral or sexual issues, did not help solve this fundamental problem. If conservatives wanted women to remain veiled and in the home, feminists exhorted men to adhere to the same moral standards they applied to women.

In the last decades of the twentieth century the problem of the linking of veiling to morality, laden with implications for the public role of women, still remained unresolved. While feminists had used the (face) veil early in the century to smooth their way into the public sphere, many women reclaimed the veil – but now mainly in the form of head covering and loose clothing – when calls for their retreat from the public sphere were raised in the 1970s and 1980s. For some conservative women the new veil signaled a withdrawal from public life, while others fell back on its use in order to facilitate their lives in public. Among those who did not reappropriate the veil were the women who identified with feminism.

Once again, discussion focused on sexuality, morality, and the reassertion of patriarchal control over women. By this time, context, practice, and terminology had changed. Where the early feminists had struggled on behalf of women under colonial occupation, now the ascendant popular conservative forces resorted to their own brand of religious interpretation with its narrow view of the place of women in society. Similarly, the definition of veiling had changed. For example, Huda Sha'rawi and Nabawiyya Musa, whose first photographs without the face veil had shown them with head and body covered, would now, if similarly covered, be described as *muhajjibat*, or veiled women, in contrast to the minority of women covering their faces, who are called *munaqibbat* (wearers of the *niqab* or face veil).

Towards the end of the 1980s there also appeared women who veiled their head and body in a seductive way, ironically calling themselves *mutahasmimat* (the modest ones), though attired in ways more reminiscent of the *mutabarrijat*, the alluring, veiled women of the turn of the century. These *mutahasmimat* wear caftans and long dresses with head veils or turbans but, while acknowledging that they are not properly adhering to the spirit of *hijab*, are pointedly not wearing Western dress. Although the revival of veiling, this time in the form of the *hijab*, is bound up with an affirmation by its wearers of a presumed Islamic or indigenous identity, it can be seen as a reassertion of the essentially sexual nature of women – upon whom, rather than upon men, the burden to preserve a conventional moral order has been placed.

With the close of the twentieth century approaching, feminists continue to assert the right of women to remain active in the public sphere. A group of professional women, occupying key positions in contemporary public life, published a booklet in 1988 reminding women of the legal, economic, political and social rights granted to them as citizens by the state, and warning that "Currents have appeared trying to take women back to the era of the harem."[76] These women are fighting to stem a reversing tide, and to preserve what

Huda Sha'rawi, Bahithat al-Badiya, and Nabawiyya Musa struggled to achieve in a critical period earlier in the century.

*   *   *

Originally published in John Spagnolo (ed.), *Problems of the Middle East in Historical Perspective*, St. Antony's College, Oxford monograph series (London: Ithaca Press, 1991), pp. 27–48. This was a *Festschrift* for Albert Hourani.

NOTES

1. As told to Myriam Harrey and cited in her "La femme orientale et son destin: l'Egyptienne," *Journal de la Femme* (Paris), 21 July 1934.
2. I would like to thank Marilyn Booth for reading this paper in its final stage and offering thoughtful comments.
3. See Margot Badran, "The Origins of Feminism in Egypt," in Jacqueline Zirkzee, Arina Angerman, et al. (eds.), *Current Issues in Women's History* (London: Routledge, 1989). For women's expression of this early feminist consciousness see Margot Badran and Miriam Cooke (eds.), *Opening the Gates: A Century of Arab Feminist Writing* (London: Virago and Bloomington: Indiana University Press, 1990).
4. The first organized feminist movement, led by Huda Sha'rawi, was the subject of my D.Phil. thesis, "Huda Sha'rawi and the Liberation of the Egyptian Woman" (Oxford University, 1977), supervised by Albert Hourani.
5. On the political dimension of feminist consciousness see Linda Alcoff, "Cultural Feminism Versus Post-Structuralism: The Identity Crisis in Feminist Theory," *Signs*, 13 (1988), pp. 405–436. Linda Nicholson, discussing Catharine MacKinnon's *Towards a Feminist Theory of the State* (Cambridge, Mass.: Harvard University Press, 1989) in "A Radical's Odyssey," *Women's Review of Books*, 8 (December 1988), p. 11, writes: "Her claim, in brief, is that feminism possesses its own method, consciousness raising. Unlike objectivist modes of knowing, consciousness raising recognizes its own involvement in the knowing process, takes as its object that which is intrinsically social, and is directly related to political practice; indeed, in consciousness raising, awareness becomes a political process." I was unable to see MacKinnon's book in Cairo while writing the essay on which this chapter is based.
6. Some feminist theorists, looking at the Western experience, even see in the social construction of sexuality the core of the problem of women's oppression. Again see Nicholson, "A Radical's Odyssey," p. 11, who noted: "If there is one idea that forms the true core of this book, it is MacKinnon's identification of sexuality with women's oppression."
7. Sharon Sievers, "Six (Or More) Feminists in Search of an Historian," *Journal of Women's History*, 2 (1989), p. 134. Sievers also has published *Flowers in Salt: The Beginnings of Feminist Consciousness in Modern Japan* (Stanford: Stanford University Press, 1983).
8. Karen Offen, "Defining Feminism: A Comparative Historical Approach," *Signs*,

14 (1988), p. 151. Among her many contributions see "Liberty, Equality and Justice for Women: The Theory and Practice of Feminism in Nineteenth-Century Europe," in Renate Bridenthat, Claudia Koonz, and Susan Mosher Stuard (eds.), *Becoming Visible: Women in European History*, 2nd ed. (Boston Houghton Mifflin, 1987), pp. 335–373.

9. Kumari Jayawardena, *Feminism and Nationalism in the Third World* (London: Zed, 1986).

10. Nancy Cott, *The Grounding of Modern Feminism* (New Haven: Yale University Press, 1987), p. 13.

11. In this chapter, feminism refers both to an understanding of the constraints imposed upon women because of their gender and to actions directed at freeing them to attain shorter- or longer-term goals in the shaping of new lives.

12. Alcoff, "Cultural Feminism Versus Post-Structuralism," p. 434.

13. See Margot Badran, "Dual Liberation: Feminism and Nationalism in Egypt, 1870s–1925," *Feminist Issues* (Spring 1988), pp. 15–34.

14. The three were, however, by no means the only ones to contribute to the early rise of feminism. I have dealt with other women in "Huda Sha'rawi and the Liberation of the Egyptian Woman." See also Badran and Cooke (eds.),*Opening the Gates*; Marilyn Booth, "Mayy Ziyadah and the Feminist Perspective in Egypt, 1908–1931," B.A. Honors thesis (Harvard-Radcliffe, 1978); and her "Mai Ziyada, Women's Biography and Feminist Consciousness: Role Models and Gender Roles in Egypt," in Nikki Keddie and Beth Baron (eds.), *Women in Middle Eastern History: Shifting Boundaries in Sex and Gender* (New Haven: Yale University Press, 1991). Many Syrian Christian women with nascent feminist consciousness contributed to the rise of the women's press in Egypt, starting in 1894. Beth Baron has studied this press from 1894 to 1919: see "The Rise of a New Literary Culture: The Women's Press of Egypt, 1892–1919," Ph.D. thesis (University of California at Los Angeles, 1988).

15. See Thomas Philipp, "Feminism and Nationalist Politics in Egypt," in L. Beck and N. Keddie (eds.), *Women in the Muslim World* (Cambridge, Mass.: Harvard University Press, 1978), pp. 277–294.

16. See Fatima Mernissi, *Beyond the Veil: Male–Female Dynamics in Modern Muslim Society*, rev. ed. (Bloomington: Indiana University Press, 1987), pp. 27–64; and Fatma A. Sabah, *Women in the Muslim Unconscious*, trans. Mary Jo Lakeland (New York: Pergamon, 1984), *passim*.

17. See Margot Badran and Midge Quandt (eds.), *Sex, History and Culture: A Double Issue of Trends in History* (New York: Haworth Press, 1990); and Pat Caplan, *Cultural Construction of Sexuality* (New York: Tavistock, 1987).

18. Quote translated by Marilyn Booth from 'Aisha al-Taimuriyya, *Nata'ij al-ahwalfi al-aqwal via al-af'al* (The results of circumstances in words and deeds, Cairo, 1305/1887–1888), in Badran and Cooke (eds.), *Opening the Gates*.

19. Quote translated by Marilyn Booth from Mayy Ziyada, "al-Ma'ra wa al-tamad-dun" (Woman and civilization), reprinted in *'Mai', al-kalimat wa al-isharat* (Mai, words and signs, Cairo, 1922), pp. 27–37, in Badran and Cooke (eds.), *Opening the Gates*.

20. See her *Mudhakkirat ra'ida al-'arabiyya al-haditha Huda Sha'rawi* (Memoirs of the modern Arab feminist pioneer Huda Sha'rawi, Cairo: Dar al-Hilal, 1981),

trans. as *Harem Years: The Memoirs of an Egyptian Feminist, Huda Shaarawi* (London: Virago, 1986 and New York: Feminist Press, 1987), ed., trans., and introd. Margot Badran.

21. On the life of Bahithat al-Badiya see Majd al-Din Hifni Nasif (ed.), *Athar Bahithat al-Badiyya Malak Hifni Nasif: 1886–1918* (Literary works of Bahithat al-Badiyya Malak Hifni Nasif, Cairo: Wizarat al-Thaqafa wa al-Irshad al-Qaumi, 1962); and Mayy Ziyada, *Bahithat al-Badiyya: bahth intiqadi* (Bahithat al-Badiyya: critical research, Cairo: Matba'at al-Muqtataf, 1920). Marilyn Booth analyses this biography by Ziyada in "Mai Ziyada, Women's Biography and Feminist Consciousness."

22. On Nabawiyya Musa see Khair al-Din al-Zirkali (ed.), *al-'Alam qamus tarajim li ashar al-rijal wa al-nisa' min al-'arab wa musta'rabin wa-al-mustashriqin*, 2nd printing (Biographical dictionary of the most famous Arab men and women, Cairo: Matba'at Kustatsumas, 1954–1959), vol. 8, pp. 321–322; Badran, "Huda Sha'rawi"; and Mona Mikhail, *Images of Arab Women: Fact and Fiction* (Washington: Three Continents Press, 1978).

23. The progressive Ahmad Lutfy al-Sayyid commented on this development in an article, "al-Haraka al-nisa'iyya fi misr" (The women's movement in Egypt), first published in *al-Jarida* in 1912; and later in *al-Muntakhabat* (Selections, Cairo: Dar al-Nashr al-Hadith, 1937), pp. 268–271.

24. See Qasim Amin, *Tahrir al-mar'a* (The liberation of woman, Cairo: Maktabat al-Taraqqi, 1899); and *al-Mar'a al-jadida* (The new woman, Cairo: Matba'at al-Ma'arif, 1901); and Murqus Fahmi, *al-Mar'a fi al-sharq* (The woman in the East, Cairo: Matba'at al-Talif, 1894).

25. See Sha'rawi, *Mudhakkirat*; also Badran and Cooke (eds.), *Opening the Gates*.

26. The development of schooling for women in modern Egypt was by no means a linear process. While some daughters of upper-class families attended the Siufiyya School, established in 1873 by Tcheshme Hanim, a wife of Khedive Isma'il, neither the experiment nor the school lasted very long. The Saniyya School, formed in 1889, incorporated both the Siufiyya School and the Qirabiyya School, which had been established in 1874. The new school became an important teacher-training institution for middle-class girls. The Egyptian school first attended by upper-class girls in the 1930s was the Kulliyat al-Banat in Zamalek. However, some upper-class girls had gone to foreign schools earlier.

27. On British policy in the early twentieth century see the Earl of Cromer, *Modern Egypt* (London: Macmillan, 1908). For an Egyptian educator's account see Amir Boktor, *School and Society in the Valley of the Nile* (Cairo: Elias Modern Press, 1936). For memories of student experiences in the government schools at the turn of the century see Salama Musa, *The Education of Salama Musa*, trans. L. O. Schuman (Leiden: E. J. Brill, 1961). See also Jirjis Salamah, *Athar al-ihtilal al-baritani fi al-ta'lim al-qaumi fi misr, 1822–1922* (The effects of the British occupation on national education in Egypt, 1822–1922, Cairo: Maktabat al-Anjalu al-Misriyah, 1966); and Robert L. Tignor, *Modernization and British Colonial Rule in Egypt, 1882–1914* (Princeton: Princeton University Press, 1966).

28. Muhammad Abu al-Hadid, "Misriyya tatahhada al-rijal" (An Egyptian woman challenges men), *al-Jumhuriyya*, 21 August 1975.

29. Foreign women were also invited to speak.

30. On the women's lectures and the founding of the Women's Intellectual Association see Shaarawi, *Harem Years*, pp. 92–94 and 98–100. On lecture topics see Mlle. A. Couvreur, *La Femme aux différentes épochs de l'histoire: conférences faites aux dames égyptiennes* (Paris: Peyriller, 1910). Couvreur was a teacher at the Lycée Racine in Paris seconded to the Egyptian University. On the Women's Refinement Union, see Nasif (ed.), *Athar Bahithat al-Badiyya*, who writes that women from Egypt, the Arab countries, and Western foreigners participated in the activities of the Union.

31. See Shaarawi, *Harem Years*, pp. 94–98; and for other founding members see Afaf Lutfi al-Sayyid Marsot, "The Revolutionary Gentlewomen in Egypt," in Beck and Keddie (eds.), *Women in the Muslim World*, pp. 261–276.

32. See Nasif (ed.), *Athar Bahithat al-Badiyya*, pp. 54–55.

33. Huda Sha'rawi, "Kalima al-Sayida al-Jalila Huda Hanim Sha'rawi" (The speech of Her Excellency, Huda Hanim Sha'rawi), *al-Misriyya*, 15 February 1937, p. 13.

34. See Badran, "Dual Liberation."

35. For a definition of *hijab* in English, see Hans Wehr, *A Dictionary of Modern Written Arabic* (Ithaca: Spoken Languages Services, Inc., 1961), pp. 156–157. Veiling, or *hijab*, has connoted both covering the female body and female seclusion. In the period we are considering, the term veiling referred to covering the face as well as the body, while *sufur*, or unveiling, meant uncovering the face. Here I use the term "veiling" as it was employed early in the twentieth century. In current usage in Egypt *hijab* does not include covering the face; the word used for veiling that includes the face is *niqab*.

36. Bahithat al-Badiya, "al-Hijab am al-sufur" (Veiling or unveiling), in Nasif (ed.), *Athar Bahithat al-Badiyya*, pp. 187–192.

37. Mernissi, *Beyond the Veil*, pp. 30–34 and 53–54.

38. For an analysis of the institutions of seclusion and veiling, deriving from research in South Asia, see Hanna Papanek, "Purdah: Separate Worlds and Symbolic Shelter," in Hanna Papanek and Gail Minault (eds.), *Separate Worlds: Studies of Purdah in South Asia* (Columbia, Mo.: South Asia Books, 1982), pp. 3–53.

39. Bahithat al-Badiya, "al-Hijab am al-sufur."

40. Ibid.

41. Bahithat al-Badiya, "al-Mar'a wa al-hijab' (Woman and the veil), in Nasif (ed.), *Athar Bahithat al-Badiyya*, pp. 275–279.

42. See, for example, Ahmad Lutfi al-Sayyid, "al-Haraka al-nisa'iyya."

43. Bahithat al-Badiya, "al-Hijab am al-sufur," pp. 188–189.

44. Bahithat al-Badiya, "Muhadara fi nadi Hizb al-Umma" (A speech in the club of the Umma Party), in *al-Nisa'iyyat* (Cairo: Matba'at al-Jaridah Press, 1909), pp. 95–100.

45. It is interesting to note that Zainab Amin Taufiq, whose husband, Qasim Amin, called for unveiling, herself did not unveil. On the other hand, Lisa Girghis 'Abd al-Malak al-Farauni, born in 1879, the same year as Sha'rawi, whose husband, Murqus Fahmi, was also a proponent of unveiling, never took up the veil. As a Copt she was part of the earlier trend away from veiling among Christians. Personal communication from Andree Fahmy, her daughter, 10 December 1988.

46. Nabawiyya Musa, *al-Mar'a wa al-'amal* (Woman and work, Alexandria: al-Matba'at al-Qawmi, 1920), introduction, pp. 3–5. There is some photographic

evidence that Musa may have stopped covering her face after she began teaching, but further documentation is necessary to confirm this. Throughout her life, however, she fastidiously adhered to modest – many would say severe – dress.

47. Bahithat al-Badiya, "al-Mar'a wa al-hijab," pp. 275–279.
48. Bahithat al-Badiya, "Hayat al-Anisa Mai," in Nasif (ed.), *Athar Bahithat al-Badiyya*, p. 320.
49. Shaarawi, *Harem Years*, part 1, pp. 33–58.
50. Even if reinterpreted in women's favor, they were sometimes unable to avoid lapsing into old categories. See Nabawiyya Musa, "al-Farq bain al-rajal wa al-mar'a wa isti'dad kull minhuma al-'amal" (The difference between men and women and their capacities for work), in *al-Mar'a wa al-'amal*, pp. 21–36, where she first claims the two sexes are the same, but later speaks about the greater compassion of women towards the weak as an indication that they are more reasonable than men.
51. Ibid.
52. Ibid.
53. Cited in ibid.
54. Ibid.
55. Bahithat al-Badiya, "Muhadara," in *al-Nisa'iyyat*, pp. 95–100.
56. Musa, "al-Farq," pp. 21–36.
57. In Nasif (ed.), *Athar Bahithat al-Badiyya*, pp. 130–135.
58. Musa, "al-Farq," pp. 21–36.
59. Nabawiyya Musa, "Ta'thir al-kutub wa al-riwayat fi al-akhlaq" (The effect of books and novels on morals), in *al-Mar'a wa al-'amal*, pp. 89–96.
60. Bahithat al-Badiya, "Muhadara," in *al-Nisa'iyyat*, pp. 95–100.
61. On the term *tarbiyya* as applied to male education, see Timothy Mitchell, *Colonizing Egypt* (Cambridge: Cambridge University Press, 1988), pp. 88–91.
62. On the term *tarbiyya* as applied to female upbringing, see Bahithat al-Badiya, "Tarbiya al-banat fil bait wa al-madrasa" (The upbringing of girls in home and school), pp. 197–200; and "Fi tarbiya al-banat" (On the upbringing of girls), pp. 136–142 in Nasif (ed.), *Athar Bahithat al-Badiyya*; and Ahmad Lutfi al-Sayyid, "Tarbiya al-banat" (The upbringing of girls), in *al-Muntakhabat*, pp. 226–228.
63. Not surprisingly, as we shall see later, one of the first demands the feminists made at the start of their movement in the early 1920s was for equal secondary school-ing for women, which was seen as a prerequisite for all other demands for new lives in the public sphere.
64. The terminological usage, however, was not always so clear cut, and *tarbiyya* sometimes also referred to the education of girls.
65. Bahithat al-Badiya, "Muhadara," pp. 95–100.
66. Musa, "al-Farq," pp. 21–36.
67. See Bahithat al-Badiya, "Asharat wasa'il lil-tariqiyat al-mar'a al-misriyya" (Ten means toward the progress of the Egyptian woman), in Nasif (ed.), *Athar Bahithat al-Badiyya*, pp. 124–129.
68. Shaarawi, *Harem Years*, pp. 94–97.
69. Nasif, (ed.), *Athar Bahithat al-Badiyya*, pp. 54–56.
70. Musa, "Introduction," in *al-Mar'a wa al-'amal*, pp. 3–5.
71. Musa, "Kaifa turabbi al-fatat al-misriyya" (How do we raise/educate the young Egyptian woman?), in ibid., pp. 37–48.

72. Bahithat al-Badiya, "Muhadara," pp. 95–100.

73. Musa, "al-Farq," pp. 21–36.

74. For an especially strong statement on this, see Musa, "Ihtiyaj misr ili tabibat wa mu'allimat wa khayyat wa ghairuhunna" (Egypt's need for women doctors, women teachers, seamstresses, and women in other professions), in *al-Mar'a wa al-'amal*, pp. 65–77.

75. Ibid.

76. *al-Huquq al-qanuniyya li al-mar'a al-misriyya bain al-nadhariyya wa al-tatbiq* (The rights of the Egyptian woman in theory and practice, Cairo: n.p., 1988).

4

EXPRESSING FEMINISM AND NATIONALISM IN AUTOBIOGRAPHY: THE MEMOIRS OF AN EGYPTIAN EDUCATOR

There are different reasons for writing autobiography, and different ways of reading autobiography. As a reader who is a historian of modern Egypt specializing in women's history and feminist history, I am interested in the feminist content of women's autobiography. Many years ago, while I was doing research on the feminist movement led by Huda Sha'rawi from the 1920s through the 1940s, a relative introduced me to her unpublished memoirs of her childhood and life up to the time she began to lead a feminist movement. Sha'rawi's memoirs helped me answer many questions about origins of feminist consciousness and nascent forms of feminist activism in Egypt.[1] Over the years, as I read writings of women in Egypt, I came to see other expressions of feminist consciousness and activism as part of daily life.[2] Through my historical study and activism in Egypt I have continued to speculate about what may have existed beyond the realm of formal feminist movements or explicitly articulated feminist ideology.[3]

In 1989, while doing research at Dar al-Kutub, the National Library in Cairo, I came across the autobiography of Nabawiyya Musa, published serially from 5 May 1938 to 2 August 1942 in her periodical, *Majallat al-Fatah* (The magazine of the young woman, which was published from 20 October 1937 to 5 June 1943), under the title "Dhikriyyati" (My memoirs). This was a major discovery for me as a feminist historian. It was the highly detailed life of a woman who was a pioneering educator and who had made a lifelong commitment to nationalist and feminist issues. Musa, of modest middle-class origins, was a self-made woman whose everyday language was Arabic, as it was for the majority of Egyptians. Huda Sha'rawi and other upper-class feminists who spoke French appropriated the ready-made feminist terminology of that language, which generated the term "feminism" in the late nineteenth century.[4] In Musa's time there was no unequivocal word for feminism or feminist in Arabic; the term *nisa'i/nisa'iyya* was used, but could mean either "feminist" or "women's," depending on the context. However, there are forms of consciousness and behaviors that can be understood as feminist without the aid of clear-cut terminology.[5] Knowing the past of feminists and how they viewed their experience helps in the task of understanding constructions of feminism. Revelations in an autobiographical text such as Musa's are critical for a fuller understanding of the history of Egyptian feminism.

Nabawiyya Musa's "Dhikriyyati" is a treasure trove. It describes concrete ways in which Egyptian women were oppressed in the early twentieth century and how one woman overcame structural and behavioral modes of oppression. Musa's autobiography enables us to demonstrate that Egyptian women's feminist consciousness and activism exceeded what most people have been able to see or willing to concede. "Dhikriyyati," a major document in the history of Egyptian feminism, also contributes to expanding and refining feminist theory.

Musa achieved her highest form of self-expression in her autobiographical writing, which she began at the age of fifty-two, long after she had established herself as a formidable educator. Much earlier in her career, at the age of thirty-four, she had published a short treatise called *al-Mar'a wa al-'amal* (Woman and work), supporting education and work for women.[6] Her feminist exposition in these two kinds of writing is strikingly different. She exhibits far freer expression in her autobiography. "Dhikriyyati" is thus critical to an understanding of the possibilities of the autobiographical mode for feminist expression in Egypt.

Musa's life and the reconstruction of her life operated as counter-discourses cutting through indigenous and colonialist patriarchal overlays. Through autobiography, Musa produced a feminist and nationalist manifesto that was bolder, more sweeping, and far more radical than the feminism and nationalism she articulated in *al-Mar'a wa al-'amal*. This early publication, which announced the author's feminist and nationalist agenda, was a brave work published at the height of the national revolution in Egypt. Her "Dhikriyyati," begun nearly two decades later, which served at once as a historical record and a feminist model, was, I argue, her supreme political work.

BIOGRAPHICAL CONTEXTS

Nabawiyya Musa (1886–1951), pioneering educator in modern Egypt, was born thirteen years after the first state school for girls was established and four years after the start of British colonial occupation. She was thirty-six years old when British occupation officially ended in 1922, and thirty-nine when the first state secondary school for girls opened in 1925. However, there were still British advisers in the government ministries, a British presence in the police, and a military presence in the Suez Canal Zone which was not expelled until 1956. That year the state granted Egyptian women the vote, according them full political rights as citizens while at the same moment, as part of a larger move to curtail free political expression, it suppressed the right of feminists to organize independently.

Nabawiyya Musa was from the modest middle class of a highly stratified society. She was a female in a patriarchal society. She was a citizen of a country under colonial occupation for her first thirty-six years and thereafter under partial occupation during the period of quasi-independence. She was born fatherless in a culture where the patriarchal family was paramount.[7] Nevertheless, she managed to build a life for herself within the heavy constraints imposed by an indigenous patriarchal society and colonial domination, as well as by family circumstances.[8] As a teacher, headmistress, and founder of girls' schools, she engaged in a life-long struggle to advance the cause of Egyptian women. Musa studied in the girls' section of the 'Abbas Primary School, passing the primary school examination in 1903, two years after girls first were allowed to take this state-administered test.[9] She then entered the Saniyya Teachers' School (established in 1889), where she took a teacher-training certificate in 1906. Triumphing over the objections of the colonial educational authorities, in 1907 she became the first Egyptian girl to be allowed to sit for the state baccalaureate examination and the last until after independence was declared in 1922.

Musa was one of the first Egyptian women to become a teacher in the state school system when she began to teach in the girls' section of the 'Abbas Primary School in 1906. She was the first Egyptian Muslim woman to become a headmistress, taking direction of the girls' school opened by Egyptian nationalists in Fayyum in 1909. She went on to become headmistress of the girls' school in Mansura also created by nationalists from 1910 to 1914. Musa gave lectures in the women's section of the Egyptian University (est. 1908), which lasted for three academic years, from 1909 to 1912.[10] (When Musa went to the new Egyptian University in 1908 seeking to enrol she was not allowed to enter the building until permission was sent to the gate by the director.)

From 1914 to 1916, Musa was assistant headmistress (the head-mistress was an Englishwoman) at the Bulaq Women Teachers' Training School in Cairo, which was part of the state school system, and from 1916 to 1924 she was headmistress of Wardiyyan Women Teachers' Training School in Alexandria. She was appointed chief inspector of female education in the Ministry of Education in 1924, the year the decision was made to create the first state secondary school offering girls the same curriculum as boys.[11] In 1926 she was dismissed from the Ministry of Education (after many complicated entanglements, apparent rivalries and jealousies, and accusations which she contested). Thereafter, she devoted herself to running the two schools for girls she had struggled successfully to found: al-Tarqiyya al-Fatah Primary School for Girls in Alexandria and Banat al-Ashraf Secondary School for Girls in Cairo.[12]

In 1923, the year after independence was declared, when the first public, organized feminist movement started, Nabawiyya Musa became a member of the newly founded al-Ittihad al-Nisa'i al-Misri (Egyptian Feminist Union [EFU]). Along with EFU President Huda Sha'rawi, and Saiza Nabarawi, she attended the conference of the International Alliance for Women Suffrage in Rome, where she spoke on women's educational needs in Egypt. This was Musa's first and last formal role in the EFU-led feminist movement, which agitated for a range of social, economic, and political rights for women for the next quarter-century under the leadership of Huda Sha'rawi.[13]

Although she appeared on the scene only for a brief moment as an EFU activist, Musa, who was gifted in Arabic, used her pen through-out her life to advance the causes of women and the nation. As a young schoolteacher she wrote articles on education for the press, under the pseudonym Damir Hai fi Jism Raqiq (A living conscience in a delicate body) because employees of the Ministry of Education were

forbidden to write for the newspapers. She published the aforemen-
tioned *al-Mar'a wa al-'amal* in 1920 and *al-Ayat al-bayyinat fi tarbiyyat al-banat* (The clear model in the education of girls) at an
uncertain date. In 1938 she published *Diwan al-fatah* (The young
woman's collection of poems) and, during the same decade, *Riwayya
Nabhutub* (Nabhutub, a novel). In 1957 Musa started her own periodical, *Majallat al-Fatah*, as a "weekly political and general magazine" aimed at a wide audience of women and men that sold for one
piaster. In her weekly editorial, "Kalima al-Muharrira" (The editor's
word), she criticized government policy, especially concerning
education.[14]

Musa's career came to an abrupt end when the Egyptian government imprisoned her for speaking out against the government's com-
promising position after British tanks positioned themselves in front
of Abdin Palace in 1942, to put pressure on the king. Her magazine
ceased publication in 1943. She died in retirement eight years later at
the age of sixty-four.[15]

In the early twentieth century, Musa sought new opportunities for
herself, and campaigned for the inclusion of other domestically confined middle- and upper-class women in the life of society. Although
she objected to the enforced seclusion of women in the home she supported the separation of the sexes in public. Musa's strict application
of the practice of gender segregation in her schools enabled women as
students and teachers to find space in the public arena where direct
male interventions in their lives could be held at bay. She operated
within the framework of the prevailing sexual and moral ideologies,
which became for her weapons to keep men in their place.

Although Nabawiyya Musa was active in Egypt for nearly half a
century and was a prominent figure in education, she has been
neglected in general accounts of modern Egypt, a fate shared with
other women. Even Amir Boktor, in his history of education in Egypt,
overlooked her. When attention later turned to women's history,
Musa began to receive some notice, but she still remains insufficiently
known.[16]

AUTOBIOGRAPHY AS AN INDIGENOUS FORM

Recording one's life story is a centuries-old practice in Egypt and elsewhere in the Arab and Islamic worlds. The earliest self-narratives date

back to the medieval period. As far as we know, however, only from the twentieth century have Arab women written accounts of their lives. It is possible, however, that future research will unearth earlier texts that are currently unknown.[17]

In Egypt the rise of the modern autobiographical tradition followed independence in 1922. It was developed by middle- and upper-class women and men who had played important roles in the political, intellectual, and cultural life of the country. The modern genre of autobiography is called in Arabic *tarjama hayat* (literally, interpretation of life) or *sira dhatiyya* (literally, self-created life story).[18] Egyptians often inscribed their life stories under the rubric of memoirs (in Arabic, *mudhakkirat* or *dhikriyyat*), suggesting the process of recall. The first modern autobiography was writer Taha Husain's *al-Ayyam* (The days), which appeared serially in *Majallat al-Hilal* from 1926 to 1927 and in book form in 1929.[19] By the 1930s both women and men were publishing autobiographies, a practice that became more common from the 1940s.

Nabawiyya Musa is one of the first two women, according to our current knowledge, to have published her life story, which she began in instalments, as noted, in May 1938. Umm Kulthum, the legendary Egyptian singer, serialized her memoirs several months earlier in the journal *Akhir Sa'a*, from November 1937 to January 1938. Hers, however, unlike Musa's, were written with the help of, or "with the pen of" Muhammad Hammad.[20] Other early autobiographical writings of women include the *Mudhakkirat* (Memoirs) of feminist leader Huda Sha'rawi, recorded around the middle 1940s but not published until 1981 by Dar al-Hilal publishing house in Cairo, and in translation in 1986 in London and 1987 in New York; and journalist and feminist Munira Thabit's *Thaura fi al-burj al-'aji: mudhakkirat fi 'ashrin 'aman* (Revolution in the ivory tower: memoirs of twenty years), published in 1945. Women's autobiographies continued into the 1950s. Actress and journalist Ruz al-Yusif's *Dhikriyyat Ruz al-Yusif* was published in 1953 and again in 1959, after her death.[21] Professor of Islamic thought and writer Bint al-Shati' (pseudonym for 'Aisha 'Abd al-Rahman) published *Sirr al-Shati'* (Life of al-Shati') in 1951 and a second autobiography in 1967 called *'Ala jisr: usturat al-zaman* (On a bridge: a myth of time).[22] 'Asma Fahmi, a teacher, published *Dhikriyyat 'an Madrasa al-Hilmiyya al-Thanawiyya lil-Banat* (Memories of the Hilmiyya Secondary School for Girls) in 1955. 'Asmahan, a singer of Lebanese origin, told about her life and singing career in Egypt from the late 1920s to the middle 1940s under the title *'Asmahan tirwi qissatuha* ('Asmahan tells her story), "with the pen of" Muhammad al-Taba'i in 1965.[23] Another well-known performer of the same period, also of Lebanese origin, Bad'ia Masabni, published *Mudhakirrat Bad'ia Masabni* (The memoirs of Bad'ia Masabni) "with the pen of" Nazik Basila.[24] The Egyptian actress Fatma Rushdi, born in 1910, recounted her story in the first half of the century in *Kifahi fi masrah wa sinima* (My struggle in theater and cinema), published in 1971.[25] The feminist Duriyya Shafiq, active in the 1940s and early 1950s, began to write her memoirs after her house arrest in 1957 and her continued period of self-imposed withdrawal from society. Her memoirs, in family hands, have not been published.[26] Feminist and social welfare activist Hawa Idris wrote about her mission starting in the 1930s in *Ana wa al-sharq* (I and the East). She completed the work in the early 1970s, making a handful of privately bound copies. Feminist and artist Inji Aflatun, who became active in the student movement in the mid-1940s, began her memoirs, but she died in 1990, before she could complete them.[27] Women continue to the present time to engage in autobiographical writing.

However, not all women were, or are, prepared to write autobiography – or, that is, straightforward autobiography. Some have appropriated distancing devices to mask the autobiographical. Women in Egypt have sometimes used biography to speak autobiographically. Writer and critic Safinaz Kazim explained to me that her series of biographies in the paper *al-Watan* in the 1980s, which included a portrait of Nabawiyya Musa, carried autobiographical overtones.[28] Marilyn Booth, a historian and literary critic, detected a similar impulse in the Lebanese writer Mayy Ziyada's biographies of three women writers published early in the twentieth century.[29] The writer Nawal al-Saadawi employed still another strategy in creating a fictional autobiography, *Mudhakirrat al-tabiba* (The memoirs of a woman doctor), published in 1960.[30]

Although women and men both participated in the creation of the modern genre of autobiography, presentation of one's life had different connotations for each. Writing about the self was a radical act for women, but not for men. Women's voices were considered *awra*, something shameful, to be covered. *Awra*, which means pudendum, carries specifically sexual connotations. Moreover, not only women's voices but their entire beings were construed in sexual terms and therefore as *awra*. The prevailing ideology held that women, as essentially sexual beings, posed dangers to men, family, and society.[31] Men secluded women in order to control them – that is, women of the middle and upper classes, Muslims, Christians, and Jews alike, whose labor outside the home was not needed. Their lives were to be private and unseen. In the early decades of the twentieth century, as a result of continuing socio-economic and technological change in the urban world, middle- and upper-class women gradually emerged from domestic confinement to become an increasing presence in society.[32] Women began to remove the face veils that had rendered them invisible, and deprived them of individual identity in society. Non-Muslims were the first to do so.[33] Around 1909, when Musa took up the position as headmistress of a school for girls in the Fayyum oasis, where veiling was generally not practiced, she quietly uncovered her face. During her employ in the colonial state school system as a teacher and then an assistant principal, she was required to veil by the colonial education authorities. At the school in Fayyum that was opened by Egyptian nationalists she was free to remove the veil from her face (she retained the head cover, however, and did so for the rest of her life). Huda Sha'rawi removed her face veil as an overt and confrontational political act in the train station in Cairo after returning from the feminist conference in Rome in 1923. Their two different ways of enacting unveiling (the face) symbolized Musa's and Sha'rawi's divergent approaches to the process of women's liberation.

For all the controversy and antagonism connected with the issue of uncovering the face, the public disclosure of a woman's own life was a far greater challenge to convention. Much of women's early practice of autobiography can be seen as a feminist act of assertion, helping to shatter the complicity with patriarchal domination that had been effected through women's enforced invisibility and silence.[34] Women's autobiography constituted exposure. It was an entry into public discourse in a very personal and individual way, and was a way of shaping it. A woman speaking about her own life constituted a form of shedding of the patriarchal surrogate voice. Many of the pioneering autobiographers just mentioned were feminists. Most, however, were entertainers whose lives were already public, and who were, because of their profession, looked at askance. Yet in shaping the narratives of their life-stories they, like the feminists, assumed agency.

THE TEXT

When Nabawiyya Musa set down episodes in her life for public con-
sumption, she embarked on a radical enterprise. She chose her own
periodical, *Majallat al-Fatah*, as the forum in which to publish her
"Dhikriyyati" in weekly instalments. Despite its title, as already
mentioned, the magazine aimed at a general readership.[35]

The mature Musa was a still feisty woman in the thick of battle
when she began to resurrect her earlier defiant and victorious selves.[36]
She opened the narrative of her life with the episode, "How I Started
my Work Life and When my Troubles Began," establishing what
would be a trope of trials and triumphs and a focus on her educational
mission. She produced ninety-one instalments, with little heed for
historical sequence. She then started a new series, beginning chrono-
logically by filling in the void of her early years, but soon abandoned
this approach. The old and new series together contain a total of 152
episodes, many of which are repeated.

Musa presented her life as a struggle, a pattern of skirmishes and
successes with her patriarchal enemies, whom she scathingly exposed
in their perpetual attacks upon her. She narrated how a young woman
invented her own life, came of age as a teacher and headmistress, and
played a role in shaping modern education in Egypt. If Musa's autobiography is the life of a pioneering educator in modern Egypt, it is
equally a testament to the evolution of her feminist and nationalist
consciousness and activism. "Dhikriyyati" affords the reader an
unprecedented opportunity to see modes of feminism and of nationalism that were not expressed in the context of a formal political organization or movement. It shows how an acute gender consciousness
heightened by nationalist awareness and a strong drive propelled her
into manipulating her environment in order to transcend the limitations that might otherwise have stifled her. Musa's feminism did not
announce itself as did the movement feminism of Huda Sha'rawi,
with its highly-visible discourse of protest and demands, and use of
explicit feminist terminology and dramatic symbolic gestures.
Although Musa had evolved a feminist consciousness and had honed
feminist tools, she did not articulate her life in the explicit language of
feminism as did Sha'rawi, who, moreover, expressed herself mainly
in French.

Musa came from the modest middle class and Sha'rawi from the
wealthy land-owning class. They observed and operated from diverse

vantage points. Musa's position in life as an educator and public personality was self-achieved, and one she had to struggle to maintain.
She was in a position of dependency on the Ministry of Education for
much of her early career. Sha'rawi, on the other hand, was born to
wealth and elite standing that gave her considerable independence
and afforded her greater protection in going against the grain as a
feminist. However, she spoke and wrote in French, the language of
the élite, and therefore had more limited reach. Musa, who communicated in Arabic, the language of the majority, enjoyed wider access
to her compatriots. If Musa had employed an explicit feminist vocabulary, which she would have had to coin in Arabic (we have already
noted the absence of a precise word for feminism or feminist in
Arabic), she might have alienated large segments of the population.
Moreover, an overt feminist stance would have risked antagonizing
her superiors in the Ministry of Education, who held power over
her.[37] Separate circumstances, combined with different personal
choices and proclivities, set these two women from different classes
on diverse paths in the service of their gender and nation.

Musa's autobiographical account affords us access to her less
explicit (in terms of deploying feminist rhetoric and demands), more
pragmatic, and idiosyncratic brand of feminism. She was not part of a
movement, and her memoirs do not indicate that she consciously considered herself a feminist, or mention her passing connection with the
EFU. Yet she clearly belongs to the history of feminism in Egypt.

SELF-CONSTRUCTION

The brief outline of Nabawiyya Musa's life confirms that she overcame barriers to self-expression in the kind of society and circumstances in which she found herself. In his memoirs, the Egyptian
writer and journalist Salama Musa (a Copt, writer, and Fabian socialist), a contemporary of Nabawiyya Musa who came from the same
town, Zagazig, in the eastern Delta, gives a sense of the world into
which she as a female was born: "Once I was struck by my sister
because I had called her name in the street. It was considered just as
improper for a girl's name to be heard in public as for her face to be
seen."[38] How did Musa overcome the barriers in front of her? Clearly
eager for her Egyptian readership to know, she tells the story of her
self-construction in "Dhikriyyati."

Musa relates that she was raised single-handedly by her mother on the pension of her army colonel father, who died while on a military mission in Sudan before her birth. Her subordinate status as a girl was impressed on her by her mother, who took Nabawiyya and her brother, ten years her senior, from Zagazig, the small town in the eastern Delta where she and her mother had been born, to Cairo to advance his schooling.[39]

Musa, however, advanced her own education through self-creation, a leitmotif in the narrative of her life. Extracting help from her brother, she acquired the rudiments of Arabic through memorization. When she had taught herself the elements of writing, progressing from the mnemonic to the creative, she triumphantly composed her first verse. She narrates a painful scene in which her brother denigrated her first effort to write, but dispels the pain by recounting that her uncle told her, "Don't pay attention to what he said. When you become educated none of us will be able to touch your writing."[40] Mastery of the word and mastery of the self converge, as domination by language becomes another trope in Musa's story of self-creation.

While memorizing served Musa in the first stages of learning and in the acquisition of basic skills, she soon insisted on using her own mind and creative abilities, even in sacrosanct matters of religion. When the young Nabawiyya proceeded from the more passive and imitative task of memorizing the Qur'an to the active and individualist enterprise of interpretation, she again incurred censure and established victory. She recounts that a male relative studying at al-Azhar, the center of Islamic learning, chastised her for trying to interpret the Qur'an on her own without a religious guide, something even he, as a (male) student of religion, would not attempt, as it was seen as tantamount to heresy. Ignoring this, she challenged him to explain a Qur'anic *aya* (verse). When he blundered through a blatant misreading of the Arabic, she pointed out his error and scorned him in a poetic composition. In a culture permeated by religion, Musa established her own ability to read the scripture for herself and rejected passive acquiescence to the not-infallible interpretation of male authority.[41]

In this episode Musa and her male relative represent two approaches to religion and authority: acquiescence in the authority of religious figures (a status which the male relative might one day attain, but which was beyond the expected reach of Nabawiyya, as a woman) and the reliance upon oneself to interpret religion. Individual rational investigation, or *ijtihad*, was an Islamic method for understanding religion resurrected by the late nineteenth-century reformer Shaikh Muhammad 'Abduh as part of his Islamic modernism, encouraging Muslims to reject non-Islamic practices and to apply religion to new circumstances. It was within this context of Islamic modernism that pioneering feminists in Egypt such as Musa and Sha'rawi articulated their approach to women's liberation.[42]

Finding her way to school (possible then only for middle-class girls, as the tuition of the élite was still strictly confined to the home) opened up a whole new life for Musa. She narrates how her brother initially played a helpful role in informing her about entry requirements for the new Saniyya School.[43] Again, there was a pattern of obstacles and resistance. When, at Musa's request for a mathematics tutor, her mother sought the help of her uncle, he, she tells readers, responded with a famous proverb, saying, "Teach them (girls) to say words of love, not to write," advocating a sexual destiny (of marriage and motherhood) for women and indicating the irrelevance, or impropriety, of literacy for females. Musa adds flippantly that her mother taught her neither, whereupon she solved the problem on her own by getting a mathematics book and teaching herself.[44]

In recounting her determination to attend school, a domain outside the domestic, family-centered world, Musa's narrative displays a break with maternal authority. When she announced her intention to go to school, her mother told her it "was a violation of decorum and modesty, and an affront to good upbringing and religion," and threatened to disown her.[45] The text then ironically discloses the unwitting collusion of the mother with the daughter's project as the young and determined Nabawiyya marched off to register at the school armed with the signet ring of her illiterate mother, and hence with her mother's "permission." When Nabawiyya learned she had passed the entrance examination, she gave her mother an ultimatum. If her mother stood in her way she would leave home and enter school as a boarder, paying her tuition out of her portion of her late father's pension. Her mother acquiesced – afraid to forfeit the income, remarks Musa. At this point her brother enters the narrative reconstruction, warning his sister, "If you go to the Saniyya School I shall cease to know you." She snapped, "Then I shall have one less [male]relative and that's fine with me."[46] Musa paid her fees as a day student with the money she received from selling the jewelry her mother had given her, the conventional gift of feminine adornment from mother to daughter. She remarks that she had found jewelry inappropriate to her new-found status as a student. The redeployment of elements of her social and cultural heritage to rewrite her gendered destiny and serve her new self-chosen objectives is yet another trope in Musa's life narrative.

In her text Musa challenges the commonplace belief that an educated girl is a frivolous girl, exploding the stereotype with her portrayal of the young Nabawiyya. Earlier, in *al-Mar'a wa al-'amal*, she had argued that education for women would make them more serious and better able to protect themselves.[47]

In Musa's youth, as we have seen, schooling was not the norm for a girl, but it was possible. Notions that female education constituted a violation of religion were attacked in state-encouraged treatises published in the final third of nineteenth century by Shaikh Ahmad Rifa'i al-Tahtawi and 'Ali Pasha Mubarak.[48] Marriage, however, was a norm backed by religious injunction. Musa's rejection of marriage was her most obvious act of defiance, but gaining an education was also integral to this rebellion, as she shows in her autobiography when she links her pursuit of education to her escape from marriage: "It [marriage] repelled me and perhaps my leaving home at the age of thirteen to go to school was because of my hatred for marriage. If I had stayed without work I could not have remained unmarried. I did not have the resources adequate to my needs."[49]

Musa relates how a series of suitors who learned of her existence through articles she published in the newspapers presented themselves for marriage. At some length she describes how she turned each down. She was earning good money that they could not match. When one suitor suggested that she continue to work after marriage, she rejected it as an absurd notion in words that showed she had no interest in what later would be called the "double burden." (In any case, women were forbidden to continue teaching after marriage until the 1930s, when the state allowed married women to teach in government-sponsored schools.)[50] The burden, Musa implies, was not simply a pragmatic one, but included the general weight of male domination that came with marriage. In the context of discussing her escape from marriage she declares: "I preferred to live as the master of men, not their servant."[51] Musa also surely rejected the specter of reconfinement in the domestic sphere from which she had adroitly escaped by going to school and finding employment.

Publication of such astonishingly blunt views on marriage as Musa's is unusual in the context of Egyptian society and culture, both in her day and now, in the next century. She makes her deep aversion to marriage evident: "I hated marriage and considered it dirt and had decided not to soil myself with this dirt. Since childhood, I had believed that marriage was animalistic and degrading to women and I could not bear [the thought of] it."[52]

When we contrast the approaches Musa takes to marriage in her treatise and in her autobiography, we see that she is careful to uphold the ideal of marriage and motherhood as women's first and paramount roles in *al-Mar'a wa al-'amal*, while in "Dhikriyyati" she gives firm reasons for her rejection – even denigration – of marriage. In her treatise, Musa's main aim was to promote schooling and work for women in the early years of the twentieth century. Accordingly, she took care to dispel fears she knew people would have that education and work might divert women from what were deemed their "natural" roles. But by the late 1930s, major battles for women in education and work had been won. Musa herself was at the pinnacle of her career, no longer an employee of the Ministry of Education but an independent educator heading her own private schools. She could more safely make her position known by presenting it as her own experience and commenting upon it.

Another contentious matter that Musa takes up in her autobiography is the controversy over *sufur* (unveiling) and *hijab* (veiling, then commonly understood to include covering the face). On this subject, her position is the same in both works. In her memoirs she borrows from her introduction to *al-Mar'a wa al-'amal*, where she had written:

> I have dealt with all subjects relating to Egyptian women except for what they now call *sufur* and *hijab* because I believe these are academic terms the meanings of which we are quite ignorant. I cannot call the peasant woman unveiled because she does not wear the transparent [face] veil that is known to us city women. The peasant woman goes about her way modestly ... I cannot call some of the city women veiled when they go out immodestly covered with ornaments and jewelry attracting the eyes of the passer-by while on their faces they wear a veil that conceals nothing but timidity.[53]

Musa wanted to shift the debate away from *sufur* versus *hijab* to a focus on *hishma*, or modesty, transcending the categories "traditional" and "modern," which saw veiling as traditional and unveiling as modern. In "Dhikriyyati," Musa illustrates her point when she narrates her encounter on a tram with a woman who asked her if she were a Christian because her face was uncovered (Christians had begun to unveil earlier than Muslims). Musa replied that she was behaving with greater modesty than the woman herself was. She recounts that she told the woman that her transparent veil did not hide her face, and continued, "I see what I should not see of your bosom and I see your arms [which according the widely accepted interpretation Muslim women were enjoined to cover] ... but you do not see anything of me but my face [which Islam does not enjoin women to cover]."[54] She also reconstructs an exchange she had with a male writer in the offices of the Cairo daily *al-Ahram*, who insisted that women should cover their faces. After reminding him that his female relatives in the village did not cover their faces (as was customary for peasant women) she said: "Sir, you claim that men are wiser and more rational than women. If women are not seduced by your faces, and some of you are indeed handsome, how could you men who are more rational be seduced by women's faces? You men should be veiled and women unveiled."[55]

At the end of the 1930s and the beginning of the 1940s, she observes in "Dhikriyyati," "What I foresaw came true. Now the women of Egypt have unveiled and men have started to attack the mentality of the veiled woman. Yes, what I envisioned came true but not in the way I had hoped. Unveiling was accompanied by flashiness (*tabarraj*), which I did not expect the respectable Egyptian woman to fall prey to, especially the educated women. But who knows, maybe it is a passing thing. Perhaps later we shall return to modest unveiling."[56] Musa's prescient speculation about the future has been realized by the renewed concern for modesty and the reveiling of the head and body that surfaced in the 1970s, two decades after her death.

By early adulthood, Musa had achieved considerable self-definition, and had secured her personal independence. She had acquired status and financial independence, and in so doing was able to thwart the social convention that would make marriage her destiny. Yet, she was still a female in a patriarchal society and subject to controls imposed, in part, by the (patriarchal) culture's code of morality. Musa, unveiled (that is, with face uncovered) and single, and hence vulnerable, upheld this code to protect herself in her everyday life even while she also made it serve her wider ends.

LINES OF BATTLE: COLONIALISM

Musa narrates her life up to the age of twenty as a "feminist project" of inventing a life for herself and not merely following convention. She represents her "feminism" as taking on a more collective and public dimension when she entered the workforce. Defying the conventional life script, and those who sought to impose it, Musa entered into a new stage of combat which was to last the rest of her life.

For almost the first two decades of her professional life, as during her school days, Musa had to contend with the omnipresent British colonial rule. Colonialism oppressed Egyptians in gender- and class-specific ways, often doubly oppressing women. At the same time, colonial authorities sometimes promoted new roles for women – and, in so doing, gave rise to tensions across (indigenous) gender lines, a largely unexplored form of colonial divide and rule.[57] In the struggle against colonialism, Egyptians played roles determined in certain ways by class and gender. Sha'rawi conducted her nationalist activism during the independence struggle, and her post-independence feminism within the framework of a political organization, and expressed it in militant slogans, demands, and demonstrations.[58] Musa's nationalist activism, like her feminist activism, was expressed mainly through her work, and was articulated more subtly. Musa's "Dhikriyyati" illuminates intersections between her feminism and nationalism, and sheds light on forms of indigenous and colonial patriarchal oppression she experienced.

Musa used her autobiography to elucidate her mode of nationalist activism. Her nationalism with a feminist dimension has to be understood in the context of her position as a middle-class teacher in a government school. Unlike Sha'rawi, whose life, as already mentioned, was secured by her upper-class status and wealth, Musa could not engage in overt political protest without incurring professional and financial risk. It was not, however, simply pragmatic considerations that motivated Musa, but the conviction that building an educated citizenry, especially educated female citizens, was integral to achieving solid independence and preserving national identity. She stresses women's central role in consolidating an Egyptian identity and in expanding the national workforce in *al-Mar'a wa al-'amal*, insisting that "the best service that can be done for the country that we are ready to die for is to direct the attention of women toward education and work." She tells her readers in her book, published at the height of the national revolution, that "this conviction has inspired me to publish this book in the hope that it will have some effect."[59]

Recounting her position and actions during the revolution of 1919–1922, when she was headmistress of the Wardiyyan Women Teachers' Training School in Alexandria, Musa reveals how class and gender operated in the nationalist struggle. During that period when (male) students and teachers were frequently out on strike, Musa did not allow herself, her teachers, or her students to participate in demonstrations. That could have led to the closure of her school and the end of her career, neither of which, she believed, would have benefited Egypt.[60] She writes:

> I have loved, and still love, education which has totally preoccupied me. It has kept me from involvement in politics because I believed that a person serves their country through the work in which they excel and through that alone … In my view schools going out on strike does not help the country.[61] We can help in our own ways such as advocating the spread of girls' education which our country greatly needs. It is a non-threatening endeavor with which no one can interfere and something noble that will greatly benefit the country and have a long-term impact.[62]

Musa also objected to women and girls going out on demonstrations with men because she believed it would endanger the women's reputations and pose a moral threat to them: "I was unhappy that nationalist activity might be a reason for women teachers to violate codes of modesty and decorum and be an occasion for frivolity."[63] Later, she states: "I explained to them [the women teachers and girls] that taking part in street demonstrations was not fitting to our dignity as oriental women."[64]

Musa discloses to her readers how the men who were her adversaries in the Ministry of Education called into question her nationalist credentials as a way to goad her into striking in order to bring about her downfall as an anti-British agitator. She reveals how gender strife perpetrated by certain Egyptian men within the Ministry overrode nationalist solidarity, even during the independence struggle.

REPRESENTING VICTORY

As an illustration of how Musa meshed issues of gender and national-ism, I consider an episode representative of her confrontation with authority. Musa had been active in state education for two decades, a period full of battles with both British and Egyptian superiors and col-leagues in the Ministry of Education. Her text is replete with tales of traps set on all fronts to bring her down and of her skillful maneuvers to maintain her position. She claims the British authorities in the Ministry of Education preferred to keep her inside the system and under their control rather than allowing her to slip into private edu-cation, where she might become a threat. In the first two decades of the century, schools were sites of nationalist agitation and resistance, and teachers and students alike were closely watched. Musa relates incident after incident in which her Egyptian foes inside the Ministry tried to create her downfall by reporting to the rulers that she was a threat to their authority.

However, it was not during colonial occupation, but four years after (quasi) independence, in March 1926, that Musa's downfall came, when she was fired by the Ministry of Education. According to one account she was dismissed for opposing new appointments of foreign headmistresses in government schools, motivating Egyptian headmistresses and women inspectors against the Ministry of Education, and accusing senior officials in the Ministry of Education of making sexual advances toward women teachers.[65] She tells her readers that the accusations leveled against her could not be substan-tiated by her employment record at the Ministry of Education. Consequently she claims a new file was fabricated, "one hundred and forty-eight pages filled with nonsense and imaginings."[66] Musa fur-ther relates how both of the lawyers she had retained allowed them-selves to be manipulated by the judges in court into agreeing that the testimony on Musa's behalf be read privately, 'in camera', rather than publicly in the courtroom. She claims that this caused her to lose her case against the government. She tells her readers how she appealed the case and decided to take up her own defense. This was the ultimate act of agency in quest of self-vindication by the woman who had cre-ated and protected herself. She wrote:

> I appealed the decision the same day. I wrote in the newspapers that I
> had dismissed my lawyers and that I would take up my own defense

in court. The announcement created an uproar in different circles. People awaited the day the court would convene to examine my case in order to see the woman defend herself in an important case against the government. That was what I wanted. I had seen that a defense conducted behind four walls would not shame the court. But conducting it before the general public could be an important force pushing the court towards justice.[67]

Musa elaborates on how she defended herself by rallying the people to her side:

I wanted to speak on the matter of the claim but the court wanted to prevent me. However, I insisted upon my right to speak. The people in the courtroom went into an uproar. Some of them shouted, "Let her speak. Let her speak. Where is justice?" I spoke and gave a full explanation of my case without the court being able to stop me. Whenever the court wanted to stop me from introducing some facts, I firmly insisted on my right to speak while the public increased its uproar and show of disgust. When the session ended, those present were convinced that I had been treated unfairly and that what I had demanded was just and that my explanations were sound. The representative of the government stood up to give the government defense but was unable to say anything significant. His arguments were weak and the public was against him. Whenever he started to speak the people went into an uproar ... When the court adjourned newspaper photographers were waiting for me and took pictures.[68]

Musa won her case for compensation. She adds that Fikri Abaza (a prominent journalist) wrote: "In doing what she did Nabawiyya blocked the way for lawyers to earn a living."[69] Musa says that succeeding in her defense and passing her baccalaureate examination, which each gained her public acclaim, were achievements that were the two happiest days of her life.

POSSIBILITIES OF AUTOBIOGRAPHY

Fatima Mernissi writes: "Memory and recollection are the dawn of pleasure; they speak the language of freedom and self-development."[70] This assessment applies to Nabawiyya Musa's "Dhikriyyati." At the peak of her life, when she began to record it with zest and fierceness, she was having, as it were, her day in court. Declarative and defiant, Musa speaks the language of freedom in "Dhikriyyati."

During the militant phase of the national revolution, eighteen years before she began her autobiography, Musa enunciated her agenda in *al-Mar'a wa al-'amal*, supporting education and work for women while upholding prevailing moral/cultural values, for the betterment of women and the good of the nation. Hers was a program for female relief from patriarchal oppression and for the rescue of the nation from colonial oppression. In her treatise Musa rejects binary oppositions: the prevailing social construction of gender that essentialized male and female as "two separate species"[71] and the contest between veiling and unveiling, with implications of modest or immodest, (morally) right or (morally) wrong, traditional or modern.

In this study I have preferred to let Musa's autobiographical voice resonate. Hers is an unfamiliar voice, long silenced through neglect of her work. It is a voice that displays the range of fine-tuning and concretizing she found possible in the form of the self-narrative but not in the treatise. "Dhikriyyati" illustrates how a feminist and nationalist project can be embedded in autobiography, and elucidates Musa's process in a highly particularized and historicized way. Autobiography enabled Musa to expound and reveal the feminism and nationalism that inflected her educational mission. Through autobiography she could delineate the contours and details of patriarchal oppressions and expose layers of hypocrisy.

At one level Musa was a historical scribe; yet she was also the shaper of the tale and the interpreter of the past. Not only had she entered the public arena of active struggle and achieved personhood in an asymmetrically gendered world, but she entered the public arena of written discourse. Her life was best represented as a struggle with the trope of trials and triumphs. As a woman Musa was refused admittance to the new Egyptian University. She was unable to fulfill her wish to become a lawyer. She was professionally buffeted by colonial authorities. She was fired by the Ministry of Education after independence. But against all odds and opposition she managed to construct a meaningful life.

Musa showed how it was a struggle to be both the same and equal in a society where difference was minutely gendered and the male was highly privileged and empowered. The male Egyptians pioneering in writing modern autobiography narrated lives lived at the center and the top of the new "democratic" order. They lived and wrote their lives as full citizens in the newly semi-independent Egypt. In writing the history of the female Egyptian, Musa celebrated struggle, using her narrative re-creation of it as both mirror and prism. Her autobiography recorded the experience and furnished a model of an Egyptian Muslim woman who had forged and sustained a life for herself. For Musa autobiography was finally "the dawn of pleasure," if pleasure is satisfaction that a life has been lived and retold with purpose.

* * *

This is a slightly revised version of a chapter published in Sidonie Smith and Julia Watson (eds.), *De/Colonizing the Subject: The Politics of Gender in Women's Autobiography* (Minneapolis: University of Minnesota Press, 1992).

NOTES

1. See Huda Shaarawi, *Harem Years: The Memoirs of an Egyptian Feminist*, ed. and trans. Margot Badran (New York: Feminist Press, 1987). I first saw the memoirs in 1967. The copy of the memoirs in the possession of 'Abd al-Hamid Fahmi Mursi was published under the title *Mudhakirrat ra'ida al-'arabiyya al-haditha Huda Sha'rawi* (Memoirs of the modern Arab pioneer Huda Sha'rawi, Cairo: Dar al-Hilal, 1981).
2. For some of these writings, see Margot Badran and Miriam Cooke (eds.), *Opening the Gates: A Century of Arab Feminist Writing* (Bloomington: Indiana University Press, 1990).
3. Two of my works that explore feminist ideologies and activisms in Egypt from the late nineteenth century to the present are "Independent Women: More than a Century of Feminism in Egypt," in Judith Tucker (ed.), *Arab Women: Old Boundaries, New Frontiers* (Bloomington: Indiana University Press, with the Institute for Contemporary Arab Studies, Georgetown University, 1993) and chapter 5 in this volume; "Competing Agenda: Feminists, Islam, and the State in Nineteenth and Twentieth Century Egypt," in Deniz Kandiyoti (ed.), *Women, Islam, and the State* (Philadelphia: Temple University Press, 1991) and chapter 1 in this volume. Also see Akram Khater and Cynthia Nelson, "al-Harakah al-Nissa'iyah: The Women's Movement and Political Participation in Modern Egypt," *Women's Studies International Forum*, 2 (1988), pp. 465–483. Concerning the meanings of feminism, see my article, "Ma hiyya ma'na al-Nisa'iyya?" (What is the meaning of feminism?), *Nisf al-Dunya* (Cairo), 21 September 1990. As a member of the Arab Women's Solidarity Association (AWSA), I participated in an AWSA conference in Cairo in 1988 where feminism was debated, and presented a paper titled "Feminism as a Force in the Arab World," which was later published in *Contemporary Thought and Women* (Cairo: AWSA Press, 1989 [Arabic]; 1990 [English]).
4. On the origin of the term feminism, see Karen Offen, "Defining Feminism: A Comparative Historical Approach," *Signs*, 14 (Autumn 1988), pp. 119–147.

5. See Margot Badran, "Gender Activism: Feminists and Islamists in Egypt," paper presented at the Roundtable on Identity Politics and Women, United Nations University World Institute for Development Economics Research, Helsinki, October 1990; subsequently published in Valentine Moghadam (ed.), *Identity Politics and Women: Cultural Reassertions and Feminisms in International Perspective* (Boulder: Westview Press, 1993) and chapter 6 in this volume.

6. Nabawiyya Musa, *al-Mar'a wa al-'amal* (Alexandria: al-Matba'a al-Wataniya, 1920).

7. Her father, Musa Muhammad, was an army colonel who died before she was born, while on a mission to the Sudan.

8. Recalling the same period, Amir Boktor wrote: "Women from the poorest homes were attracted to the teaching profession ... Only in the last ten years [mid-1920s to mid-1930s] have more Egyptian girls come into the profession," *School and Society in the Valley of the Nile* (Cairo: Elias Modern Press, 1936), p. 185; "Work for a girl of a middle class family, or even of a lower class status, is an act of indecency," ibid., p. 75.

9. Musa was 78th out of a total 2,783 male and female students. She did better in the Arabic examination than the future writer Muhammad 'Abbas al-'Aqqad, who came out 166th overall, and a future prime minister, Muhammad al-Nuqrashi, who was 64th overall. See Ahmad 'Atiya 'Abd Allah, "al-Taliba alati tafqwwaqat 'ala al-Nuqrashi and al-'Aqqad" (The female student who topped al-Nuqrashi and al-'Aqqad), clipping dated 11 May 1951, in Nabawiyya Musa file 3 2357, Dar al-Hilal (the source of the clipping was not appended). The author was then director of the Education Museum.

10. On the beginnings of the Egyptian University and the women's section, see Donald Reid, *Cairo University and the Making of Modern Egypt* (New York: Cambridge University Press, 1990), pp. 51–56; on Musa's lecturing experience, see Nabawiyya Musa, "al-Muhadarat al-nisa'iyya fi al-jam'ia al-misriyya" (Women's lectures in the Egyptian University), *al-Ahram*, 16 April 1912 (reprinted in *al-Ahram*, Shuhud al-'Asr 1876–1986 [Cairo, 1986], pp. 38–42; cited in Reid, *Cairo University*, p. 244); Margot Badran, "The Origins of Feminism in Egypt," in Arina Angerman, Geerte Binnema, Annemieke Keunen, Vefie Poels, and Jacqueline Zirkzee (eds.), *Current Issues in Women's History* (London: Routledge, 1989); Margot Badran, "From Consciousness to Activism: Feminist Politics in Early Twentieth Century Egypt," in John Spangolo (ed.), *Problems of the Middle East in Historical Perspective* (London: Ithaca, 1991) and chapter 3 in this volume.

11. A secondary school for girls with the same curriculum as that for boys had been one of the first two demands the EFU made in 1923.

12. The information on Musa's life is obtained mainly from her "Dhikriyyati" (henceforth referred to as NM). Brief biographical profiles include Khair al-Din al-Zirkali, *al-'Alam qamus tarajam li ashar al-rijal wa al-nisa' min al-'arab wa must'aribin wa mustashriqin* (Biographical dictionary of the most famous Arab men and women), 2nd printing (Cairo: Matba'at Kustatsumas, 1954–1959), vol. 8, pp. 321–322; Ahmad Zaki 'Abd al-Halim, *Nisa' fawq al-qima* (Extraordinary women, Cairo: Dar al-Faisal, n.d.), pp. 18–24.

13. It is interesting that Musa speaks only once of Huda Sha'rawi in her memoirs, in "Musa'adat al-sayyida al-lalila Huda Hanim Sha'rawi" (The help of Huda Sha'rawi), First Series, no. 14. (The autobiographical instalments of

"Dhikriyyati" that appeared in *Majallat al-Fatah* are cited throughout according to series and number.) She tells how, in response to Musa's request, Sha'rawi made emergency funds available to Musa to secure new premises for her school. Huda Sha'rawi's feminist movement was the subject of my D.Phil. thesis, "Huda Sha'rawi and the Liberation of the Egyptian Woman," Oxford University, 1977.

14. The first issue of *Majallat al-Fatah* appeared on 20 October 1937. It is worth noting that the EFU's Arabic-language journal, *al-Misriyya* (The Egyptian woman, counterpart to the EFU's *l'Egyptienne*, established in 1925) was first issued seven months earlier, on 15 February 1937.

15. The government put her in prison alongside prostitutes. Safinaz Kazim has spoken of this indignity in "al-Ra'ida Nabawiyya Musa wa in'ash dhakirrat al-umma" (The pioneer Nabawiyya Musa and the reviving of the nation's memory), *Majallat al-Hilal* (January 1984).

16. For example, she is mentioned briefly in Ijalal Khalifa, *al-Haraka al-nisa'iyya al-haditha* (The modern feminist movement, Cairo: al-Matba'at al-'Arabiyya al-Haditha, 1974). Musa has received more attention over the years in short articles in the Egyptian press than in books.

17. Early autobiographies in the Islamic Middle East include, for example, al-Ghazzali (d. 1111), *al-Munqidh min al-dalal*; and Ibn Khaldun (d. 1406), *al-Ta'rif*. On early or "traditional" autobiography, see Franz Rosenthal, "Die arabische Autobiographic," *Analecta Orientalia*, 14, Studie Arabica (1937); Gustave E. von Grunebaum, "Self-Expression: Literature and History" and "The Human Ideal," in *Medieval Islam*, 2nd ed. (Chicago: University of Chicago Press, 1953), pp. 221–293; Fadwa Malti-Douglas, *Blindness and Autobiography* (Princeton: Princeton University Press, 1988), pp. 9–10. On Arab women's autobiographies, see Badran and Cooke (eds.), *Opening the Gates*, p. xxxv. For an example from South Asia, see Stephen Frederic Dale, "Steppe Humanism; The Autobiographical Writings of Zahir al-Din Muhammad Babur, 1483–1530," *International Journal of Middle East Studies*, 22 (February 1990), pp. 37–58.

18. I cannot date the start of the use of the terms *tarjama hayat* or *sira dhatiyya*, although the term *sira* (biography) is ancient, *al-Sira* being the biography of the Prophet Muhammad. It is interesting to note that the English word autobiography first appeared in print only in 1809. On autobiography, see Shawqi Dayf, *al-Tarjama al-shakhsiyya* (Personal life story, Cairo: Dar al-Ma'arif, 1979); Ihsan 'Abbas, *Fann al-sira* (Artistic biography, Beirut: Dar al-Thaqafa, 1956).

19. See Malti-Douglas, *Blindness and Autobiography*.

20. "With the pen of" is a direct translation from the Arabic; it can indicate merely scribal help or possibly further assistance in shaping the narrative. Awad says that "Umm Kulthum wrote it [her memoirs] out for me." However, ascertaining the extent of assistance that "with the pen of" represents for the other autobiographies mentioned below in the text would require further research. Umm Kulthum's memoirs published in *Akhir Sa'a* were republished in Mahmud Awad, *Umm Kulthum alati la ya'rifuha ahad* (The Umm Kulthum nobody knows, Cairo: Mu'assat Akhbar al-Yaum, 1971) with added more material by Awad; an English translation of the memoirs, "Excerpts from *The Umm Kulthum Nobody Knows*," is found in Elizabeth Fernea and Basima Qattan Bezirgan (eds.), *Middle Eastern Muslim Women Speak* (Austin: University of Texas, 1977), pp. 135–167.

21. Her autobiography was written by the then young journalist Ahmad Baha al-Din. See Sonia Dabbous, "Studying an Egyptian Journalist: Rose al-Youssef, a Woman and a Journal," *Islamic and Mediterranean Women's History Network Newsletter*, 1 (Spring/Fall 1988), pp. 11–12.

22. See C. Kooij, "Bint Al-Shati': A Suitable Case for Biography?" in Ibrahim A. El-Sheikh, C. Aart van de Koppel, and Rudolf Peters (eds.), *The Challenge of the Middle East: Middle East Studies at the University of Amsterdam* (Amsterdam: Institute for Modern Near Eastern Studies, University of Amsterdam, 1982).

23. 'Asmahan, *'Asmahan tirwi qissatuha* (Asmahan tells her story), with the pen of Muhammad al-Taba'i (Cairo: Mu'assat Ruz al-Yusif, 1965).

24. Bad'ia Masabni, *Mudhakirrat Bad'ia Masabni* (The memoirs of Bad'ia Masabni), with the pen of Nazik Basila (Beirut: Dar Maktabat al-Hiyat, n.d.).

25. Fatma Rushdi, *Kifahi fi masrah wa sinima* (My struggle in theater and cinema) (Cairo: Dar al-Ma'aris, 1971).

26. See Cynthia Nelson, "The Voices of Doria Shafiq: Feminist Consciousness in Egypt, 1940–60," *Feminist Issues* (Fall 1986), pp. 15–31. Appearing after this chapter was written is Nelson's book *Doria Shafiq, Egyptian Feminist: A Woman Apart* (Gainsville: University Press of Florida, 1996).

27. A leftist and feminist in the student movement after World War II, she was jailed under Nasser from 1959 to 1963, and afterward kept a low profile, working exclusively as an artist. In an interview in 1988 Aflatun told me she was working on her memoirs. She published *Thamanun milyun imra'a ma'na* (Eighty million women with us) in 1948 and *Nahnu al-nisa' al-misriyyat* (We Egyptian women) in 1949. Michelle Raccagni has written an unpublished paper titled "Inji Efflatoun, Author, Artist, and Militant: A Brief Analysis of Her Life and Works."

28. Personal communication, Cairo, March 1989.

29. Marilyn Booth, "Biography and Feminist Rhetoric in Early Twentieth-Century Egypt: Mayy Ziyada's Studies of Three Women's Lives," *Journal of Women's History*, 3 (Spring 1991), pp. 38–64.

30. Since this chapter was originally written Fatima Mernissi published *Dreams of Trespass: Tales of a Harem Girlhood* (New York: Addison-Wesley, 1994) a memoir, as the author acknowledged, in the form of a novel.

31. See Fatna A. Sabah, *Women in the Muslim Unconscious*, trans. Mary Jo Lakeland (New York: Pergamon, 1984).

32. On the life of an upper-class woman, see Sha'rawi, *Mudhakirrat ra'ida al-'arabiyya al-haditha Huda Sha'rawi* and *Harem Years*.

33. See Beth Baron, "Unveiling in Early Twentieth Century Egypt: Practical and Symbolic Considerations," *Middle Eastern Studies*, 25 (July 1989), pp. 370–386.

34. About Huda Sha'rawi's memoirs I have said: "Writing about her life during the harem years was a final unveiling. It can be seen as Huda Shaarawi's final feminist act," Shaarawi, *Harem Years*, p. 1.

35. Musa had also called her poetry collection *Diwan al-fatah* (Collected poems of the young woman). *Al-fatah* means "young woman," but it could also signify an unmarried woman. Using *al-fatah* could be an assertion of her independent status, which she fought to preserve in a society expecting every woman to marry. *Diwan al-fatah* celebrated the status of the independent woman. *Majallat al-Fatah* was a woman speaking to women and men, and not in the tradition of the women's journals aimed at female audiences. And as an Arabic periodical, its largest audience was middle class. On the early Arabic women's press, see Beth

Ann Baron, "The Rise of a New Literary Culture: The Women's Press of Egypt, 1892–1919," Ph.D. thesis, University of California, Los Angeles, 1988.

36. By the time she began to publish her memoirs, Musa had long since been the butt of ridicule in the press and the subject of numerous cartoons portraying her covered from tip to toe in the traditional *abaya* (the long black wrap that by then was worn mainly by more conservative women and those of the lower class), bespectacled and "ugly," usually in a haranguing posture. She actually appropriated this kind of caricature in her own magazine, turning it to her own advantage. The woman who broke convention in writing about her own life had already gained a notoriety that gave her a certain freedom.

37. For an analysis of the sociocultural significance of language for the transmission of feminist thought, see Irene Fenoglio-Abd El Aal, *Defense et illustration de l'Egyptienne: aux debuts d'une expression feminine* (Cairo: Centre d'Etudes et Documentation Economique, Juridique, et Sociale, 1988).

38. Boktor, *School and Society*, p. 7.

39. NM, "Tufulati" (My childhood), First Series, no. 70, and Second Series, no. 1.

40. NM, "Tufulati," Second Series, no. 1.

41. Ibid.

42. On Islamic modernism, see Albert Hourani, *Arabic Thought in the Liberal Age* (Cambridge: Cambridge University Press, 1983), pp. 130–163.

43. The Saniyya School was created in 1889, incorporating the Siufiyya School founded by Tcheshme Hanim, a wife of Kehdive Isma'il, in 1873 (the first state-connected school for girls) and the Qirabiyya School, founded the following year. At the beginning of the twentieth century the Saniyya School became the training ground for middle-class women in Egypt to become teachers. For reminiscences on the early classes, see NM, "Nahda ta'lim al-banat fi misr" (The renaissance of girls' education in Egypt), Second Series, no. 3.

44. NM, "Kaifa dakhaltu Madrasat al-Saniyya" (How I entered the Saniyya School), Second Series, no. 3.

45. Ibid.

46. Ibid.

47. "Ta'thir al-kutub wa riwayyat fi al-akhlaq" (The effects of books and novels on morals), in Musa, *al-Mar'a wa al-'amal*, pp. 89–96.

48. See Shaikh Ahmad Rifa'i al-Tahtawi, *Tariq al-hija wa al-tamrin 'ala qawaid al-lugha al-'arabiyya* (The intelligent way and exercise in employing the rules of the Arabic language) (Cairo: n.p., 1869) and 'Ali Pasha Mubarak, *al-Murshid al-amin lil-banat wa al-banin* (The faithful guide for girls and boys) (Cairo: n.p., 1875).

49. NM, "Athar husuli 'ala al-bakkaluriyya wa madhhabi fi al-zawwaj" (The result of my success in the baccalaureate examination and my view of marriage), Second Series, no. 18.

50. NM, "Madhhabi fi al-zawwaj" (My view of marriage), First Series, no. 22.

51. Ibid.

52. Ibid.

53. Musa, "al-Muqaddima" (Introduction), in *al-Mar'a wa al-'amal*, quoted in NM, "Sufuri" (My unveiling), Second Series, no. 15.

54. NM, "Sufuri," Second Series, no. 15.

55. Ibid.

56. Ibid.

57. On women's new roles, see Judith Tucker, *Women in Nineteenth Century Egypt* (Cambridge: Cambridge University Press, 1985).

58. See Margot Badran, "Dual Liberation: Feminism and Nationalism in Egypt, 1870s–1925," *Feminist Issues* (Spring 1988), pp. 15–34.

59. Musa, "al-Muqaddima," pp. 3–5.

60. A woman who had been a teacher in one of Musa's schools recalled in a latter period how Musa instilled a nationalist spirit in her students and that she invited outside speakers to talk on current events. See "Mudhakkirat Mudarissa" (Memoirs of a teacher), *al-Jumhuriyya*, 16 November 1970. The teacher's name is not given.

61. NM, "Wathifa wakila" (The job of deputy headmistress), Second Series, no. 61.

62. NM, "Insha' Madrasat Tarqiyya al-Fatah" (The establishment of the Tarqiyya al-Fatah School), Second Series, no. 75.

63. NM, "Kaifa kuntu u'aqab 'ala al-qiyam bi-wajab siyanat al-akhlaq" (How I was punished for performing the duty of maintaining morals), First Series, no. 9.

64. NM, "Insha' Madrasat Tarqiyya al-Fatah."

65. Muhammad Abu al-Hadid, "Misriyya tathada al-rijal" (An Egyptian woman who challenged men), *al-Jumhuriyya*, 21 August 1975.

66. NM, "Qissa al-dhi'ab wa al-hamal" (The story of the wolf and the lamb), First Series, no. 37.

67. NM, "Yaum al-mahkama" (The day in court), First Series, no. 38.

68. Ibid.

69. Ibid.

70. Fatima Mernissi, *Women and Islam: An Historical and Theological Enquiry*, trans. Mary Jo Lakeland (Oxford: Basil Blackwell, 1991), p. 10.

71. Musa, "al-Farq bain al-rajil wa al-mar'a" (The differences between men and women), in *al-Mar'a wa al-'amal*, pp. 21–36.

5

INDEPENDENT WOMEN: MORE THAN A CENTURY OF FEMINISM IN EGYPT

We can look back on a long tradition of feminism in Egypt. Women expressed the first stirrings of feminist consciousness in the final third of the nineteenth century. In the 1890s, a feminist ideology began to take shape, while the earliest signs of a new gender awareness can be detected in women's writings that predate this decade. At the beginning of the twentieth century, pioneering women engaged in discreet forms of feminist activism. In the early 1920s, women inaugurated an era of open, organized feminism. Egyptian women, as feminists, have maintained a strong tradition of independence (from the state and political parties) unparalleled elsewhere in the Middle East. They have also maintained an unbroken tradition, for although the public movement was suppressed during most of the Nasser period, and is beleaguered at present, feminism has persisted in Egypt.

Here I survey the feminism of women in Egypt from the latter decades of the nineteenth century to the last decade of the twentieth. In contrast to the widely held view that feminism in Egypt began with men, that it was/is Western, and that early feminism was restricted to upper-class women, I shall demonstrate that feminism began with women, that it has been indigenous, and that there has been broader cross-class cooperation among feminists than commonly acknowledged.[1] From the colonial era to the present day, women across the spectrum from right to left have continued to ground their feminism in Islam and nationalism, as they have persisted in challenging a patriarchy transcending, in different ways, political and class formations.[2]

Feminists in Egypt have been most successful in the public sphere, and most thwarted in the private. This is not, however, to imply a neat division between the public and private.³ While patriarchy's control over women for the last century and more has loosened in the societal arena, it has remained more firmly entrenched within the family. This is most vividly expressed in the preservation of personal status laws repressive to women. Each generation of feminists has had at the head of its agenda the transformation of personal status legislation.

There are certain considerations to bear in mind when analyzing feminism in Egypt. Egyptian feminism is closer to that of other Third World countries than to that of the West. Feminism in the Third World usually first arose following the shift from an agrarian subsistence economy to capitalism, and incorporation into the Western-dominated world economy. It often became organized and publicly visible following national independence struggles. Third World feminisms, which have had distinct nationalist dimensions, and have typically incorporated religious reformism in their agenda, have had to endure from their own patriarchies the condemnation of being Western, and thus at best accusations of irrelevance and at worst of cultural and political subversiveness.⁴

In the Third World, the time frame of feminist evolution has been more compressed than in the West. In the United States, for example, women made significant advances in education and inroads into paid work some half-century before they stepped up the suffrage movement.⁵ At the start of organized feminism in Egypt, women simultaneously demanded social, economic, and political rights, sequentially spacing out their campaigns in these areas only to a limited extent. Moreover, in Egypt, as in other Third World countries, feminists have had to juggle their feminist struggle with anti-colonialist and anti-imperialist ones, a dual battle unknown to Western feminists.⁶

In Egypt, as in most other Middle Eastern and Islamic countries, feminism emerged from within the urban and middle-class world where sex segregation and the domestic seclusion of women were in force. To add to the burden of Muslim women, these practices had, incorrectly, been presented as Islamic. In Turkey and Iran, the state assisted this process, whereas in Egypt women took the initiative largely on their own, and in this respect they were not only pioneers in their own country, but set an example in the region. Egyptian feminists have had to fight for changes in the personal status laws, a struggle that has continually frustrated them, while in Turkey, Tunisia, Iran, and the People's Democratic Republic of Yemen (PDRY) the state issued liberal personal status laws. In Iran, however, the Islamic

Republic withdrew the liberal legislation later in the century. (In the new Republic of Yemen, following unification of the north and south in 1990, the liberal personal status law of the PDRY gave way to a conservative new draft law, as seen in chapter 11.)[7]

There are two distinct stages in the history of feminism in Egypt. The first, from the final decades of the nineteenth century to 1923, was an era of emerging feminist consciousness and early social feminism, largely invisible to male society. During this period, most Muslim (upper- and middle-class) women continued to wear the (face) veil, a symbol and function of sex segregation and female seclusion, signaling continued adherence to inherited conventions that women with a feminist consciousness had come to see, in whole or in part, as oppressive. Under "traditional camouflage," however, women were taking initiatives in expanding their lives into public space. This was also the period when progressive men advocated the liberation of women alongside their calls for the liberation of the country.

The second stage is that of highly-visible, organized activism, from 1923 to the present, with the exception of the Nasser regime proving the rule. This era began when women formed their first feminist organization, and soon after two members removed their face veils in public as a political act, declaring their rejection of the system of female domestic seclusion and gender segregation. This announced the start of an open campaign by feminists to realize a broad program of goals they set for themselves. This occurred after Egypt achieved quasi-independence in 1922, when pro-feminist men turned their attention to national politics and their own careers. Nationalist men's formerly highly visible calls for women's liberation largely ceased, leaving only a few who worked discreetly for women's advancement. In 1923 Egyptian women activists began to use the term "feminism," and publicly call themselves feminists.

Within the second stage of feminism there are four overlapping phases: (1) radical liberal feminism, from the 1920s through the 1940s; (2) populist feminism, in the 1940s and 1950s; (3) sexual feminism, in the 1960s and 1970s; and (4) the resurgent feminism of the 1980s. I shall focus on well-known leaders associated with these phases. These include Huda Sha'rawi and Saiza Nabarawi, associated with radical liberal feminism; Fatma Ni'mat Rashid, Duriyya Shafiq, Saiza Nabarawi, and Inji Aflatun with populist feminism; and Nawal al-Saadawi with sexual feminism and resurgent feminism. However, within the context of resurgent feminism I shall also mention new groupings of feminists who eschew hierarchical formations that produce high-profile leaders. I conclude by mentioning the recent phenomenon of the new invisible feminism of individuals.

Before proceeding further it is important to discuss terminology and definitions. During the first stage, the terms "feminism" and "feminist" were not used. However, during the second stage, when they began to be employed, there were no unequivocal terms for feminism or feminist. The noun *al-nisa'iyya* and the adjective *nisa'i/nisa'iyya*, which were used, could mean, in the first instance, either "of women" or "feminism" and, in the second instance, either "women's" or "feminist"; the meanings were understood from the context. When I use the terms "feminism" and "feminist" in reference to the first stage, I employ them as analytical constructs. The pioneers of the feminist movement who first publicly declared themselves feminists (through the name of their new organization, the Egyptian Feminist Union, when they established it in 1923) announced this in French, the everyday language of the upper class, which many educated members of the middle class also knew (although Arabic was the common language of middle-class women) and the language in which the terms "feminism" and "feminist" had first been coined in the 1880s.[8]

Embedded in the project of writing the history of feminist movements and forms of feminist consciousness and ideologies is the act of defining feminism. Meanings must be recovered from historical investigation, and thus we define Egyptian feminisms within the context of the Egyptian experience.[9] I use a broad working definition of feminism that includes an awareness of constraints placed upon women because of their gender and attempts to remove these constraints and evolve a more equitable gender system involving new roles for women and improved relations between women and men. Below I shall look at different formulations of feminism in Egypt.

A major problem with the little that has been written about feminism in Egypt, and that has contributed to the misconceptions mentioned earlier, is the neglect of women's sources. Only in the last few decades has this begun to be redressed. This study is based on women's memoirs, private papers, journal articles, books, oral histories, and personal interviews with four of the six feminist leaders noted above.

THE STAGE OF RISING FEMINIST CONSCIOUSNESS

The nineteenth century was a time of dramatic societal transforma-tions that wrought enormous changes in the lives of all classes and both sexes, in urban and rural Egypt alike. Early in that century, Egypt was incorporated into the European-dominated world market system. The year 1882 saw the start of British colonial occupation.

By the end of the century, the lives of Cairene women of the upper and middle classes were marked by growing contradictions and strains. On the one hand, the ideology supporting female seclusion, face veiling, and gender segregation remained largely in force among Muslim women, supported by family patriarchs (and elder female surrogates).[10] On the other hand, state-instigated economic, social, and technological changes ushered in new patterns of everyday life for upper- and middle-class women which eroded these restrictive prac-tices. Alterations in domestic architecture disrupted internal patterns of female seclusion, while new designs and use of urban space broke down tight patterns of gender segregation as well as geographical divi-sions by creed and ethnicity. There were new educational and recre-ational outlets for middle- and upper-class women. Expanded movement for both sexes within the city and country was made pos-sible by the new carriageways and railroads. Unprecedented profes-sional and vocational opportunities beckoned to these women. The new conditions under which women were starting to live, their new experiences, and comparisons with the possibilities open to men in their families gave rise to a nascent feminist awareness.[11] Women such as 'Aisha al-Taimuriyya from the upper class, and Zainab al-Fawwaz in the middle class, born in the middle of the century, were the first generation to reveal this through their writings.[12]

By the 1890s, the tight grip of patriarchy over women within the family had been loosened by the projects and developments encour-aged by the rise of the modern state, itself a new patriarchal phenom-enon.[13] But while some forms of patriarchal control within the family were eroded, others tightened. In this context some women in the cloistered world of upper- and middle-class Cairo and Alexandria began to deepen their feminist consciousness. We know about this expanding awareness, which was invisible to the outside world, from the memoirs of Huda Sha'rawi, who recalls the debates in the first salon for women hosted by Eugénie Le Brun Rushdi, a French woman and convert to Islam, who, as the wife of an upper-class

Egyptian, had been thrust into the segregated harem world. Women discovered that the face veil and female seclusion were not required by Islam, but were merely a function of patriarchal control. They also understood that they as women had rights within Islam, which patriarchy withheld from them.[14] This awareness was assisted by the Islamic modernism Shaikh Muhammad 'Abduh had begun to expound earlier.

At the same time as some upper-class women were experiencing a feminist awakening, some women in the middle class were evolving a feminist consciousness influenced by their expanding formal education. Middle-class women had begun to attend new schools for girls that opened in the nineteenth century. (With the exception of a few girls from elite families who attended the Siufiyya School opened by Tcheshme Harem, a wife of Khedive Isma'il, in the 1870s, upper-class girls received their education at the hands of family-hired tutors in the harems until about the 1930s.) During the latter half of the 1880s, middle-class women began to publish their writings in men's journals and papers. By the early 1890s, middle-class women had begun to found their own women's journals.[15] The writings of many of these women reveal a feminist consciousness with a religious and nationalist dimension.[16]

The decade after the emergence of a women's feminist consciousness saw the rise of social feminism. Upper-class women founded the Mabarrat Muhammad 'Ali (1909) to bring medical assistance and health instruction to poor women in their own neighborhoods. Sha'rawi and some other women explicitly placed this project in a feminist context, seeing it as the first step in the process of liberating the lives of lower-class women and, at the same time, expanding their own lives beyond the harem. Sha'rawi's memoirs reveal a distinct nationalist impulse motivating her and other women to pioneer in public philanthropy.[17] This, not the widely visible participation of women in the 1919 nationalist demonstrations, was the first time that upper-class women's unconventional extra-domestic behavior was legitimized as a nationalist act. Middle-class women also participated in social feminism through societies they founded on their own, or with upper-class women, such as Jam'iyyat al-Mar'a al-Jadida (New Woman Society, NWS), created in 1919 (a month after the start of the revolution against the continued British occupation), which taught working-class girls literacy, hygiene, and crafts.[18] A recurring theme in the history of Egyptian feminism was the breaking of convention by women in the cause of nationalism, accompanied by an increase in their practical experience.

Women of the middle and upper classes also came together in "public" lectures (that is, outside the harem but in places exclusively reserved for women) organized by women for women from 1909 to 1912 at the new Egyptian University and in the offices of the progressive paper *al-Jarida*. Sponsored by upper-class women and given by middle-class women, Bahithat al-Badiya (Malak Hifni Nasif), Nabawiyya Musa, and Mayy Ziyada, a poet and writer of Lebanese and Palestinian origin, were among the speakers.[19] In these lectures feminist consciousness was further expanded and feminist bonds among women across class lines were forged.

Bahithat al-Badiya (whose untimely death in 1918 brought Huda Sha'rawi to the podium for the first time to deliver a eulogy) was the first woman to make public feminist demands in Egypt. Because she was unable as a woman to appear before the all-male Egyptian Congress of 1911, a man presented her agenda, which included the demand that women be allowed into mosques (as in the early days of Islam), and have access to professions, especially those that cater to other women.[20] This, and her reluctance to favor unveiling (which then meant uncovering the face), indicated her strategy of promoting women's development within the system of sex segregation, a stand shared at the turn of the century by Nabawiyya Musa, who, however, had by 1909 removed the veil from her face.

Nabawiyya Musa, a life-long teacher and school administrator and founding member of the Egyptian Feminist Union (EFU), argued for more education, appealing to upper-class women to finance schools for girls. She also called for better jobs for women, both for their own sake and as a nationalist strategy to reduce foreign workers and the loss of Egyptian capital. Both women argued for controls on men's tyrannical use of divorce and polygamy.[21] These demands were aimed at an area of patriarchal control in the private sphere, where male dominance was strongest and women's (patriarchally prescribed) family roles were most threatened. Proponents of feminism and defenders of patriarchal principles have remained severely polarized in a century-long struggle around issues relating to the family.

While feminism in Egypt began with women in a world segregated by sex, its radical threat to patriarchy was hidden by the very barriers that obscured and obstructed its proponents.[22] When a man, Qasim Amin, made public in a widely-read book, *Tahrir al-mar'a* (The liberation of woman, Cairo, 1899), concerns at the center of Egyptian women's early feminism, patriarchal forces rose up in fury in a public counter-attack, for the time being missing the radical force that was evolving more invisibly.

THE STAGE OF PUBLIC FEMINIST ACTIVISM

Radical liberal feminism

When middle- and upper-class women participated in the Egyptian nationalist movement (1919–1922), in street demonstrations, political organizing, communications, and morale boosting, the patriarchy did not construe these as radical acts.[23] On the contrary, the patriarchy considered women's unconventional behavior as defensive national acts – an extension of the notion of woman as defender of the home. Despite women's crucial roles (which men needed and welcomed) in the nationalist struggle, and male nationalists' liberation rhetoric and promises to women, when the militant struggle was over patriarchy hastened to consolidate its hold, and expected women to retreat to the home. While women's nationalist experience did not itself produce feminism (as has already been seen), it did give women valuable political experience, consolidated their claims on the nation, and quickened expectations. Women argued that patriarchal domination was tantamount to foreign imperialist domination and that national liberation was incomplete without women's liberation.[24]

With the achievement of (partial) independence came a new constitution and parliamentary democracy. However, the electoral law denying women the right to vote and their banning from attending the opening of parliament – except as wives of ministers and high officials – signaled to women that they were expected to retreat into the private sphere of house and family. Women might defend Egypt during times of crisis, but in "normal" times men must govern and command the public sphere.

Egyptian women understood the message, and after several decades of hidden feminist evolution they were prepared to act. Huda Sha'rawi and Saiza Nabarawi inaugurated the era of open feminist activism in 1923 by removing their face veils at the Cairo train station after returning from an international feminist conference, in a bold gesture declaring their determination to put a final end to sex segregation and female seclusion in the home. Shortly before, Sha'rawi had led other upper- and middle-class women in forming the EFU. It declared an agenda for political, social, and economic transformation to integrate (urban) women into public life on a level with men and enhance women's lives in the private sphere. The feminists were aware that the lives of peasant women were not confined to the private sphere, and used the presence of these women in public space to argue their case. The EFU grounded its arguments for women's rights within the Islamic modernist and nationalist frameworks along the lines already worked out in the stage of unseen feminism.

The feminism of Huda Sha'rawi, Saiza Nabarawi, and other EFU feminists can be called radical liberal feminism. The act of helping finally to dismantle the system of segregation and female seclusion through the dramatic gesture of publicly unveiling (uncovering the face) – and by implication the ideology associated with this – was clearly radical.[25] The EFU feminist agenda called for political rights for women, changes in personal status laws (especially for controls on divorce and polygamy), equal secondary school and university education for women, expanded professional opportunities for women in the fields of law, medicine, and education, and new work opportunities for women in factories and commercial establishments. It called for protective legislation for workers and support systems (childcare and health care), and also demanded an end to legalized prostitution. The EFU itself trained poor women in health, hygiene, and childcare, and ran a daycare center and a medical clinic for working mothers. Women had to act outside the formal political system. While regular EFU tactics included lobbying government offices and leaders, petitioning, speaking, and writing, EFU women also occasionally employed the more militant activities of picketing and street demonstrations (some EFU women were even briefly jailed in 1930). The EFU's agenda for legal, social, and political transformation was more comprehensive and revolutionary than the men's project for the construction of the new nation-state. After independence, men quickly became locked in the scramble for power within the new parliamentary system, resulting in a protracted struggle between the Wafd, Liberal Constitutionalists, the Palace, and the British authorities – and in the process most lost sight of their earlier expressed ideals of the liberation of women.

The EFU membership included both upper- and middle-class women, but the former were more numerous. The EFU had two journals, *l'Egyptienne* (est. 1925) and *al-Misriyya* (est. 1937) and an impressive headquarters (inaugurated in 1932), and commanded substantial funds of its own (much of it deriving from landowners' wealth, especially Sha'rawi's inheritance), which helped to sustain the movement for a quarter of a century.

Feminism typically starts from the social location where its proponents are situated within the patriarchal order, and then widens out. The first Egyptian feminists emerging from Cairo harems led an urban-based movement. Yet from the beginning, feminists were ideologically committed to lessening the patriarchal grip over all Egyptian women. In the mid-1930s, the EFU leadership accelerated its campaign for political rights for women. It also tried to extend feminist activism to the provinces. Sha'rawi opened a school and health clinic in a village near Minya and a model farm in Giza in an effort to spur other EFU women to do the same. However, by then rank-and-file EFU members had grown complacent and were uncooperative, thwarting the leadership in its efforts to broaden the movement in Egypt.[26] The EFU met with better results in advancing Arab feminism, and in 1945 the Arab Feminist Union was created in Cairo under the presidency of Sha'rawi.

By the time of Sha'rawi's death in 1947 the EFU had witnessed successes for women in education and work. Political rights were not achieved and women continued to be sexually exploited through legalized prostitution. The minimum marriage ages for both sexes were raised, but there was no control over men's easy access to divorce and polygamy. The latter were the bitterest disappointments of the EFU movement, Nabarawi told me in the late 1960s.

Populist feminism

By the end of World War II, the serious economic problems that had afflicted the lower and middle classes in the cities since the 1930s remained unresolved. From the 1930s onward, the Muslim Brotherhs attracted a wide following among women and men who were economically deprived. Poverty continued to plague the peasants, who still lacked the health and educational services enjoyed by other Egyptians. The new generation of feminists was moved by these conditions. Meanwhile, there was continued and deepening political turmoil in Egypt and renewed impatience with the prolongation of the British presence. In 1952, a revolution occurred and a republic was created, and in 1956 the Suez Canal was nationalized and the British and French expelled from the Canal Zone. During the eighteen years of Nasser's rule, socialism replaced the capitalism of the previous period.

In the second half of the 1930s, the EFU membership not only failed to respond to the initiative of Sha'rawi and Nabarawi to serve the needs of a broader base of women, but also displayed an elitist unwillingness to welcome the more active feminists of the middle class into their ranks. However, Sha'rawi and, especially, Nabarawi were linked to a new populist feminism that the EFU itself was unable to disseminate within its own organization. Despite major achievements there were many pressing issues that needed addressing. The moment had come for a new thrust. This came from the populist feminists, predominantly middle-class women, who accelerated the campaign for political rights for women and conducted direct action among poor urban and rural women to help spur them on to struggle for economic and social liberation. They also kept up the quest to reform personal status laws.

Fatma Ni'mat Rashid, Duriyya Shafiq, and Inji Aflatun emerged as leaders of three strands of populist feminism.[27] All three used their pens in the cause of feminism. Two founded organizations and their own journals. One wrote books and contributed to the journals of others. One as a feminist and a communist was unwilling to be subsumed within patriarchal leftist organizations.[28]

The journalist Fatma Ni'mat Rashid had written for the EFU's *l'Egyptienne* and had edited its Arabic journal, *al-Misriyya*, before breaking with the organization in 1937. In 1944, she founded the Hizb al-Nisa'i al-Watani (National Feminist Party, NFP), whose name indicated its attempt for the first time ever to form a women's political party, intended to step up the campaign for women's political rights.[29] The NFP, which maintained close links with the Workers' and Peasants' Parties, also adopted a broad agenda of economic and social reforms. It worked to spread literacy and training in hygiene among lower-class women of Cairo, and was the first feminist group to advocate birth control and abortion.

The NFP had a predominantly middle-class membership, comprising lawyers, journalists, writers, and teachers. Although its membership and agenda showed a broadening feminist base, the party did not have the wide appeal the second populist organization elicited.

A more dynamic feminist initiative came from Duriyya Shafiq, another middle-class woman, younger than Rashid and a protégée of

Huda Sha'rawi, who had supported her studies at the Sorbonne. Shafiq, with the highest level of formal education of the feminists to date, returned from an extended stay in Paris with her doctorate in 1945.[30] Sha'rawi welcomed Shafiq, but the Feminist Union members were not receptive to her. In 1948, the year after Sha'rawi's death, Shafiq created the Ittihad Bint al-Nil (Daughter of the Nile Union, DNU), and founded three journals to serve the association's purposes.[31] Shafiq's organization adopted a feminist agenda similar to that of the NFP, giving priority to political rights for women and favoring a broad social and economic program.[32]

Shafiq was far more successful than Rashid in mobilizing middle-class women. Moreover, the DNU was the first feminist organization to establish a broad base in the provinces, where centers were opened for teaching literacy and hygiene to poor women. Shafiq herself was a far bolder and more compelling leader than Rashid. She was also the most directly confrontational of all the feminists. In campaigning for political rights she led a women's march on parliament and a three-hour sit-in in 1951. Later, as she grew increasingly impatient, she mounted hunger strikes. She had also, meanwhile, taken up the campaign to transform the personal status laws begun earlier by the EFU and which had proven so difficult to advance. Shafiq ridiculed the practice of high dowers by publicizing the acceptance of a *mahr* of twenty-five piasters on the occasion of her marriage, and she debated with al-Azhar shaikhs on divorce and polygamy.

Meanwhile, the third strand of populist feminism further to the left was in the making, and emerged in the context of the Egyptian women's peace movement. The two principal leaders of this populist feminism of the left were EFU feminist Saiza Nabarawi (from 1947 to 1953 vice president of the Feminist Union) and a young upper-class woman, Inji Aflatun.

Aflatun, as a student at the Lycée Français in Cairo, became imbued with a strong social consciousness. She was a fervent anti-imperialist at a time when, following World War II, leftist groups were on the rise in Egypt. Aflatun helped found the University and Institutes' Youth League in 1945, and afterwards became a member of the National Women's Committee. She used both direct action and her pen to further the cause of women's liberation. Aflatun went to textile factories in Shubra to meet with women workers about their rights. She also drew wider attention to the economic and social problems of workers and peasants as well as to the patriarchal domination of women in the home and workplace in her book, *Nahnu al-nisa' al-misriyyat* (We Egyptian women, 1949).[33] She located class and gender oppression within the framework of imperialist exploitation. Like the other feminist leaders, Aflatun also insisted on political rights for women and on improved personal status laws. Although a communist, she situated her call for women's rights within an Islamic framework. This may seem contradictory to those more familiar with Western experience. However, Aflatun understood the importance of religion to the masses, and that it was necessary to locate their struggle against patriarchy within an Islamic framework. A supporter and member of leftist groups that included members of both sexes, Aflatun, in the tradition of independent feminism, also understood the political imperative for women to work within their own groups in order to keep feminist goals and priorities up front.

The Harakat Ansar al-Salam (Movement of the Friends of Peace) brought the young feminist activist Aflatun and the veteran EFU feminist Nabarawi together for the first time in 1950. Aflatun then joined the EFU youth group which Nabarawi had organized to work with lower-class women in Cairo. This gave Aflatun a framework within which to continue the activity she had begun earlier among working women in Shubra. The following year, when violence broke out in the Canal Zone, Nabarawi led women in setting up the Lajnat al-Nisa' lil-Muqawama al-Sha'biyya (Women's Committee for Popular Resistance) to coordinate women's active resistance. Nabarawi, Aflatun, Hawa Idris (an EFU member and cousin of Huda Sha'rawi), Hikmat al-Ghazali (a communist, whose sister, Zainab al-Ghazali, had founded the Muslim Sisters), and other women went through British lines to Ismailiyya to agitate. Later, women – feminists and non-feminists alike – from communists to Muslim Sisters, staged an anti-imperialist demonstration. At this moment, women's feminist and nationalist activism was expressed jointly.

Meanwhile, the 1952 revolution led by army officers took place, followed by the installation of the Revolutionary Command Council, and soon afterwards Nasser consolidated his power. The most immediate repercussion for Nabarawi, Aflatun, and other feminist militants was a clampdown on their activity in the context of a move against the left. During this period, however, all independent political groupings and forms of public expression were suppressed. The Women's Committee for Popular Resistance was outlawed, and the EFU youth group, which was seen as too leftist, was dissolved.

Nabarawi, considered too radical, was forced out of the EFU in 1953 by a timid membership, exactly thirty years after she had helped create the feminist organization.

However, Nabarawi and Aflatun continued their feminist and nationalist activism through their writing as well as less visible ways of organizing. In 1956, with mounting tension connected with the Egyptian nationalization of the Suez Canal and the tripartite invasion of Egypt by Britain, France, and Israel, Nabarawi, Aflatun, and others formed the Popular Resistance Committee, which gave paramilitary and political training to women. However, this would be these women's final public activist work.

The new revolutionary government under Nasser implemented a socialist program which bestowed benefits on both sexes. In 1956 an electoral law gave women the vote they had first asked for three decades earlier. Education and health benefits were distributed more fully to all classes and throughout the country. University education was made free, and all graduates were guaranteed jobs. Within this context, women as citizens enjoyed gains, but they felt the effects of lingering patriarchal domination. Apart from token figures, women did not make it to the top echelons of the government bureaucracy or professions, and were virtually segregated to areas of work deemed more fitting for females.[34] Moreover, the state, while welcoming those women it needed as workers, did not provide them with sufficient support services to ease the double burden they now bore – working long hours in their jobs as well as for their families.[35] The personal status laws, both symbolically and practically oppressive to women, remained in force.

In the face of continued patriarchal domination Nabarawi, Aflatun, and others formed the Ittihad al-Nisa'i al-Qawmi (National Feminist Union, NFU), appealing to a broad coalition of women across the political spectrum. However, the government blocked their efforts by refusing the organization a permit. The state that had finally granted women full political rights withdrew from them the freedom to organize politically. Feminist organizations, along with all other independent political organizations, were banned. The EFU was forced to confine itself to welfare work and to change its name. It became the Huda Sha'rawi Association – gone was the radical word "feminist." The following year Aflatun, as a communist, was sent to prison, where she remained for four years. Shafiq, an outspoken feminist and critic of the regime, was placed under house arrest. Rashid's feminist party was dissolved. Nabarawi was silenced. Women's activist feminism, inaugurated in the aftermath of the 1919 nationalist revolution, was suppressed after three-and-a-half decades of independent struggle. Women, however, kept their independent feminism alive behind the scenes in Egypt (reminiscent of the early invisibility of the feminism of the harems) – but their voice was heard internationally, especially in the person of Saiza Nabarawi, who regularly participated in the international conferences of the communist Democratic Federation of Women.[36]

Sexual feminism

At the beginning of the 1970s, with the coming to power of Sadat and the rise of open-door (*infitah*) capitalism, along with a more broad opening up, feminism reappeared on the public scene. It also coincided with the acceleration of the second wave of Islamic "fundamentalism" or Islamism, that had begun to make its appearance following the war in 1967, mainly among university students of the lower middle class, both male and female, many of whom came from rural areas. Resurgent Islamism was expressed by women in the form of a return to the veil (typically covering the head and body but not the face) amid calls for them to return to the home.[37] This signaled a reassertion of the patriachal notion of women's exclusive sexual and family roles, the lauding of which was used to send women back to their "place."[38]

At the very moment some women were returning to the veil, publicly calling attention to women as essentially sexual beings, women's bodies and female sexuality emerged as a feminist issue, marking the public reassertion of feminism, which was allowed to re-surface following the death of Nasser in 1970. This new feminist concern was expressed by a medical doctor and feminist, Nawal al-Saadawi, who published a book titled *al-Mar'a wa al-jins* (Woman and sex) the year after Sadat succeeded Nasser in power. In this book and subsequent writings, al-Saadawi discussed in public what was most private and, indeed, taboo.[39] This took special courage and involved great risk. Al-Saadawi lost her job at the Ministry of Health, and before long went into self-imposed exile. Not since Qasim Amin's *Tahrir al-mar'a* (1899) had there been such an impassioned outcry from patriarchal forces. But, as before, there was also a positive resonance among progressive women. Al-Saadawi, in fighting against the then widespread (and now resurgent) practice of clitoridectomy (among the issues she addressed), and Amin before her, in opposing the veiling of the face – both issues connected with sexuality and the female body – demonstrated that these practices had been falsely attributed to Islam, and were simply forms of patriarchal control of women.

Earlier feminists had focused solely upon the sexual exploitation of poor women as prostitutes, but al-Saadawi addressed sexuality more comprehensively. The sexual exploitation of women occurred in both public and family spheres, and was not confined to a single (that is, the lower) class. Al-Saadawi located sexual issues in larger political and economic contexts. With the authority and clinical evidence of a doctor – and, more particularly, a woman doctor with a feminist consciousness – she publicly deplored physical assaults on women's bodies connected with obsessive fears about female virginity and sexual purity, and condemned both the public commercial exploitation of the female body and private forms of aggression against women's bodies.

Al-Saadawi publicized the physical and psychological harm done to women's bodies by clitoridectomy, and argued for its eradication. She emphasized that this extreme form of patriarchal control of female sexuality was wrongly sanctioned in the name of Islam. A number of feminists in Egypt struggled to wipe out the practice. However, a similar campaign by feminists in Sudan has been far more visible and widespread.[40]

Al-Saadawi pointed in public to the operation of a double standard whereby the Islamic prescription confining sexuality to the conjugal relationship was applied to women but not men. She exposed the sexual exploitation of women in the sanctity of their own homes with disturbing evidence that this was more widespread than commonly admitted. Like feminists before her she decried the public marketing of women's bodies, but rather than focus more exclusively on matters of the law and policing, she exposed the economic and social roots of prostitution and its effects in her writings, most notably in her novel *Woman at Point Zero*, based on a real-life case.

Al-Saadawi bravely brought to light the subject of the sexual domination and abuse of women, placing the onus on men and society at a time when women were increasingly being told that the responsibility was theirs (as omnisexual beings who threaten society or as sources of *fitna*) to cover (that is, veil) themselves and distance themselves from the public arena to safeguard morality, while also returning to their "proper place." Meanwhile, with the appearance of open-door capitalism women's bodies were being used for commercial exploitation – as seen, for example, in blatant forms of advertising. Al-Saadawi forced the "private" subject of sexuality into the public arena. During the 1980s, matters concerning sexuality became less visible but by no means less significant. A new awareness had been raised, and there was no going back.

New resurgent feminism

In the 1980s, feminism in Egypt, which had been returning to public visibility, was becoming organized anew. In 1985, the Jam'iyyat Tadamun al-Mar'a al-'Arabiyya (Arab Women's Solidarity Association, AWSA) officially came into being, although it had started to coalesce earlier. The organization, under the presidency of Nawal al-Saadawi, was headquartered in Cairo with branches in several Arab countries and in some Arab communities in the West. Egyptians, as members of AWSA, located their feminism within an Arab framework. AWSA feminism issued the declaration that "women's active participation in the political, economic, social, and cultural life of the Arab world is essential for the realization of true democracy in Arab society," and demanded an end to gender discrimination, both in the family and in society.[41] AWSA members included a wide spectrum of feminists.

The rescinding of the revised Personal Status Law of 1979 (the first major revision since 1929), which had been issued by a decree from Sadat (who had been pressured by his wife, Jihan), and had given women greater benefits in the case of divorce and made it easier for women to initiate the dissolution of their marriages, galvanized a large number of women during the first year of AWSA's existence. A broad feminist coalition formed the Lajnat al-Difa'i 'an Huquq al-Mar'a wa al-Usra (Committee for the Defense of the Rights of the Woman and the Family), to fight for the reinstatement of the law. They achieved the restoration of the law, although in a watered-down form.[42]

While the broader feminist coalition subsequently fragmented, AWSA continued, and strengthened itself institutionally. It conducted monthly seminars, organized international conferences held in Cairo, and in 1989 founded its own journal, *Nun* (the letter "n" in Arabic, which is the first letter in *nisa'* (woman) and *nisa'iyya* (feminism); it has also been pointed out that it is the first letter in al-Saadawi's given name, Nawal). AWSA feminism was highly visible and confrontational, and outspokenly critical of conservative Islamist positions on gender. In 1990, after its president, al-Saadawi, and other women had protested against the build-up to the first Gulf War, the government ordered *Nun* to cease publication, and the following year shut down AWSA itself. AWSA has taken the case to court and after many imposed delays on the hearings still awaits action. (It eventually lost its case but continues its existence abroad.)

Other – informal – feminist groups also formed in the mid-1980s. Two were initiated by women in their twenties and thirties who did not attempt to officially register under the Ministry of Social Affairs but coalesced more informally around their publications. A third included women in their forties and fifties who organized around a specific project.

In 1984, some women who had been active in the democratic student movement of the 1970s formed a study group in Cairo. Two years later the group issued *Majallat al-mar'a al-jadida* (New Woman Magazine) to disseminate their feminist views. The group later formed committees to deal with the everyday needs of ordinary women, including health, legal literacy, and income generation.[43] The group announced itself in a 1990 communication: "The New Woman Group is a progressive and democratic feminist group of women who believe that while Egyptian and Arab women share with men the hardships brought about by backwardness, dependence and economic crisis, they have to carry a double burden and suffer from various forms of subordination, oppression and suppression arising specifically from their position as women."[44]

Another group of women of the same generation sprang up in Mansura in the Delta when young women who had organized public protests against the Israeli invasion of Lebanon in 1982 went on to form Jam'iyyat Bint al-Ard (Society of the Daughter of the Earth), and two years later brought out *Majallat Bint al-Ard* (Daughter of the Earth magazine). The group works with women in the town of Mansura and surrounding villages in feminist consciousness-raising and income-generating projects. Bint al-Ard members connect with local women within their own milieu, trying to meet the needs women themselves define as urgent.[45]

Meanwhile, in the second half of the 1980s, several professional women in their forties and fifties came together to work on a legal literacy project. Calling themselves A Group of Women Concerned with Affairs Relating to the Egyptian Woman, they pooled their expertise to produce a booklet called *al-Huquq al-qanuniyya lil-mar'a al-misriyya bain al-nadhariyya wa al-tatbiq* (The legal rights of the Egyptian woman in theory and practice) to help make women aware of their rights guaranteed by law. They devoted an entire chapter to explaining the Muslim personal status code, and instructed women about including protective conditions in their marriage contracts. They also, among other things, explained labor law.[46]

By not being officially registered but remaining informal, new women's groups do not risk dissolution by the government, as happened to AWSA. The contemporary climate is not receptive to feminism. For reasons of expediency and because of uncertainties about feminism and its meanings, and surely also because feminism is tainted, many progressive women work for the advancement of women within the context of their professions and service-oriented associations more discreetly, eschewing labels and public identification with feminism. Thus, today in Egypt, invisible and visible feminisms exist side by side.

The most striking feature of more than a century of feminism in Egypt is the maintenance by women of an independent feminist tradition. The feminists, who started by understanding that patriarchy, not Islam, kept women down, have made the distinction between patriarchy and Islam in arguing their cause throughout the century. They have rejected the attempts of their opponents to impose restrictions on women in the name of Islam. This has been as true of the radical liberal EFU feminists as of the most leftist of the populist feminists. Women have not allowed their feminism and Islam to be polarized, and have certainly been aware of the political consequences of this. Women as feminists used Islamic arguments in the effort to end patriarchal tyranny in the private sphere and to legitimize their full entry into the public sphere.

Both within the segregated system and outside it, women have conducted their own nationalist activities. When these caused them to contravene conventional behavior, they stressed their nationalism to legitimize their actions (as they did in their early philanthropic work). However, during the period of nationalist militancy, women did not have to justify their unprecedented actions in the public sphere. There was a clear (political) crisis. Patriarchy, threatened on the national front, welcomed and encouraged women's actions.

Following quasi-independence, when efforts by secular nationalists were made to push women back into the private sphere, some feminists marshaled nationalist arguments to justify their continued presence in the public sphere and their rights there. In the 1970s, when Islamists called for women to retreat to the home, some women confronted this call in the name of Islam. Throughout the century, women have placed their feminism within the nationalist context and within the framework of Islam. Through argument and action they have defended the nation against foreign occupation and economic, political, and cultural imperialism. However, patriarchy has had the temerity to label feminism in Egypt as Western, *ipso facto* un-Islamic, to discredit feminism by undermining its national and cultural-cum-religious legitimacy.

Feminism in Egypt has been far less class-bound than observers and critics have claimed. From the start, women of the middle and upper classes have evolved similar feminist ideologies and strategies, and have worked together to further their goals.

Feminists have made most gains in the public sphere, where the grip of family patriarchy was weakened by the rising state itself, albeit a new but different patriarchal formation. In building a modern state and society, the patriarchal state required the labor of all its citizens; some of the needs and goals of the state and of women coincided, typically in education and work. Accordingly, the state granted some of the feminists' demands over the century, but the timetable was mainly controlled by the state. It was not in the state's interest – and politically problematic – for the state to grant women the vote in the decades from the 1920s to the early 1950s, but the new socialist state under Nasser found it expedient to grant women the vote in 1956 while suppressing organized feminism. However, patriarchy clung to its privileges, and continued to dominate in the private sphere. State patriarchy did not need or wish to challenge family patriarchy.

This overview of feminism over the *longue durée* in Egypt clearly demonstrates that, irrespective of political and economic formations and forms of imperialist presence and penetration, patriarchy survives and reshapes itself according to its own needs and in order to deflect feminist opposition. The most striking achievement of Egyptian feminism perhaps is that it has understood this well and has fought to preserve an independent tradition, keeping its cause alive against all odds.

* * *

Originally published in Judith Tucker (ed.), *Arab Women: Old Boundaries, New Frontiers* (Bloomington: University of Indiana Press, 1993). It originated as a paper presented at a symposium on Arab women at the Center for Contemporary Arab Studies, Georgetown University, in 1986.

NOTES

I would like to thank the Fulbright Islamic Civilizations Program and the Ford Foundation for supporting some of research that has gone into the paper on which this chapter is based.

1. Juan Ricardo Cole, "Feminism, Class, and Islam in Turn-of-the-Century Egypt," *International Journal of Middle East Studies* 13 (1981), pp. 397–407, misses the early debates of feminists and cross-class feminist bonds among women. Thomas Philipp, "Feminism in Nationalist Politics in Egypt," in L. Beck and N. Keddie (eds.), *Women in the Muslim World* (Cambridge, Mass.: Harvard University Press, 1978), pp. 295–308, wrongly describes EFU women as being exclusively upper-class.

2. For an overview of feminist positions on "the woman question" from the late nineteenth century to the 1980s juxtaposed with nationalist and Islamist positions see Margot Badran, "Competing Agenda: Feminists, Islam, and the State in Nineteenth and Twentieth Century Egypt," in Deniz Kandiyoti (ed.), *Women, Islam, and the State* (Philadelphia: Temple University Press and London: Macmillan, 1991), pp. 201–236, and chapter 1 in this volume. On articulations of feminism by women in Egypt over the period dealt with in this paper see Margot Badran and Miriam Cooke (eds.), *Opening the Gates: A Century of Arab Feminist Writing* (Bloomington: Indiana University Press and London: Virago, 1990).

3. Public and private are not conceptualized as strictly split domains but are at many levels intimately interconnected, as Cynthia Nelson has demonstrated in an early article, "Public and Private Politics: Women in the Middle Eastern World," *American Ethnologist*, 1 (1974), pp. 551–565. For a recent discussion on this issue see Suad Joseph, "Women and Politics in the Middle East," *MERIP*, 138, 16, 1 (January–February 1986), pp. 3–8.

4. On the rise of feminism in Asian countries see Kumari Jayawardena, *Feminism and Nationalism in the Third World* (London: Zed, 1986).

5. For comparisons see Jane Rendall, *The Origins of Modern Feminism: Women in Britain, France and the United States, 1780–1860* (New York: Shocken Books, 1984) and Richard Evans, *The Feminists: Women's Emancipation Movements in Europe, America and Australia, 1840–1920* (London: Croom Helm and New York: Barnes & Noble, 1977).

6. See Jayawardena, *Feminism and Nationalism in the Third World*. Concerning the Indian experience, see Geraldine Forbes, "Caged Tigers: First Wave Feminists in India," *Women's Studies International Forum*, 5 (1982), pp. 525–536; Gail Minault (ed.), *The Extended Family: Women and Political Participation in India*

and Pakistan (New Delhi: Chanakya, 1981); and Gail Omvedt, *We Will Smash This Prison: Indian Women in Struggle* (London: Zed, 1980).

7. See Deniz Kandiyoti, "End of Empire: Islam, Nationalism and Women in Turkey," in Kandiyoti (ed.), *Women, Islam and the State*, pp. 22–27; and in the same book, Afsaneh Najmabadi, "Hazards of Modernity and Morality: Women, State and Ideology in Contemporary Iran," pp. 48–76; Eliz Sanasarian, *The Women's Rights Movements in Iran* (New York: Praeger, 1982); and Michelle Raccagni, "Origins of Feminism in Egypt and Tunisia," Ph.D. dissertation (Ann Arbor, Mich.: University Microfilms, 1982). On certain parallels with feminist experience in Egypt see Khawar Mumtaz and Farida Shaheed, *Women of Pakistan: Two Steps Forward, One Step Backward?* (London: Zed and Lahore: Vanguard Books, 1987).

8. On Arabophone and Francophone articulations of feminism in Egypt see Irene Fenoglio-Abd El Aal, *Défense et illustration de l'Egyptienne: Aux débuts d'une expression feminine* (Cairo: Centre d'Etudes et de Documentation Economique, Juridique et Sociale, 1988). On the origins of the term "feminism," see Karen Offen, "Defining Feminism: A Comparative Historical Approach," *Signs*, 14 (Autumn 1988), pp. 119–147.

9. On this challenge see Sharon Sievers, "Six or More Feminists in Search of an Historian," *Journal of Women's History*, 1, 2 (Fall 1989), pp. 134–146.

10. Face veiling, a symbol and function of female seclusion and the distancing of the sexes, began to disappear first among Christians in Egypt. See Beth Baron, "Unveiling in Early Twentieth Century Egypt: Practical and Symbolic Considerations," *Middle Eastern Studies*, 25, 3 (July 1989), pp. 370–86.

11. Ethel Klein, in *Gender Politics: From Consciousness to Mass Politics* (Cambridge, Mass.: Harvard University Press, 1985), argues that feminist ideology arises from concrete experiences rather than abstract philosophy. On the rise of feminism up to the time of the start of the organized feminist movement, see Margot Badran, "The Origins of Feminism in Egypt," in Arina Angerman et al. (eds.), *Current Issues in Women's History* (London and New York: Routledge, 1989), pp. 153–170.

12. See al-Taimuriyya's *Nata'ij al-ahwal fi al-aqwal wa al-af'al* (The results of circumstances in words and deeds, Cairo: Matba'at Muhammad Afandi Mustafá, 1887/8) and *Mirat at-ta'amul fi al-umur* (The mirror of contemplation on things, Cairo: n.p., *c.*1890s); and Fawwaz's *al-Rasa'il al-Zainabiyya* (Zainab's letters, Cairo: al-Matba'a al-Mutawassita, 1905), a collection of her writings. For translations into English of writings by these two women (by Marilyn Booth) see Badran and Cooke (eds.), *Opening the Gates*.

13. The rise of state patriarchy offered women of the middle and upper classes opportunities for new education and certain new jobs while while simultaneously blocking other opportunities. The state patriarchy had more adverse effects on lower-class and peasant women. On the latter during the nineteenth century, see Judith Tucker, *Women in Nineteenth-Century Egypt* (Cambridge: Cambridge University Press, 1985).

14. See Huda Shaarawi, *Harem Years: The Memoirs of an Egyptian Feminist*, ed., trans., and introd. Margot Badran (London: Virago, 1986 and New York: Feminist Press, 1987).

15. Women's articles began to appear, for example, in the second half of the 1880s in *al-Muqtataf* and *al-Lata'if*. The first women's journal was founded in 1892 by

Hind Naufal. Beth Baron has examined the early women's press in "The Rise of a New Literary Culture: The Women's Press of Egypt, 1892–1919," Ph.D. dissertation, University of California at Los Angeles, 1988.

16. Byron D. Cannon, "Nineteenth Century Arabic Writings on Women and Society: The Interim Role of the Masonic Press in Cairo (al-Lata'if, 1885–1895)," *International Journal of Middle East Studies*, 17, 4 (1985), pp. 463–484, sees women's articles before the 1890s as being pre-feminist, while I would argue that they express the beginnings of a feminist consciousness.

17. Sha'rawi, *Harem Years*. For a comparative perspective on women's social feminism see Geraldine Forbes, "From Purdah to Politics: The Social Feminism of the All-India Women's Organization," in Hanna Papnek and Gail Minault (eds.), *Separate Worlds: Studies of Purdah in South Asia* (Columbia, Mo.: South Asia Books, 1982), pp. 219–244.

18. Sha'rawi donated money to the NWS, as well as equipment for its crafts workshop, and because of this was made honorary president.

19. Bahithat al-Badiya and Nabawiyya Musa went to the Saniyya Teachers' Training School, and taught and wrote while still observing harem conventions. See Bahithat al-Badiya, *al-Nisa'iyyat* (Cairo: al-Jarida, 1910); Majd al-Din Hifni Nasif, *Athar Bahitha al-Bad'iyya Malak Hifni Nasif, 1886–1918* (Cairo: Wizarat al-Thaqafa wa al-Irshad al-Qaumi, 1962); and Nabawiyya Musa, *al-Mar'a wa al-'amal* (Alexandria: al-Matba'a al-Wataniya, 1920). Mayy Ziyada maintained links with Sha'rawi and other EFU feminists until Ziyada's death in 1941. The EFU published a commemorative volume, *Dhikra faqida al-adiba al-nabigha Mayy* (Commemoration of the late distinguished writer Mayy), in 1941.

20. The year before, at the National Party Congress in Brussels, a nationalist message from Inshira Shawqi was read out by a man, who commented that custom prevented her from being there in person. Shawqi's niece, Fatma Ni'mat Rashid, is one of the populist feminists discussed below.

21. Bahithat al-Badiya, whose husband, unbeknownst to her, already had a wife before she married him, was particularly outspoken against polygamy. She said: "the husband of two or more wives ought to be appointed Minister of the Colonies" (*Nisa'iyyat*, p. 41).

22. On the invisible feminist activism at the beginning of this century, see Margot Badran, "From Consciousness to Activism: Feminist Politics in Twentieth Century Egypt," in John Spagnolo (ed.), *Problems of the Middle East in Historical Perspective*, St. Antony's College, Oxford monograph series (London: Ithaca Press, 1991) and chapter 3 in this volume.

23. Lower-class women also participated in the revolution, especially in the street demonstrations. Some of them were killed for the cause. On the tradition of lower-class and peasant women's revolts see Judith Tucker, "Insurrectionary Women: Women and the State in Nineteenth Century Egypt," *MERIP*, 138, 16, 1 (January–February 1986), pp. 9–13.

24. See Margot Badran, "Dual Liberation: Feminism and Nationalism in Egypt, 1870–1925," *Feminist Issues* (Spring 1988), pp. 15–34.

25. The term "liberal feminism," associated with Western experience, does not capture the radical nature of liberal feminism in Egypt, hence my term "radical liberal feminism."

26. In personal communications, Saiza Nabarawi discussed the problem of EFU

reluctance to broaden its base and welcome new middle-class women into the organization and how eventually she went her separate way.

27. The term "populist feminism" seems to broadly capture this new feminism, which had different specific forms yet basic similarities, although the feminism of Nabarawi (by this time) and Aflatun was to the left of Rashid's and Shafiq's.

28. On this period see Akram Khater and Cynthia Nelson, "al-Harakah al-Nisa'iyah: The Women's Movement and Political Participation in Modern Egypt," *Women's Studies International Forum*, 2, 5 (1988), pp. 465–83.

29. See Ijlal Mahmud Khalifa, *al-Haraka al-nisa'iyya al-haditha* (The modern feminist movement, Cairo: al-Matba'a al-'Arabiya al-Haditha, 1973); and Raccagni, "Origins," pp. 247–57.

30. Duriyya Shafiq wrote her major dissertation on the Egyptian woman and Islam, her academic interest prefiguring women's studies to become a serious academic discipline some four decades later.

31. Shafiq recounted to me her last encounter with Sha'rawi before her death, saying that Sha'rawi had told her to carry on the feminist movement after her. She saw herself as carrying out that mandate.

32. On Duriyya Shafiq, see Cynthia Nelson, "The Voices of Doria Shafiq: Feminist Consciousness in Egypt, 1940–1960," *Feminist Issues* (Fall 1986), pp. 15–31.

33. Michelle Raccagni is preparing her translation of this book, with an introduction, for publication. For Aflatun see Raccagni, "Origins," pp. 274–278 and Michelle Raccagni, "Inji Afflatun, Author, Artist and Militant: A Brief Analysis of Her Life and Works" (typescript).

34. Hikmat Abu Zayd, Aisha Ratib, and Amal Uthman all achieved the post of minister of social affairs, but women had more difficulty achieving middle-level appointments and positions. See Clement Henry Moore, "Sexual Equality amid Professional Impoverishment," in *Images of Development* (Cambridge, Mass.: MIT Press, 1980), pp. 131–143, and Kathleen Howard-Merriam, "Women, Education and the Professions in Egypt," *Comparative Education Review*, 23, 2 (June 1979), pp. 256–270.

35. See Mona Hammam, "Women and Industrial Work in Egypt: The Chubra El-Kheima Case," *Arab Studies Quarterly*, 2 (1980), pp. 50–69; and the same author's "The Continuum of Economic Activities in Middle Eastern Social Formations, Family Division of Labor and Migration," paper presented at the Symposium on the Sex Division of Labor, Development, and Women's Status, 1980.

36. I first met Nabarawi, Shafiq, and Aflatun during this period. All three kept the ideology of feminism very much alive and were generous with their time in transmitting the feminist heritage to all those who came to them, showing concern for the preservation of the feminist past. Of the three, at that time (1967 and afterwards) only Nabarawi remained publicly active, carrying on feminist activities internationally but remaining low-key at home.

37. There was a heavy concentration of Islamist women in the medical faculties who were tending to refrain from practicing medicine. The state had paid for their education, and society was in need of their services, especially in the rural areas.

38. On the construction of women as omnisexual beings see Fatna A. Sabah, *Women in the Muslim Unconscious* (New York: Pergamon, 1984), trans. Mary Jo Lakeland.

39. See, for example, *al-Mar'a wa al-jins* (Beirut: al-Mu'assasa al-'Arabiya lil-Dirasat wa-al-Nashr, 1974); *The Hidden Face of Eve*, ed. and trans. Sherif Hetata (London: Zed, 1980); and *Woman at Point Zero* (London: Zed, 1983).

40. Interviews with Asma El Dareer and many other women in Khartoum and throughout Kordofan. See Asma El Dareer, *Woman, Why Do You Weep? Circumcision and its Consequences* (London: Zed, 1982). For accounts by Egyptian women (in addition to al-Saadawi) on their personal experience of clitoridectomy, see Nayra Atiya, *Khul-Khaal: Five Egyptian Women Tell Their Stories* (Syracuse: Syracuse University Press, 1982).

41. "Challenges Facing Arab Women at the End of the Twentieth Century," an AWSA publication, ed. Nahid Toubia, trans. Miriam Cooke, in Badran and Cooke (eds.), *Opening the Gates*, p. 367.

42. See Sarah Graham-Brown, "After Jihan's Law: A New Battle over Women's Rights," *The Middle East* (June 1985), pp. 17–20; and Nadia Hijab, *Womanpower: The Arab Debate on Women and Work* (Cambridge: Cambridge University Press, 1988).

43. Information on the group comes from an interview with Hala Shukrallah and 'Aida Saif al-Dawla, 1 September 1990 and from *Majallat al-Mar'a al-Jadida.*

44. Letter to women from the New Woman Group, July 1990 (unpublished).

45. Information on the group comes from an interview with Jihan al-Sayyid, 6 September 1990, and from *Majallat Bint al-Ard.* The group includes 'Aziza Husain, Magda al-Mufti, Inji Rushdi, Saniyya Salih, Mervat al-Tallawi, Awatif Wali, and Muna Zulfiqar.

46. The group includes 'Aziza Husain, Magda al-Mufti, Inji Rushdi, Saniyya Salih, Mervat al-Tallawi, Awatif Wali, and Muna Zulfiqar. See *al-Huquq al-qanuniyya li al-mar'a al-misriyya bain al-nadhariyya wa al-tatbiq* (Cairo: n.p., 1988 [privately printed]), pp. 5–6. The introduction, trans. into English by Ali Badran and Margot Badran, appears in Badran and Cooke (eds.), *Opening the Gates*, pp. 373–374.

6

GENDER ACTIVISM: FEMINISTS
AND ISLAMISTS IN EGYPT

INTRODUCTION

In the 1990s in Egypt, among a number of intellectual women across the ideological spectrum, one now detects a kind of "feminism" or public activist mode without a name. This activism transcends ideological boundaries of politically-articulated feminism and Islamism. I shall refer to it as "gender activism." It is a response by women deciding for themselves how to conduct their lives in society. Thus many whom I shall refer to in this chapter as feminist, pro-feminist, and Islamist women are taking similar positions on women's societal roles and engaging in common forms of activism. In periodizing Egyptian women's activism, I call this the third wave of feminism and Islamism.

The second wave of feminism and Islamism, from the late 1960s to the late 1980s, was characterized by polarization expressed in ideological combat, with women lined up on opposing sides.[1] The first wave of feminism and activism occurred from the 1920s to the 1950s: organized feminism emerged in the 1920s, and women began to participate in the Islamic movement in the 1930s. Although first-wave women made choices between the two movements, the period was not marked by adversarialism.

The present third wave – evolving in the 1990s – constitutes a new configuration of female forces, and has collapsed some of the hard-drawn lines that emerged during the second wave. This is not to suggest that the grounding of women's gender activism in divergent ideologies is insignificant. On the contrary, the ideological context of gender activism is crucial, as ultimately it separates the basic agendas of the feminist and Islamist women. The term "gender activism" intends to capture women's common "feminist" modes of thinking and behavior in the public sphere without denying the reality of distinct feminist and Islamist "movements" and the separate experience of uncommitted (pro-feminist) women.

Feminists include women who publicly declare their (feminist) identity as well as those who privately admit to being feminists but do not make open affirmation of this. Pro-feminists are those who take various stands that can be understood as feminist but who reject, both in private and public, any identification as feminists. Islamist women publicly declare themselves by wearing a head veil (*hijab*) and are called *muhajjabat,* or wear a face veil (*niqab*) and are known as *munaqqabat.* Women who cover represent a wide range, from those who accommodate themselves to veiling (I use this term to include the range of "covering practices") as part of a general social current, to those with a profound commitment to Islam. It is the latter with whom this chapter is concerned.

Contemporary feminists and pro-feminists are mainly from the middle and upper-middle class, while Islamist women come from a broad background ranging from the lower-middle class to the upper-middle class. The base of feminists of the second and third waves has remained typically middle class, while the class background of Islamist women has expanded since the 1970s from an early base of women from the modest middle class to include more women from the upper strata of the middle class. Islamist intellectual women, however, are from the more privileged strata of the middle class, as are their feminist and pro-feminist counterparts.

Many women who are pro-feminist shy away from the feminist label for pragmatic reasons, saying they find it too confining or misleading. Others among the leftists find feminism incompatible with their socialist ideology, yet may have various pro-feminist leanings. Islamist women in Egypt reject the notion of feminism as superfluous or heretical, and accordingly preclude the possibility of an "Islamic feminism." The exception so far has proved the rule. Many feminist and pro-feminist women also have problems with the term feminism, largely because of Western associations, even though they concede that this belief is misguided. Egyptian feminists and Islamists alike have difficulties with the stereotype of feminism prevailing in Egypt – which Islamists believe to be true and feminists reject – as aggressively anti-men and in conflict with the culture's moral code, and do not wish to be associated with such views of gender and culture.

The gender activism which I describe is for the most part not a social movement, but mainly involves individuals or a few loosely structured groupings. It is mainly pragmatic rather than political in the more highly organized or self-conscious sense, and low-profile and subtle rather than public and confrontational. (The exception to the above characterization is the Arab Women's Solidarity Association (AWSA), which has suffered from government repression.) Feminist women would regard this as feminist activism; pro-feminist women might do so; but Islamist women would not.

What is the significance of gender activism? It means that many women across a broad spectrum insist on maintaining or increasing their own roles in society and promoting a public presence of women in general. It means that many women insist on their own growth, productivity, and creativity in diverse spheres. It means that women are fighting back against retrogressive forces that wish to push them to the margins of society. It means some erosion of a bifurcation among women and some lessening of the tensions arising from ideological polarization within the Muslim community and among Egyptians more generally. It means a certain freeing of women from patriarchal dominance in the family. It does not mean a lessening of women's concern for the family. Finally, it indicates a certain opening out within the Islamist movement.

This chapter draws on numerous interviews as well as more informal conversations and debates in Egypt from 1988 to 1990, with women of different ages who are feminists, pro-feminists, and Islamists. These women are intellectuals, writers, and professionals, mainly from the middle class. I also conducted interviews with a number of men who could be designated as pro-feminist or Islamist. I chose to interview persons who were active in society and concerned with the question of women's public roles. Although I have included writers I also wanted to obtain the views of those who do not express themselves in print or public speaking. As I was eager to be oriented toward what people thought were important aspects of the subjects under discussion, the interviews were conducted in an interactive fashion. As a result, lively debates ensued and broader comparisons were made. It was out of these encounters, my research, and in the course of daily living that I developed my understanding of what I came to call gender activism. What I learned through previous historical investigation about what I have called the "gender politics" of women in Egypt early in the twentieth century has had compelling echoes, which have also helped focus my thinking on the subject.[2]

THE CONTEMPORARY CONTEXT

Since the 1970s there has been a growing Islamist climate in Egypt, with critical implications for women. Until recently, the Islamist movement was mainly associated with populist ideologues and militants who focused on the issue of an Islamic state, and who stressed female morality and expected women in the movement to be passive followers.[3] The circumference of the Islamist sphere has broadened, and more mainstream and liberal male religious writers and speakers are now becoming part of the movement. At the same time, there are efforts to attract more women, who are now encouraged to play active roles in the movement.[4]

Historically there has been room in Egypt for the competing discourses of the state, Islamists, and feminists on the "woman question." This continues into the 1990s.[5] The state and the feminists have had to take Islamist social and political sensibilities into account. Indeed, Islamist forces have tempered the agendas and public discourses of the state and many feminists. At the same time, the state has curtailed the movements and public expression of Islamists, who are themselves hostile toward both the state and feminists. Alternative or competing discourses have previously coexisted in Egypt in a variety of political and cultural climates. At the moment the broad conservative atmosphere in Egypt, permeated by populist Islamist influences, tempers explicit public feminist expression.

Since the 1970s conservative social ideology articulated by Islamists has been clashing with imperatives arising from economic need, producing strains and tensions that are further exacerbated by the ostentation of a small section of the newly, and inordinately wealthy. During the 1980s economic conditions continued to deteriorate. Many middle- and lower-class families came to require the income of more than one working member. Households have had to draw on the income-generating capacities of women as well as men, who often hold down more than one job. This poor economic situation does not show signs of abating in the foreseeable future.

This is the broad context in which we must locate the current gender activism. Since the end of the 1980s there has been some liberalization on gender issues within Islamist ranks, or possibly political expediency concerning women. I do not, however, see gender activism as springing exclusively from these socio-economic phenomena. I do believe that gender activism may help spawn an Islamic "feminist" activism in Egypt during the decade of the 1990s.

IDENTITY: GOING PUBLIC AND REMAINING PRIVATE

The prevailing conservative Islamist climate in Egypt influences what may be called the politics of disclosure or concealment. Is one's identity to be proclaimed or disguised in public?

Islamist women insist upon public identification of themselves as committed Muslims, with the *hijab* or, less frequently, the *niqab* being the most obvious sign of their commitment. While the *hijab* is usually understood to be an Islamic requirement, the *niqab* is seen as being excessive and not prescribed by scripture.[6] Islamists claim that women cannot be true and committed Muslims without the external symbol of the veil. Veiling, however, is seen not only as a religious requirement but as a symbol of cultural authenticity. Kamila al-'Arabi, a television announcer fired for donning the veil, says, "The hijab is ... a matter of identity and self-discovery after a long fall and being lost in Westernization when colonialism imposed its clothes on us ... that is why the hijab was and must be a national issue of great importance."[7] Islamist women, including religiously observant Muslims as well as purely nominal Muslims, call Muslim women who do not veil "secularists," often implying much more. Islamists, however, make distinctions between *'almaniyya bila din*, or secularism without religion, and *'almaniyya*, or secularism within religion. Non-Islamist women often resent being labeled as secularists and being negatively judged by (Islamist) co-religionists about their relationship with Islam, which they do not see as befitting a Muslim.

It is striking how many contemporary women who identify with feminism are reluctant to publicly affirm this, in contrast to first- and second-wave feminists. The reasons for current behavior seem to be pragmatic and political. Feminists today feel freer, both personally and professionally, by being less explicit. Some shrink from taking a public stand because of family and/or societal pressures in today's conservative atmosphere. Many feminist and pro-feminist women with whom I talked over and over expressed their difficulty with the feminist label, insisting that it was confining. Development specialist Sumaiya Ibrahim Huber recalled her reactions a few years ago, saying: "I didn't want to be put in a corner ... I think I had a problem with labels ... I think people use the term badly and I thought that a feminist was like a fanatic." She added: "I [still] wouldn't call myself a feminist but I don't react as strongly as before."[8] Publisher Eva Elias put it succinctly: "I think labels limit you."[9]

Many also fear the negative consequences of being associated with feminism. Even when women reject public perceptions of feminism as stridently anti-male and in defiance of moral norms, they are anxious about being associated with these perceptions. In Egypt, feminism is also widely branded as Western. This notion is reinforced in part because the term itself is a Western coinage, and so far no unequivocal word for feminism has been minted in Arabic. Heba al-Khouly, a development specialist and a feminist, said, "I think there is a real problem with the term feminist because it is a Western term. I think it is a fear about loss of identity. It is not so much that it [feminism] is radical."[10] Hala Halim, a graduate student in comparative literature, confessed, "There seems to be something mutually exclusive about being a feminist and being an Egyptian, as if you reject your bonds to your own country."[11] Historian Huda Lutfy admitted: "We are made to feel guilty [if we are feminists] about [allegedly] being Western, as you know."[12]

Other ideological problems inhibit women. Pro-feminist women confess to being unclear about what feminism means. Some equate feminism with activism and contend that they cannot be feminists if they are not activists. Socialist women (with the major exception of self-proclaimed socialist Nawal al-Saadawi) and current or past members of the Taggamu Party hold that women's causes must be furthered within the framework of socialism, broadly speaking, or more specifically within the context of the Taggamu Party. Although they may take positions similar to those of feminists on particular issues, their ideological and political orientation precludes their coming out as feminists. For these women feminism is not a comprehensive analysis dealing with the whole of society but a partial approach which they see as privileging women and as a luxury in a Third World country like Egypt. Writer and professor of literature Radwa Ashur asserted, "To talk about women's rights as such seems to the majority of Egyptians a kind of luxury."[13] Similarly, Latifa Zayyat, a writer and Taggamu Party member, insisted, "We cannot afford the luxury of a feminist movement."[14]

While many people project the sense that feminism in Egypt is monolithic, some speak of a plurality of feminisms. Hala Halim said, "This may be taking things too far but I think there is a feminism for every woman."[15] For her this means that until she has worked out her own version of feminism she eschews a feminist identity, a stance which seems common among a number of pro-feminists.

Today's feminists in Egypt are women with layered identities, only one of which is feminist. By publicly asserting one identity they might be seen as giving priority to that one over others, and this most are unwilling to do. In contrast to feminists and pro-feminists, Islamist women claim a single paramount identity which, according to their ideology, must be publicly asserted.

Unlike Islamists, feminists have no obvious external ways of proclaiming their identity. Many committed feminists do make a public declaration of their identity, and are known through their words and actions. Feminists are largely identified through their affiliation with the Jam'iyyat Tadamun al-Mar'a al-'Arabiyya (Arab Women's Solidarity Association, AWSA), or with collectives producing journals such as *Majallat al-Mar'a al-Jadida* (New woman magazine) and *Majallat Bint al-Ard* (Daughter of the earth magazine), published in Mansura in the Delta. Similarly, the group of professional women who published *al-Huquq al-qanuniyya li al-mar'a al-misriyya bain al-nadhariyya wa al-talbiq* (The legal rights of the Egyptian woman in theory and practice) have made their feminism known. For women associated with such groups, taking a public stand is integral to their feminism. Other committed feminists – and this applies to pro-feminists as well – who are not formally involved with a group might acknowledge their feminism when the occasion calls for it, but otherwise their stand would not necessarily be known.

ESSENTIALIZING CULTURE AND FORGETTING HISTORY

Islamist women are seen as having cultural norms on their side, while feminist women appear to be challenging indigenous culture. The burden of proof of authenticity, or correctness, is on feminists. They have to show that they are not tainted by alien – mainly Western – influences. This is a problem feminists have virtually everywhere in the Arab and Islamic worlds, if not everywhere in the Third World. As Algerian feminist Nassera Merah notes about Islamists *vis-à-vis* feminists in Algeria, "their supreme reproach [to the feminists] is their association with the West." Islamists, on the other hand, are *ipso facto* indigenous and authentic.[16]

In the current popular Islamist discourse in Egypt there is an essentializing of culture, an allocation to women of timeless attributes. The Muslim woman is first and foremost, if not only, a good daughter, wife, and mother, ideally spending her life in the home ministering to her family. This is an ageless model for women exhorted by Islamist men and, to a lesser degree, by Islamist women.[17]

Quite different was the Islamic modernist movement of the late nineteenth century led by Shaikh Muhammad 'Abduh. He called for renewal and reform, advocating the practice of *ijtihad*, individual rational investigation of religion in order to consider it in the context of new socio-economic needs. Ushering in a liberal era when judicious innovation in various areas of life was regarded as Islamic, this brand of Islam prepared the ground for the rise of Egyptian feminism elaborated within a religious framework. During this period, too, Egyptian feminism drew support from liberal Egyptian nationalists.[18] At the turn of the twentieth century, women with a feminist consciousness and activist agendas such as Nabawiyya Musa and Bahithat al-Badiya articulated their programs in the discourses of Islam and of nationalism.[19] Equally, the early organized feminist movements led by Huda Sha'rawi and Duriyya Shafiq operated within an Islamic framework.[20]

Feminist movements in Egypt in the first half of the century and public policy under Nasser's program of Arab socialism assisted women across the class spectrum in making vast inroads into society. Today women are found in virtually every sector of the economy and at all levels, although generally not heavily clustered at the top.[21] In the 1970s, with the state-encouraged shift away from Arab socialism during Sadat's rule, Islam was used as a counter-ideology which fed the rise of social conservatism. Only toward the end of the twentieth century, with the ascendancy of a conservative popular Islamic culture, did feminism in Egypt come to be widely branded as anti-Islamic.[22]

With the Islamist wave unfolding from the late 1960s and accelerating in the 1970s there was some reversal of previous gender trends in society. The second Islamist wave idealized women's family and domestic roles, reassigning women to the home and urging them out of the workplace.[23] The movement among women to re-veil set some Muslim women apart from others, serving as a political as well as religious statement. The new veiling fed a discourse of modesty that further endangered women's public roles, even though many women argued that the veil facilitated their presence in public.[24] Segregation of the sexes and a return to the home were part of this rising discourse of modesty articulated in the name of Islam.[25] In Egypt the move to the veil has been widespread among educated women.[26] The conservative Islamic discourse in Egypt has been mainly articulated by men; however, there have been some women who have also contributed to it. Prominent among them are Zainab al-Ghazali, the founder of the Muslim Women's Society (MWS) in 1936 (which in 1948 became the Society of the Muslim Sisters when it allied with the state-suppressed Muslim Brothers) and Safinaz Kazim, theater critic for *al-Musawwar*, a columnist for the Islamic paper *al-Hilal al-Dawli* (published in London) and mainstream Egyptian papers, and author of several books. Both have extolled women's conventional family roles. But they have also spoken out in support of women's roles in society. Moreover, both have insisted upon playing active roles in society themselves.

Al-Ghazali and Kazim have been antagonistic to feminism. Before leaving to form the MWS, al-Ghazali in 1935 was briefly a member of al-Ittihad al-Nisa'i al-Misri (the Egyptian Feminist Union, EFU), founded and headed by Huda Sha'rawi. She told me recently, "The Egyptian Feminist Union wanted to establish the civilization of the Western woman in Egypt, the Arab world, and the Islamic world."[27] Kazim agrees with this view. In her book *Mas'alat al-sufur wa al-hijab* (The question of unveiling and veiling, published in 1982), she argued that the feminist movement led by Sha'rawi pulled women away from Islam. Sixty years after Sha'rawi publicly unveiled her face, leading to the final removal of face veils by women of the middle and upper class, Kazim asserted that women's unveiling was an aberration, not the norm.[28]

SECOND-WAVE FEMINISM

Coincident with the ascendancy of conservative Islam was the rise of second-wave feminism, associated with Nawal al-Saadawi, whose writings took feminism in a new direction. Her feminism, calling for a social, economic, and cultural revolution, was not initially articulated within an Islamic framework, although she drew on certain Islamic arguments. A medical doctor, her 1972 book *al-Mar'a wa al-jins* (Woman and sex) focused on sexual oppression of women resulting in physical and psychological ills. She likewise attacked the sexual double standard. She enlightened many women in Egypt, and helped to raise the consciousness of a whole generation of women students in the democratic movement.[29] However, because she entered an area of taboo she also evoked intense popular criticism. Often misunderstood, her feminism was associated with encouraging the immorality of women and violating religion. Indeed, feminism *per se* came to be widely seen in this light. Just as al-Saadawi put the spotlight on sexual abuses, the nascent Islamist movement, by advocating a return to the veil, accentuated the notion of women as sexual beings (both vulnerable and dangerous). Islamists and other conservatives have linked feminism with sexual freedom, and the link has yet to be broken.[30]

Organized feminism resurfaced in Egypt in the early 1980s – three decades after the EFU and other feminist associations had been silenced – with the creation of AWSA, headed by Nawal al-Saadawi.[31] Meanwhile, in 1984, some young women who as students had been part of the democratic movement of the 1970s formed a study group. They investigated the history of feminist movements in Egypt led by Sha'rawi and others. In the face of the growing Islamist movement they wanted to recover some of the gains of the Nasser period, but rejected state authoritarianism and felt women themselves should identify their own needs. Two years later, the group created *Majallat al-Mar'a al-Jadida* to reach out to other women. This group later became the New Woman Society. Another collective effort emerged in Mansura, where a group of women who had organized with others in public protest over the Israeli invasion of Lebanon in 1982 went on to form Jam'iyyat Bint al-Ard (Society of the Daughters of the Earth) to continue their activism along feminist lines. They encouraged girls in this Delta city and surrounding rural areas to develop their minds and take part in the life of their communities. In an effort to make wider contact, they started *Majallat Bint al-Ard* in 1984. The first issue addressed the problem of women being pushed back into the home. The problem was examined again in the sixth issue in 1990. The editorial collective proposed a debate in print between two veteran activists, the feminist Amina Sa'id and the Islamist Zainab al-Ghazali, but the latter did not agree.[32]

The crisis provoked in 1985 by the rescinding of the liberally revised personal status law of 1979 led to the formation of a broad feminist coalition called Lajnat al-Difa'i 'an Huquq al-Mar'a wa al-Usra (Committee for the Defense of the Rights of the Woman and the Family) to fight back. On the eve of the Egyptian delegation's departure for the Nairobi conference marking the end of the United Nations Decade for Women, the coalition succeeded in obtaining the reinstatement of the law, albeit in truncated form.[33] Later disagreements among feminists split the united front, and the coalition fragmented.

GENDER ACTIVISM

The gender activism of the end of the 1980s and beginning of the 1990s signals a pragmatic moment for Islamist, feminist, and pro-feminist women. Committed feminists proceed with their projects: seminars, conferences, and publications. They maintain high visibility while working to achieve their goals, as do Islamist intellectual women. Pro-feminist women advance women's causes within the framework of their professions, but keep their feminism largely out of sight. Non-association feminists talk more about their activism and less about their ideology, contrary to the practice of association feminists and Islamists.

At a time when the major chorus of populist (mainly male) Islamist voices continues to call for women's retreat to the home, some Islamist women challenge this by insisting upon women's rights in the public sphere. Veteran Islamist Zainab al-Ghazali continues her earlier activism, after six years in prison under Nasser, inspiring and mobilizing young women who gather at her home and who read her writings – including her weekly column for *al-Liwa al-Islami*. While she has always exalted women's roles as wives and mothers, she also demonstrates, by personal example and encouragement, the importance of *da'wa* – that is, winning people to the true Islam to achieve an Islamic state and society. For professional women, who consititute many of her followers, this could be conducted within the context of their work.[34]

Safinaz Kazim, who started out as a leftist in the 1960s, has remained on the scene as a writer and journalist (with three periods of imprisonment). She prefers to view women and men simply as Muslims rather than gendered beings, and does not favor institution-alized gender separations. For example, she decried the idea of start-ing an Islamic journal for women saying, "Dividing the forces of society into male and female is a Western practice." (It is interesting to note that she discredited gender segregation by branding it Western).[35]

Kazim has promoted women's work and other societal roles in her column, "Personal Papers" in *al-Hilal al-Dawli,* a London-based Islamist journal. In an article entitled "Turuk al-mar'a li al-'amal da'wa shar'a islamiyya" (Women's methods in the work of propagat-ing Islamic doctrine, which appeared on 16 October 1987), she indicted as un-Islamic the call for women to quit their work. In "Quwwa al-mujtam'a al-islami" (The power of Islamic society, pub-lished in two parts: on 16 September and 1 October 1987), she reminded Muslims that women and men together constitute society and they must build it together. Kazim writes for Islamist papers abroad and for "secular" publications at home, which have usually been reluctant to accept articles with an Islamic tone from her. However, in November 1990, the wide-circulation women's maga-zine *Nus al-Dunya* (Half the World) published her article "Bi al-tafkir al-islami la tujid qadiyya li al-mar'a" (In Islamic thinking there is no woman question). Here she articulates both a gender-free and gen-dered approach to society, stating that "there is no woman question," while acknowledging that "the woman has to regain her lawful rights guaranteed to her by Islam," including the right to work, to elect lead-ers, and "participation in building an advanced Islamic society." As a deputy editor at Dar al-Hilal publishing house, a member of the edi-torial staff of *al-Musawwar,* and through the very act of writing itself, Kazim engages in gender activism.

Some Islamists, many of whom are young women, have taken advantage of the new forum for airing their views provided by the first Islamist magazine for women, which appeared in October 1990. A sis-ter magazine to the Islamist men's *al-Mukhtar al-Islami,* it is called *Hajir.* While women's magazines are typically under the editorship of women, *Hajir* is run by a male editor-in-chief called Jamal Sultan. He announced that the magazine intends to counter the negative influ-ences of the women's and feminist magazines by providing an Islamic alternative. Female contributors to this new Islamic magazine include both conservatives and liberals. Among the issues discussed in the early issues are public voices and roles for women. In "al-Adab al-nisa'i wa al-ham al-qaumi" (Women's literature and national anxiety, in January 1991), Miral al-Tahawi stressed that women's writings are key in countering "the current of rigidity" and getting to "the root of problems." Hiba Su'ad al-Din, in "al-Mar'a wa al-siyasiya" (Woman and politics, in November 1990), argued that the Islamic path to women's freedom is through politics, and that work is a woman's issue. Al-Din claimed that if a woman or members of her family suffer because she works, it is not the woman but the state that is to blame, for not providing proper support systems.

Meanwhile, Islamist progressive discourse on gender is being moved in a new direction by a young Islamist graduate student in political science at Cairo University, Hiba Rauf, who is attempting to develop a feminism within Islam. Rauf is examining the early sources of religion and Islamic history to evolve a theory of women's liberation. She rejects the term feminism because she sees it as anti-men, but not because of its allegedly Western origins. Like the feminists, and like Kazim, she recognizes that women do not enjoy the rights accorded them by religion. For Rauf, as for Kazim, Muslim women's practice of their lawful rights is a step toward the realization of a true Islamic society.

Like all Islamists, Rauf is critical of the West; however, unlike most of them, she tends to critically examine phenomena attributed to the West rather than to reject them wholesale. Concerning feminism she says:

> Feminist questions can be very useful to us. When I read some feminist writings and saw what they were about, they helped me very much and gave me some ideas. But, I always go back to my Qur'anic dictionary, if I can use the term. The Qur'an is my dictionary and I can't move without it so for every term they use I go back and for every idea of theirs I go back and if I can find some legitimacy for them from the Qur'an I go on with them and see how they can help me with [new] ideas ... It is the [universal] humanitarian things that concern me, but what is peculiar to them and is the result of Western ideas or experience and is not universal, I leave to them.[36]

She confesses: "As far as I know feminism negates religion." Although Rauf rejects the term feminism, she is looking for a way to express much of what feminism at base connotes. The challenge for her is to liberate women and to stay within the parameters of Islam as she understands it. While reading about women's experience in the West she discovered the American New Right, and commented: "The New Right can be of more use to Islamist scholars than radical feminism. The New Right doesn't reject Christian values and family life. Maybe we can find something in common and can raise some questions and have a debate but we have no starting point with radical and Leftist feminism."

Rauf is willing to admit that "Western" feminist movements have met with certain successes in Egypt, and tries to analyze why rather than condemn them outright in the manner of mainstream Islamist discourse, produced mainly by men but also by Islamist women such as Safinaz Kazim and Zainab al-Ghazali. The latter said in an interview, "The Egyptian Feminist Union [in the 1920s, 1930s, and 1940s] wanted to establish the civilization of the Western woman in Egypt and the rest of the Arab and Islamic worlds."[37] Rauf says:

> They [conservative Islamists] say women's liberation movements were dominated by the West and were the tools of Westernization but they don't say why they succeeded to some extent. That [success] was simply because we as Muslims [kept] women in a very bad condition. They say that women have such and such [rights] in Islamic societies. But they didn't [enjoy their rights]. When women's liberation movements started it was because Muslims had so much trouble in their family life and in society so that they [the feminist movements] had something to say and they were listened to. They don't analyze it that way ... The problem is how can the Islamic movement initiate women's liberation from within? ... I would like very much to create such a movement. But this movement must liberate the entire society, women and men alike, and not be a separate movement for women. I would like this movement to be an item on the Islamic agenda.

Among the Islamists I interviewed only one called herself a feminist. She admitted that she did not find any contradictions between feminism and Islam. Maha Saʿud, a university graduate now engaged in development work, was a stewardess with Saudi Arabian Airlines for nine years before she took up the veil and as a result was obliged to quit her job. Feminism for her is an everyday matter. It is an attitude and a way of conducting daily life. Women should have the freedom to choose how to live their lives and to freely express themselves in a way that is in general harmony with society. She believes this is possible. Saʿud does not see feminism as Western, but rather as a universal that finds particular forms of expression in different societies. In this she stands out, not just among Islamist women but among many feminists and most pro-feminists as well.[38]

The pro-feminists mainly include women who typically are not concerned with ideology but are pragmatists who have carved out lives and careers for themselves and in the context of their professions tend to promote the general interests of women. Pro-feminists also include women who are committed to socialist ideology and, while attuned to matters relating to women, have mainly subsumed their gender concern within their socialist ideology and politics. The pro-feminists with whom I talked participate in public life through their professions and their literary production. They are trying to counter-act what they see as a menacing regressive environment for women and to place their individual work in a larger perspective. Rather than debating feminism they address gender issues and explore new directions. Hanna Ayub, who is part of the development community, remarked:

> Nowadays we are starting to get together as women interested in women's issues to discuss these things. We are a group of educated young women who happen to know each other. We are trying to net-work to make the group wider. We got together because we have one thing in common which is our interest in women's issues and because we realize what is happening to women ... such as asking women to go back to the home ... The group is trying to counter-balance what is happening to other women. We see other educated women going backward in big steps. Our generation are women in their twenties and thirties.[39]

Development specialists Sumaiya Ibrahim Huber and Heba al-Khouly are members of the group. Both work with poor women in income-generation projects. Huber works with Bedouin women in Sinai and al-Khouly works among poor Cairene women. Huber, al-Khouly, and Ayoub share a general perspective on the importance of women's roles in the workplace. Women in the group include both pro-feminists and feminists (such as al-Khouly), but the emphasis is on practical issues rather than on ideological debate.

Experience has taught women like Ghada al-Howaidy that women can make practical gains in everyday life which have incremental effects in opening out their lives on public and private fronts alike. Al-Howaidy, who works in bi-national educational and cultural exchange, does not call herself a feminist "because to me it's linked with [political] action."[40] She says that if a particular issue affecting women, such as the revocation of the revised Muslim personal status code, mentioned above, arose she would get in involved as an activist. Generally, however, she believes that women should not be singled out as a separate category. This is a common position among pro-feminists.

Gender activism at the university, where Islamism started to grow in the 1970s and is still strong, presents challenges. Huda Sadda is a professor of English literature at Cairo University, where many of the students are conservative and the Islamist movement has many adherents. She and the many other women professors at Egyptian universities, including several as department heads, serve as female role models by their very presence. The challenge is to open up new forms of awareness among students. Sadda says: "If you shock students they don't listen to you and brand you Western, too affected by Western ideas, and then shut you out completely."[41] Her approach is to be sensitive to where they are coming from and proceed cautiously.

Among the ideological pro-feminists are writers Latifa Zayyat and Radwa Ashur, both leftists. Zayyat was active in the student and the nationalist movements in the second half of the 1940s. In the early 1950s she joined the faculty at the Teacher Training School for Women at Ain Shams, which later became the Kulliyat al-Banat (Girls' College). In 1960 she published her much-acclaimed novel, *al-Bab al-maftuh* (The open door), about a young middle-class woman who found freedom from restrictions upheld by her family and society through participation in the nationalist movement. Although the author of a novel with a feminist theme, Zayyat has until recently shrunk from identifying with feminism, which had no place in her socialist and nationalist ideology. However, in 1990 she confessed: "I have come more and more to realize that the status of women has been of great importance to me."[42] Her recent collection of short stories, *Shaikhukha* (Old age), is "a celebration of self-reconciliation," which, she insists "no man could have written." She speaks of a woman's acceptance of old age and interrogates women's different kinds of relationships. In her writing she probes and expresses gender issues, and acknowledges her writing as a gendered enterprise.

Radwa Ashur, part of the 1960s student generation, a university professor in comparative literature, writer, and critic, like Zayyat, finds feminism as a separate ideology problematic. She explains:

I am very much preoccupied with women's liberation in the context of social liberation as part of national liberation ... My feminist consciousness is one thread of a rich texture. I don't take this thread out of the material and say this is the whole texture. That is why I don't conceive of myself as a feminist ... I am aware of my problem as a woman. It is obvious in what I write because my personal experience makes me conscious of my womanhood and whatever hinders my womanhood but I am also aware that I am Egyptian, Arab, and Third World. Being all three and a woman go into the making of me.[43]

Like Zayyat, a fellow writer, Ashur illuminates gender problematics in her books, and like Sadda and other women professors, her very presence as a university professor constitutes an important statement about gender.

Among the self-acknowledged feminists many operate in their everyday lives in ways not very different from pro-feminists. Meanwhile, others try to build and increase forms of collective activism. The Arab Women's Solidarity Association (AWSA) under Nawal al-Saadawi maintained the highest profile among feminists. AWSA feminism has been the most provocative and controversial in Egypt. AWSA's membership had grown in the mid-1980s at the time of the crisis over the Muslim personal status code, but later decreased when rifts among women occurred. Nevertheless, the organization has evolved as a forum for feminist debate and outreach through its publications, including a quarterly magazine, *Nun,* launched in 1989, international conferences (in 1986, 1988, 1990), and monthly *nadwas* or seminars. These events have attracted women of different ages, especially younger women, as well as men concerned with gender issues. Typically, the seminar speakers have been feminists or pro-feminists. However, early in 1990, an Islamist voice was heard when Safinz Kazim spoke on veiling and women's rights in Islam, drawing a particularly large audience. The talk provoked angry debate between AWSA feminists and Islamists, revealing the depths of the ideological polarization between them concerning the role of Islam in everyday life and the nature of the ideal state and society. However, there was no disagreement about women's economic and political roles as such. The government grew increasingly uneasy with AWSA, and in the spring of 1990 prevented publication of the fourth issue of *Nun.* The following year, after al-Saadawi participated in protests against the impending first Gulf War, the government closed down the association. AWSA, which is currently taking legal action [it subsequently lost its case and was shut down by the government], has received support from the Egyptian Organization for Human Rights.

Feminists who are members of the establishment and have made it to the top of their professions have confronted the call for women to retreat to the home. A group comprising lawyers, journalists, professors, and Egypt's first woman ambassador collaborated in publishing a booklet entitled *al-Huquq al-qanuniyya lil-mar'a al-'arabiyya bain al-nadthariyya wa al-tatbiq* (The legal rights of the Egyptian woman: theory and practice), spelling out for women the rights guaranteed to them by laws and conventions so that they may enjoy them in practice. The first chapter deals with laws concerning work. The third chapter, on the Muslim personal status code, makes the link between the "private" and "public," reminding women that they can stipulate in their marriage contract the right to work outside the home. The booklet explains:

> The inclusion of a provision to that effect [the right to work outside the home] in the marriage contract in no way implies that a wife's right to work outside the home is contingent on her husband's approval. As explained above, this right is guaranteed by the Constitution and by law. However, it is advisable to include this provision to safeguard the wife's right to alimony in case of divorce as husbands have been known in some cases to use the wife's exercise of this right as an excuse to avoid making alimony payments, claiming that they were opposed to her working outside the home.[44]

The feminist authors of the booklet came of age in the 1950s and 1960s. Younger feminists, who were at university in the 1970s, have also taken initiatives to spearhead forms of collective activism. Members of the group that produced *Majallat al-Mar'a al-Jadida* circulated a letter in July 1990 clarifying their position and inviting collaboration:

> The New Woman Group is a progressive and democratic feminist group of women, who believe that while Egyptian and Arab women share with men the hardships brought about by backwardness, dependence and economic crisis, they have to carry a double burden and suffer from a variety of forms of subordination, oppression and suppression arising specifically from their position as women. Moreover, while we believe in the equal right of men and women to fight all forms of oppression and exploitation, we similarly believe

that women's struggle will remain incomplete without their very own battles for freedom and equality and their rights to express themselves, to participate in public life and to take their own life decisions, their right to work and to equal pay, to mention just a few. We also stress women's right in determining what they want to do with their lives whether in the public or personal sphere. We claim that this freedom will not be achieved unless women learn to organize themselves in a wide democratic movement, that has place for all Egyptian women in general and Egyptian women of the popular classes in particular. We are working with the objective that the New Woman Group which is one of several democratic women's groups in Egypt will be able to join together the widest possible number of those women interested in the women's question and who work in fields related to women's concerns, interests, and rights and who fight to win those rights.[45]

Their strategy is to mobilize women in order to share with them their skills, expertise, and experience in a number of concrete fields, including adult education, health, childcare, legal aid, income generation, and general information for the benefit of the broad mass of underprivileged women.

Meanwhile, other feminists have been involved in individual forms of activism. These include the writer Salwa Bakr, who attended university and participated in the students' democratic movement of the 1970s with many members of al-Mar'a al-Jadida (New Woman) group. She says, "I object to the role of the woman being only in the home doing secondary work rather than doing effective work in society. She can't choose her life, her career, and her behavior." For these reasons, and others, Bakr calls herself a feminist. She is pessimistic, however, about the possibilities in the foreseeable future for an effective feminist movement. "Now there is no movement to develop society in general and so it is difficult for a women's rights movement to emerge." Bakr expresses her activism through her novels:

All the characters in my books are women ... I know the world of women ... I worry about the role of women which society forgets all the time so I speak about women going out on strikes, women in the hard times in our country. Everything in [recorded] history is related to men but this is not the way it was and so I write about women ... I worry about the situation of women because I am suffering from it.[46]

While Bakr records women's recent history in fictional form, Huda Lutfy uses her historian's skills to look deeper into the past and write the history of Egyptian and Arab women. She does this as a self-conscious act of retrieval and validation of modes of indigenous feminist consciousness and behaviors:

> I explore Middle Eastern history and try to find out how women felt, and perhaps sometimes try to identify with these women, psychologically, especially women who tried to assert themselves and to say, yes I am a woman but yes I can be influential, I can have my say, I can be a poet, a singer, I can be a musician, I can be a politician, a successful merchant and so on. By finding examples of these women even though they are rather exceptional, I don't have to deal with this guilt that it [women's assertion and accomplishments] is all Western, that women belonging to Middle Eastern society never questioned, never felt frustrated by the restrictions placed on them ... It is not just in the historical experience of the West that women started to assert themselves and express themselves and to say that we want to do more than the role society imposes on us.[47]

Sensitive to this same issue, al-Khouly said: "I get very upset that the West should monopolize the concept of feminism ... We had feminism in our history too."[48]

Feminists are active in the provinces as well as in the capital. In the Delta, in and around Mansura, as previously mentioned, members of al-Bint al-Ard (Daughter of the earth) group are engaged in various forms of practical outreach, such as training women in income-generating work. Jihan al-Sayyid, a member of the collective, articulates their approach and agenda: "Any movement like ours, in order to make contact with the masses, must work within their environment. We must work from below. It is long work and very difficult work. Writing is not enough; we must work with the people. The Daughter of the Earth must work with all classes: peasants, workers, and professionals."[49] It is not only feminists who belong to al-Bint al-Ard collectives; some members are Islamists. In the Delta village of Kamshish, Shahinda Maqlad, a hero in the peasant uprising in the 1960s during Nasser's agrarian reform, is involved in similar forms of activism. In addition to her regular work, Maqlad recently organized a committee to plan a conference marking the twenty-fifth anniversary of the uprising. For Maqlad, women's liberation can only occur in the context of national liberation via socialism.[50]

Another gender activist working among women in the rural areas of Egypt is Algerian-born Zohra Merabet. Permanently settled in Egypt, she heads her own development consulting firm. She says that her feminist consciousness first emerged during her childhood in the Aures Mountains of southeast Algeria and evolved more fully during her days in the student and women's movements in France in the late 1960s. Merabet's activism finds expression in the women's development projects she works on in different parts of the country. She has observed a number of rural women who have become affiliated with Islamic groups in both Upper and Lower Egypt, and sees this at some level as a "feminist" function. She says:

> It is hard for me to have a position on it. One has a functional reaction to it ... The Islamization process is a process of [developing] awareness of the personality and one's position in society. It is very difficult for me to handle. In a way, I see it as a kind of progress. The women [who become Islamists] have discovered certain things and want to make a mark on society. I can understand it because I took a certain path to make a mark on my society. [She described how important going to engineering school and becoming an engineer had been to her feminist actions.] These women I met in the rural areas took a different means, something that helped them to walk out of the family unit into a group to discuss and think. There's a certain group educational factor. Women who become leaders [as she observed in villages in the Nile Valley and oases] become *muhajjabat*. It [becoming more overtly identified with Islam by veiling] enables them to take a stand, to do something. What goes on in the countryside is very different from what goes on in Cairo ... Maybe the framework is too big in the urban setting. In smaller societies it is a very positive action because it gives women the chance to start articulating some ideas. They might not remain Islamists their whole lives. At the village level, Islamism empowers women. In Cairo the opposite may happen because one may be controlled by higher forces who are doing the articulating of ideology. In a complicated way village women [by becoming outwardly identified with Islam] are inventing themselves.[51]

CONCLUSIONS

This chapter has attempted to show that since the end of the 1980s, the positions of intellectual women as feminists, pro-feminists, and Islamists concerning women's roles in Egyptian society have been converging. Although women's rights to play roles in society, and the importance of these roles, have historically been central to feminist and pro-feminist thinking in Egypt, this has not been part of standard Islamist thought. Increasingly however, some women in the Islamist movement are advancing the cause of women's public roles through word and deed. I have used the term "gender activism" to describe this common approach toward women's public roles by feminists, pro-feminists, and Islamists. This has been an attempt to solve the problem of capturing the advocacy and practice by feminists and Islamists alike of women's roles in society as a basic right – and one legitimized by Islam – by means of a new, and therefore unencumbered, analytical construct. Yet, I have cautioned that although women across the ideological spectrum engage in gender activism, which is essentially a common pragmatic approach, women's moorings in divergent ideologies remain significant.

With the third feminist and Islamist phase from the late 1980s into the 1990s, the more stark adversarialism of the second phase from the 1960s well into the 1980s has been tempered. What accounts for this change? I would argue that this represents a pragmatic and political response on the part of feminist, pro-feminist, and Islamist women alike. At the end of the twentieth century, society in many ways is up for grabs: feminists and pro-feminists want to hold ground and Islamists want to gain ground. Whereas committed feminists have evolved analyses of patriarchal supremacy, Islamist women have either internalized patriarchal thinking, even while at times acting on their own in contrary ways, or they have silently eschewed it. Both stances on the part of gender activists signal some awareness of patriarchal hegemony. While older Islamist women have not directly confronted this hegemonic framework, younger Islamist women are beginning to question male dominance, and to see it as transgressing the bounds of what they consider to be the correct Islamic parameters. Although this will probably not lead the new generation of intellectual women out of Islamism, it will probably produce a gender reconfiguration from within.

Not only are there treacherous patriarchal shoals in Egyptian society, but the Egyptian state impedes the free flourishing of feminism and Islamism alike. Thus women like those mentioned operate in a pragmatic mode: non-movement feminism holds out while liberal inroads are made within the Islamist movement. In Egypt, intellectual women will continue to articulate their positions, to stand their ground in society, and try to reach out across class, regional, and ide-ological divides. Their gender activism will remain grounded in divergent ideologies which in turn reflect their different configura-tions of identity and their overlapping yet distinct visions of the good society.

Egyptian women as feminists, pro-feminists, and Islamists all have a stake in retaining their presence in society and in promoting the public presence of other women. They have many common gender interests and common goals, despite the different primary contexts in which they locate their projects. For feminists religion is primarily an individual and personal matter. They do not advocate an Islamic state, and they have a pluralist attitude toward society. For the more ideologically concerned Islamists, the goal of an Islamic state and society is fundamental. They believe that when this is achieved women, and all other members of the *umma* (Islamic nation), will enjoy true liberation. Their differences, however, have not precluded feminist, pro-feminist, and Islamist women from engaging in com-mon forms of activism.

* * *

Originally published in Valentine Moghadam (ed.), *Identity Politics and Women: Cultural Reassertions and Feminisms in International Perspective* (Boulder: Westview Press, 1993).

NOTES

I would like to thank the Fulbright Islamic Civilization Program and the Ford Foundation for support during the late 1980s when I collected material that appears in this chapter. I would also like to thank Dr. Ann Radwan, Executive Director of the Fulbright Commission in Cairo, for her help in facilitating my research and Dr. Valentine Moghadam for organizing the Roundtable on Identity Politics and Women at the United Nations University World Institute for Development Economics Research (WIDER), where my research was presented and for her careful editorial attention to the final version of my paper.

1. I made comparisons between the first two waves of feminism and Islamism in "Feminism and Fundamentalism: Emergence and Resurgence," paper delivered at Bard College, 1986 and in "Feminists and Islam in Egypt: An Historical Perspective," seminar paper for the Institute of Islamic Studies Research, McGill University, 1987. In "Competing Agendas: Feminists, Islam, and the State in Nineteenth and Twentieth Century Egypt," in Deniz Kandiyoti (ed.), *Women,*

Islam, and the State (London: Macmillan and Philadelphia: Temple University Press, 1991) and chapter 1 in this volume, I have examined feminist and Islamist experience under various state formations. In "Independent Women: More Than a Century of Feminism in Egypt," in Judith Tucker (ed.), *Arab Women: Old Boundaries, New Frontiers* (Bloomington: Indiana University Press, 1993) and chapter 5 in this volume, I discuss the feminist continuum in Egypt from the late nineteenth century to the present, distinguishing various phases and their leaders. I dealt with the first feminist wave in "Huda Sha'rawi and the Liberation of the Egyptian Woman," D.Phil. thesis, Oxford University, 1977.

2. See Margot Badran, "From Consciousness to Activism: Feminist Politics in Early Twentieth Century Egypt," in John Spagnolo (ed.), *Problems of the Middle East in Historical Perspective*, St. Antony's College, Oxford monograph series (London: Ithaca Press, 1991), and chapter 3 in this volume.

3. See, for example, Hamied N. Ansari, "The Islamic Militants in Egyptian Politics," *International Journal of Middle East Studies*, 16, 1 (1984), pp. 123–144. See also the following by Saad Eddin Ibrahim: "Contemporary Islamic Militancy," in *Ideen unserer Zeit* (Zurich: Rugger Verlag, 1987), pp. 109–127; "Anatomy of Egypt's Militant Islamic Groups," *International Journal of Middle East Studies*, 12, 4 (1980), pp. 481–499; and "Islamic Militancy as a Social Movement: The Case of Two Groups in Egypt," in Ali Dessouki (ed.), *Islamic Resurgence in the Arab World* (New York: Praeger, 1982), pp. 117–137.

4. For a broad treatment of the Islamist movement see Saad Eddin Ibrahim, "Egypt's Islamic Activism in the 1980s," *Third World Quarterly*, 10, 2 (April 1988), pp. 632–657. Books by Islamist men who take liberal views on women's roles in society include Muhammad al-Ghazali's *Istiqlal al-mar'a fi al-islam* (The independence of the woman in Islam, Cairo: Dar al-Mustaqbal al-'Arabi, n.d.) and his *Qadaiya al-mar'a bain al-taqalid al-rakida wa al-wafida* (Issues of the woman between stagnant and alien traditions, Cairo: Dar al-Shuruq, 1990). Jamal al-Din 'Aliya, in a talk at a girls' school in Constantine, Algeria, on 19 March 1990 entitled "Muqarana bain al-usra al-muslima wa al-namudhij al mithali" (A comparison between the Muslim family and the ideal model), in addition to discussing women's family roles, spoke in favor of women's work and other public roles, and noted the need for an Islamist women's liberation movement. In an interview in Cairo in 1989, the Islamist intellectual and writer Muhammad Yahia told me of the Islamist movement's need to draw women into active participation.

5. See Badran, "Competing Agendas."

6. Women who wear the *niqab* are particularly zealous. However, the issue of *niqab* is highly sensitive. In 1991 a series of articles was published in *al-Nur* under the heading "Tahrim al-niqab" (The face veil is forbidden) by Ismail Ben Mansur, which elicited an impassioned outcry. The author published an article called "Hiwar al-ashab hawla man'a al-niqab" (Dialogue with friends about forbidding the face veil), *al-Nur*, 19 August 1990, discussing the thirty-eight letters he had received from professionals and some students, including at least one woman student, which attacked him for his position on the *niqab*. There is controversy among religious thinkers concerning the *niqab*; many write in favor of it; however, Muhammad al-Ghazali attacks it in *Istiqlal al-mar'a fi al-islam*, p. 7. It is important to mention here that I did not speak with any *munaqqabat* (women who wear the *niqab*), nor did I attempt to, since I was led to believe they would not welcome this.

7. Kamila al-'Arabi, "Tuba li man taghatta ghadan bi al-hijab" (Blessed is she who is covered tomorrow with the *hijab*), *Hajir*, 1 October 1990.

8. Interview with Sumaiya Ibrahim Huber, Cairo, 16 July 1990.

9. Interview with Eva Elias, Cairo, 29 March 1990.

10. Interview with Heba al-Khouly, Cairo, 16 July 1990.

11. Interview with Hala Halim, Cairo, 12 August 1990.

12. Interview with Huda Lutfy, Cairo, 22 May 1990.

13. Interview with Radwa Ashur, Cairo, 24 May 1990.

14. Interview with Latifa Zayyat, Cairo, 3 May 1990.

15. Interview with Hala Halim, Cairo, 12 August 1990.

16. Nassera Merah, "Women, Equality, and Fundamentalism in Algeria," paper prepared for the UNU/WIDER Roundtable on Identity Politics and Women. Not only feminists but secularists in general are often accused of leading society astray and promoting Western culture by not veiling. An example of a grassroots Islamist view is 'Abd al-'Aziz al-Najjar, a science teacher from Kafr al-Shaikh in the Delta, who said in an article entitled "Iftira'at Ibrahim Madkur wa Amina Sa'id" (Fabrications of Ibrahim Madkur and Amina Sa'id), *al-Nur*, 19 August 1990, that the stand against veiling taken by Ibrahim Madkur, former president of the Arabic Academy, and Amina Sa'id would lead Egypt to become like Europe with all its immorality.

17. Huda Lutfy demonstrated this in "A Study of Muslim Popular Literature on the Role of Women in Contemporary Egyptian Society," a paper presented at the Conference of the Middle East Studies Group, London, 1988. Concerning a similar approach in publications in the 1970s see Yvonne Haddad, "The Case of the Feminist Movement," chapter 5 in *Contemporary Islam and the Challenge of History* (Albany: State University of New York Press, 1982) and "Traditional Affirmations Concerning the Role of Women as Found in Contemporary Arab Islamic Literature," in Jane Smith (ed.), *Women in Contemporary Muslim Societies* (Lewisburgh, Pa.: Bucknell University Press, 1980), pp. 61–86; and Valerie J. Hoffman-Ladd, "Polemics on the Modesty and Segregation of Women in Contemporary Egypt," *International Journal of Middle East Studies*, 19, 1 (February, 1987), pp. 23–50.

18. See Albert Hourani, *Arabic Thought in the Liberal Age, 1798–1939* (Cambridge: Cambridge University Press, 1983).

19. See Margot Badran, "The Origins of Feminism in Egypt," in Arina Angerman et al. (eds.), *Current Issues in Women's History* (London: Routledge, 1989), pp. 143–170; and Badran, "From Consciousness to Activism."

20. See Badran, "Independent Women."

21. See Kathleen Howard-Merriam, "Women, Education and the Professions in Egypt," *Comparative Education Review*, 23 (1979), pp. 256–270; and Clement H. Moore, "Sexual Equality amid Professional Impoverishment," in *Images of Development: Egyptian Engineers in the Search of Industry* (Cambridge, Mass.: MIT Press, 1980), pp. 131–143.

22. See, for example, Muhammad 'Atiyya Khamis (ed.), *al-Harakat al-nisa'iyyat wa silatuha m'a al-ist'mar* (Feminist movements and their relations'with colonialism, Cairo: Dar al-Ansar, 1978); and Safinaz Kazim, *Mas'alat al-sufur wa al-hijab* (Questions of unveiling and veiling, Cairo: n.p., 1982). I analyzed this phenomenon in "Feminism as a Force in the Arab World," in *Contemporary Arab Thought and the Woman* (Cairo: Arab Women's Solidarity Association, 1990; and 1989 in Arabic).

23. This was observed and decried by many Egyptian women. See, for example, 'Aziza Husain, Inji Rushdi, Saniyya Salih, Awatif Wali, Mervat Ittalawi, Muna Zulfiqar, and Magda al-Mufti, *al-Huquq al-qanuniyya li al-mar'a al-misriyya bain al-nadhariyya wa al-tatbiq* (The legal rights of the Egyptian woman: theory and practice) (Cairo: n.p., 1988); and Nawal al-Sadaawi, "The Political Challenges Facing Arab Women at the End of the 20th Century," in Nahid Toubia (ed.), *Women of the Arab World: The Coming Challange*, trans. Nahed El Gamal, papers of the Arab Women's Solidarity Association Conference (London: Zed, 1988), pp. 8–26. Analyses of second-wave Islamist discourse on women include those by Yvonne Haddad and Huda Lutfy (see note 17 above).

24. Amina Sa'id was one of the first to attack the move to take up the veil which she saw as a large step backwards. Among her articles in *Hawwa'* in the 1970s are: "This Phenomenon, What Does It Mean?" (18 November 1972); "Back to the Issue of the Dress, This Show of Fuss ... What does it Mean?" (25 November 1972); and "Feast of Unveiling, Feast of Renaissance" (24 March 1973). The latter commemorated the political unveiling by Huda Sha'rawi and Saiza Nabarawi fifty years earlier at the beginning of the first organized feminist movement in Egypt. Analyses of the return to the veil in the earlier years of the second Islamist wave include Fadwa El Guindi, "Veiling Infitah with Muslim Ethic: Egypt's Contemporary Islamic Movement," *Social Problems*, 28, 4 (April 1981), pp. 465–485; Zainab Radwan, *Bahth zahirat al-hijab bain al-jam'iyyat* (A study of the phenomenon of the veil among university women, Cairo: National Centre for Sociological and Criminological Research, 1982); and John Alden Williams, "A Return to the Veil in Egypt," *Middle East Review*, 11, 3 (1979), pp. 49–54. These studies accepted women's explanations that veiling helped smooth their movements in public, stressing a positive functionalist approach. They did not elaborate the negative implications of the ideology accompanying the veil or possible longer-term implications.

25. See Hoffman-Ladd, "Polemics."

26. It is interesting to note that the opposite is true in Algeria, where Nassera Merah notes that many Islamist women are illiterate or semi-literate: see Merah, "Women, Equality, and Fundamentalism in Algeria."

27. Interview with Zainab al-Ghazali, Cairo, 12 February 1989.

28. Christian women in Egypt had started to unveil at the end of the nineteenth century. Among Muslims, Nabawiyya Musa, who unveiled around 1909, was in the vanguard. It was not until after the unveiling of Huda Sha'rawi, and with her Saiza Nabarawi, in 1923, as an overt political act, that most Muslim women would finally end the practice.

29. Interview with Hala Shukrallah, a member of al-Mar'a al-Jadida group, Cairo, 1 September 1990, during which she said how she and other students were influenced by the book. In an interview with the writer Salwa Bakr in Cairo on 18 May 1990, she spoke of the importance of the book, saying it was "very brave and useful."

30. At the 1988 AWSA Conference on Contemporary Arab Thought and the Woman, the Syrian literary critic Samar Attar presented a paper on themes of sexuality in the Thousand and One Nights, which – although a literary analysis of fiction – gave rise to angry accusations of feminist promotion of immorality.

31. On the creation of AWSA see Toubia (ed.), *Women of the Arab World.*

32. Jihan al-Sayyid, Suraya 'Abdul Rad'i, and Hala Isma'il, "Taqrir 'an al-tajriba *al-Majalla Bint al-Ard*" (Report on the experience of the Daughter of the Earth Magazine), paper presented to the AWSA Conference on Arab Women in Publishing and Journalism; interview with Jihan al-Sayyid, Cairo, 6 September 1990.

33. See Nadia Hijab, *Womanpower: The Arab Debate an Women and Work* (Cambridge: Cambridge University Press, 1988); and Sarah Graham-Brown, "After Jihan's Law: A New Battle Over Women's Rights," *The Middle East* (June 1985), pp. 17–20.

34. Interview with Zainab al-Ghazali, Cairo, February 1989. During the interview several of her followers were present, which gave me the opportunity to talk with them as well. An indication of al-Ghazali's influence may be seen by the fact that her prison memoirs, *Ayyam fi al-hayyati* (Days in my life), are now in their tenth printing. On al-Ghazali's dual message to Muslim women see Badran, "Competing Agendas." Also see Valerie J. Hoffman, "An Islamic Activist: Zaynab al-Ghazali," in Elizabeth Fernea (ed.), *Women and the Family in the Middle East: New Voices of Change* (Austin: University of Texas Press, 1985), pp. 233–254.

35. Safinaz Kazim, "Quwwa al-mujtam'a al-islami," *al-Hilal al-Dawli*, 16 September and 1 October 1987.

36. This and subsequent quotes come from an interview with Hiba Rauf, Cairo, 8 September 1990.

37. Interview with Zainab al-Ghazali, Cairo, 12 February 1989. For a similar view see Khamis (ed.), *Harakat nisa'iyya*.

38. Interview with Maha Sa'ud, Cairo, January 1990.

39. Interview with Hanna Ayub, Cairo, 29 March 1990.

40. Interview with Ghada al-Howaidy, Cairo, 20 August 1990.

41. Interview with Huda Sadda, Cairo, 5 May 1990.

42. Interview with Latifa Zayyat, Cairo, 3 May 1990.

43. Interview with Radwa Ashur, Cairo, 25 May 1990.

44. Husain et al., *al-Huquq al-qanuniyya*.

45. Letter from al-Mar'a al-Jadida group, Cairo, July 1990.

46. Interview with Salwa Bakr, Cairo, 18 May 1990.

47. Interview with Huda Lutfy, Cairo, 22 May 1990.

48. Interview with Heba al-Khouly, Cairo, 16 July 1990.

49. Interview with Jihan al-Sayyid, Cairo, 6 September 1990.

50. Interview with Shahinda Maqlad, Cairo, May 1990.

51. Interview with Zohra Merabet, Cairo, 7 September 1990.

7

BODY POLITIC(S): WOMEN, POWER, AND SEXUALITY IN EGYPT

Through an investigation of female genital mutilation (FGM) in Egypt, this chapter explores how women's bodies become contested sites of power, politics, and ideology.[1] The imposition of FGM has been one of many mechanisms of control over women which helps sustain patriarchal power. This form of patriarchal control constitutes a direct violation of women's bodily integrity and sexuality. A complicated web of discourses and politics has grown up around the issue of FGM, which has also been referred to as "female circumcision." For women as feminists and human rights activists the abolition of female circumcision, or what they prefer to call FGM, is an issue in its own right; it is of direct concern to activist women (some of whom are themselves circumcised), as well as part of a system of patriarchal domination to which they are subject and which they consciously oppose. For men, as advocates, abolitionists, or accommodationists,[2] female circumcision, as most call it, is bound up in complicated sets of politics, economics, and power. This chapter is an account and analysis of discourse, debates, practices, and politics at the time of the 1994 United Nations International Conference on Population and Development (UNICPD) in Cairo and immediately following – years when the question of FGM was center-stage.

The FGM abolitionist movement in Egypt came to the fore with the International Conference on Population and Development (ICPD) held in Cairo in 1994. Egyptian feminists, most notably Nawal al-Saadawi, had drawn attention to FGM (earlier often referred to as female circumcision) in the 1970s and 1980s; however, it was during the ICPD that FGM became highly politicized in Egypt and on the world stage. Once wide national and global attention was drawn to the practice of FGM, and when it became obvious that it had become the focus of a feminist/human rights campaign in Egypt, others suddenly made it their concern as well, among them the state, the Islamic religious authorities and Islamists, and the medical profession.

This chapter is an attempt to uncover the complicated layers of politics and divergent agendas around FGM. At one level it is a battle of feminists against patriarchalists. Feminist and human rights FGM abolitionists are clear about their oppositional stance to FGM and the patriarchal order in which it is embedded. The agendas and politics of the patriarchalists,[3] liberals, moderates, and extremists are less patent. FGM appears to be pawn in the contest between the secular state and society, on one side, and the Islamist or "fundamentalist" movement, on the other. Divergent stands on FGM signal power struggles between the majority of religious scholars centered on the bastion of Islamic learning at al-Azhar, who form the traditionally recognized scholarly cadre (*'ulama*), and those who belong to the populist Islamist opposition seeking to "re-Islamize" the state and society. The question of FGM also reverberates within the world of modern medical science, where issues of health and capital are of central concern.

For women the contested terrain is their bodies and sexuality. For men it is the bodies and sexuality of the other. Into the web of politics come cultural constructions of gender and sexuality. Feminist and human rights activists historicize operations of gender and sexuality, questioning these cultural constructions as part of a patriarchal system they seek to dismantle. Patriarchalists tend to leave these products of (patriarchal) culture unexamined, honoring essentialized notions of "the woman" and sexuality, and are in no hurry to undo masculinist hegemony.

FGM in modern Egypt has been variously constituted within shifting patriarchal cultures over the last one to two centuries. In the late nineteenth and early twentieth centuries (the liberal moment) it was construed as part of the private realm, and thus not for public debate. In the 1950s and 1960s (during the socialist period) it was the hidden part of indigenous culture, that was to be left alone.[4] In the 1970s, 1980s, and into the 1990s Islamist culture proclaimed it religiously ordained. It was at the beginning of the 1970s that second-wave feminist Nawal al-Saadawi took the lead in bringing the issue of FGM onto the public agenda, as just noted, doing so in the context of her advocacy for female bodily rights and integrity.[5]

While feminists and other progressives had previously confronted FGM, it was only in the mid-1990s that they were able to broadly politicize the issue. The occasion of the ICPD in Cairo in 1994 provided a configuration of crucial elements: intense international attention; state concern for Egypt's national reputation; Islamist insistence on demonstrating a hold over issues of gender, family, and private domain; and a ripe feminist/human rights discourse. During the international conference in Cairo, CNN aired a documentary on FGM produced in Egypt, filming the live performing of genital mutilation on a fourteen-year-old girl, which exposed both the horrors of FGM and of CNN's collusion in violating a female body while producing financial gain for the television network. This brought many parties/interest groups out into the open.[6]

I argue that above all it was when activist women in Egypt located FGM firmly within a feminist and human rights discourse that they were able to create a serious FGM abolitionist movement. This alarmed the custodians of patriarchy, drawing them into unprecedented public debate – or, more accurately, into public exposure. The intensity, persistence, and reformulation of patriarchal discourses (and patriarchal in-fighting) has kept FGM a public issue – indeed, an intriguing media event – thus garnering wider audiences for feminist and human rights campaigns.

CULTURAL AND POLITICAL VOCABULARIES: WOMAN, SEXUALITY, AND FGM/CIRCUMCISION

In classic Islamic juridical, philosophical, and medical texts, and in popular lore, sexuality is not simply tied to procreation, but is associated with pleasure. Sexual pleasure is an equal right for women and men, which both may equally demand.[7] Learned Islamic texts and popular belief also hold that women possess enormous sexual appetites (far greater than those of men), and that women's whole being, body and voice constitutes a sexualized entity. The word describing "the sexualized" in Arabic is *awra*, which literally means genitalia. That which is *awra* must be covered, and since in the traditional conservative view "the woman" is construed as an "omnisexual being," to use Fatima Mernissi's term, women's entire bodies must be hidden, and in traditional conservative culture even their voices. While woman is thus culturally (but not religiously) constructed as an "omnisexual being," man is not, and hence his *awra* is restricted to his genitalia, in keeping with Islamic religious prescription.[8]

Notions of woman as an omnisexual – and highly sexualized – being permeate the entire culture in Egypt. This is to say that such thinking is shared by both Christians and Muslims, who generally believe that women's sexuality is the product of "nature." Women, as omnisexual creatures, have been associated with disorder or chaos (*fitna*) connected with sexuality, and, as Mernissi reminds us, a beautiful woman may be called *fitna* (as *femme fatale*).[9] Women must be contained, therefore, to preserve social order. The need to control women is made more urgent still by linking male and family honor to the chastity of women (chastity as sexual behavior confined to marriage is religiously prescribed by Christianity and Islam alike for both sexes, but in these religious cultures is not in practice imposed on men). Chaste women's bodies must bear the weight of patriarchal honor. The honor of men is not produced through their own chastity, but through association with the chaste bodies of their women – the women in their families.

Because of these popular beliefs about women and their sexuality, the threat they pose, and the linkage between women's sexual purity and the honor of males and the family, women have been highly controlled in traditional patriarchal culture. In Egypt (and elsewhere) women have been controlled by being kept hidden and silent. In urban Egypt, and in the strata where women's labor outside the house has not been an economic necessity, the domestic seclusion of women was traditionally practiced, and if women did leave the sanctity of their homes they went out with faces and bodies fully veiled. The widespread belief in both learned circles and popular culture that these practices were ordained by Islam gave them great weight. Christians in Egypt historically followed the social conventions of the mainstream Muslim majority.[10] If women could not be domestically sequestered because their labor outside the house was needed, as has been the case historically for the majority of village dwellers and the urban poor, other controls were placed on women, mainly forms of community surveillance and sanctions.[11]

FGM has been one of the mechanisms of patriarchal control of the woman's body/sexuality, and thus a "guarantee" of male and family honor. FGM is an ancient custom, thought to go back to Pharaonic times, practiced by all strata in urban and rural areas alike. Face veiling, historically a practice of the middle and upper urban classes, has been another mechanism through which women have been regulated by patriarchy. In the late nineteenth century, their encounters with the socio-economic and technological transformations of modernity led some women to develop a feminist consciousness. They began to remove their face veils, refusing to hide their faces as well as their voices, effectively rejecting notions of *awra* associated with these practices.[12] Activist leaders signaled the start of the first organized feminist movement in Egypt in 1923 with a public unveiling of their faces, as part of a larger movement aimed at reducing patriarchal dominion of women. This was also the moment when activist women first publicly used the term "feminism."[13]

Unlike face veiling, FGM constitutes physical violence perpetrated against the female body, and one that leaves a permanent trace. There is an extensive literature on female circumcision detailing the range of genital invasions – from the most extreme form, infibulation, which involves total excision of the clitoris and major and minor labia and a stitching together of skin walls, leaving only a small aperture for urination, to the least invasive, which is the removal of skin at the tip of the clitoris.[14] In Egypt circumcision is typically performed on girls between the ages of six and twelve years (that is, both before and after puberty). The majority, who live in rural areas, are subjected to mutilation by untrained village midwives and barbers. Only in towns and cities are doctors or health practitioners with modern training available, but their outreach is limited.[15]

The cultural and political vocabulary of "female circumcision" is telling. A brief look at terminology is a way to explore deeper meanings. By noting the terminology individuals and groups use we can read their attitudes and politics. Conventional words used in Arabic in the past and present in Egypt include *khitan, khifad,* and *tahara.* Of the three, only *khitan,* a word in the lexicon of classical Arabic, is used for the circumcision of both females and males. The root of the word carries the notion of cutting, and implies a clinical process. The other two words, purely colloquial terms, which are used exclusively for female circumcision, are more loaded. The root of *khifad* means to lower, diminish, decrease, subdue, "as to subdue a voice" [or sexuality].[16] The diverse terms for FGM can be confusing. A girl from Upper Egypt told researchers that when the terms "female genital mutilation" and *khitan* were used on television, "nobody understood they were referring to what is known to us as tahara [purification]."[17]

FGM passed into Arabic in Egypt as "al-intihaq al-badani lil-sighar al-inadh" (literally, the physical violation of young females). *Al-intihaq* is also a term used for rape.[18] Activists in Egypt employ a dual vocabulary in Arabic and English. The Egyptian Task Force, created in 1994 to fight FGM, is known in English as the FGM Task Force, while in Arabic it calls itself Quwwat al-'Amal lil-Munahaddat li-Khitan al-Banat (The task force to fight the circumcision of girls). Task Force head Marie Assaad explained that in working with ordinary people in a country where the vast majority of women are circumcised, using the term circumcision rather than a vocabulary of mutilation is less harsh on women. But the activist women insist upon identifying as the FGM Task Force in English, to fully express their perspective.[19]

ICPD AS CATALYST, FGM AS PRISM: PANDORA'S BOX OPENS

When Egypt, a pivotal state in the region, influential in the Islamic world, and a significant geopolitical player on the global stage, agreed to host the prestigious International Conference on Population and Development in 1994, it took on a tangle of issues. The international NGOs preparing for the ICPD made it clear to the Egyptian government that planning for the conference could not proceed without the efforts of local NGOs. Long-time social activists 'Aziza Husain, working since the 1950s in the Family Planning Association and in community development projects, and Marie Assaad, with decades of experience in a range of local associations and locally, nationally, and transnationally through the YWCA, brought together NGOs and individual women activists to form a task force to coordinate local preparations. The task force, in turn, set up focal groups in various governorates throughout the country. The operation constituted a broad collaboration between Egyptian feminists, human rights activists, and development workers, including some two hundred individuals and sixty NGOs, in what has been described as "a moment of exhilaration."[20] Lending critical support and tightening regional links, Sudanese feminist and anti-FGM activist Nahid Toubia, founder of the Research, Action, and Information Network for Bodily Integrity of Women (RAINBOW), comprised of African women

activists headquartered in New York, visited Cairo during preparations to insure that FGM was placed on the agenda of the conference
that was being organized around themes of reproductive rights and
female sexuality.[21] Toubia drew upon experience in Sudan where
(unlike Egypt) there had been a broadly active FGM eradication campaign in the 1970s and 1980s, which was, however, dismantled in the
1990s with the ascendancy of the Islamist government.[22]

The Egyptian government was compelled to give progressive
activist forces the opportunity to organize themselves, public space to
operate in, and facilitation of international contacts. The government, in short, had to demonstrate to the international community
that democracy, especially freedom of speech, existed, and also had to
provide strong security when religious conservative forces threatened
disruption. The ICPD vehemently condemned FGM in the safe public forum the Egyptian government was obliged to create.

The broadcasting of the CNN documentary on FGM in Egypt,
mentioned earlier, pushed the issue to center-stage both nationally
and globally. The documentary made FGM a public spectacle and,
together with the high-profile ICPD, set off a train of events in which
feminists, human rights activists, doctors, religious leaders, grassroots activists, and the state all participated.

In the wake of the ICPD and the CNN film, with its exposure of
dangers to girls at the hands of untrained practitioners, the minister
of health, 'Ali 'Abd al-Fattah, issued a decree permitting female circumcision to be performed in hospitals, overturning a 1959 ban.[23]
This led to a spate of lawsuits, including cases against doctors.
Feminists and human rights activists immediately filed a suit against
the minister of health for allowing female circumcision to be done in
hospitals. It was dismissed on the grounds that the contesting parties
did not have a direct interest. However, after the widely-publicized
death of a fourteen-year-old girl during an FGM operation by a medical doctor, the new minister of health, Isma'il Sallam, withdrew his
predecessor's decree, reinstating the ban on the practice of female circumcision in hospitals. This led to new lawsuits filed by Munir Fawzi,
a gynecologist at 'Ain Shams University Hospital and Shaikh Yusif al-
Badri, of the Higher Council for Islamic Affairs, against the prime
minister and minister of health. In July 1997 the Administrative
Court of the State Council ruled against the minister of health's ban
on circumcision in the hospitals. The minister of health contested this,
and on 29 December 1997 the court of highest appeals overturned the

previous decision, ruling in favor of the ban (I return to these suits below). The ongoing legal saga guaranteed the question of FGM high publicity. The FGM debates, well reported in the press, became sites for various agendas.

A HOUSE UNITED: FEMINISTS AND HUMAN RIGHTS ACTIVISTS

The permanent FGM Task Force, which formalized the relatively spontaneous coalition of women feminist, human rights, and health activists that came together in the preparatory task force for the ICPD, included women of different generations and classes, both Muslim and Christian. The FGM Task Force also maintained solid links with women and men living and working in rural areas. The Task Force, led by Marie Assaad, worked under the umbrella of two organizations headed by 'Aziza Husain: the National Commission of Population and Development (NCPD), designated by the Ministry of Health to follow up on the ICPD; and the Egyptian Society for Population and Development (ESPD), under the jurisdiction of the Ministry of Social Affairs. The Task Force enjoyed considerable independence; it had clearly received the green light from the government.

While the Task Force, along with the think tank it spawned, which met more frequently to strategize, constituted the key focal point, its members also worked within other professional and associational contexts. Many Task Force members were medical professionals active in feminist and human rights organizations. Siham 'Abd al-Salaam worked through the Task Force umbrella organization, the Center for Development and Population Activities and the Cairo Institute for Human Rights (CIHR). Amal 'Abd al-Hadi, who also worked at the CIHR, was active in the New Women's Research Center,[24] as was 'Aida Saif al-Dawla and Nadia 'Abd al-Wahhab. 'Afaf Mar'ai and Amal Sharif were from the Coalition for Women's Issues. Task Force members hold higher degrees in various disciplines. For example, Siham 'Abd al-Salaam has an M.A. in film studies, while Marlyn Tadros holds a Ph.D. in English literature. Tadros, a member of the Legal Research and Resource Center, was founder and managing editor of *People's Rights/Women's Rights*, which maintained a web page and ran extensive coverage of FGM.

The Task Force took a firm stand against FGM in any form, demanding its full and immediate stoppage. Its 1997 position paper declared: "Our position regarding FGM is its unconditional denunciation. It is based on a strong belief in a woman's right to maintain the integrity and wholeness of her body and the freedom of her mind; to choose her life and to base her choices on her own evaluation of what should or should not be done."[25]

The FGM Task Force's statement on feminist/human rights was clear. It cited the condemnation of FGM as a human rights violation at the United Nations Human Rights Conference in Vienna in 1993, and in the Platform for Action endorsed by the United Nations World Conference on Women at Beijing in 1995. Then Egyptian ambassador to Japan, and later minster of social affairs, Mervet al-Tallawy, chaired the subcommittee on Health and Reproductive Rights at the Beijing conference, in which the issue of FGM was debated.[26] In Egypt Task Force members, who spent three years combining activism with analysis, articulated a feminist critique of FGM and the patriarchal system in which it is embedded. They declared:

> We are also aware that the prevalence of FGM in our country [97% of ever married women according to the last demographic survey, done in 1996[27]] shows that we are not dealing with an occasional practice, but a social phenomenon, a cognitive and behavioral construct, which has a social function of maintaining a patriarchal hierarchy of society. Our goal is to challenge this hierarchy and to work towards a reconsideration of the prevailing value system governing gender relations in general and women's sense of entitlement in particular.[28]

By virtue of its Muslim and Christian composition and concern with the bodily mutilation of both Muslim and Christian Egyptians, the FGM Task Force was a secular entity in the sense that it was non-sectarian and its basic discourse was not religious. Because of the stridency of political Islam, however, the FGM Task Force eventually found it imperative to publicly declare its position on "religion and FGM." It did so as follows: "We believe the role of religion is to realize justice and equity between people, to promote their happiness and welfare. Any use of religion to the detriment of that happiness is an abuse of religion based on interest, whether personal or political." The Task Force made clear that it was "not in a position to interpret religious texts," nor did it pretend to issue religious pronouncements (*fatwas*). However, it insisted: "It is the responsibility of those who set themselves the task of interpreting religious texts to do so in a way that promotes the well-being of mankind [*sic*], women and men."[29]

The Task Force's anti-FGM discourse revealed its politics and strategy. As a unified coalition, it decided on a common approach, but as it comprised members who had their own individual approaches and who were active in other contexts, there was a certain operational diversity, which was a strength. Task Force members agreed collectively, after trial and error, that the most effective way for it to confront the issue of FGM was to attack it as a socially constructed, historical custom. Activists stressed FGM's pre-Christian and pre-Islamic roots to show that it was a custom that simply persisted after the advent of these religions. The challenge facing activists was to deconstruct the mesh of popular discourses of gender, sexuality, and honor that surround FGM.

FGM feminist/human rights activists used the same argument that feminists in Egypt had employed early in the twentieth century in combating face veiling. Female chastity and honor are protected by women and men's own behavior and not by external controls such as a piece of cloth or genital mutilation. They stressed the role of human will and discipline of both sexes in the maintenance of chastity and honor. Activists found that girls and younger women (most of whom now have some formal education), as well as many men of the rising generation, were sensitive to this issue of individual will. Anti-FGM activists working in rural areas observed how the notion of self-responsibility and the realization that it is within the power of women and girls to protect themselves and assume responsibility for their own inviolability and honor enhances their self-esteem. A young woman in the village of al-Tayiba in Minya Province said: "When parents circumcise their daughters it is as if they do not trust them, but an uncircumcised girl knows how to protect herself and this is an honor for her."[30]

Tahara connotes ritual cleanliness, and also implies beautification. Ritual purification is achieved when the "unclean" and "ugly" parts of the female genitals are removed. Activists, especially when speaking with rural women, countered this by speaking in a religiously neutral language of the sanctity of the body that God created. They also employed the discourse of science, declaring that modern medicine understands that parts removed by FGM are actually beneficial to the body and should be left intact.

While activists preferred not to employ religious arguments they did attempt to de-link FGM and religion. They favored demonstration through example, often citing the admission by the current Shaikh al-Azhar that he had not circumcised his own daughters. Muslim activists sometimes pointed out that female circumcision is not mentioned in the Qur'an. However, FGM abolitionists generally prefer not to use the discourse of Islam in public debates, arguing that being drawn into protracted religious arguments would be counter-productive and that, not being *'ulama* (Islamic scholars), they lack the recognized authority that would strengthen their case. Muslim abolitionists, however, did point to inconsistencies in Islamic religious arguments as part of their strategy to undermine FGM. In a broader movement now underway in Egypt and elsewhere, Islamic feminists are claiming the right of all believers to exercise *ijtihad* (independent rational investigation of sacred texts) and to constitute themselves as authoritative voices.

CLOSING RANKS: URBAN ACTIVIST WOMEN AND RURAL COMMUNITIES

The ICPD provided the occasion for an unprecedented breakthrough in expanding anti-FGM activism in rural communities. A perennial problem for social activists has been how to reach rural populations. The ICPD provided a forum for bringing together NGOs working in villages with social activists working in the urban areas. Urban–rural links formed at the time of the ICPD have been maintained and strengthened.

The organization with the longest continuing experience working with villagers on FGM eradication is the Coptic Evangelical Organization for Social Services (CEOSS), founded in 1950. FGM is one of the "harmful practices" that CEOSS has worked to eliminate in the context of community development projects.[31] The organization has operated for several decades in the governorate of Minya in Upper Egypt, where it has claimed an eradication rate of more than 70 percent in eight villages. CEOSS strategy has been based upon community initiative and control of the eradication process. A village must send a written invitation to CEOSS if it wishes the organization to render support. CEOSS workers live in the village for an initial period, helping to set up a general village committee to work on local issues in general and a women's committee to work on FGM eradication. They do not try to attract village notables so much as ordinary people, often young adults, who show initiative and the will to work. In rural areas, men and women together collaborate in the FGM abolitionist movement. Villages have always been more highly gender-integrated in everyday life and work, unlike urban society, which still exhibits varying degrees of gender separation and isolation of women, which have both increased with the spread of Islamism. When men, who typically enjoy greater prestige, become part of the abolitionist movement they can use the weight of their customary status in countering FGM proponents. CEOSS community workers favor gradual withdrawal from the village, aiming in the long run to leave anti-FGM work fully in the hands of the villagers.

Some villages have imposed their own, highly successful, village-wide bans on FGM. Villagers themselves have refashioned traditional attitudes about honor and shame, sexuality, and mechanisms of control. Thus a new message about an old practice is transmitted and enforced through both traditional and modified community structures. Once the idea of female circumcision as genital mutilation takes root, it becomes shameful for a family to admit or be known to practice circumcision of their girls. In villages where a local ban was imposed on FGM, infractions against the ban were punished by the community through public humiliation. Contrary to notions that the rural population is deeply wedded to FGM as a venerable custom, activists found that villagers exposed to new thinking about the practice had been known to abandon it with remarkable speed.[32] Villagers thus take control to prevent FGM, and women assume responsibility to protect their own sexuality through self-responsibility and self-discipline.

FGM Task Force members have reported that villagers often asked why the Task Force had only recently come to their assistance. The urban activists explained that they were too organizationally and politically weak to reach them before. In Egypt, as elsewhere, rural inhabitants are often neglected, and are the last to receive modern health and education services. They are kept out of the loop of modernity and then represented as being tied to old habits. Feminist educator Nabawiyya Musa, early last century, made the same argument concerning women: they are neglected; and then blamed for "backwardness"; and neglected still more, in a repetitive cycle.[33] The villages that have eradicated FGM present a challenge to conservatives and reactionaries, who claim that they support the desire of villagers to uphold female circumcision.

FGM AND ISLAM: A HOUSE DIVIDED

The "re-Islamization" of FGM was underway in Egypt before the time of the ICPD. This happened in the context of the spreading Islamist movement and its attempts to strengthen the patriarchal culture. Highly visible "re-Islamizing" moves regarding FGM coincided with the intensifying politicization of FGM as a woman's rights issue in 1994 by the vibrant, well-organized feminist and human rights movement.

FGM, or female circumcision, is not prescribed by Islam, according to classic Islamic jurisprudence and standard Islamic interpretive methodologies.[34] Activists have been quick to note that there is no mention of female circumcision in the Qur'an. There exist only a few weak *hadith*s (sayings of the Prophet Muhammad) referring to female circumcision. The practice was known in Arabia at the time of the Prophet Muhammad (it was thought to have come from Ethiopia into Yemen), but has long since died out, except for a few pockets, while it has never been known to the majority of the world's Muslims.[35] Although weak or questionable *hadith*s carry no authority, Islamist advocates have used these to "prove," or to create the impression, that circumcision for girls is Islamic. Promoting an Islamic justification of FGM is reminiscent of the earlier spurious Islamic "justification" of face veiling (not an Islamic prescription) in Egypt, which the Islamic modernist movement of the late nineteenth century, initiated by the progressive al-Azhar-trained scholar and later Mufti of Egypt, Shaikh Muhammad 'Abduh, exposed as un-Islamic.[36]

FGM became a site of political contestation between Islamists and liberals. This was exhibited at the highest levels. The two top official religious posts in Egypt are that of Mufti of Egypt (dispenser of religious judgments, *fatwa*s) and Shaikh al-Azhar, the head of the revered, liberal institution of Islamic learning. Both posts are state appointments. Stands that the persons occupying these posts take on specific issues are read politically as being pro- or anti- the secular state. During the ICPD, and in its aftermath, a pro-female circumcision stance became one of the markers of Islamists, who seemed to fear that they were losing control as the definers and keepers of female sexuality, and other forms of social control.

The first public contestation at the top was staged at the time of the ICPD. Gad al-Haq 'Ali Gad-al-Haq, who was then Shaikh al-Azhar, declared female circumcision a religious requirement, and made the provocative claim that to speak against female circumcision was to speak against Islam. The then Mufti, Muhammad Sayyid al-Tantawi (who later became Shaikh al-Azhar), meanwhile, used his authority as official dispenser of religious judgments to issue a *fatwa* pronouncing female circumcision to be non-Islamic. He also drew upon personal experience when he publicly admitted that he had not circumcised his own daughters. Tantawi's *fatwa* saying female circumcision was not Islamic, and another *fatwa* declaring interest on money lawful, as well as a later meeting with the Chief Rabbi of Israel, Yisrael Lau, were all read by the oppositional Islamists as "proof" that he was the state's man.[37] Because of such moves it was said in Islamist quarters that Tantawi's credibility, and thus his authority on issues such as female circumcision, were lost. Progressive opinion meanwhile worked in the opposite direction. The refusal by al-Tantawi to declare female circumcision an Islamic prescription was applauded, and seen as part of a drive to check both FGM and the Islamist project.

Within the Islamist camp itself there was also a sign of a divergence from the predominant pro-FGM position. Space appeared to be opening up for more liberal views, if the stand of the widely known and respected Islamist lawyer Muhammad Salim al-'Awwa was an indication. This Islamist lawyer presented Islamic juridical proofs and philosophical arguments against female circumcision in an article entitled: "Khitan al-banat laisa sunna wa la makruma" (Circumcision of girls is neither required nor praiseworthy) published in 1994 in *al-Sha'b* (mouthpiece of the coalition that had formed between the Labor Party and the Muslim Brothers).

Most *'ulama* and others who use religious arguments, did not, like Gad-al-Haq, pronounce female circumcision to be an Islamic requirement. They simply declared that it was not a religious requirement, but added that the practice was not forbidden by Islam. These religious scholars also used a social constructionist argument when they claimed the circumcision of girls served to temper the so-called hyper-sexuality of females.

It has been Islamist men and male religious scholars who have taken friendly stances toward female circumcision. There are no women religious scholars who have publicly pronounced in favor of it, nor have women intellectuals among the Islamists done so; but they have also not spoken out against it. In other parts of the Islamic world, for example in Malaysia, Muslim women intellectuals and activists have marshaled Qur'anic arguments to confront another kind of physical violence against women – battery by husbands – which many insist is prescribed by Islam. [38]

It remains to be seen whether the "Islamization" of FGM will take hold in the rural areas, where the practice has flourished without this religious justification. It is possible that the contest between FGM feminist and human rights abolitionists, on the one side, and Islamists, on the other, could eventually play out in the rural areas, where eradication attempts have begun to make headway. But these minimal successful inroads have not as yet been widely visible in the larger world of rural Egypt.

Political Islam sought to increase its adherents by supporting a practice it claimed the majority insists upon, while also claiming to have God on its side. An example of the Islamists' boldness is seen in an article published less than two weeks after the higher court decision to dismiss cases against the ban on female circumcision in hospitals with the inflammatory title "Circumcision [of girls] is Legislated by God despite its Prohibition by the Courts," in *al-Usbu'a* (The weekly) by Dr. Abu 'Umaiyra, former dean of the College of Usul al-Din (principles of religion) at al-Azhar.[39]

Shaikh Nasr Farid Muhammad Wasil, the new Mufti, appointed at the time when the cases against the ban on FGM in hospitals were being heard, stated in his first public interview after taking office, published in the mass-circulation daily *al-Akhbar* on 13 November 1996: "There is no retreat on the previous *fatwas* on female circumcision issued by Dar al-Iftah which confirmed that there are no religious texts within the domain of the Islamic *shari'a* which command or prevent female circumcision." He shifted the focus away from religion to the family, with its own "traditions and habits," saying: "If the family finds there is a compelling reason not to perform circumcision of [their] girls, it is their decision, beyond the realm of religion. Likewise, if the family finds a compelling reason for circumcision [of their girls] they should do it without bringing religion into the matter." The Mufti, however, was not about to leave matters exclusively in the hands of families, and thus shifted the question to another set of professionals – the modern medical elite. He insisted that it was incumbent upon the family to take the opinion of "the trusted and just medical doctors who in their profession are considered truthful and knowledgeable."[40]

FGM AND DOCTORS: A HOUSE DIVIDED

Women constitute a significant presence in the medical profession. Females who have entered medical school in Egypt have been high achievers. Only students with top scores in the state qualifying examinations are admitted to the medical faculties. The influx of large numbers of women into the medical faculties began after the 1952 revolution, when free universal education through university was opened to both genders and all classes.[41]

There was a direct link between women's presence in the medical profession and second-wave feminism in Egypt in the early 1970s. The founding text of second-wave feminism was written by a woman medical doctor who broke through the wall of imposed silence to name the violations committed against the female body. The most systemic and universal of these aggressions was FGM, perpetrated in the name of protection (of the woman) and honor (of the man). The already-mentioned Nawal al-Saadawi, in *al-Mar'a wa al-jins* (Woman and sex), published in 1972, drew upon her experience as a doctor and as a circumcised woman when she exposed the physical and psychological ravages of FGM committed against girls, and located this bodily aggression within the context of patriarchal dominion.[42] *Al-Mar'a wa al-jins*, which became a cult book for Egyptian university students in the democratic movement of the 1970s, cost the doctor-cum-author her job in the Ministry of Health.[43]

Women doctors, as noted, have been at the forefront of the FGM abolitionist movement. They combine knowledge of health and the human body with a feminist analysis of patriarchal operations in Egypt. Siham 'Abd al-Salaam, for example, articulated a trenchant critique of the collusion of the patriarchalist medical élite in perpetuating aggressions against the female body.[44] For feminist abolitionists FGM is a physical violation of women's right to bodily integrity and a brutal mechanism of patriarchal control. Abolitionists are well aware that FGM is hard to disengage from the set of beliefs and practices that compose women's quotidian universe. Women physicians among the abolitionists call for immediate and total cessation of what they unequivocally term female genital mutilation. For them as doctors and as women there is no such thing as a partial (or benign) excision of genitals: mutilation is mutilation. This is reflected in Egyptian law: removal of any part of the body for non-medical reasons is a criminal offense, and thus to be a "gradualist" is to be a perpetrator.

A minority of male doctors are also abolitionists. As noted, minister of health Isma'il Sallam came out against FGM, reimposing the ban on its practice in hospitals. He also (like the Shaikh al-Azhar) publicly stated that he did not circumcise his own daughters, and that in his official capacity he is as responsible for all Egyptian girls as for his own daughters. His official status necessitated that Sallam take a public stand, but others who were not so positioned could choose to remain silent.

The majority of male doctors, as well as many women doctors who are complicit with the patriarchal order, favor the medicalization of FGM. Abolitionists publicly insist that to modernize FGM is not to gradually phase it out, but to entrench it more deeply. Doctors who favor medicalization make a health argument, pointing to "the social reality" that the majority of girls will undergo circumcision, and that therefore it is preferable to provide safe conditions with doctors performing circumcisions in hospitals. However, there is a different social and economic reality that they ignore. As the doctors are well aware, the majority of Egyptian girls, who are either rural villagers or from the urban lower class, do not have access to modern doctors and hospitals. Medicalizing female circumcision brings financial profit to doctors, as it enacts a shift from traditional to modern practice.[45] Doctors advocating or performing safe circumcisions are not concurrently engaging in activism aimed at ending female circumcision. They perpetuate the practice while claiming, or appearing, to oppose FGM and await its elimination.

At the beginning of the chapter I drew attention to the opposing positions of two successive ministers of health concerning the performance of female circumcision in hospitals – one allowing, and the other banning the practice. The question can be asked to what extent this indicates real differences within the medical leadership, or whether the divergent decrees are more illustrative of the vacillating attitude and political maneuvers of the state, at times appearing to appease pro-female circumcision Islamists, and at others to expediently assert its own authority to curb or eradicate the practice.

THE MEETING OF PATRIARCHIES: MEDICAL AND RELIGIOUS

"The Necessity to Uphold Religious Instructions and an Immediate Plan for Emergency Medicine," was the title of an article that appeared in the prestigious Cairo daily *al-Ahram* in October 1994. In it the author, Salim Nigm, deputy head of the Doctors' Syndicate, announced that medical doctors and religious scholars (*'ulama*) concurred that circumcision as a surgical operation could be performed on a girl after the age of puberty, with her consent and that of a parent or guardian.[46]

Two years later, in 1996, the reinstatement of the ban on female circumcision in hospitals occasioned an assertion of the convergence between medicine and religion that attracted intense public attention, and put FGM at the core of a fierce contest between the Islamists and the state. While feminist and human rights activists celebrated the renewed ban on FGM in hospitals, conservative opponents in the medical and religious establishments struck back.

Gynecologist Munir Fawzi, and Shaikh Yusif al-Badri, a member of the Higher Council for Islamic Affairs, filed suits against the minister of health Isma'il Sallam's 1996 ban on female circumcision. They argued that the ban violated the 1971 constitution, which declared the Islamic *shari'a* to be the source of all laws in Egypt, making the claim that female circumcision falls within the *shari'a*. Fawzi backed up his claim by citing the authority of the former Shaikh al-Azhar, Gad-al-Haq. He also used non-religious arguments, claiming that because the majority of village women practice circumcision the ban runs contrary to the customs of the people. Fawzi also employed a health argument in favor of medicalization. Shaikh Yusif al-Badri backed up his claim that Islam condones female circumcision with detailed arguments based on his readings of Islamic jurisprudence. To further shore up his stand he also used a social argument that female circumcision preserves a woman's dignity.[47]

When the case reached the State Council, the highest court of appeal, it was found that the ban did not violate the constitution, because female circumcision is not a matter falling within purview of the *shari'a*. Violations against the ban on female circumcision would come under the jurisdiction of criminal law, except if the circumcision were performed at the request of the girl and her parents, following a statement by a hospital chief of gynecology claiming it a medical necessity. The state, in delimiting the borders of Islamic legal jurisdiction, protected its own body politic/s and, in the process, up to a point, the female body.[48]

WHOSE BODY POLITIC(S)?

There is a tug-of-war over women's bodies: to whom do they belong? And to whom does the body politic belong? Women as feminist and human rights activists are claiming women's bodies belong to women themselves, and that they have the right to unviolated bodies as women and as human beings. For them female circumcision is female genital mutilation. Egyptian activist women, however, sometimes as we have seen, use "politic" language in Arabic, rather than the radical, political language they use in English.

When women politicized FGM, members of the religious and medical élite entered the contest. With the exception of female doctors at the forefront of the abolitionist campaign, and some male practitioners, doctors advocated medicalization under the guise of favoring gradual elimination. But medicalization, in modernizing FGM, perpetuates the practice and entrenches it more deeply. It brings economic gain to willing medical practitioners and sustains patriarchal control over women and their bodies. Those clerics who advocate female circumcision outright are Islamists who attempt to "Islamize" the practice as a way to entrench it more deeply and to extend the reach of political Islam, and in so doing extend power over women's bodies and the entire body politic. The men of religion who state that female circumcision is not Islamic do not call unequivocally for its eradication, but leave the task to the modern medical profession. In this way they lend passive support to its perpetuation, while at the same time some refuse to circumcise their own daughters.

The state currently does not favor medicalization of FGM. It also does not condone the "Islamization" of the practice. It does not accept female circumcision as falling with the purview of the *shari'a* and therefore to be protected by the constitution. The state is aware that Islamists are using this argument as one means to extend their political control over the body politic, which the state assiduously tries to resist. It therefore becomes an ally of women abolitionists, up to a point, when it suits its own interests.

Women abolitionists understand the connection between FGM and patriarchal control of women, as do the advocates of FGM. The former try to dismantle patriarchal control over women's bodies, while the latter aim to sustain this control over women and their bodies. The former use the discourse of women's/human rights, while the latter marshal their own formulations of religious and medical discourse. The power politics over women's bodies are still heavily controlled by men – of the state, medical profession, and religious elite – all of whom use women and their bodies to further their own projects. Women anti-FGM campaigners are unmasking their projects, exposing FGM as a profound violation of women and their bodies as they articulate a compelling – or disturbing – discourse of justice and rights.

* * *

Originally presented as a paper at the Workshop on Sexuality, Power, and Religion organized by the Park Ridge Center for the Study of Health, Faith, and Ethics, Chicago, March 1998.

NOTES

1. Part of the research for the paper on which this chapter is based was carried out under a grant from the American Research Center in Egypt, which I gratefuly acknowledge.
2. Accomodationists refer to those who, when necessary or politic, go along with the practice.
3. My term for those who uphold patriarchy, both in general and in any of its various specific manifestations or operations.
4. The 1962 Mithaq (literally, "covenant"; usually known as the national covenant) issued by the Nasser government outlining its program of Arab socialism called the family the "basic nucleus of society" which "should be provided with all forms of protection to preserve *national customs* and to reproduce its [the family's] fabric" (emphasis added). This "protection" of the (private) family and its "sphere" was a concession made explicit at a time when the state extended the public sphere (and its direct control over it) in an unprecedented way. While an aggressive state-sponsored birth-control program constituted an intrusion into the family sphere of control over procreation, the state did not make such an intrusion regarding FGM. In 1959 the Nasser-led state prevented female circumcision from being performed in government hospitals and clinics, a measure which later abolitionists favor, and which can be read as keeping FGM firmly within the private, family arena. The tendency of states to forfeit female citizens' issues in the interests of their own power and even survival has been elucidated in the literature. See, for example, Deniz Kandiyoti (ed.), *Women, Islam, and the State* (London: Macmillan and Philadelphia: Temple University Press, 1991).
5. Nawal al-Saadawi, *al-Mar'a wa al-jins* (Cairo: al-Nashirun al-'Arab, 1972) and *The Hidden Face of Eve* (London: Zed, 1980).
6. Marlyn Tadros, "Female Genital Mutilation: Next Case Please!" *People's Rights, Women's Rights*, 5 (July 1997), pp. 14–15.
7. See Abdel Wahhab Boudiba, *Sexuality in Islam* (London: Routledge & Kegan Paul, 1975); Fatna Sabah, *Woman in the Muslim Unconscious*, trans. Mary Jo

Lakeland (New York: Pergamon, 1984); Bassam Musallam, *Sex and Society in Islam: Birth Control before the Nineteenth Century* (Cambridge: Cambridge University Press, 1983); and Monica Green, "Essay Review: Female Sexuality in the Medieval West," *Trends In History*, 4, 4 (1990), pp. 127–158.

8. Fatima Mernissi, *Beyond the Veil: Male–Female Dynamics in a Modern Muslim Society*, 2nd ed. (Bloomington: Indiana University Press, 1987).

9. Ibid., p. 31.

10. I have written about this in my book *Feminists, Islam, and Nation: Gender and the Making of Modern Egypt* (Princeton: Princeton University Press, 1995).

11. Ibid.

12. When Hind Naufal founded the first women's journal, called *al-Fatah* (The young woman) in Egypt in 1892 and invited contributions from Egyptian women, she said in her opening editorial: "But, do not imagine that a woman who writes in a journal is compromised in modesty or violates her purity and good behavior." See Hind Naufal,"The Dawn of the Arabic Women's Press," in Margot Badran and Miriam Cooke (eds.), *Opening the Gates: A Century of Arab Feminist Writing* (London: Virago and Bloomington: University of Indiana Press, 1990), pp. 216–19, quotation on p. 218. On the dual unveiling of faces and voices in Iran see Farzani Milani, *Veils and Words: The Emerging Voice of Iranian Women Writers* (Syracuse: Syracuse University Press, 1992).

13. The first feminist movement in Egypt is the subject of my book *Feminists, Islam, and Nation.*

14. Of the general scholarly and activist literature see, for example, Nahid Toubia, *Female Genital Mutilation: A Call for Global Action* (New York: Woman Ink, 1995). On recent documentation for Egypt see, for example, F. El-Zanaty et al., *Egypt Demographic and Health Survey 1995* (Calverton, Md.: National Population Council [Egypt] and Macro International [USA] 1996); *Facts about Female Circumcision* (Cairo: Cairo Family Planning Association, 1991); and *Scientific Facts on Female Genital Mutilation* (Cairo: Egyptian Society for the Prevention of Harmful Traditional Practices to the Woman and Child, 1993).

15. Zanaty et al., *Egypt Demographic and Health Survey, 1995.*

16. Hans Wehr, *A Dictionary of Modern Written Arabic* (Ithaca: n.p., 1961), pp. 227 (*khitan*) and 250 (*khifad*).

17. Samiha el Katsha, Sherine Ibrahim, and Noha Sedky, *Experiences of Non-governmental Organizations Working towards the Elimination of Female Genital Mutilation in Egypt* (Cairo: Female Genital Mutilation Task Force, 1997), p. 50.

18. See Wehr, *Dictionary*, p. 1004, for a full range of meanings, some of which include: enervation, depletion, abuse. *Intihaq al-hurma* (literally, physical violation of the woman/lady/wife) is translated as "sacrilege."

19. The issue of using different vocabulary in Arabic and English on the subject of FGM recalls the different vocabularies used by first-wave feminists in Arabic and French in the 1920s, 1930s, and 1940s. Early feminist activists used a less radical vocabulary in Arabic. On this see Badran, *Feminists, Islam, and Nation* and Irène Abd al-Aal, *Défense et illustration de l'Egyptienne aux débuts d'une expression féminine* (Cairo: Centre d'Etudes et de Documentation Economique, Juridique et Sociale, 1988).

20. Interview with Marie Assaad, 7 February 1998.

21. Interview with Marie Assaad, 7 February 1998 and with Amal 'Abd al-Hadi, 12 February 1998; See Aida Seif El Dawla, "The Political and Legal Struggle

over FGM in Egypt before and after the International Conference on Population and Development," in *Intersections between Health and Human Rights: The Case of Female Genital Mutilation* (New York: Research, Action, and Information Network for Bodily Integrity of Women, 1995), pp. 10–17.

22. In 1979 at a conference on the Changing Status of Sudanese Women, women doctors and feminists from Sudan spoke about the FGM abolitionist campaign in their country. I participated in this conference, where I gave a paper entitled "Women's Movements as Vehicles for Women's Development: Reflections from the Egyptian Experience." In the early 1980s, when I participated with Sudanese doctors, midwives, and nurses in gathering data on health issues, including FGM, in North and South Kordofan, I witnessed at close quarters anti-FGM efforts in western Sudan.

23. See the article "'Amaliyyat al-khitan fi al-mustashfahat" (Circumcision operation in hospitals), in *Akhbar al-Yaum*, 29 October 1994, p. 13; the operation was to be performed by a gynecological surgeon and an anesthetist, a tacit admission of the pain involved. The cost was set at ten Egyptian pounds.

24. Now called the New Women's Foundation.

25. FGM Task Force, "FGM Task Force Position Paper," October 1997; in Arabic "Mawqifna min khitan al-untha" (Our position on female circumcision).

26. On Egypt as signatory to international conventions relating to women's rights see Mervat Tallawy, "International Organization, National Machinery, Islam, and Foreign Policy," in Mahnaz Afkhami and Erika Friedl (eds.), *Muslim Women and the Politics of Participation: Implementing the Beijing Platform* (Syracuse: Syracuse University Press, 1997), pp. 128–140. On Egypt and the implementation of the Platform for Action signed at the United Nations Fourth World Conference in Beijing see Hoda Badran, *The Road from Beijing* (New York: UNDP, 1997).

27. Zanaty et al., *Egypt Demographic and Health Survey, 1995*.

28. FGM Task Force, "Position Paper."

29. Ibid.

30. El Katsha, Ibrahim, and Sedky, *Experiences of Non-governmental Organizations*, p. 22.

31. Information on CEOSS from interviews with Marlyn Tadros, 6 February 1998; Marie Assaad, 9 February 1998; and Amal 'Abd al-Hadi, 12 February 1998; and el Katsha, Ibrahim, and Sedky, *Experiences of Non-governmental Organizations*, pp. 17–27.

32. Interview with Marie Assaad, 7 February 1998.

33. Musa speaks of this in her book *al-Mar'a wa al-'amal* (Women and work, Alexandria: Matba'a al-Qawmi, 1920). A translated excerpt appears in Badran and Cooke (eds.), *Opening the Gates*, pp. 263–269.

34. In the aftermath of the ICPD an article by Islamist lawyer Muhammad Salim al-'Awwa was published discussing Islamic legal and philosophical views on female circumcision: "Khitan al-banat laisa sunna wa la makruma" (Circumcision of girls is neither obligatory nor praiseworthy), *al-Sha'b*, 8 November 1994. For a review of female circumcision in classical Islamic jurisprudence see Jonathan P. Berkey, "Circumcision Circumscribed: Female Excision and Cultural Accommodation in the Medieval Near East," *International Journal of Middle East Studies*, 28 (1996), pp. 19–38.

35. Muslim feminists and other women have used this observation in their activist

discourse. See for example, Seema Kazi, "Muslim Law and Women Living under Muslim Laws"; and Anne Elizabeth Mayer, "Aberrant 'Islams' and Errant Daughters: The Turbulent Legacy of Beijing in Muslim Societies," both in Afkhami and Friedl (eds.), *Muslim Women and the Politics of Participation.* pp. 141–146 and 29–42 respectively.

36. The notion that face veiling was not Islamic was forcefully expressed in Qasim Amin's book *Tahrir al-mar'a* (The liberation of woman, Cairo: Maktabat al-Taraqqi, 1899) in arguments that are believed to have originated from 'Abduh. For thinking on this and related subjects see Muhammad 'Imara (ed.), *al-Imam Muhammad 'Abduh: siratahu, akarahu, a'malahu* ([The complete works of Muhammad 'Abduh,] Beirut: Dar al-Quds, 1978).

37. The meeting with the Chief Rabbi occurred on 15 December 1998. Islamists are against normalization of relations with Israel within the framework set up by the Oslo accords (as are many secular progressives). The Egyptian government at the moment is far from happy about the off-track peace process and therefore has a complicated view on "normalization." The state is known for sending out contradictory signals on all contentious issues (peace process, FGM). See Amira Howeidy, "'He Was Here ... and we Met'," *al-Ahram Weekly,* 18–24 December 1997, p. 3; and Amira Howeidy, "Political Strife in al-Azhar," *al-Ahram Weekly,* 12–18 February 1998.

38. A group called Sisters in Islam, comprised of Islamic and Islamist women who are reinterpreting the Qur'an and performing critical investigations of the *shar'ia,* published a pamphlet in the 1980s entitled "Is Wife Beating Condoned by Allah?" FGM has not been practiced in Malaysia.

39. *al-Usbu'a,* 9 February 1998, p. 18.

40. "Fatawwa al-khitan al-sabiqa al-sahihi wa amr matruk lil-'usur wa atiba'a" (Previous *fatwas* concerning circumcision [*khitan*] are correct and the matter should be left to families and doctors), interview with Dr. Farid Muhammad Wasil by Hisham al-Agami, al-Akhbar, 13 November 1996, p. 10.

41. The first women graduated from the faculty of medicine at Fuad I University (later called Cairo University) in 1936, although Egyptian women had previously trained abroad as doctors. The Egyptian Feminist Union feted the new doctors returning from training abroad along with the first women to graduate from Fuad I university (in the faculty of arts) in 1933. See Badran, *Feminists, Islam, and Nation,* pp. 149–150.

42. Al-Saadawi's internationally best known writing on female circumcision and other issues relating to women's bodies, discussed in a feminist context, is her *Hidden Face of Eve.* For semi-fictional accounts of her experience in medical school and as a doctor see her *Mudhakkirat al-tabiba* (Memoirs of a woman doctor, Cairo: Dar al-Ma'rif, 1965) and *Imratain fi al-imra'a* (Two women in one, Beirut: Dar al-Adab, 1979).

43. I discussed how al-Saadawi put female sexuality, and especially FGM, on the feminist agenda for the first time in Egypt in "Feminism, Sexuality, and the Egyptian Woman Intellectual," a paper presented at a panel on Arab Women Intellectuals, Middle East Studies Association Conference, Boston, 1986. I also discussed al-Saadawi's views on the female body and sexuality in the context of the history of feminism in Egypt in "Independent Women: More Than a Century of Feminism in Egypt," in Judith Tucker (ed.), *Arab Women: Old Boundaries, New Frontiers* (Bloomington: University of Indiana Press, 1993) and

and chapter 5 in this volume and "Competing Agenda: Feminists, Islam, and the State in Nineteenth and Twentieth Century Egypt," in Kandiyoti (ed.), *Women, Islam, and the State,* and chapter 1 in this volume.

44. Siham 'Abd al-Salaam is a medical doctor who also has an advanced degree in film criticism. An example of her writing is "Women's Sexuality and the Discourse of Power: The Case of FGM," unpublished paper for panel on Arab Women Intellectuals, Middle East Studies Association Meetings, Boston, 1996.

45. In a televised debate on female circumcision a woman doctor said that some of her male colleagues admitted that female circumcision is financially rewarding and that they encourage people to keep up the practice by pretending that it is Islamic. See 'Abd al-Salaam, "Women's Sexuality and the Discourse of Power," p. 21.

46. *al-Ahram,* 12 October 1994, p. 10.

47. See Tadros, "Female Genital Mutilation."

48. Decision published on 29 December 1997.

8

GENDER JOURNEYS INTO ARABIC

INTRODUCTION

Concepts have always circulated across cultures and geographical areas, as Edward Said reminds us in his much-cited paper "Traveling Theory." Analytical concepts travel from one location to another because they possess expressive or analytical power or crystallize an idea or set of related ideas. The journeys of new concepts or analytical terms may be smooth or rough, usually both. Words that express them journey along particular paths as they circulate from one culture to another, or within cultures. In the process they become "naturalized." To continue with Said, "Such movement in a new environment is never unimpeded. It necessarily involves processes of representation and institutionalization different from those at point of origin. This complicates any account of the transplantation, trans-ference, circulation, and commerce of theories and ideas."[1]

Here I shall consider the journey of "gender" as a new construct and theoretical tool from an anglophone to an arabophone universe. It is a journey that began in the final two decades of the twentieth cen-tury and is still in process. First, I discuss the political and intellectual contexts of the emergence of the new concept and analytical tool called gender in the anglophone world, and the contexts of gender in its travels to the arabophone world. Second, I examine the question of terminology. I note the structural differences between English and Arabic, observe the freight words carry, and analyze the strategies and methods adopted to express gender in Arabic. Third, I look at a par-ticular historical moment and site of entry of gender into the arabo-phone world in order to chart specific experience in its travels as a concept, analytical tool, and new term in Arabic. In this section I look at the demonization of the term gender as part of a larger political struggle.

Three arguments underpin this chapter. (1) The new construct and analytical tool called gender has universal meanings and applications; it is generic and as such cannot be the exclusive property of, or relevant only to, any particular group or culture. (2) Historically, a notion of gender (and the idea of cultural construction more broadly) existed in the arabophone world centuries before the concept of gender was distilled and named in the twentieth century. What we now call gendering or gender analysis has long been practiced in the arabophone world, and especially within Islamic discourse. (3) Related to the second argument is that the named and defined concept of gender, in the process of traveling, becomes naturalized as it enters into and engages with a particular (cultural, local) universe or epistemological system. Yet gender, like many new constructs and terms, in the process of their early circulations, may also be denigrated or trivialized. This happened in the arabophone world when gender was still new, during its tortuous movements within the academy, and while voyaging out into society at large.

MULTIPLE MOTHERS OF "GENDER" AND ITS EARLY TRAVELS

The new term "gender" emerged in academic circles in the United States in the final decades of the twentieth century in the wake of social liberation movements.[2] Universities, along with the street, were key sites of the women's liberation movement, the civil rights movement, and the anti-Vietnam war movement, as well as movements in support of African and Asian national liberation. Out of these movements emerged new areas of study, new academic disciplines, and new theory: women's or feminist studies and later gender studies, African-American studies, Third World studies, and post-colonial studies.

Women scholars in the American academy distilled the idea of gender as a new analytical category connoting the cultural construction of man and woman, or masculinity and femininity, as distinct from the biological categories of male and female (sex). Historians, who were researching and analyzing women's historical experiences as distinct from men's, were in the forefront of the pioneering efforts that gave rise to formulation of the new concept and term "gender." Thus, gender became a device facilitating the analysis of our everyday practices as women and men within specific contexts – for example, of religion, culture, nation, and society.[3] In a landmark paper at the Conference of the American Historical Association in New York in 1985 entitled "Gender: A Useful Category of Historical Analysis," Joan Scott brought to the attention of the wider academic community the power and potential of the new theoretical concept of gender that feminist scholars had been working to develop in the past several years.[4] Since the word gender was coined there have been intense academic debates in the anglophone world, as elsewhere, as intellectuals and activists continue to shape ideas of gender and to hone it as an analytical tool.[5]

In the arabophone world, as in other parts of the Third World, it has been claimed, as a de-legitimizing gesture, that gender is a Western construct, or more simply that gender is Western. The early formulations and theorizations of gender in the academy in the United States were not simply the work of Westerners. This would imply the absurd notion of a hermetically sealed-off Western world (or Eastern world, etc.). Such thinking simplistically conflates place or geographical location with people – and, more specifically, with those who do intellectual work – and presumes little or no significant movement in and out of space. Among the women pioneering in gender analysis, before the term gender had begun to circulate, were scholars from Africa and Asia engaged in innovative intellectual research and analysis. One of the best known is the distinguished Moroccan scholar Fatima Mernissi, whose research in the 1970s as a graduate student at Brandeis University resulted in one of the foundation texts of gender studies, now a classic, called *Beyond the Veil: Male–Female Dynamics in a Modern Muslim Society*. Another is the United States-based Indian scholar Chandra Talpende Mohanty, whose path-breaking work on gender is also among the foundational texts of women's studies, post-colonial studies, and culture studies.[6] These and many other examples testify that "thinking and doing gender" from the start was not merely a Western practice, and that it was not simply based on Western experience and exported with an indelible Western imprint to other parts of the globe.[7] Since the 1970s numerous arabophone scholars working in the West (temporarily or permanently) have engaged in gender analysis of aspects of their own societies.

In the arabophone world, as within the Third World generally, gender traveled most widely and rapidly through the development community, more particularly through Women in Development (WID) and later Gender and Development (GAD) projects. The United Nations Decade of Women from 1975 to 1985, as well as new policies in bilateral contexts, helped accelerate the spread of gendered development projects in the Third World. Within the international development community, the term gender traveled in English. Efforts meanwhile were made to find words in local languages, either as loan words or new coinages. In the development world, English as a global language is employed in tandem with local languages, with significant implications for understandings and uses of gender. "Gender work" has been most prominent and widespread, and least threatening, within the context of development projects. Within the framework of development, gender has been most directly controlled, as well as most protected, by the state. Arab countries have accepted billions of dollars for development in the name of gender. In the context of development, moreover, ordinary citizens have, as beneficiaries, welcomed gender projects.

Gender also traveled into the arabophone world with the creation of women's studies programs and centers. Typically these have not been established in the state universities that constitute the core of higher education in the Arab world, but rather in private colleges and universities. Private institutions of higher education – and, more specifically, women's studies programs and centers – have received multiple sources of funding, both local and international. Private institutions are freer from government control, in its more direct forms, but they fall prey to state curbs on civil society.

The longest-lived – and, indeed, the first – women's studies center established in the Arab world is the Institute for Women's Studies founded at the Beirut College for Women in 1973, a good decade before the emergence of gender as a named concept. Although the Institute for Women's Studies has shown wide-ranging interests, it has always been concerned with women's literary production, located as it has been in an important intellectual and artistic center. Another early pioneering women's studies center was created at Ahfad College (now Ahfad University) in Khartoum in the late 1970s. It became known for its focus on development as WID and GAD were being refined – and indeed, Ahfad has made salient contributions in this field. The Women's Studies Center created at Bir Zeit University in

Palestine in 1994 has taken initiatives in scrutinizing state-building policies and practices from a gender perspective. These are just three examples, taken from the eastern part of the Arab world, of how gender has been introduced into the private academy. A different private site of what might be called "public women's studies" are programs (public lectures and publication projects) set up within the framework of NGOs, as well as workshops and conferences, which are also conduits through which notions of gender pass.[8]

In the Arab world, a notable exception to the practice of creating women's studies in private academic space is the Empirical Research and Women's Studies Center (ERWSC) created in 1996 (growing out of the Women's Studies Unit begun three years earlier) at the University of San'a', which is part of the state-run system of higher education in Yemen.[9] The ERWSC was not only located in a state university, it also received massive bilateral funding (from the Netherlands government). Being part of the state system, however, did not accord it some of the immunities enjoyed by programs in private institutions. It also positioned the ERWSC more precariously in terms of national politics with critical implications for gender, as I discuss in the final section.

As part of academic women's studies, gender probes into the deep recesses of culture and society. Gender analysis provides a tool for critiquing received conventions. It is a tool of empowerment for citizens and civil society. For all of these reasons gender is threatening to entrenched centers of power and authority, and to political groups seeking power.[10]

Gender work in an academic context, as within the context of development in Arab countries, is carried out in English, and/or French, along with Arabic. At Ahfad University instruction is conducted in English. At the Women's Studies Institute in Beirut, Arabic, English and French are employed. The women's studies centers at Bir Zeit and the University of San'a' use both Arabic and English, although Arabic is the major language of instruction. Gender work conducted in English and gender work in Arabic inform, refine, and stretch expression in each language. It is wrong, indeed naive, to assume that there is a one-way street from the anglophone world to the arabophone world. Proponents of such a position frame "gender" (which seems to become some kind of free-standing phenomenon) as cultural invasion, unwittingly presuming an astonishing lack of agency in the arabophone world, or positing it as a victim.

There have been those among both secularists and the religiously oriented who have shared the view that gender is a concept alien to religion. In the arabophone world gender circulated mainly, and earliest, in the secular contexts of development and of academic women's studies. Many of the religiously oriented have not participated in the debates that have been circulating around gender, nor has the new construct of gender been seriously engaged with by the *'ulama* (religious scholars). On the other hand, many secularists who are more familiar with gender are often unfamiliar or unconcerned with Islamic epistemology. Moreover, the politicization of the secular and the religious as antagonistic have thrust "gender" as a tool into opposing ideological camps.[11] Secularists find it a useful tool of analysis, while the religiously oriented see it as a destructive weapon of cultural assault.

In the arabophone world, there have been important works of gender analysis of religion and religious texts. An Egyptian specialist in religious studies, Zainab Radwan, conducted the earliest extensive study of the *hijab* (head covering), the politics surrounding its early use and its multiple meanings.[12] Fatima Mernissi was a pioneer in conducting a gendered analysis of *hadith* (traditional sayings of the Prophet).[13] A Moroccan professor of law, Farida Bennani, and an Egyptian professor of comparative jurisprudence, Suad Salih, have done numerous penetrating gender analyses of *fiqh* (Islamic jurisprudence). There has been seminal research and gendered analysis of the Qur'an and other sacred texts conducted in Arabic and written and published in English, such as the American scholar Amina Wadud's *Qur'an and Woman.*[14]

The movement of Islamic feminism has been underway since the final decade of the twentieth century, bringing gender to the fore within Islamic contexts. The seminal contributions of Islamic feminists (with or without the label, and often the latter) to cultural debates, activist causes, and societal development have been both applauded and maligned. Against this background, I would now like to consider problems of meanings and namings in the gender journeys from the anglophone to the arabophone universe.

"GENDER" BY ANY OTHER NAME

Naming "gender" in Arabic is in many ways more problematic than the idea of gender itself. Yet, of course, naming and meaning are interconnected. Trying to find a word in Arabic for the English "gender" as a term that connotes cultural constructions of masculinity and femininity as distinct from sex as a biological category opens up a plethora of problems. The epistemological differences are, of course, reflected in linguistic terms – the "word vessels" and what fills them, so to speak. Another kind of problem concerns the structure of the two languages, Arabic and English. Words in Arabic, as a Semitic language, are built around a root of consonants: the standard triliteral root, as well as, in some cases, a quadriliteral root. In this way, a universe of meanings becomes associated with the root consonants configured in various morphological forms. Related words built from the same root indicate the range of meanings flowing from a shared stem. Morphological mappings can also help in constructing histories of words and meanings, or at least give us some tantalizing hints.

AL-JINS: MORE THAN SEX

Al-jins is the word in modern Arabic that designates sex as the biological categories of male and female, as does the English word "sex."[15] But, unlike the word sex in English, *al-jins* possesses multiple meanings. *Al-jins* is more than sex. Or, to put it another way, there has never been a discrete word in Arabic for sex as designating the biological categories of male and female. Moreover, linguists and historians of the Arabic language believe, and the Arabic dictionaries offer strong evidence for this, that *al-jins* only began to include sex amongst its meanings in modern times, possibly as late as the nineteenth century.

Al-jins is a loan word in Arabic. Some scholars claim the term first came into Arabic from the Syriac word *genso*, which is known to have been in circulation in the fourth century c.e. *Genso* in the singular signified "nation," in the sense of a group of believers and, in the plural, "pagans" (the non-believing other "nation").[16] However, *al-jins* as an early Syriac loan word does not appear to have circulated widely, in the view of some scholars.[17] The word *al-jins* does not exist in the Qur'an or in classical *fiqh*.

Other scholars believe that *al-jins* came into Arabic in the eighth century c.e. as a Greek loan word connoting genus or category of classification (as in genus and species), while at the same time acknowledging a prior connection with the Syriac *genso*. It is surmised that the

Greek *genos* found its way into Arabic through the learned communities, while the preexisting Syriac loan may also been in wider popular circulation at that time. Whatever its provenance(s), *al-jins* makes its first appearance in Arabic classical dictionaries, starting with *al-Misbah al-munir fi gharib al-sharq al-kabir lil-rafa'i*, compiled by al-Fayumi, who died in 770 A.H. (thirteenth century C.E.) where it is defined as genus, with the word for species being *al-naw'*.

In *Assas al-balagha*, an Arabic dictionary compiled around the same time as *al-Misbah*, the word *al-jins* signifies people and in the plural means "the impure" (it seems in the sense of connoting "pagan"), a definition echoing that of the Syriac *genso*.[18] Was the wider use of the term *al-jins*, both in the sense of genus and of "nation" or "race" during the Abbasid period associated with the rise of non-Arabs in the Islamic caliphate and the need to order by "race," "ethnicity," and "nation" and the need for this ordering mechanism to be named? A detailed investigation of this question is beyond the scope of this present work and, moreover, requires the attention of linguistics specialists. I have raised the matter here to indicate to purists objecting to the English loan word *al-jandar* (gender) that many words now taken as "pure Arabic words" were in fact loans, and that loans come into a language when what they signify or conceptualize carries some epistemological power. I have also made this excursion into the history of *al-jins* as a reminder of how fluid and multiple its meanings have been. This dynamism can be read as a sign of cultural vitality and the need to continue to question and to analyze in the light of shifting environments. The construct gender carries with it something of what *al-jins* constituted earlier in its pre-modern moment and continues to convey to this day. Gender as social construction is not alien to the arabophone world. It is "gender" as focused on cultural construction built around the biological categories of male and female that is innovative.

In its modern construction *al-jins*, and various morphological forms of its root, carry connotations relating to nation, race, and ethnicity. *Al-jinsiyya*, for example, is "citizenship." *Al-jins* runs the gamut from the biological (biological sex and biological physical type or race) to the constructed (nationality, citizenship, the process of naturalization, etc.). Gender as an analytical concept takes as its central focus constructions of the masculine and feminine, which are always inflected by other factors, such as race, nation, class, ethnicity. Part of the problem of translating the English "gender" (as a construct distinct from sex) into Arabic has to do with the different, vaster range of meanings connected with the root of the Arabic word that came to connote sex. The English "sex" and the Arabic "*al-jins*" are not simple equivalents. The English term gender in some way is closer to *al-jins* in that it signifies (cultural) construction, a mode of classification (and therefore possessing analytical capacity). It is somewhat ironic that the Arabic word *al-jins* originally embodied a meaning and ana-lytical capacity more closely resembling the notion of the English word gender than it now does by primarily designating sex, and that the English term gender is taken as alien or culturally invasive and dis/credited as "Western."

"SEX" AND "GENDER" AS CONCEPTS – BUT NOT WORDS – IN THE QUR'AN

In the Qur'an, male and female as biological categories are rendered as *al-dhakar* (dual, *dhakarain*; plural, *dhukur* and *dhukran*) and *al-untha* (dual, *unthayyaini*; plural *inath*). Categories constructed around biological sex but carrying religious/cultural prescription in the Qur'an include: *rajul* (man: dual, *rajulan*; plural, *rijal*); *imra'a* (woman [also wife]: dual, *imra'atani*; plural for women *nisa'* and *niswa*), and many other familial categories. In the Qur'an, religiously constructed duties, responsibilities, and possibilities for Muslims are often (though not always) indicated with specific reference to male or female (*al-dhakar* and *al-untha*) and man or women (*al-rajul* and *al-mar'a*). Interpretations or understandings of Qur'anic pre-scriptions relating to women and men, relations between them, etc. are gained through exegesis (*tafsir*). Thus, *tafsir* focusing on matters pertaining to Muslims as males or females is a form of gender analysis. To put it slightly differently, using the methodology of *tafsir* to work out what is enjoined upon, allowed, preferred, forbid-den, etc. to Muslims as males or females constitutes a mode of "gender analysis."[19]

Thinking in categories relating to (biological) male or female, or (cultural) man and woman (etc.) has been highly developed in the Islamic/arabophone universe, and certainly more thoroughly articu-lated than in the secular arabophone universe. There is much to learn from, and to interrogate, concerning cultural construction, or gen-der, within Islamic religious discourse. Islamic methodologies such as *tafsir* and *ijtihad* (the rational investigation of sacred texts) may be used, and indeed are being used by gender analysts who aim to bring into practice the social justice they insist the Qur'an and other religious sources guarantee. As mentioned earlier, American Islamic theologian Amina Wadud has pioneered the use of *tafsir* to enact a gendered analysis of the Qur'an.[20]

PUTTING GENDER INTO ARABIC: ARABIZATION OR ASSIMILATION?

Two strategies have been adopted for expressing gender in the Arabic language: Arabization (by which is meant finding a term in Arabic to signify gender) and assimilation (as a loan word). With Arabization, gender is more immediately linguistically domesticated or "naturalized" (*mutajannis* for "naturalized" derives from the same root as *al-jins*). With assimilation the alien origins of the term are more directly signaled or apparent, and the "naturalization" process is longer. In some instances, prestige attaches to the assimilation of foreign words; in other cases, the "foreignness" of a foreign loan word can be delegitimizing. In the case of technological terms, "foreignness" or "Westernness" is valued, but when it comes to concepts, associations with the foreign or Western raise the specter of cultural invasion and illegitimacy. Often names for objects are assimilated before the issue even becomes a question, as with telephone (the term invented in Arabic, *hatif*, never took off, and indeed is seen as silly by those who even know of the word, which is now virtually extinct), mobile telephone or cell phone, television, computer, fax, and the like. Often terms for concepts are Arabized, such as *niswiyya* (feminism), *abawiyya* (patriarchy), *jumhuriyya* (republic), and *watan* (nation). It is interesting to note that of all these concepts, *niswiyya* alone is controversial – which indicates that some terms, even if Arabized, raise hackles because of their meanings.

SEEKING AN OPTIMAL WAY TO EXPRESS GENDER IN ARABIC

There are linguistic, cultural, and political dimensions inherent in the question of rendering the term gender in Arabic. I first consider

Arabization. Efforts to Arabize include either finding a term among existing words or coining a neologism. Arabization has generally been the preferred strategy in Egypt, as well as other countries of the Eastern Mediterranean. Gender burst on the scene in Egypt in the 1980s, initially mainly as a development-driven term, and was rendered in Arabic as *naw' al-jins*, literally, a kind (species) of sex. Within the development context the term *naw' al-jins* was rejected at the local level, not only but especially in rural areas, as development workers, both male and female, observed at first hand. Local recipients of "gender training" were quick to grasp the significance and analytical use of gender, development trainers observed, but balked at the term *naw' al-jins* because it was shameful ('*aib*) to utter the word *al-jins*, or sex, in public, especially in the mixed presence of women and men. This also illustrated how using the word *al-jins* (however modified) causes a pivot around the idea of sex. Before long, *naw' al-jins* was modified, and *naw'* alone came to signify gender. Meanwhile, in some of the other countries of the Eastern Mediterranean, *al-jins al-ijtima'i* (literally, social sex) came into circulation.

There are serious problems with both *naw' al-jins* and *naw'*. The term *naw' al-jins* seems to sustain the fusion, or better the confusion of (biological) sex with (socially constructed) gender. Moreover, as just noted, there are also reasons of cultural propriety for not using the word *jins*. The word *naw'* on its own is also inadequate. It is too vague or generic, and does not supply connotations of the (construction of) masculine or feminine which inhere in the term gender. The English word gender was adopted precisely because it did convey the notion of woman and man as constructed categories, deriving from the grammatical term connoting a linguistic construction of the masculine and feminine. There has been widespread dissatisfaction with both *naw' al-jins* and *naw'*, while the term *al-jins al-ijtima'i* does not eliminate the problems associated with the word *al-jins*, and using *al-ijtima'i* (social) gives rise to other complications.

Fabricating a neologism, the other mode of Arabizing, has also been tried. This was attempted more than a decade after the earlier terms had been in circulation. The *Journal of Comparative Poetics: Alif*, a publication of the American University in Cairo, announced in 1999 (issue 19) that "after lengthy discussions with linguists, critics and poets" it had opted for coining a new word for gender in Arabic. *Alif* proposed the term *janusa*. The journal explains:

While the biological factor is present in gender, the term is not biolog-ical in the first place, but cultural. Thus, we rendered gender (the col-lective formalization of the image, status, tasks, potential rights and responsibilities of males and females in a given culture at a certain his-torical moment) in Arabic in the neologism *janusa* which corresponds morphologically to *unutha* (femininity) and *dhikura* (masculinity). *Janusa* (gender) incorporates notions of the masculine and the femi-nine as they are perceived in a given time and place, with all the ideo-logical twists and politics that such a construction and vision imply.[21]

The term *janusa*, however, sustains the problems associated with *al-jins* as sex, even though, as *Alif* itself iterates, there are a range of meanings associated with different morphological forms deriving from the stem *jns*. While *janusa* has been used in some translations from English into Arabic, it is still too early to determine whether it will enter into wide usage. [Since this was written five years ago *janusa* has not passed into broad use.] Many Arabic speakers I have talked with find it jarring (as loan words are often accused of being) and con-fusing, perhaps the more so because it is "Arabic" yet strange.

The other strategy for solving the linguistic problem is opting for a straightforward loan word, thus the phonetic rendering of gender in Arabic as *al-jandar*. This has been the preferred mode in Yemen. *Al-jandar* entered Arabic as part of academic discourse at the ERWSC at the University of San'a', as already noted. In 1997, when the Women's Studies Center invited me to teach an introduction to women's stud-ies, the issue of how to express gender in Arabic arose immediately. In order for students to be able to access the debates and research on gen-der in English it was decided that core courses would be taught in English, with simultaneous translation. I taught the course in English and the Center director, Raufa Hassan, translated and provided Yemeni examples by way of local contextualization. After careful con-sideration and lengthy discussion, it was agreed that gender was best rendered simply as a loan word, hence *al-jandar*.[22] The word first entered the academic discourse orally, and very quickly passed into broader conversational use in society.

In academic women's studies, as with earlier experience in dis-cussing and using "gender" in the field of development, there was a quick grasp of the analytic power of the new construct. The term *al-jandar* itself was also embraced with alacrity and ease. It avoided socially objectionable and analytically confusing associations with *al-jins*, making clear the distinction between gender as cultural construction and sex as biology. *Al-jandar* slipped so smoothly into Arabic that before long students could be heard using the word in their everyday Arabic.

In January 1999 the ERWSC ran a Gender Terminology Workshop, inviting participants from several Arab countries to discuss ways of expressing a range of words and phrases used in women's studies and gender studies. There was considerable debate on how to express gender in Arabic. Many views were aired, but no consensus was reached. In any case, whatever the roles of specialists or the élite in proposing terms, ultimately, it is only through wider usage that a term passes into the vernacular.

ARABIZATION CUM ASSIMILATION

The experiences just cited of finding and using a word for gender in Arabic are efforts made from within arabophone society. There has also been an attempt from beyond, notably through the United Nations. This is part of a larger effort to standardize vocabulary in Arabic as one of the official languages of the UN, in which there are more than twenty participating arabophone nations. A look at a UN handbook of gender terms reveals a vacillation between rendering gender in Arabic as *al-jandar* and *naw'*. This is reflected in the title of part one of the handbook: *al-Jandar-al-naw' al-ijtima'i* (the title alone indicating a lack of consensus concerning terminology.) In the list of terms, however, gender appears simply as *al-jandar*. Yet, gender awareness (or consciousness) is *al-wa'i bil-naw'* (a kind of awareness). Gender goals are *ahdaf al-jandar*. Gender blindness is *al-'ama al-naw'* (a kind of blindness). Gender impacts is *athar al-jandar*. Gender analysis is *al-tahlil al-naw'*. One of the odder terms is *al-musawwa bain al-naw'*, literally "equality between kind," by which is meant gender equality. The UN handbook reflects at once the lack of consensus about gender and related terms and an attempt to standardize gender terminology in the development field.

GENDER MORPHOLOGY IN ARABIC

The morphological structure of Arabic aided the easy passage of *al-jandar* into the language, as the word produced the quadriliteral root *jndr,* This made possible multiple linguistic configurations. I give examples of this in the following section. I would like to point out, however, that there exist in the Arabic language two words built around the root *jndr.* These are the verb *jandara,* meaning to smooth or polish, and the noun *jandara,* a wooden device for smoothing cloth, also used for the later ironing device called a mangle. However, these words are by now archaic. (It is also likely that they are loans from either Farsi or Urdu.) Most people would probably only discover them, as this author has done (and the *Alif* group did), by resorting to dictionaries to discover if any words with the root *jndr* existed.

One of the reasons *Alif* opted for the word *janusa* was, in their words, because it "corresponds morphologically to *unutha* (femininity) and *dhikura* (masculinity)." But how does this assist the morphological manipulation of *janusa,* or its ability to spawn other forms around a core meaning? The stem of *janusa, jns,* moreover, constitutes a return to *al-jins* and the associations with sex. Moreover, verbs (in different forms) built up from the stem *jns* with their own established meanings already exist. The terms *naw' al-jins* and *jins al-ijtima'i* clearly preclude morphological exploits.

AL-JANDAR BECOMES A HOUSEHOLD WORD

Terms enter the vernacular by various routes and at different speeds. Some enter slowly and discreetly. Others burst on the wider scene by a sensationalist route, as happened with *al-jandar* in Yemen. I recount the Yemeni experience to illustrate the volatile trajectory of a new term.

I mentioned earlier that it has been in the context of academic and intellectual work that gender has been most threatening in the Arab world. In some instances there have been nationalist or culturalist outcries against "gender" as constituting some kind of alien invasion, an intrusion of the unwanted, the unnecessary, and the actually or potentially disruptive. If gender analysis is about opening up new potentials for women and for men, for understandings and practices of their rights, it has fundamental implications for the project of democracy, and with it the potential for disturbing hegemonic power arrangements. When confined to development, with the economic and technical aid this brings, governments not only view gender as unthreatening, but actively welcome it in the context of development aid – as long as it is controlled and monitored by the government.

As an intellectual and academic enterprise, gender interrogates and analyzes cultural assumptions and practices. Although gender analysis may be put to conservative ends as well as more progressive uses, enabling people to question and debate "fundamental cultural issues" can be seen by many in the state and society as a politically and culturally subversive enterprise. It is with these observations that I proceed with the "gender journey" in Yemen.

In Yemen in the fall of 1999 a vicious campaign pivoting around gender/*al-jandar* was mounted against the ERWSC at the University of San'a', which soon led to the closure of the center. The specific occasion for the hostile attack (the most virulent and widespread, but not the first) was the highly public and successful International Conference on Challenges for Women's Studies in the Twenty-First Century organized by ERWSC and under the sponsorship of the president of Yemen. The conference, on 9–14 September, occurred three weeks before the holding of national presidential elections. There was simultaneous translation of all sessions in three languages: Arabic, English, and French. The sessions, moreover, appeared live on the web. The Islamist Islah Party, which was the weak partner in a coalition with the ruling A-Mu'tamar Party, seized the moment by attacking the conference, ERWSC, its organizer, and, by implication, its sponsor, the president of Yemen. The Islahis struck at the ruling party in the run-up to the national elections, in an effort to show that they controlled the street and to make a show of concern about national culture and morality, which they took it upon themselves to defend. They were able to openly attack ERWSC in a way they could not attack the ruling party. The Islahis struck a direct blow at a successfully growing and rapidly expanding site of free intellectual inquiry at San'a' University that was steadily attracting increasing numbers of students, and indirectly struck a blow at the ruling party. National party politics play out intensely on university campuses in Yemen, as elsewhere in the Arab world. While the Islah Party had gained significant support among students in various disciplinary departments, most of the faculty and students at the Women's Studies Center remained aloof from partisan politics; meanwhile the center was attracting increasing numbers of students.

The war cry in this game of high-stakes national politics was *al-jandar*, which was attacked as a way to spread alarm in society – and, in the process, to smear the ruling party and discredit ERWSC. Detractors reduced *al-jandar* to *al-jins* – and, moreover, illicit forms of sex as defined by Islam – as they intensified their attack upon ERWSC. While the frenzied attention paid to gender brought ERWSC to a halt, gender components of internationally-supported development projects remained unscathed. (It might be added that ERWSC was heavily supported by aid from the Netherlands, but this was not an ordinary development project.)

In September 1999 it was put about that gender was a foreign evil that ERWSC had helped unleash against the local culture.[23] Literate and illiterate audiences alike were targeted. This was done by means of sermons, first from mosques in San'a' and soon from *minbar*s (pulpits) throughout the country. Tape cassettes of the sermons were sold in the streets. Cassettes, which are widely available in Yemen, have tremendous power to deliver messages to widespread audiences. Anthropologist Flagg Miller, who has studied "cassette culture" in Yemen, says: "In their sensitivity to local sound-scapes, they [cassettes] can amplify chords that are potentially fractious."[24] Meanwhile, scathing attacks were escalating in the press. Rashad al-Shara'bi published an article entitled "'al-Jandar' haqiqa wa al-khatar!" ("Gender": the truth and the danger) in the newspaper *al-'Asima* (17 October 1999) warning that "genderists" (*al-janadira*) had arrived in San'a'. These genderists were a disruptive force, out "to change the basic social order under the pretext of educating us." Standard forms of attack were to brand something as being against Islam, culture, traditions, and the nation. 'Abd al-Rahman Bafaddal, an Islahi political leader, insisted in the *Yemen Times* in October 1999 (issue 14, 4–10 October) that gender has "no place in our culture or language" and, moreover, "insults our constitution, our religion, and our culture."

Zaid bin 'Ali al-Shami wrote in the Islahi paper *al-Sahwa* (14 October 1999):

> It [gender] means making the human being one by erasing the differences and barriers between males and females in order to give women equality with men. Disciples of gender (*ansar al-jandar*) are out to deform nature [by issuing] an invitation for marriage between men and men, and women and women ... Those who demand to erase the differences between males and females despise the woman and so they want to transform her into a man. Moreover, to achieve equality they want men to become women.

Muhammad al-Khamisi wrote in *al-Sahwa* (14 October 1999):

> Philosophers of gender (*falasafit al-jandar*) are spreading immoral-
> ity, corruption, and harm to the family ... They advocate deviant sex-
> ual behavior: adultery, homosexuality, and lesbianism. They want to
> destroy the legal marriage contract between the woman and the man,
> which includes rights, duties, and responsibilities. How can this term
> be spread in academic centers in the name of knowledge in a country
> of faith and wisdom?

In their zeal to discredit gender, writers and speakers engaged in
imaginative morphological exploits of the root *jndr*. Not only did
they use the term *al-jandar* (gender), but they invented *jandara* (genderism), *jandari* (male genderist), *jandariyya* (female genderist), and
janadira (collective plural for genderists). Verbs included:
jandara/ujandiru (to gender) and *tajandara/yatajandaru* (to make
into a genderist). There was also the adverb *jandariyyan* (genderisti-
cally). With the exception of the words "gender" and "to gender,"
none of the above-mentioned words exist in English. Yemeni Arabic
thus bequeaths to the anglophone lexicon the reverse loan words genderist, genderism, and genderistic, enriching the gender vocabulary
in English.

From September 1999 through the first several months of 2000 an
impressive repetoire of phrases surfaced in the Arabic press in Yemen.
These included: *ansar al-jandar* (disciples of gender); *ahl al-jandar*
(people of gender); *thaqafa jandariyya* (gender culture); *al-qada'iyya
al-jandariyya* (gender issues); *al-wa'i al-jandari* (gender consciousness); *mustaqbal jandari* (gender future); *quwwa jandariyat al-
tarikhhiyya* (historical gender power); and even *aja'ib jandariyya*
(gender wonders). One person wrote that the genderists even go so far
as "to gender her (Balqis)" ([an] *yujandiruha*), although what was
meant by this was not clear. In these phrases and examples of the morphological range above there could hardly be a more convincing display of how "naturally" *al-jandar* slips into dynamic use in Arabic.

The demonization campaign put gender on the lexical map in
Yemen, firmly securing its place in the vernacular. *Al-jandar* suddenly and tumultuously became a household word, however negatively defined. Yet, politicization – that is, hyper-politicization – of
al-jandar gave rise to doubts and suspicions. I observed this during
my ordinary movements in San'a' in the months following the crisis,
when people discreetly raised questions about the meaning of gender

when they realized I was associated with San'a' University. Whatever its meanings, it appeared that *al-jandar* was there to stay.

This chapter has been the attempt of a historian and a women's studies scholar to reflect, through study and first-hand experience, upon the journeys of gender into Arabic. I think it is instructive to chart journeys of ideas and words as they are in progress and to note the contexts of the debates and politics surrounding these flows.

* * *

Originally published in *Langues and Linguistique: Revue Internationale de Linguistique*, special issue on Language and Gender in the Arab World, ed. Margot Badran, Fatima Sadiqi, and Linda Stump al-Rashidi, 9 (2002: Fes, Morocco).

NOTES

1. In Edward Said, *The Word, the Text, and the Critic* (Cambridge, Mass.: Harvard University Press, 1983). After finalizing my book, including my 2002 work, I was told that the following article was scheduled to appear in *JMEWS*: Samia Mehrez, "Translating Gender," *Journal of Middle East Women's Studies*, 3, 1 (2006), pp. 106–127.

2. A good account of the history of women's studies in the United States is Marilyn Jacoby Boxer, *When Women Ask the Questions: Creating Women's Studies in America* (Baltimore: Johns Hopkins University Press, 1998). On gender studies and religion see Janet R. Jakobsen and Ann Pellegrini, "Gender Studies," in Serenity Young (ed.), *Encyclopedia of Women and World Religions*, 2 vols. (New York: Macmillan, 2000), vol. 1, pp. 365–366.

3. See Kwok Pui-Lan, "Liberation Theologies," in Young (ed.), *Encyclopedia of Women and World Religions*, vol. 1, pp. 591–593.

4. See Joan Scott, "Gender: A Useful Category of Historical Analysis," *American Historical Review*, 91, 5 (December 1986).

5. For a recapitulation of gender debates see Linda Nicholson, "Gender," in A. Jagger and I. Young (eds.), *Blackwell Companions to Philosophy: A Companion to Feminist Philosophy* (Oxford: Blackwell, 1998), pp. 289–297. For a recent interrogation of sex and gender as analytical categories see Tina Chanter, "Gender Aporias," *Signs*, 25, 4 (2000), pp. 1237–1241.

6. See, for example, Chandra Talpade Mohanty, Ann Russo, and Lourdes Torres (eds.), *Third World Women and the Politics of Feminism* (Bloomington: Indiana University Press, 1991).

7. Women's studies in the United States focusing on Middle Eastern societies was created by both women from the region and Western women. For an early account see Margot Badran, "The Institutionalization of Middle East Women's Studies in the United States," *MESA Bulletin*, 22 (1988), pp. 9–18; and for a more

recent assessment see Simona Sharoni, "Women and Gender in Middle East Studies: Trends, Prospects and Challenges," *Middle East Report* (October–December 2000).

8. For what I have called "public women's studies" located within NGOs there has been intense, and indeed acrimonious, debate over the issue of accepting foreign funding.

9. A women's studies research center was set up at the University of Aden in the late 1990s, but it does not engage in teaching.

10. I would like to stress the analytical distinction between thinking and writing in gendered terms without the awareness of "gender" and theorizing "gender" as a mode of analysis. Many, whether the religiously oriented or secularists, use gender categories without being aware of "gender" as an explicit mode of analysis. See Miriam Cooke, "Gender in Arabic Literature," in *The Oxford Encyclopedia of the Modern Islamic World* (New York: Oxford University Press, 1995), vol. 1, pp. 103–105.

11. I have explored this in "Towards Islamic Feminisms: A Look at the Middle East," in Asma Afsaruddin (ed.), *Hermeneutics and Honor: Negotiating Female "Public" Space in Islamic/ate Societies* (Cambridge, Mass.: Harvard University Press, 2000), pp. 159–188 and chapter 9 in this volume; and "Locating Feminisms: The Collapse of Secular and Religious Discourses, a Selective Look at the Mashriq," in Fatima Sadiqi et al. (eds.), *Mouvements féministes: origines et orientations* (Fes: Centre d'Etudes et de Recherches sur la Femme, Université Sidi Mohamed Ben Abdellah, 2000), pp. 73–88.

12. Zainab Radwan, *Bahth zahirat al-hijab bain al-jami'iyyat* (A study of the phenomenon of the veil among university women, Cairo: National Centre for Sociological and Criminological Research, 1982).

13. Fatima Mernissi, *Harem politique* (Paris: Albin Michel, 1987), trans. Mary Jo Lakeland and published in the United Kingdom as *Women and Islam: An Historical and Theological Enquiry* (Oxford: Blackwell, 1991) and in the United States as *The Veil and the Male Elite* (Reading, Mass: Addison-Wesley, 1991).

14. Amina Wadud, *Qur'an and Woman: Rereading the Sacred Text from a Woman's Perspective* (New York: Oxford University Press, 1999); an earlier edition was published in 1992 in Kuala Lumpur. See also Amina Wadud, *Inside the Gender Jihad: Women's Reform in Islam* (Oxford: Oneworld, 2007).

15. I would like to thank Ahmad Mukhtar Umar, a specialist in the history of the Arabic language, Professor Emeritus, Dar al-'Ulum, Cairo University, for his information and insights concerning the word *al-jins*.

16. This is similar to the Hebrew *goyim* (literally, "nations") for pagans. I wish to thank Syriac scholar Joseph Phillip Amar for sharing his knowledge of Syriac with me.

17. See, for example, *Dictionnaire Arabe–Francais–Anglais (Langue classique et moderne): Arabic–French–English Dictionary*, compiled by Regius Blachère, Moustafa Chouemi, and Claude Denizeau (Paris: G.-P. Maisonneuve et Larose, 1967), vol. 3, fascicule 28, pp. 1782–1788.

18. *Assas al-Balagha*, 2 vols. (Cairo: Dar al-Kutub, 1972), vol. 1, p. 138.

19. 15 In 2002, the year this article first appeared, I published "Gender in the Qur'an," in Jane McAuliffe (ed.), *Encyclopedia of the Qur'an* (Leiden: Brill, 2002), vol. 2. Also in 2002 Asma Barlas published *"Believing Women" in Islam: Unreading Patriarchal Interpretations of the Qur'an*. A new gender-sensitive

translation of the Qur'an by Laleh Bakhtiar was published by Kazi Publications in Chicago in 2007.

20. See her *Qur'an and Woman*. I discuss her work in "Islamic Feminism: What's in a Name?" and "Islamic Feminism on the Move," chapters 10 and 14 respectively of this volume. Vincent Cornell, in "The Qur'an as Scripture," *Oxford Encyclopedia of the Modern Islamic World*, vol. 3, pp. 387–394, gives a cogent brief account of her gender analysis on p. 392.

21. Quotation from the English version of the introduction, entitled "Gender and Knowledge: Contribution of Gender Perspectives to Intellectual Formations," *Alif: Journal of Comparative Poetics*, 19 (Cairo, 1999), pp. 6–7, on p. 6. The Arabic introduction is titled "al-Janusa wa al-ma'rifa siyakha al-ma'arif bain al-itanith wa al-takhkir," pp. 6–7. The journal contains articles published in Arabic and English; each of the two sections have their own pagination.

22. I taught at ERWSC first in 1997, and also taught and helped develop the core courses in gender theory and methodology for the diploma and master's degree students, and supervised Ph.D. students as a Fulbright lecturer at the University of San'a' from 1998 to 2000. The courses included Introduction to Women's Studies, Gender Research Methodology, Advanced Gender Research Methodology, and Historical Research Methodologies.

23. I have recounted this in "Gender: Meanings, Uses, and Discourses in Post-Unification Yemen," which I gave as a public lecture in June 2000 at the American Institute for Yemeni Studies and which was simultaneously read in Arabic ("al-Jandar: ma'naha wa istikhdamatiha wa khitabatiha fi al-yaman b'ad al-wihda") as a public rebuttal and answer to the scurrilous attacks upon ERWSC, its director, various faculty and visiting scholars, and the demonization of the concept "gender." On this occasion heavy armed security was provided. The lecture was subsequently published in three parts by the *Yemen Times*: 19–25 June, 26 June–2 July, and 3–9 July 2000. I left the Arabic version to be published after my departure. The English version was also circulated on the web by NAD (Niswa' and Development). At the Emerging Democracies Forum held the previous June in San'a' under the sponsorship of the president of Yemen in which "gender" was prominent, and which was attended by high-level Islahis, there was no public attack mounted, although Islahi views on "gender" were made known in some of the workshops.

24. W. Flagg Miller, "Convention (Ittiba') or Invention (Ibtida')? Islamist Cassettes and Tradition in Yemen," paper presented at the American Anthropology Association conference, San Francisco, 2000.

Part II

Muslim World – Late Twentieth and
Early Twenty-First Centuries:
Widening Circles, New Directions

9

TOWARD ISLAMIC FEMINISMS: A LOOK AT THE MIDDLE EAST

Muslim women's engagements with modernity in its diverse forms from the nineteenth to the late twentieth centuries have both produced and been driven by new forms of consciousness about gender that surfaced at various moments. The basic argument of this chapter is that Muslim women's feminisms in the Middle East have emerged in the context of encounters with modernity, and that Islam has been implicated in the construction of these feminisms, as have notions of transnationality. This chapter considers how women, through their own reinterpretations of religion, culture, and modernity, informed by experience and referenced by sacred scripture, have constituted their own subjectivity within transnational contexts.[1]

Feminism as a new consciousness of gender and women's subordination first emerged among the upper and middle classes in the crannies of unevenly gendered modernity at different moments in various countries of the Middle East. Feminism, especially in stages of open activism, constituted uncomfortable challenges to masculinist scrambles to control the construction of modernity – its processes and its class and gender privileges. Men of the middle and upper classes would "get to modernity first," control the space, transfer power and privileges, and, in short, define (a patriarchal) modernity.[2] It has often been argued that women were made to constitute or preserve "the traditional" at moments when customary ways were in danger of disappearing. I think it was not so much that women should act as symbols of an endangered old order so that men could be less (culturally) anxiously "modern" as that women must not compete for the benefits of modernity and define it in egalitarian terms.

In the late nineteenth and twentieth centuries, pioneering women constructed new feminisms out of attempts to engage more fully with modernity, appropriating the discourses of Islamic modernism and secular nationalism.[3] In the final third of the twentieth century some women, as recent beneficiaries of, or aspirants to, a new modernity, are questioning mainstream masculinist positions and developing a "feminist" consciousness from within Islamist movements. Historically, women have both created their own independent movements and have participated in male-dominated movements as they critiqued them and also subverted them in certain ways. This gives rise to certain analytical challenges. How do we talk about women's activism within independent feminist movements without exaggerating the notion of free agency?[4] How do we talk about women's agency as "feminists" within masculinist movements without underestimating the possibilities of their independent agency?

Coloring projects and processes of modernity in Middle Eastern societies has been the chiaroscuro – the light and shadow – of the West. In the Middle East, modernity has always been complicated by association with a colonializing and imperialist West, and has played out differently across class and gender lines. The earliest beneficiaries of modernity were the upper strata, and particularly men. Women were both more restricted in their access to the benefits of modernity and more tainted by its Western associations. The uneven gendering of modernity and its implications cast deep shadows on women's modernist discourse, especially their feminist discourse: it was "Western" and therefore non-indigenous. During the colonial and early postcolonial periods, its Western associations implicated feminism as nationally subversive and treasonous.[5] A dichotomy was set up early (by opponents of Islamic modernism within the Muslim Middle East) between Islam and modernity, constructed as an East–West antagonism. This opposition has been sustained not only in certain quarters in Middle Eastern societies but also by Westerners hostile toward or ignorant of Islam.

In the Middle East, Muslim women who claimed a feminist identity did so as one of a number of identities: Muslim, nationalist, etc. There have been other Muslim women who have claimed a single public identity, such as nationalist, socialist, or Islamist, adamantly refusing any other label. While everyone possesses multiple identities, making a particular identity visible or invisible is a political decision. This is often controlled by the dominant discourse, whether it is nationalism, socialism, or Islamism, which makes the articulation of a simultaneous identity a treacherous act. Late nineteenth-century Islamic modernism opened up space for multiple identities, so that one could be, for example, an Islamic reformer, a secular nationalist, and a feminist. Late twentieth-century Islamism – certainly the patriarchal mainstream – is in contention with other identities, especially nationalism and feminism, aiming to subsume the former and to obliterate the latter.

Relations between Muslim women as feminists and Islamists have been uneven. At certain moments, they have been highly polarized, with each viewing the other as implacable adversaries.[6] I think, for example, of second-wave feminists and Islamists in Egypt in the 1970s and 1980s, or of feminist and Islamist women in Algeria or Sudan today. There has also been another pattern of relations between some more open Muslim feminists and Islamist women. This is a tolerant strand that acknowledges some common ground and mutual concerns, fostering space at certain moments for shared struggle. During the period of first-wave feminism in Egypt in the 1930s and 1940s, there were cordial relations between feminist and Islamist women, who shared many goals. Later instances include the following three examples: (1) In the "headscarf debate" in Turkey in the mid-1980s, second-generation feminists supported emergent Islamist women's right to wear *hijab*, in the form of a headscarf, at the university and in other public sites;[7] (2) Yemeni feminist and Islamist women's common activism has promoted women's participation in the 1997 parliamentary elections, with both sets of women using the discourse of Islam to politically mobilize women.[8] Yemeni feminist and Islamist women have also banded together to fight reactionary items in the 1997 draft for a revised personal status code or family law, which, like the existing law, is based on the *shari'a*, or religious legal corpus[9]; (3) the first feminist book fair in Cairo in 1995 displayed books by both feminist and Islamist women, and drew women together in panel discussions across the feminist–Islamist spectrum.[10] Some third-wave Islamists have admitted that there are lessons to be learned from Egyptian feminist history – and even from critical readings of Western feminist literature – in the effort to construct an Islamic theory of women's liberation.[11]

While the nationalist dimension of Muslim women's feminisms has been widely recognized, this has not been true of the Islamic dimension. I argue that the feminisms of most Muslim women have historically been more Islamic than commonly alleged. (First-wave Turkish

feminists have been the major exception to this tendency.) This argument intersects with the notion that plural identities and loyalties are
operative in everyday life, but have often been obscured at the level of
public discourse and in the politics of positioning. In trying to understand Muslim women's feminisms we have to a certain extent been
imprisoned by an inadequate vocabulary. A word for feminist (used
adjectivally) first appeared in Arabic in 1923 in Egypt – but this word,
nisa'iyya, ambiguously connoted either "feminist" or "women's." Its
meaning had to be discerned from the context or from feminists' direct
translations of the Arabic word into French or English. In the early
1990s (in the period leading up to the United Nations women's conference in Beijing in 1995), a new, unequivocal Arabic word for "feminism" began to circulate in Egypt: the word is *niswiyya*. In Turkish and
Persian there are loan words for "feminism." A lack of critical deconstruction of concepts, especially gendered deconstructions, and insuf-
ficient historicization has hampered understanding of Muslim
women's feminisms. Serious debates in public forums have been put
off course by the persistent circulation of disparaging and degrading
stereotypes of feminism (most frequently turning feminist critiques of
masculinist domination into feminism as man-hating projects sowing
discord between genders). Orientalist notions first articulated around
the turn of the twentieth century and echoed later in the century
by mainstream Islamists, both contending that Muslim women
"cannot possibly be feminists," have also skewed discussions.

To demonstrate my arguments about feminist – Islamist juxtapo-
sitions and imbrications I look at the experience of Muslim feminists
in Egypt early in the twentieth century and of Islamist women in
Turkey at the end of the century. I draw on my own historical work on
Egyptian feminism, especially my book *Feminists, Islam, and Nation:
Gender and the Making of Modern Egypt*, and on research on contemporary Islamist women in Turkey by Turkish sociologist Nilüfer Göle,
published in an English translation under the title *The Forbidden
Modern: Civilization and Unveiling* (1996) from the Turkish *Mödern
mahrem: medeniyet ve örtüme* (1991).[12]

Both books reveal strikingly similar gender activist modes, goals,
and strategies. I note how early Egyptian feminist and contemporary
Turkish liberal Islamist discourses both emerged from within the
framework of Islamic movements (early reformist or later resurgent),
in which Muslim women, through revisiting sacred scripture (in
the late nineteenth and early twentieth centuries mainly via men's

reinterpretations, in the final decades through their own direct rein-
tepretation), seek to constitute modern lives for themselves. I discuss
the divergent public identities that both sets of women have assumed,
and their positions within the dominant discourses of their respective
moments.[13] I conclude this comparative reflection with a broader
look at Muslim women's re-visioning of Islam through *ijtihad* (independent investigation of Islamic sacred texts) as part of the global
project in which feminist and Islamist women are engaged today.
Both religiously oriented women and feminist women are rereading
the Qur'an and other religious texts, bringing to bear their own experiences and new critical methodologies to enact readings that are
more meaningful to modern women, such as the work of theologian
Amina Wadud, author of *Qur'an and Woman: Rereading the Sacred
Text from a Woman's Perspective.*[14]

I speculate on the future to encourage thinking of the broader and
longer-term implications of my discussion. I suggest that the new
radical feminism in Muslim societies – and I include diaspora societies – as we begin the twenty-first century will be "Islamic feminism."
My arguments for this are the following:

1. Islam is becoming a paramount cultural and political paradigm.
2. Muslim women, who are more highly educated in greater numbers than ever before, have begun gender-progressive readings of
   Islamic sacred scripture that will achieve – and indeed have
   already achieved – significant "feminist" breakthroughs.
3. Only the language of an "Islamic feminism" can potentially reach
   women of all classes and across urban–rural divides – or, to put it
   slightly differently, the majority of Muslims can associate only
   with a "feminism" that is explicitly "Islamic."
4. Because of increasing globalization and growing Muslim diaspora
   communities, Muslim women who practice Islam and want to
   embrace feminism need an Islamic feminism.
5. The globalized media and technology revolution produces a de-
   centered and denationalized feminism, and connects Muslim
   women both inside and outside predominantly Muslim nations or
   communities with each other.

The conceptual and political location of this "Islamic feminism" will
be a middle space, or independent site, between secular feminism and
masculinist Islamism. I suggest that "Islamic feminists" will come to

acknowledge plural identities, and that "secular feminists" will make more explicit an Islamic dimension of feminism that will link them to other Muslim women as theorists and activists of gender. "Islamic feminists" will acknowledge positionings and linkages beyond those created by religion and cease to shy away from the feminist label; rather, they will acknowledge such an identity. Globalization and diasporization are producing multiple identities and sliding intersections of "feminist" concern that are increasingly hard to deny.[15] I believe that the new radical feminism in Muslim societies – that is, "Islamic feminism" – will play a salient role in (1) the re-visioning of Islam; (2) the constitution of a new modernity in the twenty-first century; and (3) the transformation of feminism itself. Feminism may even get a new name.

Historically, feminism has been – implicitly or explicitly – part of other discourses, such as religious reformist or nationalist discourses. It gendered these discourses in ways that take as central concerns the constructions and positionings of women and their rights, choices, and opportunities. Feminism is a reformative and transformative strategy. Within Judaism and Christianity, feminist reinterpretations of sacred scripture and activisms have refigured the practice of religious ritual, opening up new roles for women as ministers and rabbis and for "unordained" women as leaders of congregational prayer. These "religious feminisms," appearing in Western countries, with a separation of religion and state or at historical moments when secular discourses hold sway, have been more specialized or compartmentalized; they have not occupied center-stage.

As we move toward the close of the twentieth century, the gender-conscious identities of Muslim women – within predominantly Muslim states and societies, in old Muslim minority communities, and in new diasporas – have become increasingly complicated. Muslim women face the conundrum of what to call their gender activism. What is legitimately possible and politically expedient within their diverse ideological and political frameworks? Women's progressive gender activisms across the feminist–Islamist spectrum are blurring as the borders between feminisms and gender-progressive Islamisms are breaking down. Actors and analysts alike face the challenge of how to characterize these gender activisms.[16]

A process is now underway to locate a feminism within a more explicit and strenuous Islamic religious paradigm, but as yet there are no center-stage religious feminisms in Islamic societies. As secularism – in the form of privatization or compartmentalization of religion and in the muting of religious cultural symbols – recedes in Muslim societies, and as Islam becomes the predominant discourse, the new feminism will be a religious feminism. A case in point is Iran, where a new Islamic feminism is becoming increasingly visible.[17]

The notion of an Islamic feminism is an uneasy one. Its constitution and practice are fraught with issues of power, authority, and legitimacy. The feminisms that evolved within Jewish and Christian religious frameworks emerged in Western societies and are seen as internal, "indigenous," or local critiques. Feminisms that evolved later in Muslim societies in postcolonial contexts were discredited in the patriarchal mainstream as Western and a project of cultural colonialism, and therefore were stigmatized as antithetical to Islam.[18] Indigenous patriarchal fear and the penumbra of Western colonialism operated to squeeze out space for feminism as part of Islamic discourse.

In the 1990s, the notion of an Islamic feminism – and, indeed, the term itself – has been surfacing in parts of the Middle East. The term, however, is controversial and not necessarily well thought out, and there is no consensus about its meaning on the part of either advocates or adversaries. Women in Iran who publish a radical paper called *Zanan* are part of what Iranian scholars Afsaneh Najmabadi and Ziba Mir-Hosseini call an emergent Islamic feminist movement.[19] Feride Acar notes the appearance of the term Islamic feminism in the Turkish popular media.[20] Saudi anthropologist Mai Yamani writes that social circumstances in her country have caused "an identifiable strand of Saudi women to make of Islam the vehicle for the expression of feminist tendencies."[21] The term Islamic feminist has occasionally been used by feminist journalists in the Egyptian anglophone press to refer to feminist acts by Islamist women.[22]

ISLAMIC AND ISLAMIST MODERNIST PROJECTS: NEW READINGS OF OLD TEXTS

Egyptian women's turn-of-the-century feminism and Turkish women's end-of-the-century Islamist "gender activism," which some call Islamic feminism, have both emerged out of broad movements of Islamic reform or re-visioning. This involved women "going back" to religious scripture to purge current practices of "deviations," "accretions," and "omissions" through fresh readings of scripture, or *ijtihad.* Such "going back" was an operation of "going forward." Women and men in Egypt, Turkey, and elsewhere have referenced sacred texts in order to engage with modernity (in the sense of new configurations of the social, economic, political, scientific, and technological). Modernity as a process always includes elements of "the before" or "the traditional." It is construed as involving new turns or departures rather than ruptures, and is uneven temporally, spatially, and indeed in the experience of individuals themselves.

It is important to clarify my use of the terms Islamic and Islamist. I employ the term Islamic in two ways: broadly, to signify anything pertaining to Islam; and more specifically, with reference to Islam (as thought and practice) from the late nineteenth century through the second third of the twentieth. I use Islamist as an adjective or noun to refer to manifestations, in the final third of the twentieth century, of "political Islam." The *hijab* (understood to be Islamically-prescribed head cover and modest dress) is a marker of the Islamist woman, but not all women who wear the *hijab* are necessarily Islamist. In Egypt today, for example, there are many women who cover but are not part of the male-led Islamist movements. Many women simply wish to conform to what they understand is a religiously prescribed mode of dress, which has by now become a popular social convention. Göle uses the term "Islamist women" in a very broad sense to include all women who wear *hijab* or "those who cover," as they are often called; these are the first generation of women to take up the new *hijab.*[23]

Islamic modernism's core idea and analytical tool is *ijtihad.* The pioneering proponent of this early movement of Islamic reform, in late nineteenth-century Egypt, was Muhammad 'Abduh, a religious scholar and later Mufti of Egypt.[24] This new movement attempted to ease the way for Egyptian Muslims (especially the more economically advantaged) to reckon with modernity – to be Muslim and modern. Islamic modernism also paved the way for secularism or an increasing privatization of religion and individually interpreted religion. In Egypt, although most law was removed from the direct jurisdiction of Islam, personal status (or family) law continued to be based on the *shari'a,* or Islamic jurisprudence. The emergent secular élite of the late nineteenth and early twentieth centuries, who welcomed a tempering of the hold of institutionalized religion, viewed this revisionist Islam as a positive, forward-looking, modernist project. The

British colonial authorities saw Islamic reform as tempering Muslims themselves, and thus serving the purposes of colonial rule.[25] It would be what was seen as "accommodationist" rather than a more "independent" Islamic reformist move that would prompt late twentieth-century Islamists to reject the 'Abduh-ian modernist project. Islamic modernism, however, provided a basis for a consolidation of a new nation-state with equal room for all Egyptians, irrespective of religion. Secular progressives of the day thus saw 'Abduh's modernist project as liberatory. Women's "feminist consciousness," which had first emerged out of the jolt of contradictory contacts with modernity, took shape as a "feminist" version of Islamic modernism at the end of the nineteenth and beginning of the twentieth century. The shadows that fell on Islamic modernism also fell on women's feminism – indeed, they were long shadows, casting a darkness on feminism to this day.

The current Islamic revisionist project in Turkey, emerging in a highly-secularized landscape, is widely seen as an ominous move backward. Atatürk, distancing himself from the previous religiously founded Ottoman imperial state and its defunct multiethnic empire, resolved to build a modern and secular nation-state in the 1920s and 1930s. He explicitly aligned modernization with Westernization, evacuating religion wholesale from his construction of modernity. A fully secular constitution or civil code (of 1926, based on a Swiss model) was imposed from on high, bringing both public and private (societal and family) spheres under the purview of secular state law. Unveiling ("de-hijabicization") was imposed by the state. Women's new dress and new lives became symbols of state-imposed Westernized modernity. The state-led unveiling, new educational and work opportunities for women, and political rights dispensed from on high constituted what has been called state feminism. (Many feminists, however, consider the notion of a state feminism to be an oxymoron). The Kemalist state did not allow for an independent women's movement. When women tried to form an autonomous feminist organization they were prevented by the state.[26] This is not to say, however, that élite women did not benefit from the "rights" bestowed on them.[27] This rigorous state-led rupture with Islamic culture took hold mainly among the urban élite – the designated beneficiaries of the secularized, Westernized modernity in whose everyday lives new transformations played out. The more modest strata and provincial and rural populace were left out of the circumference of the new Westernized modernity. For them Islamic culture remained alive.

It has been argued that the assault on religious culture, and the élitist scripting of Kemalism, planted the seeds for an eventual populist resurgence of Islam among the unsecularized non-élite, mainly from the Anatolian provinces, who did not benefit socially or economically from republican modernization. The populist reappropriation of religion, by women and men alike, half a century later, constituted an attack on the legacy of Kemalist modernity with its fervent secularism and exuberant Westernicity. Such a "return" to Islam and its scriptures for a reaffirmation of cultural legitimacy and renewed identity is seen by Kemalist loyalists in Turkey and anxious "Islam-watchers" in the West as retrogressive.[28] There are analysts, such as Nilüfer Göle, Yeşim Arat, and other social scientists, for example, who see in the Islamist movement elements of a forward-looking modernist project: a populist attempt to redefine modernity in Islamic terms.[29]

GENDERING ISLAMIC MODERNIST PROJECTS: EARLY TWENTIETH-CENTURY EGYPTIAN FEMINISTS (SECULAR AND ISLAMIC)

In *Feminists, Islam, and Nation* I demonstrated how Muslim Egyptian women's reinterpretation of Islam (influenced by the example of the Muslim reformer Muhammad 'Abduh) paved the way for cloistered middle- and upper-class women to gain access to public space, to remove the veils from their faces, to claim a public voice, and to demand educational, work, and political rights. Such maneuvers and claims, legitimized by new readings of Islam, or women's *ijtihad*, constituted an explicit feminist project through which women aimed to constitute themselves as modern citizens in a modern state and society – and, indeed, to help construct the new state and society itself. (If Muslim women in Egypt located their feminism firmly within the parameters of their Islamic religion, Coptic feminists in Egypt likewise evoked a religious justification within their own Christian tradition for the feminist activism they shared with Muslim women. However, there was no Christian reform movement; thus Coptic women's religious arguments for feminist activism remained at a general rhetorical level.)

There was another discourse at work during the originary moment of feminism in Egypt, which only slightly postdated the emergence of Islamic modernism: this was the discourse of secular nationalism. Following British colonial occupation in 1882, women and men in Egypt created a nationalist movement to expel the British from Egyptian soil. Egyptians constructed "the nation" in territorial terms, grounded in the equality of Muslims and Copts as citizens and common inhabitants of the land. This replaced the older construction of "nation" along religious and ethnic lines (the *millet* system) under the Ottomans (under whose loose jurisdiction Egypt remained until 1914). This nationalism was called secular nationalism, expressing another dimension of the term secular – inclusivity of persons of different religions as citizens with equal rights. At the same time, this construction of the secular provided space for religious difference – an equality in difference: the equal rights of Egyptian citizens to be different in religion and to be governed or regulated communally in matters of religion. (It is interesting to note that the Arabic for "secularism" [*'alamaniyya* or *'almaniyya*] comes from the word for "world" [*'alam*], while "secular" in Latin-based languages comes from the Latin word for "age" [*saeculum*]. The Arabic term has a spatial signification, while the Latin has a temporal one; this suggests two different constructions of the term and a need to consider the possibility of salient differences between the two terms.)

Egyptian women gendered the nationalist discourse; furthermore, as Muslims, they wove it into their gendered discourse of Islamic modernism. Muslim women who, as feminists and as women, struggled to be modern held Islamic modernism and secular nationalism together in interactive tension in the colonial period and in the early postcolonial era, preserving this often torturous link to this day.[30] Meanwhile, secular nationalist men moved farther down the secular road, abandoning religion to the purview of the *'ulama* (the religious scholars).[31]

Egyptian women's feminism has been called secular to signify the inclusion of Muslims and Copts within its circumference. This kind of secularism mirrored the secularism of (secular) nationalism that articulated the equality of Muslims and Copts as citizens in the land of Egypt. Like secular nationalism, progressive women's articulation of secularism did not connote an evacuation of religion from the feminist project, but accorded space to religious difference. Secular nationalist men, with their eyes most fixed on the politics of the public arena, relegated religion to the sidelines and the sphere that it still controlled – the "private" sphere, where personal status codes (with separate codes for Muslims and Christians) regulated family life. While secular nationalist men saw this in general as politically expedient and as advantageous to themselves as men, as secular nation-state builders, and as family patriarchs, (secular) feminist women could not ignore religion and the "private" sphere, which was a site of inequality or inequity – and a location where a continued application of premodern masculinist interpretation of religion was condoned. The preservation of a premodern masculinist hegemony in the "modern era" created conflictual everyday lives for women, thwarting their abilities to access the full rights of modern citizens in the public arena that as Egyptians was their due under the constitution. Patriarchal authorities in families could, and did, control women's public access.

As feminists, Muslim Egyptian women operated simultaneously to modernize the state and society (the public sphere) and to modernize the family (the private sphere) and, in so doing, functioned both as secular feminists and as Islamic feminists. Secular feminists operationalized "secularism" in the public sphere by fighting for the rights of all citizens, keeping a central (but not exclusive) focus trained on gender, irrespective of religious affiliation. Secular feminists operationalized "secularism" in the private sphere, by upholding religious difference and acknowledging the importance of religion and, as Muslims, the need to push Islamic reformist inquiry forward into implementation. Muslim Egyptian women's feminism, to repeat, was at once a "secular feminism," in the sense of being inclusive of both Muslims and Christians and in according space to a common struggle of Egyptian women to enjoy their equal rights as citizens, as well as an "Islamic feminism" that placed Islamic reform and modernism at the center of the debates around the regulation of personal status laws, referencing sacred texts in their project to modernize the legal regulation of the family.

In the colonial (1882–1922) and quasi-postcolonial (1922–1956) periods, Egyptian (secular) nationalism prevailed as the paramount public discourse but never eradicated Islamic discourse. Muslim women as feminists – who continued to identify with and practice their religion – called themselves simply feminists, assuming their affiliation with and upholding of Islam to be self-evident and not in need of public declaration. Women in the late nineteenth and early twentieth centuries could be Muslim, modern, and secular.

GENDERING ISLAMIST MODERNIST PROJECTS:
TWENTIETH-CENTURY TURKISH GENDER ACTIVISTS
(ISLAMIC AND FEMINIST)

Unlike in Egypt, where women's secular feminist activism in the early twentieth century, which explicitly called itself "feminist," sprang from the ground prepared by the Islamic modernist movement but not directly from within the movement itself, a women's gender-sensitive discourse surfaced from within the Islamist movement in Turkey in the 1980s and 1990s.[32] Contemporary Turkish "gender activists," who do not identify themselves explicitly as feminists, surfaced from within the Islamist movement itself.

The new Islamist women in Turkey, according to Göle's research in the second half of the 1980s, initially sprang from that segment of society that had not profited from the Kemalist secularized Westernized modernity. They had been virtually consigned to a space beyond the pale of this version of modernity, remaining within the circumference of Islamic culture represented in the Kemalist discourse as "backward."[33] Meanwhile, second-wave feminists also made their appearance on the scene in the 1980s; they were the daughters of the élite Kemalist women whose identity and feminism had been largely designed and delivered by the state, although women welcomed the new opportunities opened to them. These new feminists were direct heirs of a prepackaged version of modernity and "state feminism," which had curtailed women's agency and cut off these élite women from their Islamic heritage and from the Turkish majority. Kemalist "state feminism" masked the preservation of salient aspects of patriarchal culture hidden under the guise of a so-called progressive Western veneer. It particularly galled this new generation to discover that male headship of the family was inscribed in the Turkish civil code, something previously obscured.[34]

Both of these groups of women of the new generation have reacted against the project of modernity and of state feminism imposed from on high. Such rejection constituted women's moves to take the initiative in constructing their own identities and shaping their everyday lives. New feminists and Islamist women alike were well aware that women's bodies had been sites for signaling Kemalist modernity: the unveiled woman was the symbol of the secular, Westernized modern nation. The new generation made their own bodies sites of opposition to the Kemalist legacy. Islamist women who took up the *hijab*, in the form of a headscarf, signaled an Islamic modernity through the new symbolism of the veiled body. Feminist women, in defense of their bodies, meanwhile rallied against the public harassment and domestic violence to which women of all classes were subjected. The defense of the body, problems of identity, and insistence on self-agency and deciding their own agendas catapulted two different kinds of women onto the stage of independent activism half a century after the introduction of the Kemalist project.

The new Islamist women (as noted, coming mainly from ordinary families in Anatolian towns and villages or working-class and modest middle-class families in the big cities outside the circumference of the Westernized modernity) surfaced in significant numbers in the 1980s in the large urban universities, where their reappropriation of the veil, in the form of a turban, signaled their existence. These women, among the high achievers at the university, were part of a broader Islamist movement aiming to restore Islam to public primacy. Inspired by new readings of sacred scripture, they articulated an Islamic modernity as a counterpoise to the "Western," secular modernity scripted by Kemalism. Through their political participation in the Islamist movement these new activists projected an Islamic modernity for women. They left behind the private sphere of the home – the *mahrem*, the private, hidden, silent, invisible space, the "traditional" space of women (of the middle and upper strata). *Mödern mahrem*, the Turkish title of Nilüfer Göle's book *The Forbidden Modern*, calls attention to Islamist women's revisioning of conventional gender symbolism. Thus, in Turkey, while Islam was restored to view with the rising Islamist movement, women made themselves publicly visible as Muslims. The two titles seem to display an unresolved tension in an Islamic construction of modernity in Turkey.

Not only were progressive Islamist women important as role models for other women, but their Islamic activism became a path to their own self-reconstruction and practice of agency. Yeşim Arat and Feride Acar, in studying the Islamist women's journals *Kadin ve Aile*, *Bizim Aile*, and *Mektup*, which are closely aligned with men's religious associations, point to contradictory imbrications of the secular and religious in their content.[35] It is not clear to what extent women have editorial control, however, or serve more as conduits for men's gendered Islamist discourse. Along with articulating the standard rhetoric of women's primary roles as wives and mothers, their positioning as believers, and appeals to wear the *hijab*, the journals also encourage women's education, even in gender-mixed settings (the existing gender-integrated schools are a Kemalist legacy, economically unfeasible to dismantle). There is a sprinkling of a rhetoric of women's rights and emancipation in Islam. Noting that Islamist women were assuming agency as editors and writers, Yeşim Arat speculates that "these activities, in due time, might become secularized sources of power for women."[36] It is not unlikely that some women will take the initiative in constructing a more liberatory discourse out of a confused welter of ideas. It might be that Islamist women will use such journals for enunciating a feminism within the discourse of Islam, or eventually create new publications for this purpose.

Göle's study indicates similarities and differences between contemporary Turkish Islamist gender activists and early Egyptian feminists. The recent emergence on the public scene of the newly veiled (*hijab*-ed) Turkish women within the Islamist movement is reminiscent of the emergence of still-veiled (so-called *hijab*-ed but more accurately, *niqab*-ed – that is, "face-covered") Egyptian women on the public scene during the militant stage of the nationalist movement. In both instances women assumed new roles as political activists, learned valuable organizing and oratorical skills, and sought new opportunities in public space. These were both gendered modernist moves.

The arguments for education and work for women that Islamist women in contemporary Turkey advance eerily echo those put forward by the secular feminists at the beginning of the century in Egypt. Progressive Islamist women's rhetoric in Turkey extolling women's roles as mothers also closely reproduces the maternalist rhetoric of early Egyptian feminists articulated within the discourse of Islamic modernism and secular nationalism.[37] For the Egyptian feminists such rhetoric can be seen in part as a preemptive strike by pioneering women who did not want the public carpet pulled from under them on the pretext that they were abandoning their "true religiously ordained" roles. Maternalist rhetoric is freighted with multiple layers of meaning that need to be contextualized. Göle observed that some Islamist women, whether doing *teblig* (spreading the religious message) or working for pay, confronted their husbands about sharing domestic burdens and thereby refigured (functional) maternalism. Early Egyptian feminists were not that radical in their gender activism, and accepted the notion of fuller maternal responsibility in the domestic sphere. But it must be added that these élite women, unlike the Turkish Islamists of more modest circumstances, relied on the domestic labor of other women to free themselves for their new activist forays.

While women are articulating and acting out new roles within the Islamist movement and claiming new rights and opportunities, shored up by scriptural reference, the difficulties women experience, and potential threats, should not be underestimated. Women face the complicated task of helping to restore Islam to cultural prominence; that involves critiquing the "old Islam" (in ways not unlike those of the early Islamic modernists in Egypt, yet in a different context) in order to help create an Islamic modernity, and to gender that modernity. To achieve all of this, they have to manipulate complicated sets of loyalties and engage in complicated gender politics within the Islamist movement itself and *vis-à-vis* secularists.

HIJAB AND MODERNITY

How does *hijab* fit into the discourse of modernity?[38] Contemporary Turkish Islamist women's new appropriation of the *hijab* constitutes a conscious act of religious observance, a reintroduction into the public realm of a symbol of Islamic public identity, and a gendered cultural statement of the right to have a distinctive presence in the collective public polity as Muslims. It is also a (consciously or unconsciously) political statement. Turkish women, it will be observed, took up the *hijab* while already present in the public sphere.

Pioneering Egyptian feminists who entered public space early this century removed what was then called the *hijab* or face covering (*niqab* is the word now used for covering the face) as a symbol of the marginality and public erasure of women of the middle and upper strata but, especially in the early years, they continued to cover their heads. For them, covering the face was not an Islamic requirement but a patriarchal practice justified in the name of Islam. Huda al-Sha'rawi and Saiza Nabarawi announced the start of the feminist movement by a public unveiling of their faces in 1923 to symbolize the rejection of a culture of female segregation and domestic seclusion. Covering their heads only, they "modernized" the *hijab* in keeping with Islamic prescription. While Sha'rawi, like most other élite women, eventually removed her head covering altogether, it is significant that she wore the *hijab*, in the form of covering her head, for her "official" portrait as a feminist leader. It is not so much the *hijab* itself as its contextualization and the discourse around it that announces or suppresses Muslim women's agency and signals modernity or its nemesis. Some third-generation feminist and Islamist women in Egypt have remarked on this "feminist *hijab*."

REFUSING MASCULINIST POLITICS OF POSTPONEMENT

It is often thought that women's "gender activism" within the context of an Islamist movement, whether in Turkey or elsewhere, is a doomed project because women's gender issues will ultimately be subsumed. This is not an unfounded fear. Göle points out that Turkish Islamist activist women operating as "missionaries" advancing the interests of the movement tend to defer solutions to problems that women encounter in their daily lives to the appearance of the future ideal Islamic society.[39] Moreover, in the examples we have of Islamists in the Middle East moving from an oppositional mode to state power, women have been initially heavily controlled – as seen in Iran and Sudan. Egyptian women's active participation in the nationalist movement early in the twentieth century, during which they juggled feminist and nationalist goals, was seen at the time as boding well for an eventual women's liberation. Yet after independence (albeit partial) in 1922, when nationalist men came into power, women's full rights in law and practice were deferred in favor of the building of a new independent nation-state. This was the moment when Egyptian feminists left the masculinist nationalist party (the Wafd) to found their own independent feminist organization and mount a highly visible movement.[40] Gender activists within Islamist states and movements have yet to mount independent movements, although some are making judicious maneuvers.

Ultimately, a liberal discourse advanced by a male mainstream (whose words often do not match their convictions) will not save women, and a conservative discourse articulated by a broad masculinist movement will not doom women.[41] What matters is what women themselves do: their own assertive independent activism. Historically, women have been both seduced by men's liberal discourses and coopted by men's conservative discourses. Women have at different times and places through their gender activisms tried to take charge of their own destinies. Both nationalist and Islamist (mainstream) discourses have de-legitimized feminism – and, especially, independent, organized feminist activisms.

GENDERED *IJTIHAD*: THE WEB OF FEMINISM AND ISLAM

Ijtihad is a methodology which feminist and Islamist women have used to reread the Qur'an and other religious texts to expose patriarchal interpretations and to advance more gender-just understandings of Islam. Early in the twentieth century, women operated within colonial contexts, early postcolonial contexts, in the case of Turkey during the collapse of the Ottoman empire, and in ascendant secular nationalist contexts. Today women are operating within late postcolonial (and late post-Ottoman period) and postmodern contexts at a time when political Islam is ascendant. In both the early and late twentieth century, women met the challenges of modernity and the need to rearticulate culture. Women who were part of the educated élite of their day and were from wealthy or comfortable circumstances took the lead in formulating and disseminating their new readings of Islam and gender. Today, ideas about élite education, the formation of classes, and the dominant political discourses are different from those of the early part of the twentieth century.

In the early moments of encounters with modernity in the Middle East – for example, Egypt in the nineteenth century – there was an inherited sense within Sunni Islam that the canon of jurisprudence had been fixed (by the tenth century c.e.); that "the gates of *ijtihad* had been closed."[42] Although interpretation did not cease over the subsequent centuries, this notion was powerful.[43] In late nineteenth-century Egypt, the Islamic reformer Muhammad 'Abduh advocated an opening of the "gates of *ijtihad*" to enact fresh interpretations of sacred scripture that took into account contemporary social, economic, and political realities. Through his call, contemporary men and women were exhorted to rethink Islam. Early feminists such as Malak Hifni Nasif, Nabawiyya Musa, and Huda Sha'rawi in Egypt followed the lead of progressive interpreters such as 'Abduh in advancing new understandings of Islam as they tried to forge modern lives for themselves. They used Islamic arguments to legitimize new forms of education and work and to gain access for women to congregational prayer in mosques.

Malak Hifni Nasif and Nabawiyya Musa possessed state primary school and teachers' training diplomas (provided by the colonial state, with courses taught in English by British teachers, except for the Arabic language and religion), while Musa also obtained a secondary school diploma (for which she had prepared at home). Sha'rawi had been given private lessons at home (taught by French and other European tutors). Nazira Zain al-Din, a Lebanese, was taught Islamic sciences by her father, who was a religious scholar. She published *al-Sufur wa al-hijab* (Unveiling and veiling, 1928) in Beirut, advancing religious arguments against face veiling, segregation of the sexes, and female seclusion. For her efforts in enacting a more gender-sensitive reading of religious texts, she was maligned in print by men of religion. She responded the following year with a second book, called *al-Fatah wa-'l-shuyukh* (The young woman and the shaykhs, 1929), and subsequently disappeared from the scene.[44]

In the final decades of the twentieth century, highly-educated Muslim women, armed with advanced educations, including doctoral degrees, are applying a combination of historical, linguistic, hermeneutic, literary critical, deconstructive, semiotic, historicist, and feminist methodologies in their rereading of sacred texts, pushing *ijtihad* to new limits as they explore their religion with fresh eyes. They are not treading safe ground. A Sudanese scholar of Islamic religion and law, Abdullahi an-Na'im, writes: "To attribute inadequacy to any part of the *shari'ah* is regarded as heresy by the majority of Muslims, who believe that the whole of *shari'ah* is divine. This widespread view creates a formidable psychological barrier, which is reinforced by the threat of criminal prosecution for the capital offense of apostasy (*ridda*), a real threat today in countries such as the Sudan."[45]

This is borne out in the case of an Egyptian professor, Nasr Hamid Abu Zayd, who taught in the department of Arabic at Cairo University. When he applied some of these techniques in rereading the Qur'an, certain individuals took it on themselves to declare him an apostate. Third parties (his Islamist detractors) pronounced him divorced from his wife (a Muslim woman, according to common interpretations of religious law, cannot be married to an apostate). The Egyptian higher court upheld this pronouncement (after it had been rejected in a lower court), and eventually he had to take refuge in exile.[46]

Muslim women, however, have pried open space to publicly rethink their religion, exposing false readings of sacred sources and articulating gender equality within Islamic discourse. In the 1980s, the Moroccan feminist scholar Fatima Mernissi of Mohammed V University in Rabat conducted research on *hadiths* (sayings attributed to the Prophet Muhammad) exposing the misogyny perpetuated over the centuries through the circulation of false *hadiths*. She published her work in French under the title *Le harem politique* (1987), which was published in Britain as *Women and Islam: An Historical and Theological Enquiry* and in the United States as *The Veil and the Male Elite: A Feminist Interpretation of Women's Rights* (both 1991).[47] A progressive Islamic feminist group composed of women of different ideological strands came together to form Sisters in Islam in Malaysia in the 1980s. After mounting their own investigations, they published booklets for wide circulation advancing Qur'anic arguments for gender-egalitarian authority in the family and arguing that the sacred text does not condone wife-battery. African-American Muslim religious scholar Amina Wadud has published her work on Qur'anic reinterpretation, *Qur'an and Woman*, in which she opened up a range of gender issues for fresh examination.[48]

Riffat Hassan, a Pakistani religious scholar who teaches in the United States, is also rereading the Qur'an. One of her earliest articles is "Equal before Allah? Woman–Man Equality in the Islamic Tradition" (1987). In South Africa, bold interpretive and activist work is being done by women such as Fatima Noordien, [49] as well as by men such as Farid Esack at the Gender Desk of the Claremont Main Road Mosque in Cape Town. Esack has published a persuasive and provocative book that takes up issues of equality and pluralism in Islam called *Qur'an, Liberation and Pluralism: An Islamic Perspective of Interreligious Solidarity against Oppression* (1997).[50]

It is becoming increasingly difficult to talk about feminisms and gendered Islamisms. Seemingly, a salient distinction to make is between those who articulate gender equality within Islamic discourse and those who do not. Hiba Rauf, an Egyptian Islamist political science graduate student at Cairo University, does not. Yet unlike Zainab al-Ghazali and Safinaz Kazim, who adamantly reject a feminism (by that or any other name) within the discourse of Islam, Rauf is trying to articulate a new "women's rights" discourse (she rejects the term feminism) within Islam.[51] Her master's thesis, which she recently published in the United States under the title *al-Mar'a wa-'l-'amal al-siyasi: ru'ya islamiyya* (Woman and political work: an Islamic perspective, 1996), uses Islamic discourse, and from within the Islamist movement in Egypt, Rauf promotes a political construction of women's maternal role, religiously legitimizing political activism for women.[52] Like early Egyptian feminists she stretches the "private" into the "public," transcending and dissolving the distinctions people have tried to make between these realms. In Rauf's case the holistic space is the Islamic *umma* (polity), and in the case of the early feminists it was the (secular) *watan* or nation-state. However, by failing to take up the issue of gender equality as a right of citizens in the holistic *umma* of the private and public, room is left for masculinist hegemony. Egyptian women who early in the twentieth century advocated a political maternal role within the nationalist-cum-Islamic modernist paradigm witnessed the subsuming of this gendered role within a "larger" (masculinist) nationalist discourse after a nationalist state was established. This may well adumbrate the eventual implications of a politicized Islamic maternity if and when an Islamist state is achieved in Egypt.

Before returning to the intellectual activism of Iranian Islamic feminists I would like to talk about positionality. Much of the innovative interpretive work, employing various feminist analytical techniques, is being published by Muslim women outside the Middle East. While Mernissi and Rauf live and work mainly in the Middle East, their books were published in France and the United States respectively. (Both have done graduate work in the West, and both travel frequently to the West to participate in intellectual exchange.) The other new interpreters and activists mentioned above conduct their work outside the Middle East, in Malaysia, South Africa, and the United States.

The bold new interpretive work Iranian women are performing and disseminating through *Zanan* is being done inside the Middle East – and, moreover, inside an Islamic state. These women have experienced political and intellectual repression in the name of Islam inside the Islamic Republic of Iran. Only in the post-Khomeini era have they been able to carry on a public debate on gender questions based on their own rereadings of the Qur'an. Enacting their own *ijtihad*, they are articulating gender equality within an Islamic framework. In an Islamic republic where the Qur'an functions as the "constitution" of the land, women have found it possible as citizens to question readings of the Qur'an that do not result in social justice for all citizens. These new Islamic feminists, who publicly claim the label, are inclusionaries who welcome intellectual debate across an

East–West divide.[53] These Iranian Islamic feminists are publicly and explicitly taking independent and risky positions on gender as they reinterpret the religion. They are not adjuncts to masculinist political projects. Quite to the contrary, they are finding a separate space between secular feminism and masculinist Islamism. It is what I call the middle ground, in the sense of "in-between space."

In this chapter I am claiming that the new radical feminism of the future in Muslim societies will be Islamic feminism. In formulating an explicit, independent feminist discourse of gender egalitarianism inside the Middle East, the new Iranian Islamic feminists are in the lead.

CONCLUDING REFLECTIONS ON FEMINISM AND ISLAM

Is any gender-sensitive project feminist? Is feminism something articulated by a self-declared feminist? Is a person who looks to the religion of Islam for models and messages of gender-sensitive behaviors an Islamist? Is a feminist or an Islamist identity something that needs to be proclaimed, or can it be inferred? If we accept that contextualization is crucial or definitional and that acts are understood in their obvious embeddedness in ideological or political projects, then how can we capture feminisms emerging within Islamist movements? Naming, self-definition, and positioning are important; yet acts carry multiple inflections or operate simultaneously on different registers. As we move into the twenty-first century, feminist–Islamic overlap on terrains of gender and culture is increasingly discernible. At present, an Islamic feminism seems to most to be an oxymoron. But as constructions (and understandings) of feminism and Islam continue to shift and become more complex, this perception will dissipate. The middle space as the site for new feminisms in Muslim societies and among many diaspora Muslims will become increasingly populated. It will be a space full of opportunity and full of danger, the location of a new feminist culture and of a new Islamic culture.

*   *   *

Originally published in Asma Afsarrudin (ed.), *Hermeneutics and Honor in Islamic/ate Societies*, Harvard Middle East Monograph series (Cambridge, Mass.: Harvard University Press, 1999).

NOTES

1. Earlier versions of this chapter were presented at the Gender and Society Workshop at the University of Chicago; at the Symposium on Gender and Sacred Texts at Northwestern University; and as a public lecture at the University of Notre Dame sponsored by the Mediterranean/Middle East Studies Program, the Department of Classics, and the Program for Gender Studies during the spring of 1997. I would like to thank the following for their comments on the versions of this chapter presented on those occasions: Jacqueline Bhabha, Faisal Devji, Gönül Ertem, Mala de Alwis, Ritty Lukose, and Kamala Visweswaran. I also thank Tikva Frymer-Kensky and Robert Shreiter for conversations on gender, secularism, and religion.

2. See Hisham Sharabi, *Neopatriarchy: A Theory of Distorted Change in Arab Society* (New York: Oxford University Press, 1988).

3. For a general look at the nexus of feminism, religious reformism, and nationalism in the late nineteenth and twentieth centuries in selected countries of the East, see Kumari Jayawardena, *Feminism and Nationalism in the Third World* (London: Zed Books, 1986). On Egyptian feminisms, see Margot Badran, "Dual Liberation: Feminism and Nationalism in Egypt from the 1870's to 1925," *Feminist Issues*, 8 (Spring 1988), pp. 15–24 (published in Dutch as "Dubble bevridjing: feminism en nationalisme in Egypte," *Socialisties-Feministiese Teksten* [Amsterdam: Fall 1987] and in Arabic as "al-Haraka al-nisa'iyya wa al-wataniyya fi misr min 1870s illi 1925," *Nun* [Cairo, 1989] and *Nun* [Algiers, 1990]); Margot Badran, "The Origins of Feminism in Egypt," in Arina Angerman et al. (eds.), *Current Issues in Women's History* (London: Routledge, 1989) (published in Arabic in *Nun* [Algiers, December 1990] and *al-Mar'a al-Jadida* [Cairo, December 1990]); Margot Badran, "Competing Agenda: Feminists, Islam, and the State in Nineteenth and Twentieth Century Egypt," in Deniz Kandiyoti (ed.), *Women, Islam, and the State* (London : Macmillan and Philadelphia: Temple University Press, 1991) and chapter 1 in this volume; Margot Badran, "Feminism as a Force in the Arab World," in *Contemporary Arab Thought and Women* (Cairo: Arab Women's Solidarity Press, 1989); Margot Badran, "The Feminist Vision in the Writings of Three Turn-of-the-Century Egyptian Women," *British Journal for Middle Eastern Studies Bulletin*, 14, 1–2 (1988), pp. 15–34; Margot Badran, "Independent Women, More Than a Century of Feminism in Egypt," in Judith Tucker (ed.), *Arab Women: Old Boundaries, New Frontiers* (Bloomington: University of Indiana Press, 1993), and chapter 5 in this volume; Margot Badran, *Feminists, Islam, and Nation: Gender and the Making of Modern Egypt* (Princeton: Princeton University Press, 1995).

4. Sherry Ortner, *Making Gender: The Politics and Erotics of Culture* (Boston: Beacon Press, 1996), p. 16.

5. Basu notes that women's activism appears to have yielded greater dividends in contemporary nationalist struggles than during the anticolonial movements of the earlier period. In Turkey and Iran, which were not colonized, the state in the 1920s and 1930s dictated a Westernized modernity, an important part of which was "state feminism." See Amrita Basu (ed.), with C. Elizabeth McGrory, *The Challenge of Local Feminisms: Women's Movements in Global Perspective* (Boulder: Westview Press, 1995).

6. Margot Badran, "Gender Activism: Feminists and Islamists in Egypt," in

Valentine Moghadam (ed.), *Identity Politics and Women: Cultural Reassertions and Feminisms in International Perspective* (Boulder: Westview Press, 1994), and chapter 6 in this volume.

7. Emelie A. Olson, "Muslim Identity and Secularism in Contemporary Turkey: The Headscarf Dispute," *Anthropological Quarterly*, 58, 6 (October 1985), pp. 161–171.

8. The author was present at an audience with Shaikh al-Azhar Muhammad al-Tantawi, in February 1997, in the company of Yemeni feminist Raufa Hassan, who taped the Shaikh's confirmation of women's right to vote and his negation of the idea that a woman's voice is *awra* ("something shameful to be covered"; *awra* literally means "pudendum"). The taped interview was reproduced on cassettes for wide distribution in Yemen prior to the April 1997 election.

9. Margot Badran, "Unifying Women: Feminist Pasts and Presents in Yemen," *Gender and History*, 10, 3 (November 1998), pp. 498–518, and chapter 11 in this volume.

10. On the feminist book fair, see Margot Badran, "Women of the Pen," *al-Ahram Weekly*, 16–22 November 1995. From the end of the 1980s and into 1990 (before it was closed) the Arab Women's Solidarity Association held public *nadwa*s or seminars where some feminist and some Islamist women gathered, but the general atmosphere between the two was strained. This was especially apparent when the Islamist Safinaz Kazim gave a presentation on *hijab* in 1985.

11. Hiba Rauf, *al-Mar'a wa-'l-'amal al-siyasi: ru'ya islamiyya* (Woman and political work: an Islamic perspective, Herndon, Va.: International Institute for Islamic Thought, 1996). See also Afsaneh Najmabadi's "Feminism in an Islamic Republic: Years of Hardship, Years of Growth," in Yvonne Haddad and John Esposito (eds.), *Islam, Gender, and Social Change* (New York: Oxford University Press, 1998), pp. 59–84, at p. 63, where she refers to a couple of articles by Mahboobe Ommi, an Iranian writer, published in 1991 in a journal called *Zan-i Ruz* (Today's woman) and says that "Ommi's rhetoric in these articles centered on accepting the historical validity and positive contributions of feminism for the West."

12. Nilüfer Göle, *The Forbidden Modern: Civilization and Veiling* (Ann Arbor: University of Michigan Press, 1996), a translation of Nilüfer Göle, *Mödern mahrem: medeniyet ve örtüme* (Istanbul: Metis Yayinlari, 1991).

13. I have explored convergences and divergences in past and present feminist and Islamist women's experience in various writings, and in public lectures such as "Three Waves of Egyptian Feminism: Gender, Islam, and Nation," a paper presented at the University of Chicago, October 1996, and in "Feminists and Islamists in Contemporary Egypt," a paper presented at the University of Toronto, March 1996. I have looked at processes of Islamist women's globalizing projects in "Gender and Islamist Globalization," a seminar presentation on religion in Africa, Northwestern University, March 1997, and in Badran, "Unifying Women."

14. Amina Wadud-Muhsin, *Qur'an and Woman: Rereading the Sacred Text from a Woman's Perspective* (Kuala Lumpur: Penerbit Fajar Bakati, 1992 and New York: Oxford University Press, 1999).

15. On the challenges and implications of these contemporary phenomena, see, for example, Suzanne Hoeber Rudolf and James Piscatori (eds.), *Transnational Religion: Fading States* (Boulder: Westview Press, 1997).

16. Badran, "Gender Activism."

17. Ziba Mir-Hosseini, "Women and Politics in Post-Khomeini Iran: Divorce, Veiling, and Emerging Feminist Voices," in Haleh Afshar (ed.), *Women and Politics in the Third World* (London and New York: Routledge, 1996); Ziba Mir-Hosseini, "Stretching the Limits: A Feminist Reading of the Shari'a in Post-Khomeini Iran," in Mai Yamani (ed.), *Feminism and Islam: Legal and Literary Perspectives* (New York: New York University Press, 1996), pp. 285–320; and Najmabadi, "Feminism in an Islamic Republic," pp. 59–84.

18. It has also been argued that "Islam did not share the misogynous underpinnings of Christianity and Judaism" and consequently "there did not seem to be any grounds for feminism in an Islamic country": see Najmabadi, "Feminism in an Islamic Republic," p. 63.

19. Ibid.; Mir-Hosseini, "Women and Politics in Post-Khomeini Iran"; and Mir-Hosseini, "Stretching the Limits." Kian discusses the new feminist phenomenon in Iran without using the term feminism: Azadeh Kian, "Women and Politics in Post-Islamist Iran: The Gender Conscious Drive to Change," *British Journal of Middle Eastern Studies*, 24, 1 (1997), pp. 75–96.

20. Feride Acar, "Women in the Ideology of Islamic Revivalism in Turkey: Three Islamic Women's Journals," *Islamic Literature in Contemporary Turkey* (1991), p. 301.

21. Mai Yamani, "Some Observations on Women in Saudi Arabia," in Yamani (ed.), *Feminism and Islam*, p. 263.

22. The term has appeared in various articles in *al-Ahram Weekly* that have been widely read in Egypt and abroad by Arabic speakers.

23. Göle, *The Forbidden Modern*.

24. Barbara F. Stowasser, "Women's Issues in Modernist Islamic Thought," in Tucker (ed.), *Arab Women*, pp. 3–28; Yvonne Haddad, "Islam, Women, and Revolution," in Y. Haddad and E. B. Findlay (eds.), *Women, Revolution and Social Change* (Albany: State University of New York Press, 1985).

25. A common position among contemporary Islamists is that 'Abduh's Islamic modernism constituted a cooption by the colonial authorities (he was exiled and then allowed reentry into Egypt and appointed Mufti) or a selling out to the colonial West. 'Abduh, in articulating his Islamic modernism, pointed out that Arabs had perfected Greek science and philosophy before transmitting it to the West.

26. In 1923, the state outlawed the Women's People's Party. The following year the state created the Turkish Women's Federation, which was dissolved in 1935 not long after the vote had been granted to women. See Deniz Kandiyoti, "End of Empire: Islam, Nationalism and Women in Turkey," in Deniz Kandiyoti (ed.), *Women, Islam, and State* (London: Macmillan and Philadelphia: Temple University Press, 1991), pp. 22–47, at p. 41.

27. Binnaz Toprak, "Women and Fundamentalism in Turkey," in Moghadam (ed.), *Identity Politics and Women*, pp. 297–298.

28. Binnaz Toprak, *Islam and Political Development in Turkey* (Leiden: Brill, 1981).

29. Yeşim Arat, "Feminism ve İslam: *Kadın ve Aile* dergisinin düşündürdükleri" (Feminism and Islam: thoughts on the journal *Kadın ve Aile*) in Şirin Tekeli (ed.), *Kadın bakîş açîsîndan 1980'ler Türkiye'sinde kadînlar* (Women in 1980s' Turkey from a woman's perspective, Istanbul: İletişim Yayînlarî, 1990); Acar, "Women in the Ideology of Islamic Revivalism in Turkey."

30. Egyptian feminists distinguished between indigenous patriarchal domination,

often articulated in religious terms, and colonial patriarchal domination. They contested both simultaneously and deftly in "two languages."

31. Nationalists such as Mustafa Kamil, who supported a renewed caliphate and thus a construction of the nation on religious terms, did not hold the day but did bequeath a different legacy, which slowly fermented underground – that is, under secular nationalist ground.

32. On the rise of Islamism in Turkey, see Sencer Ayata, "Patronage, Party, and the State: The Politiczation of Islam in Turkey," *Middle East Journal*, 50 (1996), pp. 40–56; Faruk Birtek and Binnaz Toprak, "The Conflictual Agenda of Neo-Liberal Reconstruction and the Rise of Islamic Politics in Turkey: The Hazards of Rewriting Modernity," *Praxis International*, 13, 2 (July 1993), pp. 192–212; Sherif Mardin, "The Just and the Unjust," *Daedalus*, 120, 3 (1991), pp. 113–130; and Feroz Ahmad, *The Making of Modern Turkey* (London and New York: Routledge, 1993).

33. See Caglar Keyder, "The Dilemma of Cultural Identity on the Margin of Europe," *Middle East Review*, 17 (1993), pp. 19–33, where he shows how the Western invention of nationalism had to be taught from the top down. See also Fuat Keyman, "On the Relation between Global Modernity and Nationalism: The Crisis of Hegemony and the Rise of Islamic Identity in Turkey," *New Perspectives on Turkey* (1995), pp. 93–120, esp. p. 102. On the rise of Islamism in Turkey, see Ayata, "Patronage, Party, and the State"; Birtek and Toprak, "The Conflictual Agenda of Neo-Liberal Reconstruction and the Rise of Islamic Politics in Turkey"; Mardin, "The Just and the Unjust"; and Ahmad, *The Making of Modern Turkey*.

34. Zehra Arat, "Turkish Women and the Republican Reconstruction of Tradition," in Fatma Müge Göcek and Shiva Balaghi (eds.), *Reconstructing Gender in the Middle East* (New York: Columbia University Press, 1994); Nükhet Sirman, "Feminism in Turkey: A Short History," *New Perspectives on Turkey* (Fall 1989); Nükhet Sirman, "Feminism and the Discovery of the Self in Turkish Politics," in Andrew Finkel and Nukhet Sirman (eds.), *Turkish State, Turkish Society* (London: Routledge, 1989); Şirin Tekeli, "The Emergence of the Feminist Movement in Turkey," in Drude Dahlerup (ed.), *The New Women's Movements: Feminism and Political Power in Europe and the USA* (New York: New York University Press, 1986); and Şirin Tekeli, *Women in Modern Turkish Society* (London: Zed Books, 1995).

35. Y. Arat, "Feminism ve İslam"; Acar, "Women in the Ideology of Islamic Revivalism in Turkey."

36. Y. Arat, "Feminism ve İslam," p. 21.

37. Malak Hifni Nasif (Bahithat al-Badiya) and Nabawiyya Musa extolled the primacy of women's roles as wives and mothers while at the same time articulating the importance of new societal roles for women.

38. Arlene Macleod puts it well when alluding to the problem of analyzing the "new veil" in Egypt, "a form located neither in the traditional nor the modern vocabulary": Arlene Macleod, *Accommodating Protest: Working Women, the New Veiling, and Change in Cairo* (New York: Columbia University Press, 1990), p. 14.

39. Göle, *The Forbidden Modern*.

40. See Badran, *Feminists, Islam, and Nation*. Other examples of the deferring of women's rights by liberal or progressive rationalist men include Algeria; see, for example, Marieme Hélie-Lucas, "Women, Nationalism and Religion in the

Algerian Struggle," in Margot Badran and Miriam Cooke (eds.), *Opening the Gates: A Century of Arab Feminist Writing* (London: Virago, 1990).

41. Bauer stresses that both fundamentalist and secular patriarchies are "suspicious of women's autonomy": Janet L. Bauer, "The Mixed Blessings of Women's Fundamentalism: Democratic Impulses in a Patriarchal World," in Judy Brink and Joan Mencher (eds.), *Mixed Blessings: Gender and Religious Fundamentalism Cross Culturally* (New York: Routledge, 1997), p. 244.

42. On the gendering of the canon, see Barbara F. Stowasser, *Women in the Qur'an, Traditions, and Interpretation* (New York: Oxford University Press, 1994).

43. Despite a widespread perception to the contrary, *ijtihad* did not cease to be practiced; see Wael Hallaq, "Was the Gate of Ijtihad Closed?," *International Journal of Middle Eastern Studies*, 18 (1986).

44. Nazira Zain al-Din, *Sufur wa al-hijab* (Beirut: Matabi' Quzma, 1928); Nazira Zain al-Din, *al-Fatah wa al-shuyukh* (Beirut: al-Matba'a al-Amirkaniya, 1929).

45. Abdullahi An-Naim, *Toward an Islamic Reformation: Civil Liberties, Human Rights, and International Law* (Syracuse: Syracuse University Press, 1990), p. 11.

46. He is presently the Ibn Rushd Professor of Islam and Humanism at the University of Humanistics in Utrecht. For some of his views, see Elliot Colla and Ayman Bakr, "Silencing is at the Heart of my Case," interview with Nasr Hamid Abu Zayd in Joel Beinin and Joe Stork (eds.), *Political Islam* (Berkeley: University of California Press, 1997), pp. 327–334; and Abu Zayd, "Cairo University and Academic Freedom," *al-Ahram Weekly*, 8–14 April 1993.

47. Fatima Mernissi, *Le harem politique* (Paris: Michel Albin, 1987), trans. Mary Jo Lakeland as *Women and Islam: An Historical and Theological Enquiry* (Oxford: Basil Blackwell, 1991); Fatima Mernissi, *The Veil and the Male Elite: A Feminist Interpretation of Women's Rights in Islam*, trans. Mary Jo Lakeland (Cambridge, Mass.: Perseus Books, 1991).

48. Wadud, *Qur'an and Woman*.

49. I met Fatima Noordien at the International Women's Forum in Khartoum in 1996; see Margot Badran, "Gendering the Islamist Global Offensive," *People's Rights, Women's Rights* (Cairo: December 1996), in Arabic "al-'Awalama al-islamiyya fi majjal qadiyat al-naw'," in Huquq al-Nass, Khartoum, 13 July –3 August 1997; and Margot Badran, "Khartoum's Answer to Beijing," *al-Ahram Weekly*, November 1996.

50. Farid Esack, *Qur'an, Liberation and Pluralism: An Islamic Perspective of Interreligious Solidarity against Oppression* (Oxford: Oneworld, 1997).

51. This is not to suggest that al-Ghazali's and Kazim's writings and actions do not indicate elements of "functional feminism." An analysis of this is beyond the limits of this chapter. I have written about these women elsewhere. See Badran, "Competing Agenda; and Badran, "Gender Activism".

52. Rauf, *al-Mar'a wa-'l-'amal al-siyasi.*

53. Mir-Hosseini, "Women and Politics in Post-Khomeini Iran"; Najmabadi, "Feminism in an Islamic Republic." [At the beginning of 2008, *Zanan* was shut down by the government.]

10

ISLAMIC FEMINISM: WHAT'S IN A NAME?

What's in a name? What's behind a name? What is Islamic feminism? Let me offer a concise definition: it is a feminist discourse and practice articulated within an Islamic paradigm. Islamic feminism, which derives its understanding and mandate from the Qur'an, seeks rights and justice for women, and for men, in the totality of their existence. Islamic feminism is both highly contested and firmly embraced. There has been much misunderstanding, misrepresentation, and mischief concerning Islamic feminism. This new feminism has given rise simultaneously to hopes and to fears. We shall look at who is producing it, where, why, and to what end.

FEMINISM

As has been rightly noted, concepts and terms have a history – and practices around concepts and terms have a history. The term "feminism" was coined in France in the late 1880s by Hubertine Auclert, who introduced it in her journal, *La Citoyenne*, to criticize male predominance (and domination), and to make claims for women's rights and emancipation promised by the French Revolution. Historian of feminisms Karen Offen has demonstrated that since its initial appearance the term has been given many meanings and definitions; it has been put to diverse uses and inspired many movements.[1]

By the first decade of the twentieth century the term had made its appearance in English – first in Britain, and then, by the 1910s, in the United States.[2] By the early 1920s it was in use in Egypt, where it circulated both in French, and in Arabic as *nisa'iyya*.[3] Yes, the term originated in the West, specifically France. No, feminism is not Western. American feminism is not French, as Americans and French alike would loudly proclaim. Egyptian feminism is not French and it is not Western. It is Egyptian, as its founders have attested and history makes clear.

Feminisms are produced in particular places and are articulated in local terms. Creators and practitioners of women's history, taking shape as a new field in the 1960s, and expanding in 1970s and 1980s, have analyzed the plethora of feminisms that have appeared in different global locations. Sri Lankan scholar Kumari Jayawardena's 1986 path-breaking book *Feminisms and Nationalism in the Third World* documented feminist movements that had emerged in diverse Asian and Middle Eastern countries, showing how they were located within the contexts of local national liberation and religious reform movements, including movements of Islamic reform.[4] Egypt, as we know, was a pioneer in articulating feminist thinking and organizing collective feminist activist campaigns. Yet despite a large literature in many languages recording and critiquing these globally scattered feminisms, the notion that feminism is Western is still bandied about by those ignorant of history – or who perhaps willfully employ it as a delegitimizing tactic. Some still speak of a "Western feminism" in essentialist, monolithic, and static terms, belying a certain Occidentalist turn of mind or, perhaps, a political project aimed at adversely "framing" feminism (pun intended). Feminism, however, is a plant that only grows in its own soil. This is not to suggest that ideas or movements anywhere are hermetically sealed.

ISLAMIC FEMINISM

The term "Islamic feminism" began to be visible in the 1990s in various global locations. It was from the writings of Muslims that I discovered the term. Iranian scholars Afsaneh Najmabadi and Ziba Mir-Hosseini explained the rise and use of the term Islamic feminism in Iran by some women, as well as men, writing in the Teheran women's journal *Zanan*, which Shahla Sherkat founded in 1992.[5] Saudi Arabian scholar Mai Yamani used the term in her 1996 book *Feminism and Islam*.[6] Turkish scholars Yeşim Arat and Feride Acar in their articles,[7] and Nilüfer Göle in her book *The Forbidden Modern* (published in Turkish in 1991 and in English in 1996) used the term

Islamic feminism in the 1990s to describe a new feminist paradigm they detected emerging in Turkey.[8] South African activist Shamima Shaikh used the term Islamic feminism in the 1990s, as did her co-activists, both male and female. By the mid-1990s, there was growing evidence of Islamic feminism as a term created and circulated by Muslims in far-flung corners of the global *umma*.

Some Muslim women, as seen from the foregoing remarks, describe the articulation and advocacy of a Qur'an-mandated gender equality and social justice as Islamic feminism. Others, however, do not call this Islamic feminism, but describe it as a woman-centered rereading of the Qur'an and other religious texts by scholar-activists (a term found in the 2001 book *Windows of Faith*, edited by Gisela Webb).[9]

The producers and users of Islamic feminist discourse include those who may or may not accept the Islamic feminist label or identity. They also include religious Muslims (by which is typically meant the religiously observant), secular Muslims (whose ways of being Muslim may be less publicly evident), and non-Muslims. I would like to add that while many Muslims use the adjectives religious and secular to label themselves or others, there are other Muslims who feel uneasy about these terms. It is important to historicize or contextualize the use of the terms secular and religious, as they mean different things in different times and places. Finally, it is helpful to remember that the terms religious and secular are porous rather than rigid categories.

Some who engage in the articulation and practice of Islamic feminism asserted an Islamic feminist identity from the start. These include contributors to the Iranian journal *Zanan*, South African exegetes and activists, and women belonging to the group Sisters in Islam in Malaysia. Others, and these include many of the key producers of Islamic feminist discourse or new gender-sensitive Qur'anic interpretation, have been reluctant to identify themselves as Islamic feminists or simply feminists. Fatima Mernissi, author of *Women and Islam: An Historical and Theological Enquiry*[10] (published originally as *Le harem politique* in 1978 and first in English in 1991), who produced what was to become one of the core texts of Islamic feminism, is a secular feminist; she would not call herself an Islamic feminist.

Some of the religiously-identified women producers of Islamic feminist texts have changed their positions in more recent years. In the past, Amina Wadud, the African-American Muslim theologian and author of the landmark 1991 book *Qur'an and Woman: Rereading the Sacred Text from a Woman's Perspective*, adamantly objected to being labeled an Islamic feminist.[11] She now shows less concern if others identify her as such. What is important to her is that people understand her work. However, Wadud does bristle when she is slammed as a "Western feminist," decrying the pejorative use of both "Western" and "feminist" in the preface to the 1999 Oxford University Press edition of *Qur'an and Woman*.[12] This devout Muslim woman asks "what's wrong with being Western?" (Let us not forget that there are large and growing numbers of Western Muslims, or Muslims in the West, of whom Wadud is one.) As for discrediting feminism, she snaps back: "No reference is ever made to the definition of feminism as the radical notion that women are human beings." Riffat Hassan, an American-based theologian of Pakistani origin, has also come to accept the Islamic feminist designation – concerned most, like Wadud, that her work be understood.

GLOBAL PHENOMENON

Islamic feminism is a global phenomenon. It is not a product of East or West. As already noted, Islamic feminism is being produced by Muslim women from both majority and minority communities in Africa or Asia as well as from immigrant and convert communities in the West. Islamic feminism is circulating with increasing frequency in cyberspace.

Globally, English is the major language in which Islamic feminist discourse is articulated and circulated. At the same time, it is expressed in a large number of languages locally. In order to do Qur'anic interpretation and closely read other Islamic religious texts, mastery of Arabic is essential. With the spread of Islamic feminist interpretation Arabic loan words, such as *ijtihad* (independent investigation of religious sources), are entering English. Since English is the common language of Islamic feminism, the feminist terminology available in that language is also being accessed.

Islamic feminism transcends and eradicates old binaries. These include polarities between "religious" and "secular" and between "East" and "West." I stress this because not infrequently there are those who see Islamic feminism as setting up or reconfirming dichotomies. In my own public lectures and writings I have argued that Islamic feminist discourse does precisely the opposite: that it closes gaps and reveals common concerns and goals, starting with the basic affirmation of gender equality and social justice. Suggestions or allegations of a supposed "clash" between "secular feminism" and "religious feminism" may result from ignorance – or, more likely, from a politically motivated attempt to impede solidarities among women.

The pioneering secular feminisms in Egypt and other Arab countries have always had space for religion. The founding Egyptian feminist discourse was anchored simultaneously in the discourse of Islamic reform and of secular nationalism. Secular feminism (often called simply feminism) offered Islamic arguments in demanding women's rights to education, work, political rights – along with secular nationalist, humanitarian (later human) rights, and democratic arguments. When feminists pleaded for changes to the Muslim personal status code they advanced Islamic arguments.[13]

Islamic feminism uses Islamic discourse as its paramount – although not necessarily its only – discourse, in arguing for women's rights, gender equality, and social justice. Islamic feminist discourse in Iran draws upon secular discourses and methodologies to strengthen and extend its claims. Wadud, in her women-sensitive interpretation of the Qur'an, combines classical Islamic methodologies with new social science tools and secular discourses of rights and justice while retaining a firm and central grounding in Islamic thought.

For many years in my talks and writings, I have discussed how Muslims' secular feminists' discourses typically included religious discourse. In more recent years, as I discovered a new Islamic feminism in the making, I observed intersections of religious and secular feminisms. I talk about this in two recent articles, "Feminisms: Secular and Religious Paradigms: A Selective Look at the Middle East in Feminist Movements: Origins and Orientations," published in Fes in 2000,[14] and "Locating Feminisms: The Collapse of Secular and Religious Discourses in the Mashriq," published in a special fiftieth issue of the African Gender Institute's journal *Agenda*.[15]

Some of the specific activist goals of Islamic feminists are the same as those articulated earlier by secular feminists, such as changes in various national Muslim personal status codes. Often, when secular and Islamic feminists try to work together for common goals, they are inhibited or pulled asunder by competing political forces. This happened in Yemen following the successful drive by a coalition of a wide spectrum of women to prevent a regressive personal status law from being enacted in 1997.[16]

CONSTITUTING A DISCOURSE

How is Islamic feminist discourse (or Islamic feminist theology, as the Lebanese researcher Hosni Abboud, examining the depiction of Mary in the Qur'an, puts it) being constituted? Islamic feminism argues that the Qur'an affirms the principle of equality of all human beings, and that the practice of equality between women and men (and other categories of people) has been impeded or subverted by patriarchal ideas (ideology) and practices. Islamic jurisprudence (*fiqh*), consolidated in its classical form in the ninth century, was itself heavily saturated with the patriarchal thinking and behaviors of the day. It is this patriarchally-inflected jurisprudence that has informed the various contemporary formulations of the *shari'a*. The Hadith – the reported, but not always authentic, sayings and deeds of the Prophet Muhammad – have also been often used to shore up patriarchal ideas and practices. Sometimes *hadith*s are of questionable provenance or reliability, and sometimes they are used out of context, with negative consequence for women. Thus a priority of Islamic feminism is to go straight to Islam's fundamental text, the Qur'an. However, while some women center their attention on interpretation of the Qur'an (Amina Wadud, Riffat Hassan, and Saudi Arabian Fatima Naseef),[17] others scutinize formulations of *shari'a*-backed laws (Lebanese Aziza al-Hibri, Pakistani Shaheen Sardar Ali),[18] while yet others reexamine the Hadith (Moroccan Fatima Mernissi, Turkish Hidayet Tuksal).[19]

The basic methodologies of Islamic feminism are the classic Islamic methodologies of *ijtihad* and *tafsir* (interpretation of the Qur'an). Used along with these methodologies are the tools of linguistics, history, literary criticism, sociology, anthropology, etc. In approaching the Qur'an, women bring to their readings their own experience and questions as women. They point out that classical, and also much post-classical, interpretation was based on men's experiences, male-centered questions, and the overall influence of the patriarchal societies in which they lived.

FEMINIST HERMENEUTICS

The new gender-sensitive or feminist hermeneutics renders com-pelling confirmation of the principle of gender equality in the Qur'an that was lost sight of as male interpreters constructed a corpus of *tafsir* promoting a doctrine of male superiority reflecting the mindset of the prevailing patriarchal cultures. There are many verses (*ayat*) of the Qur'an that declare male–female equality. *Aya* 13 in *sura* 49 (al-Hujurat): "Oh humankind. We have created you from a single pair of a male and a female and made you into tribes and nations that you may know each other [not that you may despise one another]. The most honored of you in the sight of God is the most righteous of you [the one practicing the most *taqwa*]." Ontologically, all human beings are equal. They are differentiated by the practice of *taqwa* or God-consciousness (sometimes translated as piety).

Feminist hermeneutics distinguishes between the universal and timeless, and the particular and contingent. Certain practices are con-trolled and condoned as a way to encourage people on the path to behaving with fuller justice and equality in their human interactions. Feminist hermeneutics has taken three approaches:

1. revisiting verses of the Qur'an to correct false stories in common circulation, such as the accounts of creation and of events in the Garden of Eden that have shored up claims of male superiority;
2. citing verses that unequivocally enunciate the equality of women and men;
3. deconstructing verses attentive to male and female difference that have been commonly interpreted in ways that justify male domination.

As an example of new Qur'anic interpretation, we can look at *sura* 4 (al-Nisa'i), *aya* 34. While fundamentally equal, humans have been created biologically different in order to perpetuate the species. Only in particular contexts and circumstances will males and females assume particular roles and functions. Woman alone can give birth and nurse, and thus, in this particular circumstance, a husband is enjoined by the Qur'an to provide material support, as indicated in 4:34: "Men are responsible for (*qawwamuna 'ala*) women because God has given the one more than the other (*bima faddala*), and because they support them from their means." Wadud, Hassan, al-Hibri, Naseef, and others demonstrate that *qawwamuna 'ala* conveys the notion of providing for, and that the term is used prescriptively to indicate that men ought to provide for women in the context of child- bearing and rearing. It does not necessarily mean that women cannot provide for themselves in that circumstance. The term *qawwamuna 'ala* is not an unconditional statement of male authority and superiority over all women for all time, as traditional male interpreters have claimed. The women exegetes thus show how classical male interpretations have turned the specific and contingent into universals. While deconstructing particular verses such as the above to dismantle the patriarchal notion of male authority over women, the exegetes also draw attention to verses that clearly affirm the mutuality of responsibilities of men and women, as in *sura 9, aya 71* (al-Tawbah) of the Qur'an: "The believers, male and female, are protectors (*'awliyya*) of one another."

TO WHAT END?

Islamic feminism serves people in their individual lives, and can be a potent force in improving state and society. Second-generation Muslim women in diaspora communities in the West are often caught between the practices and norms imported from the original home cultures of parents who migrated from Middle Eastern or South Asian countries and imposed in the name of Islam, and the ways of life in their new countries. Islamic feminism helps such women untangle patriarchal customs and religion. It gives them Islamic ways of understanding gender equality, societal opportunity, and their own potential. Meanwhile, Islamic feminist discourse is also relevant in predominantly Muslim countries in parts of Africa and Asia as people try to construct a new and more egalitarian understanding of their religion in order to change old mind-sets and cultural practices that purport to be Islamic.

In reexamining the Qur'an along with Hadith, Islamic feminists, answering back to those who allege otherwise, are making cogent arguments that Islam does not condone wanton violence against women; they underscore that violence against women is indeed anti-Islamic. This alone will not put an end to violence, but it is one of several weapons against it. The Malaysian group Sisters in Islam is one among many (and one of the earliest to be outspoken in print) that have decried violence against women perpetrated in the name of Islam in a pamphlet called "Is Wife Beating Permissible in Islam?" which they widely distributed. South African Saʿdiya Shaikh has also completed a study on this subject in the form of an M.A. thesis for the University of Cape Town (1996) entitled "Battered Wives in Muslim Society in the Western Cape: Religious Constructions of Gender, Marriage, Sexuality and Violence." In her Ph.D. dissertation, she looks at notions of sexuality in Islamic religious texts.[20]

Islamic feminism is more radical than Muslims' secular feminisms. Islamic feminism insists on full equality of women and men across the public–private spectrum. Secular feminists historically accepted the idea of equality in the public sphere and the notion of complementarianism in the private sphere. Islamic feminism argues that women may be heads of state, leaders of congregational prayer, judges, and muftis. In some Muslim-majority countries, Muslim women function as judges, some as prime ministers and heads of state. Islamic feminism stands to benefit us all, Muslims of both sexes, as well as non-Muslims living side by side with Muslims everywhere.

It is important to focus on the content of Islamic feminism, on its goals, and not to get bogged down with distracting issues about who has the right to think/analyse and to speak. It is important not to be too defensive or proprietary about Islamic feminism. The way I see it, Islamic feminism is for all.

* * *

This originated as a talk at the American Research Center in Egypt, and was subsequently published in *al-Ahram Weekly*, 17–23 January 2002. It has been translated into Bosnian, Dutch, Flemish, French, and Italian.

NOTES

1. See Karen Offen, "Defining Feminism: A Comparative Historical Approach," *Signs*, 14, 1 (1988), pp. 119–157; and Karen Offen, "On the French Origin of the Words Feminism and Feminist," *Feminist Issues*, 8, 2 (1988), pp. 45–51.
2. See Nancy Cott, *The Grounding of Modern Feminism* (New Haven: Yale University Press. 1987), pp. 15–17.
3. Margot Badran, *Feminists, Islam, and Nation: Gender and the Making of Modern Egypt* (Princeton: Princeton University Press, 1995), pp. 19–21. On the politics of feminism and language from the late nineteenth to the mid-twentieth century

in Egypt see Irene Fenoglio-Abd El Aal, *Defense et illustration de l'Egyptienne: aux débuts d'une expression feminine,* dossier 2 (Cairo: Centre d'Etudes et de Documentation Economique, Juridique et Sociale, 1988), and also Margot Badran, "Preface," pp. 6–12.

4. Kumari Jayawardena, *Feminisms and Nationalism in the Third World* (London: Zed Press, 1986).

5. Afsaneh Najmabadi, "Feminism in an Islamic Republic: 'Years of Hardship, Years of Growth," in Yvonne Haddad and John Esposito (eds.), *Islam, Gender, and Social Change* (New York: Oxford University Press, 1998), pp. 59–84; Ziba Mir-Hosseini, "Stretching the Limits: A Feminist Reading of the Shari'a in Post-Khomeini Iran," in Mai Yamani (ed.), *Feminism and Islam: Legal and Literary Perspectives* (London: Ithaca Press, 1996), pp. 285–320.

6. Yamani (ed.), *Feminism and Islam.*

7. Yeşim Arat, " Feminism and Islam: Thoughts on the Journal *Kadīn ve Aile,*" in Şirin Tekeli (ed.), *Women in 1980's Turkey from a Woman's Perspective* (Istanbul: İletişim Yayīnlarī, 1990); Feride Acar, "Women in the Ideology of Islamic Revivalism in Turkey: Three Islamic Women's Journals," *Islamic Literature in Contemporary Turkey* (1991), pp. 280–303; Feride Acar, "Women in the Ideology of Islamic Revivalism in Turkey: Three Islamic Women's Journals," *Islamic Literature in Contemporary Turkey* (1991), pp. 280–303.

8. Nilüfer Göle, *Mödern mahrem: medeniyet ve örtüme* (Istanbul: Metis Yayīnlarī, 1991), trans. as *The Forbidden Modern: Civilization and Veiling* (Ann Arbor: University of Michigan Press, 1996).

9. Gisela Webb (ed.), *Windows of Faith: Muslim Women Scholar-Activists in North America* (Syracuse: Syracuse University Press, 2000).

10. Fatima Mernissi, *Women and Islam: An Historical and Theological Enquiry,* trans. Mary Jo Lakeland (Oxford: Basil Blackwell, 1991).

11. Amina Wadud-Muhsin, *Qur'an and Woman: Rereading the Sacred Text from a Woman's Perspective* (Kuala Lumpur: Penerbit Fajar Bakati, 1992; New York: Oxford University Press, 1999).

12. P. xviii.

13. See Badran, *Feminists, Islam, and Nation,* esp. pp. 124–135.

14. "Feminisms: Secular and Religious Paradigms: A Selective Look at the Middle East in Feminist Movements: Origins and Orientations," in Fatima Sadiqi et al. (eds.), *al-Harakat al-nisa'iyyat: al-'asl wa al-tawjihat/Mouvements feministes: origines et orientations Feminist Movements/Origins and Orientations* (Fes: Centre d'Etudes et de Recherches sur la Femme, Université Sidi Mohamed ben Abdallah, 2000), pp. 73–88.

15. "Locating Feminisms: The Collapse of Secular and Religious Discourses in the Muslim Mashriq," *Agenda* (South African feminist journal), special 50th issue on African Feminisms, 59 (2001), pp. 41–57.

16. See Margot Badran, "Unifying Women: Feminist Pasts and Presents in Yemen," *Gender and History,* special issue on Feminisms and Internationalism, 10, 3 (November 1998), and chapter 11 in this volume.

17. Wadud, *Qur'an and Woman;* Riffat Hassan, for example, "Equal before Allah? Woman–Man Equality in the Islamic Tradition," *Harvard Divinity Bulletin* (January–May 1987), pp. 2–4; Fatima Umar Naseef, *Women in Islam: A Discourse in Rights and Obligations* (Cairo: International Islamic Committee for the Woman and Child, 1999).

18. See, for example, Aziza al-Hibri, "Islamic Law and Muslim Women in America," in Marjorie Garber and Rebecca Walkowitz (eds.), *One Nation under God? Religion and American Culture* (New York: Routledge, 1999), pp. 128–44; and Shaheen Sardar Ali, *Gender and Human Rights in Islam and International Law: Equal before Allah, Unequal before Man?* (The Hague: Kluwer Law International, 2000).
19. Mernissi, *Women and Islam*; Hidayet Şefkatli Tuksal, *Kadin karşiti söylemin İslam geleneğindeki izdüşmleri* (Traces of misogynist discourse in the Islamic tradition, Ankara: Kitâbiyât, 2000).
20. Her Ph.D. dissertation is entitled "Spiritual Cartographies of Gender: Ibn 'Arabi and Sufi Discourses of Gender, Sexuality and Marriage," Temple University, 2004.

11

UNIFYING WOMEN: FEMINIST PASTS AND PRESENTS IN YEMEN

In campaigns to achieve national sovereignty and to establish new state systems women have participated as active agents, promoting gender-egalitarian notions of citizenship.[1] States themselves have both mobilized women to serve their own internal political agendas and used women to signal to the outside world an egalitarian and democratic construction of citizenship they do not necessarily deliver.[2] There is a distinct tension between states' needs to articulate the equality that is fundamental to democracy and (patriarchal) states' intentions to reproduce gender inequalities. This tension constitutes a potent site for feminist exploitation.

The literature on women's activisms and on gender and the state in Middle Eastern Muslim societies produced in the 1980s and 1990s has brought into view complicated politics and projects. In her introduction to *Women, Islam, and the State* (1991), Deniz Kandiyoti writes: "The ways women are represented in political discourse ... and the social movements through which they are able to articulate their gender interests are intimately linked to state-building processes and are responsive to their transformations."[3] Marnia Lazreg, Sondra Hale, Parvin Paidar, and I show ways women both came forth as active participants in national liberation and revolutionary movements and were used by states for their own purposes in analyses of gender politics in Algeria, Sudan, Iran, and Egypt.[4] The equality of citizens was promoted when women's active support was needed, such as in campaigns for national independence, or in oppositional movements aimed at radical state transformation. When new state power was sufficiently secured the avowed equality of citizens was replaced by expressions of gender inequality. Shifts to gender-inegalitarian discourse occurred in early postcolonial contexts, such as liberal nationalist Egypt and socialist Algeria;[5] at moments of the ascendancy of political Islam to state power, such as Iran and Sudan; and at a time of recuperation of lost state sovereignty, as in Kuwait.[6]

Gendered citizen inequalities around the globe exhibit certain basic historical patterns, albeit in highly different contexts. These have included differential access to political rights and discriminatory laws regarding such matters as marriage, divorce, child custody, and property rights – called personal status laws in Muslim societies.[7] Modern states have often been quicker to grant equal political rights to women than to institute gender-egalitarian personal status laws.[8] Modern nation-states have typically accorded high visibility to gender-equal political rights as indices of democracy. However, they have been less open concerning the small numbers of women elected to legislative bodies. States have also tended to be silent about their gender discrimination in laws regulating rights in the family. Personal status rights or persons' rights in the context of the family are often not conceptualized as citizens' rights.

Activist women's discourses and politics of citizenship in the West and in the Middle East have varied in significant ways. In Western countries women organized movements exclusively directed toward obtaining female suffrage. Campaigners for women's right to vote or suffragists in the West developed discourses of citizenship and equal gender rights around the trope of political rights. Western women have organized separate campaigns to reform laws regulating family relations and property rights. In contrast, activist women in the Middle Eastern countries, whose earliest organized movements appeared in the context of national liberation struggles and during post-independence state formation, articulated discourses of political rights and personal status rights or rights within the context of the family in a broader framework of calls for citizens' rights. For example, Egyptian feminists in the early 1920s[9] and feminists from countries of the Arab East in the mid-1940s simultaneously demanded equal political rights and more egalitarian personal status rights (they accepted a gender-complementarian model in the context of the family rather than a model calling for full equality).[10] In the 1990s Palestinian feminists are participating in the building of a new state, calling for gender egalitarian citizens' rights across a broad public–private spectrum.[11]

Although Arab feminists in postcolonial societies have articulated a comprehensive gender-egalitarian construction of modern citizenship, they have faced fundamental difficulties which have yet to be resolved. In most postcolonial countries of the Middle East, secular law (often based on the French model) governs the "public sphere," while religious law is left to regulate matters of personal status construed as belonging to the "private sphere." In this way "the citizen" is constituted as a "public citizen" and member of the secular state, and the equality central to democracy is confined to the (public) citizen. Individuals are constituted as members of a religion in the private sphere, to be governed by personal status codes constructed out of readings of Islam (or Christianity). Male religious specialists entrusted with the interpretive task have conducted patriarchal readings of Islam which have formed the bases for gender-inegalitarian personal status laws. This has created an awkward dichotomy for nationals who are cast as equal (public) citizens but unequal (private) members of religions. Arab feminists Nawal al-Saadawi and Fatima Mernissi have decried the oppressiveness of this split for women.[12]

Exceptions among Middle Eastern countries where the notion of gender-egalitarian citizenship was expressed across public–private divisions were states that opted for secular laws in the domain of personal status or family law. These states enacted from above remarkably (if imperfect) egalitarian personal status codes, through which they intended to signal their political projects of secular modernity. They included Turkey (1926), Tunisia (1956), and the People's Democratic Republic of South Yemen (1974). Although the specifics of national experience varied, these secular codes had differential consequences across classes and regions within these countries. With the discourse for gender equality in personal status matters located strictly within a secular modernist context, there was no space for a "religious modernity." In the 1980s and 1990s, Islamists, speaking the language of religion and ordinary people, attacked "secular modernity."[13] During this same period, feminist activists and scholars in the Middle East assailed the limits of "state feminism" and exposed its patriarchal dimensions.[14] ("State feminisms" have been discredited elsewhere as well, following the collapse of communist and socialist regimes.[15])

At the end of the twentieth century, with movements of political Islam more than two decades old and continuing to spread, new discourses of citizenship and of modernity are being more widely defined and are taking new approaches to religion. Postcolonial secular states and secular political parties understand the political imperative to rethink Islam. They are aware that Islam is the major political and cultural idiom of the popular classes. The split between a "secular public sphere" and a "religious private sphere" (never as sharp as alleged but nevertheless vexing) is collapsing. In the 1990s, women from within Islam and Islamist movements in far-flung places around the globe – from Malaysia, to South Africa, to Iran, to the United States – began to articulate a holistic gender-egalitarian construction of citizenship within the framework of an Islamic modernity.[16] I have argued elsewhere, along with Ziba Mir-Hosseini, Afsaneh Najmabadi, and others, that this "Islamic feminism" constitutes the new radical feminism within the Muslim world.[17]

UNIFYING YEMEN: THE EQUALITY PROJECT

The Republic of Yemen (ROY), which is neither a postcolonial secular state nor an Islamic republic, offers a different political and cultural space for feminist expression. In the new unified Yemen, the constitution and all laws – civil, personal status, commercial, and criminal – are based on the *shari'a* ("Islamic law"), and consequently all the courts are *shari'a* courts. There is no secular–religious dichotomy and no related public–private distinction. This of necessity changes the nature of the gender debates. Yemeni women in their gender activism are not bogged down in public–private and religious–secular debates (as are women from postcolonial Muslim societies); rather, as Yemenis, they articulate their feminism from the location of "integrated space." They do not have to justify their feminism as culturally authentic, as most women in postcolonial societies feel compelled to do. Positioned within a (national) religious culture but not from within a (national) Islamic republic, Yemeni women activists, and others, take "Islamic embeddedness" for granted. Yemeni feminists are not engaged in re/interpretation of Islamic religious texts, as are, for example, Iranian feminists. Yemeni women, as feminists within a culture of religious modernity, are pointing to contradictions in men's discourse and practice of citizenship, and exposing their patriarchal politics.

In 1990, the ROY was forged from the former Yemen Arab Republic (YAR, or North Yemen) and the People's Democratic

Republic of Yemen (PDRY, or South Yemen). The amalgamation of the nationalist republican regime of the north and the socialist regime of the south signals for many the supremacy of the former over the latter. In the project of fashioning unity, the trope of equality – of all citizens under the law – permeates contemporary debates. Taking a gendered look at the project and process of unification, this chapter suggests that women both act as its primary agents and reflect its deepest inequities. While they have multiple identities, affiliations, and allegiances which might divide them, women are united by gender – by experiences of gender – in ways men are not. For women gender is not merely a card in the game of political expediency in which the state and political parties engage.

Women behaving as feminists (without labels) are exposing and contesting re/assertions of patriarchal excesses that threaten national unity and the equality of citizens fundamental to the state-declared democratic project. Equality, seen through the prism of gender, is most striking in the arena of the constitutional affirmation of formal political rights. Gender inequality is most apparent in the personal status code, which preserves patriarchal hegemony.[18] I argue that Yemeni women, in functioning as feminists seeking full equality for all citizens, are at the forefront of the struggle to unify the new republic. I do not suggest, however, that women do not have differences, for they do. Rather, I claim that women, through their gendered experiences, share common issues with which they identify that furnish them with an existential unity upon which to build. To demonstrate this I look at two signal events in the recent history of gender and nation: the parliamentary elections of 1997 and the simultaneous attempt to impose a revised personal status law. In the run-up to the political elections women mobilized themselves to exercise their political rights, and were also mobilized by the state and male-dominated political parties which, however, were more sanguine about attracting women as voters than encouraging them to be candidates for election. When the attempt was made to make conservative amendments to the personal status law, women rose up in protest, while most men took cover. An examination of these two events reveals the split patriarchal agenda in the construction of the new state and how the equality declared to be at the core of this project is subverted. At the same time, it illuminates the dynamics of Yemeni women's feminism.

ONE STATE, TWO PASTS, AND TWO PRESENTS FOR WOMEN AND NATION

Yemeni women today are heirs to two separate feminist pasts. The YAR in the north was created in 1962, ending the Zaidi imamate, which had been established in 1918 following the demise of Ottoman rule (imposed in 1872). Influences of Nasserite Egypt, which had supported the republicans in the revolution against the imamate, were discernible in the construction of the new nationalist state. In the south, the PDRY was established in 1967 following an anti-colonial struggle against long-standing British administrative rule. The Aden Colony and Protectorate, which had fallen under the control of the British Colonial Office in 1839, experienced more direct colonial rule from 1937 to 1967.

While the story of women's part in the nationalist struggle to drive the British out of the south is still to be written, the pattern of intersecting nationalist and feminist awareness and activism seems to echo that of women in Egypt at the beginning of the twentieth century and in Sudan at mid-century.[19] With its creation as a socialist state, the PDRY embarked on the most progressive social program to date in the Arab world. Its constitution of 1978 made it the state's responsibility to deliver rights to women within a framework of equality. Article 36 read: "The State shall ensure equal rights for men and women in all fields of life, the political, the economical and social, and shall provide the necessary conditions for the realization of that equality." The Family Law, promulgated in 1974, was legendary in the Arab and Muslim world, rivaling the Turkish and Tunisian codes already alluded to as an egalitarian instrument.[20]

The gender equality that the Family Law confirmed, however, was diminished by a provision in the constitution indicating that the state upheld the conventional ideology of women's work in the home, affirming women's family and domestic responsibilities. It was not sufficient for the constitution to declare that men also had responsibilities in the home. Concerning women citizens the constitution read: "The State shall also work for the creation of the circumstances that will enable the woman to combine participation in the productive and social work and her role within the family sphere." This resembled the Egyptian constitution promulgated in 1971 at the beginning of the Sadat era (in the transition from Arab socialism to open-door capitalism), specifying that a woman's public roles and responsibilities must be coordinated with her family roles. This, as Egyptian feminists had been quick to point out, constituted a shift away from the more gender-egalitarian Nasserite constitution of 1963.[21]

In socialist Yemen there was no room for competing ideologies or for independent political parties. The General Union of Yemeni Women, which was formed in 1968 under the aegis of the state, became an instrument of "state feminism."[22] The Union organised literacy classes and provided instruction in practical skills, including health and childcare, sewing, and typing. Meanwhile, through its government agencies, the socialist state provided new educational and work opportunities for women. They were offered jobs in the government bureaucracy – mainly clustering in the lower levels, however, where they were employed in clerical positions. A small cadre of professional women was also formed. The most notable departure from convention occurred when women were enabled to occupy the post of judge, something still beyond the reach of women in many Arab countries.[23]

Religion was not abolished in the PDRY. Article 47 declared Islam the state religion. However, religion was made a private matter. During the period of Arab socialism in Egypt, Islam was likewise declared the state religion. There is a distinct difference between religion furnishing a dominant political idiom and religion operating as a matter of individual belief and moral guidance. There is no necessary connection between socialism and atheism, as anti-progressives would later allege when the political framework of the state shifted with the establishment of the unified state in 1990.[24]

Following the creation of the YAR in the north in 1962, the project of building a new state and society was impeded by the fighting that persisted for most of the remainder of the decade between republicans backed by Nasser's Egypt and royalists backed by neighboring Saudi Arabia.[25] The new YAR constitution of 1970 declared the equality of rights and duties of all citizens. The state exhibited certain Nasserist influences, especially during the presidency of Ibrahim al-Hamdi (from 1974 to 1977, when he was assassinated). The Family Law issued in 1978, which preserved patriarchal privileges,[26] bore resemblance to the conservative Egyptian personal status code that Nasser's socialist state had preserved and that Egyptian feminists had been trying to reform for half a century.[27]

Although the principle of equality was enshrined in the constitution, the state never made gender equality part of a vocal discourse.

Women, however, staked out new lives for themselves with quiet assistance from the state, which in certain ways smoothed their entry into public life. In the 1960s (before the promulgation of the constitution) and, especially, the 1970s, women pioneered in obtaining primary and secondary school education. Some continued their higher education at Sana'a' University (est. 1970) or abroad, especially in Egypt. They also broke ground by taking up jobs in teaching and radio broadcasting (doing children's and family programs) and later in television announcing.[28] In 1965 women established the Yemeni Women's Association (YWA) with branches in different parts of the country. The YWA created a social program similar to that of the Women's Union in the south, providing instruction in literacy, health, childcare, and practical skills. The YWA branches offered sites for women to gather outside the house, and also helped in the building of a national women's network.

Yemeni women's separate feminist pasts have left a dual legacy. Northern women acquired a set of lessons about patriarchal culture and power. They had to enact a piecemeal feminism, pioneering incrementally to stake out new roles and a claim on public space. Women from the north received limited help from the state, which was unable and unwilling to play a prominent role in their support. At the same time the state accorded women as feminist activists (in function but not in name) room to maneuver. Northern activist women, taking nothing for granted, acquired political acumen that has stood them in good stead. They had few illusions about the power or endurance of patriarchal relations and beliefs. These northern women operated largely with their own vision of how they wished to constitute their lives in a new society they were helping to shape.

Women of the south, as beneficiaries of gender gains within the project of the socialist state, were stranded with its decline. The state feminism of the PDRY did not penetrate very deep into the patriarchal bedrock, nor very far from Aden into the hinterland. In the mid-1980s, at the time of the factional strife in the PDRY, signs of incipient conservatism began to appear in Aden as women's dress grew more modest.[29] The 1980s was also a time when university enrolments of women increased dramatically.[30] Women in the south who had benefited from the opportunities and protections of the socialist state seemed to believe their gains would never be rescinded. They behaved as feminists, if by that is meant shaping lives of their choice by accessing the new options offered them. But they did not embrace a feminist ideology or identity, as this was preempted by the state. When the socialist regime collapsed, the fragile gains of state feminism went with it.[31] Women in the south, who had not honed feminist skills or refined a feminist sensibility and politics to draw upon, were bereft when the umbrella of state protection closed. Some women managed to hold their own, but many of the older generation fell by the wayside. It would be the task of the younger generation more recently, equipped with the educational opportunities the state had offered, to forge a feminist future.

Northern women had acquired an acute gender consciousness and developed practical feminist skills through their experience in piecemeal pioneering, but they had no legitimate political space. Southern women had been able to exploit the educational and professional benefits conferred under state feminism, but they did not have the independent ideological space in which to develop a feminism of their own.[32]

The two Yemens were united in 1990 to form the ROY, which constituted the realization of long-held vision and was the result of a fraught political process.[33] The constitution of the new republic, approved by referendum in 1991, provided for a parliamentary democracy. It explicitly stipulated that all citizens had "equal political, economic, social, and cultural opportunities."[34] The Electoral Law of 1992 declared both men and women eligible to vote from the age of eighteen and to be elected to parliament at the age of thirty-five.

Islam was declared the religion of the state, as it had been in both the YAR and the PDRY. Now, however, the *shari'a* was declared "the main source of legislation."[35] (The Islah Party had boycotted the 1991 constitutional referendum, insisting that the *shari'a* be "the only" source of legislation.[36]) The constitution explicitly declared that the equality of women and men must be understood within the context of the *shari'a*.[37] It was noted earlier in the united Yemen (ROY) that all laws – civil law, personal status law, commercial law, and criminal law – are cast within the framework of the *shari'a*, and that all courts are *shari'a* courts. This is unlike other constitutional states (except for the Islamic republics of Iran and Sudan) which declare Islam to be an important or sole source of legislation. Egypt, for example, where the constitution affirms Islam to be "the" source of legislation, retains a complicated secular and religious legal system. *Shari'a* courts handle only personal status cases, while national (or secular courts) handle all others. I would like to stress again that in the ROY there is no debate about secular versus religious law, and therefore no dichotomization of a "secular public sphere" and a "religious private sphere." Gender issues are debated within a holistic Islamic framework.

During the year of the unification a plethora of political parties surfaced.[38] The major parties included the General People's Congress (GPC, founded by President Ali Abdullah Salih in the 1980s); the Yemen Socialist Party (YSP) a carry-over from the former PDRY; and the Yemen Islah (Reform) Party (YIP), an Islamist grouping.[39] Each of these parties formed women's divisions, but the highest decision-making levels were retained by the male hierarchy. The Yemeni Women's Organization (YWO) was formed out of a combination of the old Yemeni Women's Association in the north (which had a feminist leadership in Sana'a' in the 1970s but was taken over by Islamist women in the 1980s) and the Women's Union of the former PDRY. The new Women's Union has continued to function at the local level in the north, where the branches have sustained their social projects.[40] In the south, the leadership of the old PDRY Women's Union in Aden, which has been in disarray, especially since the civil war of 1994, is trying to regroup.[41] The YWO has been all but moribund at the national level. Lack of state support of this quasi-governmental organization and an old-guard leadership with split residual loyalties have contributed to this.[42] The National Women's Committee (NWC), formed in 1996 under a decree from the prime minister, now constitutes the paramount quasi-governmental women's organization at the national level.[43]

Parliamentary committees were created to formulate laws for the unified state. The notion of equality of citizens, enshrined in the constitution and upheld by the political parties, was to be the guiding principle. Islah, for example, in its Political Action Programme issued in 1997, states: "The essence of equality is the equality under the law between members of society," and goes on to pledge: "The YIP shall work effortlessly [sic] to strengthen the principle of equality among all members of society."[44] The drafting of the new Personal Status Law (as the Family Law would be called in the unified Yemen) became the official responsibility of the men of the constitutional committee and the *shari'a* committee of the unified parliament. In shaping the new Personal Status Law there was a contest between northern liberals and conservatives, while southerners did little to defend the previous PDRY law.[45]

Women, who were missing from the official parliamentary committees designated to examine personal status legislation, tried by other means to influence the shaping of a new law. Raufa Hassan accepted the request of a GPC–Islah coalition to chair a conference to discuss a new law. After making a surprise appearance at the conference, the president of the country asked her to form a committee of women and men from north and south, including representatives from the Women's Union, Ministry of Justice, Ministry of Legal Affairs, and independent lawyers to study the question further. The committee tried to find a middle way between the previous family laws of the north and south. As Raufa Hassan put it, they wanted "a law society would accept without having women lose the ground they had gained in the Family Law of the south." They submitted their report in timely fashion, but, as Hassan put it, "debate lasted forever."[46]

In Ramadan 1992, at a moment when popular attention would be elsewhere, a Personal Status Law was "suddenly" enacted.[47] The new law was devoid of any suggestions made by the men and women of the committee Raufa Hassan chaired. Later, she and Radiyya Shamshir, a lawyer from the south, discovered that a deal had been struck between the GPC and the Socialist Party.[48] The Socialists would get a free hand in designing the education law but would give way on the personal status code (this was a move by the GPC to court the Islah Party).[49]

When the new law was announced, women in the south mounted strong public protest. Under the banner of the recently formed Organization for the Defense of Democratic Rights and Freedoms, hundreds went out in protest demonstrations.[50] Women in the north, despite their strong disappointment, made little overt public outcry. Instead, activist leaders continued to forge ahead from their professional bases, settling in for a long haul.

The gender-egalitarian model of the PDRY Family Law of 1974, which was bypassed in the construction of the new law for the YAR, had included such provisions as minimum marriage ages for females and males of sixteen and eighteen, respectively; free choice in marriage for both women and men; the abolition of polygamy, except under extreme conditions; divorce to be initiated by either spouse in front of a judge; and court-determined child custody.[51] The 1992 Personal Status Law of the united Republic of Yemen sustained a patriarchal model of the family, in a slightly improved version of the 1978 Family Law of the YAR. The law set the minimum marriage

age at fifteen for females. It did not protect the principle of free choice of spouses, but simply declared that marriage by force was invalid. Polygamy was allowed; however, the existing wife was to be informed of her husband's intention to marry another woman. A man's ability to end a marriage by repudiation (*talaq*) was still permitted, but a woman could obtain financial redress if a judge considered the repudiation to be unfair. A woman could also petition a court to end her marriage.

The new personal status law regulating gender relations and controlling women within a restrictive legal framework reflected the dominant post-unification political culture. In this law, equality was subverted both in principle and practice. This was done stealthily and under the justification of a narrowly interpreted *shari'a*. It was an adumbration of what was to come.

HIGH-PROFILE POLITICAL RIGHTS: FIGHTING FOR EQUAL PRACTICE

If the ability of Yemeni women to vote and be elected to parliament is an indicator of equality and democracy, as the highly vocal attention paid to women's political rights in Yemen would have it, a closer look is required. In the parliamentary elections of 1993 and 1997 the state and the political parties made highly visible efforts to mobilize women to vote for the success of male-dominated political parties.[52] Women's votes were crucial in the coming to power of the GPC–Islah coalition in 1993 and in the victory of the GPC as the paramount party in 1997.[53] Islamists candidly acknowledge the critical support women's votes had offered to Islah.[54]

Women mounted their own campaigns to support the exercise of their rights as voters and candidates in the elections in 1993. With the benefit of experience and a heightened sense of urgency, they continued even more vigorously in 1997.[55] Raufa Hassan, a parliamentary candidate in 1993, organized a nation-wide project for the Support and Increase of Women's Participation in Elections.[56] The project conducted political awareness campaigns among women throughout the country. The effort extended into remote mountain villages, where tribal leaders were often enlisted to help the female coordinators in rallying local women.[57] The group organized the training of a large network of women as governorate and constituency coordinators, first to help women register as voters and then to encourage them to cast their votes on election day. In doing this their intention was to create a permanent structure to protect and stimulate women's active participation in the political process.[58] Activist women employed Islamic discourse in promoting women's exercise of their political rights. Raufa Hassan taped an interview with Muhammad Tantawi, the Shaikh al-Azhar (rector of al-Azhar University), in which he confirmed women's right to vote and to be elected to parliament. It was later distributed as cassettes during the 1997 parliamentary elections.[59] The group also conducted seminars on women's right in Islamic law to vote and to be elected.

If the male mainstream was mobilizing women and eagerly courting their support at the ballot box, men were decidedly more resistant to supporting women as candidates for parliament. Rashida al-Qiyali, an outspoken Islahi, pointed to false promises of political support made by the male-dominated parties, saying: "They told us they would take our hands. They took our hands, not to parliament, but to the voting booths."[60] If the GPC was not vocal about its hesitancy to promote women as candidates, Islah made no pretence in opposing the idea of women running for parliament. Islah, however, did not advance Islamic justifications for women's exclusion from parliament. On the contrary, they acknowledged that women's membership in parliament was permitted by the *shari'a*. Rather, they claimed an instrumental reason, saying they did not want women to be exposed to the rough and tumble of campaigning. At the same time they expediently insisted they did not wish to support women as candidates unless they could win.[61] Despite the GPC's liberal rhetoric, its real stance was manifest in its lack of serious backing for women candidates.

Women activists worked hard to support women candidates. The project for the Support and Increase of Women's Participation in Elections ran workshops for women candidates, offering practical training on how to conduct a campaign. The project also created the Women Candidates' Fund to offer material support to the contestants. The composition of the Fund's executive committee, which included heads of women's divisions in the GPC, Islah, the National Women's Committee, and independents, testified to an element of unified activism among women on one level, and to women's complicated political maneuvers on another, simultaneously expressing loyalty to gender and party.[62]

In the first national elections in 1993, women ran for parliament and came out to vote in large numbers. However, in 1997, only twenty-one ran as candidates, less than half the number in the previous election.[63] Without serious support from men in the political parties, women stood very little chance of success. In both elections it was women from the south who were elected, and each time there were only two. In 1993 the two new women parliamentarians were both from the Socialist Party: Hawla Sharaf and Muna Basharahi.[64] After a bitter and bloody civil war between the YAR and PDRY, which began in 1994, Socialist men and women abstained from the 1997 elections. In these election the two successful candidates were from the GPC: Oras Sultan Naji and Uluf Bakhubaira.

LOW-PROFILE DRAFT PERSONAL STATUS LAW: WOMEN RESPOND

The high visibility that the state and political parties accorded gender equality in citizens' political rights, if only actively backing women as voters in the 1993 elections, renders more striking the invisibility surrounding the 1997 revised draft for a modified personal status law, encoding still less egalitarian relations between women and men than provided for in the 1992 law.[65] The supporters of this new draft kept it highly secret. They apparently hoped that with the distractions of Ramadan and preoccupation with the coming elections less than three months away, the Personal Status Law draft revision would pass in parliament without notice. However, word of the proposed revision leaked out.

When women learned of the regressive draft for a modified personal status law they swung into action. Since unification nothing had united women like the specter of this draft law. Women from the north and south, from the GCP to the Islah Party, to the independents, and across generations, joined forces. It was only after extreme difficulty that women were able to obtain a copy of the proposed draft in order to examine it thoroughly. The proposed changes included, among others elimination of a minimum marriage age; removal of the requirement that a man inform his wife of his intent to marry another woman; ending women's ability to act as legal witnesses; and the validation of a marriage by force if the partners subsequently agree.

There was limited time to halt the process. Women organized themselves from their professional bases and from within their political organisations, using all the resources available to them to mount a swift campaign. There were several focal points of activity. The Empirical Research and Women's Studies Center (ERWSC) at San'a' University, under the direction of Raufa Hassan, formed a Law Committee to examine the new draft. Composed of female and male graduate students, who included a judge and several lawyers, it was headed by a professor in the faculty of *shari'a* and statutory law, Ahmad Sharaf al-Din, a professor in the Women's Studies Center.[66] The Committee addressed the most repressive articles, marshaling Islamic arguments in formulating their refutations.

The women lawyers' office, called al-Ra'idat (the pioneers), the first and only one of its kind (est. March 1996), adopted a similar strategy of singling out the most offensive articles and preparing Islamic arguments against them. Al-Ra'idat founders Nabila al-Mufti (from Ibb in the north) and Shada Muhammad Nasir (from Aden in the south) held *nadwa*s (seminar-like discussion groups) for women during Ramadan to spread the word and debate the issues. They also used the press to widen the scope of action, contacting such papers as *al-Ayyam* and *al-Shura*.

Women's homes likewise became sites of activism. Suad al-Amri (whose father is ambassador to London) held meetings in her house, gathering friends, acquaintances, and colleagues among the young generation, along with rising professionals. Many of these women have been engaged in development work.[67] Lawyers Nabila al-Mufti and Shada Muhammad Nasir attended these meetings, offering detailed explanations of the proposed changes contained in the draft. The women also invited a prominent religious scholar and specialist in Islamic jurisprudence, Murtada al-Mahadhwari, to one of their gatherings. Shada Nasir, who took her law degree from Aden University in the 1980s (continuing advanced studies in Prague), stressed the importance for women to be well-grounded in Islamic law in order to help shape the personal status law.[68] (Her colleague Nabila al-Mufti predicts that women will become specialists in Islamic jurisprudence and in the future will help formulate codes responsive to women's needs.[69])

Members of the women's section of the Islah Party, like the other women who had been kept in the dark (although it was widely believed that Islah was behind the regressive modifications), expressed concern, and they too conducted their own investigation.[70] During Ramadan the Islahi women invited women of various political and ideological persuasions to an *iftar* (the meal breaking fast at the end of the day), which became another venue for women to collectively air their complaints about the prospective law. The women's section also quietly pressed the Islah Party leadership not to support the proposed draft.[71]

When supporters of the regressive draft bill succeeded in getting it passed through parliament, the only recourse for the women was to persuade the president not to sign the bill. The Women's Studies Center contacted 'Abd al-Karim al-Aryani, the minister of foreign affairs.[72] Al-Ra'idat, meanwhile, lobbied a counselor to the president (the minister of legal affairs in the government).[73] It was suggested to the president that efforts were under way to alienate women from the GPC. The women's interventions succeeded. The president did not sign the bill. If the GPC had previously been willing to back the proposed personal status law for political gain, either to curry favor with Islah or to be seen more widely as supporting a "religious project," the public exposure of the draft and widespread outcry by women rendered it no longer expedient to do so. Islah publicly feigned ignorance of the draft. However, tucked away in the party's Political Action Program was an item calling for "Overcoming obstacles in the way of early marriage," a euphemistic call to eliminate the legal minimum marriage age and a hint that Islah had indeed had a hand in the regressive draft.[74]

Women had not only saved the day, but were put on alert. The Women's Studies Center, which had already targeted law as one of its four major areas of study, planned to intensify its research on women and law. This is yet another expression of a wider move underway among women activists in different Muslim countries to reexamine the Qur'an and other religious sources upon which the *shari'a* is formulated in order to help achieve more gender-egalitarian laws.[75] The Center also planned to continue to closely monitor future draft laws. Center director Raufa Hassan affirms: "The next task will be to help create a [personal status] law that will come out of the society itself. This must be done through a process of intellectual and cultural development."[76] The women lawyers, for their part, believe they have important work to play in implementing the present law and promoting legal literacy.[77] Female activists agree with Nabila al-Mufti that women cannot play a role in formulating laws that promote the equality the Yemeni constitution and democratic project proclaims until they are sufficiently represented in parliament.[78]

There is a dissonance between people's perceptions and the purveyors of a conservative personal status discourse, certainly within the urban population. Research conducted among women and men in diverse neighborhoods of San'a' in 1997 disclosed widespread ignorance of the personal status law both the 1992 law and the 1997 revised draft. Strikingly, the research also revealed that people assumed that the proposed changes would constitute a liberalization of the law.[79]

When government officials, members of parliament, and politicians promote conservative (or reactionary) policies and legislation, such as the Personal Status draft, a typical justification they advance is that the people would not accept a liberal law. They blame the culture and conservative social habits. Political power brokers attempt to construct and control the discursive representation of the people, and especially women, for their own political ends. Their loud proclamations of the principle of equality and their muted impositions of inequality announce their awareness that they are manipulating, and not merely responding to, the wishes of the people in general – and of women in particular.

There is a consistency in Yemeni women's embrace of the ideals of democracy and in their resolve to put these ideals into practice. It is significant that women in Yemen have the right to vote and to be elected to parliament. Yemen can justly take credit for being the first country in the Arabian Peninsula to grant women full political rights. Yet there is a gender difference in efforts to influence application of these rights. Yemeni women encouraged their female compatriots to exercise their right to vote. Yemeni men attempted to rouse women to vote, largely as a function of partisan politics. Women also encouraged other women to run as candidates; however, in this there was not a full consensus, as most Islahi women did not support the idea of women running for parliament. However, across the board men did not encourage women to run for parliament, while some – notably Islahis – actively opposed the idea of women running. In men's views, women running for parliament would not serve men's interests.

PRACTICING FEMINISM: LIBERAL AND ISLAMIST COALITION ACTIVISM

It was not ideology or constituency politics that brought women across a wide spectrum together in militant activism. It was transgressing the bottom line of what was acceptable in women's everyday lives. Moreover, it was the crossing of the bottom line in exactly what women had always been told was their sphere: home and family. The conservative personal status law that had been intended to control women produced quite the opposite effect of politicizing them. Their unleashed fury empowered them and dissolved barriers among them. This is not to say that women retracted other loyalties, especially party loyalties, but that they coalesced around a gender issue.

When they collectively mobilized to oppose the regressive personal status draft, women had acted on an issue that directly affected their everyday lives. Women established a linkage between democracy and the principle of equality inherent in it, in both public life and private life. They insisted on the principle and practice of equality of citizens in both political rights and personal status. Linking what male politicians wanted to keep distinct and separate was made more dramatic as the national elections and efforts to enact a new regressive personal status law occurred simultaneously. Yemeni activist women insist that equality is indivisible as a democratic principle. Selective equality is illogical and anti-democratic, and is threatening to Yemen's unification process.

At this moment in Yemeni history, when women have attained equal rights to vote and to be elected, it is a blatant form of masculinist expediency to promote women's ability to vote only to harness it for male political purposes, and to impede women's ability to become members of parliament. A significant number of women in parliament might create a force that would change the politics of gender. At a time when women have legally come to enjoy their political rights (if not yet fully in practice), one way to contain women is through a conservative personal status law that reinforces male control over them in the context of the family. Activist women understand this very well.

In Yemen, women practice feminism. They do not label it. They grasp the patriarchalist manipulations of discourse and practice. Women are exposing the fraudulent contradictions between rights given in principle and withheld in practice, between equality declared and equality subverted. Yemeni women are not allowing themselves to be merely pawns in the game of patriarchal politics. This is a prag-matic rather than ideological moment for Yemeni women. They are engaging in a practical politics that does not call attention to itself. Yemeni feminist activists are refusing to get caught up in a binary sec-ular–religious framework. Activist women across the spectrum speak an Islamic language as they practice their feminism, and a feminist language as they practice their Islam. Women have consolidated forces around personal status legislation based on the *shariʿa.* In broad outline, they agree on a more advanced interpretation than men across the political and ideological spectrum. Is this feminism? Is this progressive Islamism? Is this Islamic feminism? These are not questions these feminist activists ask. They do not, as noted, call themselves feminist activists. Rather, the term describes their actions.

Through their activism Yemeni women are making a distinctive contribution to the discourse of feminism in Middle Eastern and Islamic societies. Unlike most women elsewhere in the region, they have been able to coalesce as women around critical gender issues while retaining their loyalty to a political party or remaining commit-ted to non-partisan independence. They have narrowed a gap com-mon elsewhere between Islamist and non-lslamist women. Yemeni women are insisting on the unitary nature of citizenship, inclusive of the public and the private, and the trope of equality in the construc-tion of the state and citizenry: equality of north and south, equality of women and men. Yemeni women activists mobilized swiftly to expose and confront the contradictory projects of the highly touted national elections with the prestige that women's ability to vote brought the country and the regressive draft for a revised personal status code, of which the surrounding secrecy belied its problematic nature – and, indeed, of the democratic process as practiced. Full equality expressed in a progressive personal status code will be achieved as part of a longer process, as will the implementation of women's right to be elected to parliament. Yemen cannot fully unify without women play-ing integral roles, nor can it become a functioning democracy without women fully taking part. Women and men alike understand this. But it will be the women who will have to make this happen – as we see they are doing. Yemeni women's activism is a vibrant illustration of the local feminisms Amrita Basu reminds us are constitutive of the story of "women's movements in global perspective."[80]

* * *

Originally published in *Gender and History*, special issue on Feminisms and Internationalism, 10, 3 (November 1998).

NOTES

1. Research for the paper on which this chapter is based was conducted in January and February, and from August to mid-November 1997 in Yemen (mainly San'a', but also in Aden) under a grant from the American Institute for Yemeni Studies. During this time I had interviews and extended conversations with many women in Yemen, to whom I wish to express my gratitude for information and insights which have contributed to the shaping of this chapter. From 23 August to 18 September, as part of my grant, I co-conducted a workshop in gender research skills with Raufa Hassan, director of the ERWSC, San'a' University. This study has benefited from research done during the workshop by the student participants: Evelyn Anoya, Narges Erami, Abd al-Hakim al Hamdani, Majda al-Qarmuti, Sabah al-Huthi, Samira Muhsin, Miryam Rashid, Nabil al-Shamsani, and Farah Usmai.

2. Many states, for example, have signed international conventions such as the United Nations Human Rights Convention or CEDAW, signaling acceptance of human rights and women's rights, while silently failing to honor them in practice.

3. Deniz Kandiyoti, "Introduction," in Deniz Kandiyoti (ed.), *Women, Islam, and the State* (London: Macmillan and Philadelphia: Temple University Press, 1991), p. 2.

4. See Marnia Lazreg, *The Eloquence of Silence* (London: Routledge, 1994); Sondra Hale, *Gender Politics in the Sudan: Islamism, Socialism, and the State* (Boulder: Westview Press, 1997); Parvin Paidar, *Women and the Political Process in Twentieth-Century Iran* (Cambridge: Cambridge University Press, 1995); and Margot Badran, *Feminists, Islam, and Nation: Gender and the Making of Modern Egypt* (Princeton: Princeton University Press, 1995).

5. Amrita Basu (ed.), *The Challenge of Local Feminisms:Women's Movements in Global Perspective* (Boulder: Westview Press, 1995), introduction, p. 14, makes an important observation when she writes: "Women's activism seems to have borne greater dividends in contemporary nationalist struggles than in earlier anticolonial movements."

6. On experiences in Algeria, Egypt, Iran, and Sudan see the works cited in note 4; and in Kuwait see Margot Badran, "Gender, Islam, and the State: Kuwaiti Women in Struggle, Pre-lnvasion to Postliberation," in Yvonne Haddad and John Esposito (eds.), *Islam, Gender, and Social Change* (New York: Oxford University Press, 1998), pp. 190–208.

7. They also include rights to retain citizenship after marriage, to assume citizenship in the country of one's spouse, and the ability to pass one's citizenship to one's children.

8. It is important to note that it should not be assumed that modern states in the Middle East (or elsewhere) necessarily promote more or less gender-egalitarian laws than premodern societies. Historical experience is complicated. For example, on law and gender in various places under Ottoman rule see Amira El Azhary

Sonbol, *Women, the Family, and Divorce Laws in Islamic History* (Syracuse: Syracuse University Press, 1996). Modern states in the West have adjusted some of their laws repressive to women before granting women the vote – as, for example, in England, where a women's property law was instituted before women were granted suffrage; but despite specific advances, women in most countries, after acquiring the vote, have had to continue long struggles to gain better divorce laws, laws relating to reproductive rights, and the like.

9. While Egyptian feminists articulated a unitary discourse on citizens' rights, they prioritized their activist struggle out of expediency, giving immediate attention to achieving personal status rights and postponing the fight for equal political rights. See Badran, *Feminists, Islam, and Nation.*

10. Ibid., chapter 12 (pp. 223–250).

11. See, for example, Palestinian Academic Society for the Study of International Affairs (ed.), *Women in Contemporary Palestine: Between Old Conflicts and New Realities* (Jerusalem: Palestinian Academic Society for the Study of International Affairs, 1996).

12. Nawal El Saadawi, "The Political Challenges Facing Arab Women at the End of the Twentieth Century"; and Fatima Mernissi, "Democracy as Moral Disintegration: The Contradiction between Religious Belief and Citizenship as a Manifestation of the Ahistoricity of the Arab Identity," both in Nahid Toubia (ed.), *Women of the Arab World* (London: Zed Press, 1988), pp. 8–26 and 36–43 respectively.

13. For example, on the Turkish experience see Nilüfer Göle, *The Forbidden Modern: Civilization and Veiling* (Ann Arbor: University of Michigan Press, 1996).

14. In Turkey, for example, male legal headship of the family was inscribed in the civil code of 1926, as second-wave Turkish feminists disdainfully pointed out. See Yeşim Arat, "Kemalism and Turkish Women," *Women and Politics*, 14 (1994); Yeşim Arat, "On Gender and Citizenship in Turkey," *Middle East Report* (1996); and Yeşim Arat, "Women's Movement of the 1980s in Turkey: Radical Outcome of Liberal Kemalism?," in Fatma Müge Göcek and Shiva Balaghi (eds.), *Reconstructing Gender in the Middle East* (New York: Columbia University Press, 1994); Nükhet Sirman, "Feminism in Turkey: A Short History," *New Perspectives on Turkey*, 3 (1989), pp. 1–34; and Şirin Tekeli, "The Emergence of the Feminist Movement in Turkey," in Drude Dahlerup (ed.), *The New Women's Movements: Feminism and Political Power in Europe and the USA* (London and Beverly Hills: Sage Publications, 1986).

15. For example, in the case of China see Mayfair Yang, "From Gender Erasure to Gender Difference: State Feminism, Consumer Sexuality, and Women's Public Sphere in China," in Mayfair Yang (ed.), *Spaces of their Own: Women's Public Sphere in Transnational China* (Minneapolis: University of Minnesota Press, 1998).

16. For example, in Kuala Lumpur, Malaysia, Sisters in Islam have issued several booklets on feminist rereadings of the Qur'an; on South Africa, Farid Esack, *Qur'an, Liberation and Pluralism: An Islamic Perspective of Interreligious Solidarity against Oppression* (Oxford: Oneworld, 1997); on Iran, Ziba Mir-Hosseini, "Stretching the Limits: A Feminist Reading of the Shar'ia in Post-Khomeini Iran," in Mai Yamani (ed.), *Feminism and Islam: Legal and Literary Perspectives* (New York: New York University Press, 1997), pp. 285–320; and Afsaneh Najmabadi, "Feminism in an Islamic Republic: Years of Hardship,

Years of Growth," in Haddad and Esposito (eds.), *Islam, Gender, and Social Change*, pp. 59–84; and in the United States, Amina Wadud-Muhsin, *Qur'an and Woman: Rereading the Sacred Text from a Woman's Perspective* (Kuala Lumpur: Penerbit Fajar Bakti, 1992).

17. See Mir-Hosseini, "Stretching the Limits"; Najmabadi, "Feminism in an Islamic Republic"; and Margot Badran, "Toward Islamic Feminisms: A Look at the Middle East," in Asma Afsaruddin (ed.), *Hermeneutics and Honor: Negotiating Female "Public" Space in Islamic/ate Societies*, Harvard Middle East Monograph series (Cambridge, Mass.: Harvard University Press, 1999); and Margot Badran, "Feminisms and Islamisms," *Journal of Women's History*, special issue on Women and Fundamentalisms, 10, 4 (Winter 1999).

18. Seema Kazi notes this common pattern in Muslim countries in "Muslim Law and Women Living under Muslim Laws," in Mahnaz Afkhami and Erika Friedl (eds.), *Muslim Women and the Politics of Participation: Implementing the Beijing Platform* (Syracuse: Syracuse University Press, 1997), pp. 141–146. Nadia Hijab, "Islam, Social Change, and the Reality of Arab Women's Lives," in Haddad and Esposito (eds.), *Islam, Gender, and Social Change*, pp. 45–56, speaks of this in the context of Arab society; and Boutheina Cheriet in the case of Algeria in "Fundamentalism and Women's Rights: Lessons from the City of Women," in Afkhami and Erika Friedl (eds.), *Muslim Women and the Politics of Participation*, pp. 11–17. Feminists in Arab countries have been less successful in obtaining equal rights in the "private sphere" than in the "public sphere," as I discuss in the case of Egypt – for example, in "Independent Women: More than a Century of Feminism in Egypt," in Judith Tucker (ed.), *Arab Women: Old Boundaries, New Frontiers* (Bloomington: Indiana University Press, 1993), pp. 129–148, and chapter 5 in this volume.

19. See Margot Badran, "Dual Liberation: Feminism and Nationalism in Egypt from the 1870s to 1925," *Feminist Issues* (Spring 1988), pp. 15–24; Badran, *Feminists, Islam, and Nation*; and Carolyn Fleur-Lobban, "Women and Social Liberation: The Sudan Experience," in *Three Studies on National Integration in the Arab World* (North Dartmouth, Mass.: Association of Arab-American Graduates, 1974).

20. For an analysis of the PDRY Family Law of 1974 see Maxine Molyneux, "Legal Reform and Social Revolution in Democratic Yemen: Women and the Family," *International Journal of the Sociology of Law*, 13 (1985), pp. 142–172 and republished in an abbreviated form as "The Law, the State and Socialist Policies with Regard to Women: The Case of the People's Democratic Republic of Yemen 1967–1900," in Kandiyoti (ed.), *Women, Islam, and the State*.

21. There is no necessary link between ideology expressed in a constitution and in personal status laws. It was also under Sadat that the 1929 Egyptian Personal Status Code was modified in a way more responsive to women's needs.

22. The Yemeni Women's Society, established in Aden in 1946 under the leadership of Ruqaiya Luqman, appears to be the first of its kind and private precursor to the GUYW.

23. See Helen Lackner, *The People's Democratic Republic of Yemen: Outposts of Socialist Development in Arabia* (London: Ithaca Press, 1985), pp. 114–118. In Egypt, for example, where women are not allowed to function as judges, there was a recent demonstration in the press of women's ability to fill positions as judges in Islam citing religious texts, including the Qur'an and Hadith. See the

two-part article in *al-Ahram Weekly* by Zainab Radwan, "Sitting in Judgement," 16–22 April 1998, p. 14, and "Robbing Wise Men of their Reason," 12–29 April 1998, p. 15. [In 2004 the first woman judge was appointed.]

24. In Egypt at mid-century, Inji Aflatun argued that there was no contradiction between Islam and leftist ideologies. See her books *Thamanun milyun imra'a ma'na* (Eighty million women with us, Cairo: n.p., 1948) and *Nahnu al-nisa' al-misriyyat* (We Egyptian women, Cairo: n.p., 1949).

25. See Paul Dresch, *Tribes, Government, and History in Yemen* (Oxord: Clarendon Press, 1989).

26. The situation before the Family Law of 1978 was complex. See, for example, Hassan al-Hubaishi, *Legal System and Basic Law in Yemen* (Worcester: Billing & Sons, 1988). Martha Mundy, in "Women's Inheritance of Land in Highland Yemen," *Arabian Studies*, 5 (1979), pp. 161–187, shows legal advantages women gained – on paper – regarding inheritance rights with the creation of the 1978 statutory law and how this was subverted in rural areas.

27. See Badran, *Feminists, Islam, and Nation*, chapter 7, "Recasting the Family" (pp. 124–142).

28. See Amatalrauf al-Sharki, "An Unveiled Voice," in Margot Badran and Miriam Cooke (eds.), *Opening the Gates: A Century of Arab Feminist Writing* (Bloomington: Indiana University Press, 1990), pp. 375–85.

29. Conversation with Valentina Alwan, 2 November 1997, and with other women from Aden.

30. These two phenomena, the increase of conservative dress and an increase of women at university, should not be taken as contradictions. The more daring entry of women into university would have come with the first path-breakers of the 1970s. Also, neo-religious conservatives typically encourage the education of women.

31. Interview with Mona al-Attas, 31 October 1997, who said: "Before the state in the South protected women but the new state does not." Maxine Molyneux, "Women's Rights and Political Contingency: The Case of Yemen, 1990–1994," *Middle East Journal*, special issue on Gender and Politics, 49, 3 (Summer 1995), pp. 418–431, notes (in a different context) that the PDRY con-stituition contained "many commitments to state intervention on behalf of women" (p. 422). She provides an analysis of the general political and economic decline of the PDRY and its gender consequences: see esp. pp. 427–429.

32. For a comparative perspective on "state feminism" see Yang, "From Gender Erasure to Gender Difference," who writes in reference to Maoist China: "State feminism also made it difficult to sustain a critical gender perspective and an independent feminist discourse mounted by women themselves, issuing from their own experiences." For a brief account of women from the previous two Yemens a year and a half into the new unified state, see Sheila Carapico, "Women and Public Participation in Yemen," *Middle East Report* (November–December 1991), p. 15.

33. On this process, see Charles Dunbar, "The Unification of Yemen: Process, Politics, and Prospects," *Middle East Journal*, 46 (1992), pp. 456–476; Siobhan Hall, *Yemen: The Politics of Unity* (London: Gulf Centre for Stategic Studies, 1991); and Fred Halliday, *Revolution and Foreign Policy: The Case of South Yemen, 1967–1987* (Cambridge: Cambridge University Press, 1990), chapter 4, "The Enigma of Yemeni 'Unity'"; and Sheila Carapico, "The Economic

Dimension of Yemeni Unity," *Middle East Report* (September–October 1993), pp. 9–14.

34. Article 18 of the 1991 constitution.

35. Article 2 of the 1991 constitution.

36. See Sheila Carapico, "Elections and Mass Politics in Yemen," *Middle East Report* (November–December 1993), pp. 2–6.

37. Article 27 of the 1991 constitution.

38. See Carapico, "Elections and Mass Politics in Yemen."

39. Muhammad Qahtan, the head of Islah's political division, in an interview with Rochdi Younsi, 9 September 1997, explained the long build-up of Islah and his own involvement in what was previously an underground network from 1974. The Islah Party constitutes an expedient amalgam of tribal forces headed by Shaikh Abdullah al-Ahmar, head of the Hashid confederation, and the Muslim Brothers with a strong urban base. It has three strands: extremely conservative, moderate, and "liberal."

40. In an interview on 3 September 1997 in San'a', Samira Muhsen described the programs of the Taiz branch.

41. Ihsan Ubaid (the president), Ruqaiyya Sayyid Muhammad Ali, Ihsan Salam, and Hawla Sharaf from the YWU, in an interview in Aden, 18 January 1997, gave a version of this tortuous process.

42. D. Dorman, A. N. al-Madhaji, M. Aidarus, S. Beatty, Z. Ismael, and M. de Regt, *Yemeni NGOs ,and Quasi-NGOs: Analysis and Directory: Part II, Directory* (San'a': Embassy of the Netherlands, 1996), pp. 81–83. Sheila Carapico stresses the divergent agendas of the northern and southern women within the new union as a primary reason for its disarray. See Sheila Carapico, "Yemen between Civility and Civil War," in A. R. Norton (ed.), *Civil Society in the Middle East*, (Leiden: Brill, 1996), pp. 287–316.

43. Headed by Amat al-Aleem Alsoswa, this body was created in the aftermath of Beijing. A fuller discussion of its complicated mandate to serve women and the state is beyond the task of this chapter.

44. Yemen Republic Islah Party, "Political Action Programme" (San'a', 1997), official English translation, a 38-page document.

45. See Molyneux, "Women's Rights and Political Contingency," p. 427, who writes that the Socialist Party "made no significant effort to defend their own law. Instead, they abandoned the 1974 code on the family much as they had other distinctive, secular, and socialist laws regulating social practices." Carapico, "Yemen between Civility and Civil War," p. 310, says the Yemeni Organization for the Defense of Democratic Rights and Freedoms, a human rights organization created in Aden in February 1992, "prepared to challenge the Personal Status Law."

46. Interview with Raufa Hassan by Sabah al-Huthi and Rochdi Younsi, San'a', 2 September 1997.

47. Molyneux, "Women's Rights and Political Contingency," p. 432, citing a Yemeni legal expert, writes that the 1990 Personal Status Law contained elements from the League of Arab States' Unified Model Arab Personal Status Law, which is an indication of their lack of enlightened legal paradigms. See the discussion of personal status and family laws in the YAR, PDRY, and ROY, in Republic of Yemen Women National Committee, "Status of Woman in Yemen" (San'a', May 1996), pp. 16–18; and also Anna Würth, "The Legal Status of

Women in Yemen," unpublished report, CID/WID Project, Bureau of Applied Research in Anthropology, department of anthropology, University of Arizona, March 1994; and Anna Würth, "A Sana'a Court: The Family and the Ability to Negotiate," *Islamic Law and Society*, 2 (Leiden, 1995), pp. 320–340. I would like to thank Anna Würth for sharing her knowledge of law and the courts in Yemen, and especially for discussing the (then) impending draft revision of the personal status law.

48. Raufa Hassan and Radiyya Shamshir were both to run unsuccessfully for parliament in the 1993 elections, running respectively as an independent and Socialist.

49. Interview with Raufa Hassan by Sabah al-Huthi and Rochdi Younsi, San'a', 2 September 1997.

50. See Molyneux, "Women's Rights and Political Contingency," pp. 428–429.

51. Interview with Raufa Hassan by Rochdi Younsi, San'a', 2 September 1997.

52. For a general account of the 1993 elections, see Renaud Detalle, "The Yemeni Elections Close Up," *Middle East Report* (November–December 1993), pp. 8–12.

53. In 1993, out of the 301 seats in parliament, the GPC won 123 and Islah 62 (*The Economist*, March 1997, p. 46). In 1997, the GPC won about two-thirds of the seats and Islah about 54 ("GPC Rides High," *Yemen Times*, 5–11 May 1997). See Carapico, "Yemen between Civility and Civil War," p. 300, who says that women played a major role in Islah's successful voter registration campaign, in which they mobilized large numbers of women voters.

54. See Janine Clark, "Women and Islamic Activism in Yemen," *Yemen Update: Bulletin of the American Institute for Yemeni Studies*, 39 (1887), pp. 13–15.

55. In 1993, 15 percent of the eligible women voted, as opposed to 77 percent of the men. Fifty women were among the 3,600 parliamentary candidates who remained in the running until the end. See Carapico, "Elections and Mass Politics in Yemen." In 1993, women were 19 percent of the registered voters, and in 1997, 30 percent. See "Yemen's Elections are Given High Marks by Observers," *Yemen Times* (5–11 May 1997).

56. On her campaign, see David Warburton, "A Campaign Rally in San'a," *Middle East Report* (November–December 1993), p. 12.

57. They concentrated on the constituencies with the lowest voter participation rate in the 1993 elections.

58. In January 1997 the author attended one of these two-day workshops which conducted training seminars for women to act as constituency coordinators from all over the country. At the closing ceremony women from different political parties, especially the GPC and Islah, as well as independents, were in evidence.

59. The author was present at the interview with Muhammad Tantawi at his office in al-Azhar in Cairo in February 1997.

60. Interview with Rashida al-Qiyali by Miryam Rashid, San'a', September 1997. She observed that all the political parties marginalize women.

61. Interview with Muhammad Qahtan by Margot Badran, San'a', January 1997. Rashida al-Qiyali told Miryam Rashid: "The good thing about Islah is that they are honest about the [woman's] issue."

62. The women on the executive committee of the Fund include Amat al-Razzaq Jahlaf (GPC), Amat al-Sallam Ali Raja (Islah), Amat al-Aleem Alsoswa (National Women's Committee), and Raufa Hassan (independent).

63. Women constituted an important presence in the voter monitoring procedures on election day.

64. Hawla Sharaf is from Aden and Muna Basharahi from Hadhramaut.
65. Molyneux, "Women's Rights and Political Contingency," p. 419, note 4, makes this point.
66. Members of the committee from the Center included Muhammad al-Qabatri, a judge; Hanan Bahmaid, Abd al-Hakim al-Hamdani, and Najat al-Shami, lawyers; and Fathiyya al-Haythami and Sa'id al-Mikhlafi. There were also human rights activists and journalists.
67. The author attended one of these meetings at the end of January 1997. In discussions with women there, and also in an interview with Suhair al-Amri and Bushra al-Mutawakkil, San'a', 15 January 1997, I learned about the concerns of the rising generation of professional women, whose gender consciousness, advocacy, and activism grows out of their own personal and work lives.
68. Shada Nasir emphasized this in an interview with Majda al-Qurmati and Narges Erami, San'a', 2 September 1997.
69. Interview with Nabila al-Mufti by Samira Muhsen and Evelyn Anoya, San'a', 3 September 1997.
70. When I interviewed members of the Islah women's division in San'a' in January 1997, they seemed genuinely to be unaware of the draft.
71. Interview with Muhammad Qahtan by Margot Badran, San'a', October 1997.
72. Interview with Raufa Hassan by Rochdi Younsi, San'a', 2 September 1997.
73. Interview with Nabila al-Mufti by Samira Muhsen and Evelyn Anoya, San'a', 3 September 1997.
74. Yemen Republic Islah Party, "Political Action Programme."
75. See note 16 above; also Barbara Stowasser, *Women in the Qur'an, Traditions, and Interpretation* (New York: Oxford University Press, 1994); and Barbara Stowasser, "Gender Issues and Contemporary Qur'an Interpretation," in Haddad and Esposito (eds.), *Islam, Gender, and Social Change*, pp. 30–45.
76. Interview with Raufa Hassan by Rochdi Younsi, San'a', 2 September 1997.
77. Shada Nasir emphasized this in an interview with Majda al-Qurmati and Narges Erami, San'a', 2 September 1997.
78. Interview with Nabila al-Mufti by Samira Muhsen and Evelyn Anoya, San'a', 3 September 1997.
79. This research was conducted by students from San'a' University and the University of Chicago during the workshop in Gender Research Skills held at the ERWSC, San'a' University, in August and September 1997.
80. This is taken from the subtitle of Basu's book, *The Challenge of Local Feminisms: Women's Movements in Global Perspective*.

12

SHARI'A ACTIVISM IN NIGERIA
IN THE ERA OF HUDUD

In 1999, the year of the return to democracy in Nigeria after years of military dictatorship, the contender for governor of Zamfara, the state with the highest poverty and lowest literacy in the north, pledged to place *hudud,* or Islamic laws of crime and punishment, into statutory law.[1] This move was billed as a "return to the *shari'a.*"[2] By 2002 twelve out of thirty-six states had instituted *hudud* laws. Under these laws sex outside marriage, or *zina,* was criminalized, and for the guilty could bring the ultimate penalty of death by stoning, while amputations were prescribed for crimes of theft.[3] Human rights activists and feminist activists in Nigeria, who had seen the disastrous effects of *hudud* in other countries over the past decades, worried that women and the poor would fall victim to these laws.[4]

As feared, it was not long before women were accused of adultery and brought before *shari'a* courts. In what became two high-profile cases, Safiyatu Husseini of Sokoto and Amina Lawal of Katsina, both from northern states with majority Muslim populations, were summarily convicted and sentenced to death by stoning in the lower *shari'a* courts. These quickly became high-profile cases, locally and globally. It did not escape attention that it was women – and, more precisely, poor women – who were brought before the law, while the men involved simply absconded. Nigerian women activists, Muslims and non-Muslims alike, together with some male supporters, immediately swung into action. Through their NGOs, Baobab for Women's Human Rights and the Women's Rights and Protection Association (WRAPA), activists offered the two women legal assistance, and simultaneously mounted wide publicity campaigns. The accused were eventually acquitted in higher *shari'a* courts of appeal in their respective states – Safiyatu Husseini in 2002 and Amina Lawal in 2003 – as a result of scrupulous application of *fiqh* (Islamic jurisprudence). It was thus in the Islamic legal system that the women were both convicted and acquitted following the strenuous work of Nigerian activists. However, Westerners who protested through petitions and via the media – until Nigerian activists asked them to desist as their support became counterproductive, especially when laced with expressions of Islamophobia – took credit for the victory as a triumph of (Western) secular discourse. Yet this is not to suggest that the intensive glare of the global media – Western and beyond – was without positive influence.

The campaigns women mounted to see justice done to Amina Lawal and Safiyatu Husseini, through organizing legal teams to defend their rights before higher *shari'a* courts, along with the public advocacy and debates that they stimulated, constitute a stunning manifestation of Islamic feminism at work. Did this activism and its positive outcomes provoke or further enhance Islamic feminist consciousness – the awareness of Qur'an-based women's rights as *insan*, as human beings? Did the successful campaigns catalyze intensified debates in Nigeria around issues of gender justice and social justice, mobilizing Islamic discourse to empower Muslim women and erode oppressive ideas about and treatment of women in the name of Islam? To seek answers to such questions I went to Nigeria early in 2005 to meet women.[5]

In this chapter I discuss briefly how the women's activism around the *zina* cases made an important contribution to the ongoing project of Islamic feminism; however, my main interest is to explore how this activist campaign catalyzed a longer-term unfolding of Islamic feminism. I seek answers to the above questions through the results of interviews and conversations with Muslim women I met in Nigeria. I place this in the context of global Islamic feminist discourse and practice. Muslim women in various locations move in strikingly parallel ways as well as along divergent paths and in different time frames in elaborating and activating Islamic feminism.

BEFORE "THE RETURN" TO *SHARI'A*

From the late 1970s, and especially from the 1980s, two diametrically-opposed discourses on women and gender generated by Muslims circulated (trans)nationally. One discourse, initially spread mainly by men as Islamists or advocates of political Islam, also called Islamic fundamentalists, was a patriarchal discourse in the language of Islam, supporting male domination and protection of women in a system of unequal gender rights, laying stress on women's family roles. The other was a gender-egalitarian discourse articulated by Muslim women as feminists and human rights advocates that stressed women's rights and public roles in the multiple and intersecting discourses of Islamic modernism, and (Muslims') secular feminism/s, human rights, and democracy.

The 1990s saw the appearance of the new Islamic feminist discourse, referred to above, based on women scholars' new Qur'anic interpretation articulating the full equality of women and men across the public–private spectrum. This Islamic feminist discourse, backed by this new exegetical work, elaborated a more radical notion of gender equality than Muslim women's secular feminisms, which had typically acquiesced in the notion of equity or balanced gender roles in the private or family sphere. The early secular feminist movements in Muslim-majority societies which first arose in the early twentieth century, fighting battles on multiple fronts, found it easier to make headway pushing for full equality in the public sphere. They accepted the new Islamic modernist approaches to ameliorating injustices in the family through pushing for optimal performance of gender-differentiated roles.[6] It would take time for societal changes and higher levels of training before women could embark on more radical interpretation on their own, as happened toward the end of the twentieth century. With the turn of the twenty-first century, the patriarchal and egalitarian discourses of Islam and their respective proponents were on a high-stakes collision course.

From the early 1980s Muslim women in different parts of the globe, joined by some non-Muslims, began to consolidate a transnational feminist/human rights culture when they formed the network called Women Living under Muslim Laws (WLUML). It began informally when Algerian women objected to not being consulted about the draft for a new Muslim family law in Algeria. Formally established in 1984, WLUML has engaged in advocacy and lobbying work around questions of laws and their implementation, issuing alerts and circulating petitions on behalf of women suffering victimization. It undertook a long-tem project gathering data on laws and women's experience in Muslim societies around the world that resulted in the publication of *Knowing our Rights: Women, Family, Laws and Customs in the Muslim World* in 2003, which had appeared in a third edition by December 2006. The women who began WLUML were (secular) feminists and human rights advocates who used international discourses, and who familiarized themselves with the various legal discourses, including religious jurisprudence, found in the societies where they operated. With the development of Islamic feminist discourse in the 1990s they accessed its insights and methods as well.[7]

As Muslim women were consolidating this transnational feminist network culture, the transnational movement of political Islam was spreading globally. Islamism, which had begun to surface in parts of the Muslim world in the 1970s, made its appearance in northern Nigeria toward the end of that decade, through a group called Jama'atu Izalat al-Bid'a wa Iqamat al-Sunna (Society for the Eradication of Innovation and the Establishment of Tradition).[8] The Izala movement has been called "neo-fundamentalist" as it did not challenge the state (like the fundamentalist movements such as the Egyptian-founded Muslim Brothers), but rather civil society and especially Sufi trends, advocating legal reform (or a return to Islamic laws). At the core of its reformist project was the spread of its own brand of Islamic education and to that end the Izala created Islamic schools throughout the north to teach religious subjects, along with what in Nigeria are called Western subjects (elsewhere often called modern subjects), to males and females alike. An unintentional result of the neo-fundamentalists' mission of teaching the religious sciences and the Arabic language was to open the way for questioning Izala's reactionary patriarchal attitude to Islam. A young woman I spoke with, after completing her studies in an Izala-run school, went on to give women lessons in religion in her home, where she introduced them to a gender-egalitarian approach to Islam. While operating as an outspoken feminist education activist – and she is not shy about claiming this label – she continued her Islamic religious studies at the university.[9]

During this same period, Nigerian women were creating their own associations and spearheading their own educational initiatives. In 1985, Muslim women from around the country with ties to the Muslim Sisters Organization and other Islamic associations came together to establish the Federation of Muslim Women's Associations of Nigeria (FOMWAN), with Aisha Lemu as its first head or *amira*. Its main purpose was to provide schooling for Muslim girls in a curriculum that combined Islamic and Western subjects. While FOMWAN laid stress on education and an overall religious formation it also provided health training and services in its various outreach programs. This grassroots association celebrated its twentieth anniversary in 2005 with a large conference in the nation's capital, Abuja.[10] Its current head is activist, writer, and journalist Bilkisu Yusuf.

Nigerian women, Muslims and Christians together, were also forming human rights and women's rights organizations in the 1990s. I mention, as examples, the two organizations that came to the rescue of the women accused in the two *zina* cases. Baobab for Women's Human Rights was established in 1996 under the leadership of Ayesha Imam, a founding member of WLUML.[11] Although autonomous, the organization has ties with WLUML. Three years later, in 1999, the year the first *hudud* laws were announced, WRAPA was founded, with activist Saudatu Mahdi assuming the position of secretary-general. Human rights and feminist activists employed multiple discourses, seeing human rights, democracy, and progressive religious discourse as mutually reinforcing women's rights and human rights, and gender justice and social justice.

Muslim women operating more fully within an Islamic framework, such as the FOMWAN women, and those functioning within multiple frameworks, such as Baobab and WRAPA members, were not adversarial, but rather their focus and their projects differed. From talking with women from both groups it appears that around the turn of the twentieth century – and especially in the aftermath of the *zina* cases – these two groups were converging more and more in their concerns about issues of women, state, and society. The problematic verdicts issued by the lower *shari'a* courts in the *zina* cases and the impressive backing by women activists from Baobab and WRAPA through the mobilization of *fiqh* readings have galvanized women across a broad spectrum in support of a common quest for gender justice and social justice in the aftermath of the instituting of *hudud* laws.

ISLAMIC FEMINISM

Islamic feminism is a global discourse that is continually fed by the local, while the global discourse likewise animates the local. In the

1990s a new feminist paradigm in the language of Islam caught the attention of Muslim women, themselves feminists, in different locations, who, often unbeknown to each other, started to call it Islamic feminism. They were noticing and naming a feminist discourse and practice grounded in rereadings of the Qur'an, seeking rights and justice for women – and for men – in the totality of their existence. Women interpreters enunciated two key concepts of Islamic feminism: gender equality and social justice. They were fundamental ideals that were to be applied in everyday life across the public–private continuum.[12]

Islamic feminism, with its paramount grounding in religious discourse, did not reject or replace what has been known as Muslims' secular feminism/s expressed in the discourses of Islamic modernism, secular nationalism, and humanitarian and – later – human rights. Islamic feminism elaborated the principle of gender equality as part and parcel of all equalities within Islamic discourse as its paramount discourse. It can be seen as building upon and extending the Islamic modernist strand of Muslims' multi-vocal secular feminism.[13] African-American scholar Amina Wadud in her book *Qur'an and Woman: Reading the Sacred Text from a Woman's Perspective* (1992, 1999) elaborated the notions of gender equality and social justice, and made clear their necessary intersection. Her work has provided powerful support in the form of strong Islamic argumentation in the struggle for the implementation of equality and justice across lines of race, gender, and class.

Patriarchal ideas articulated in the language of Islam have subverted the practice of gender equality and social justice which the Qur'an puts forward. Pakistani-American Asma Barlas faced the problem head-on when she defined patriarchy and unmasked its invidious work in eroding the notion and practice of Qur'anic equality of human beings (*insan*) irrespective of their physical attributes (anatomy, skin color, etc.) and various socially constructed differences. Removal of the structures of inequality that patriarchy sustains is fundamental to the project of understanding and practicing equality. Barlas's *Unreading Patriarchal Interpretations of the Qur'an*, the outcome of work begun in the 1990s, was published in 2002.

Other scholars concerned about inequitable or problematical laws enacted in the name of Islam turned their attention to Islamic jurisprudence (*fiqh*) deriving from interpretation of the Qur'an and other sources such as Hadith (sayings and deeds attributed to the

Prophet Muhammad). Ziba Mir-Hosseini, a London-based scholar from Iran, scrutinized *fiqh* and its application in the enacting of Muslim personal status codes, also called family law in statutory law.[14] These codes, claiming firm grounding in Islamic jurisprudence, support a patriarchal family structure.

Complicating the reform of *fiqh*-backed laws, commonly called "*shari'a* laws" and often simply, "the *shari'a*," (as the elision of *fiqh* and *shari'a* as divinely guided "path" illustrates) is the widely-held belief that to alter the Muslim personal status or family laws is to tamper with the sacred. This has long been an effective way to inhibit people from engaging in critique of and attempts to re-cast *fiqh*-based laws. This is not to say, however, that there have not been serious and sustained movements by feminists to reform *fiqh*-based Muslim family law, nor that some successes have not been achieved.[15]

Islamic feminists have taken pains to make the distinction between the *shari'a* as the path discerned from the Qur'an that Muslims are exhorted to follow in life (*shari'a* as divine inspiration and guiding principles) and so-called "*shari'a* law(s)" (laws deriving from understandings of *fiqh* that are man-made, and therefore open to questioning and change). The *shari'a*, as "the path" indicated in the scripture as the word of God, is sacred; but it needs to be ascertained through human effort. By stressing the distinction between man-made law(s) and the divine path, Islamic feminists strive to remove an obstacle in the way of those who feared – indeed, were encouraged to fear – that they might be challenging divine law if they questioned *fiqh* and laws deriving from it.[16]

SHARI'A AS PATH AND AS POLITICS

In Nigeria, with the politicization of the *shari'a*, the distinction between *shari'a* as "the path" and *shari'a* as man-made law was expediently kept blurred by states that came to be called the "*shari'a* states" after instituting *hudud* laws and declaring "a return to the *shari'a*."[17] While the label "*shari'a* states" was originally conferred by non-Muslims to refer to states that had instituted *hudud* laws, and was then taken up by the media, it was soon brandished by the so-called "*shari'a* states" themselves as if in confirmation of their self-arrogated task to reestablish the *shari'a*.

It is important to note parenthetically that the notion of the "*shari'a* state" as a state within a sovereign state is peculiar to Nigeria. "The *shari'a* state" should not be confused with a sovereign "Islamic state," which declares its constitution and all of its laws to be based on the *shari'a*. Unlike in the self-styled Islamic states, the notion of the "*shari'a* state" in Nigeria simply pivoted around the institution of *hudud* laws, a law-and-order approach to Islam.

By making the claim and igniting hope for a new "coming" of *shari'a* to be ushered in through the "gate of *hudud*," state authorities set themselves on a course they did not chart. In short, they misread the politics. The rapid and zealous implementation of *hudud* witnessed by the condemnations of the two poor women in the *zina* cases flung open a Pandora's box of confusions and contractions swirling around "the *shari'a*" and actions taken in its name, and vividly linked two kinds of oppressions: that of women and the poor. With the explosion of the two *zina* cases on the scene women who came to the rescue of their condemned sisters put forward another definition of *shari'a* and opened up a fresh look at *fiqh*.

HUDUD

Hudud have remained traditionally operative, but were never codified in Saudi Arabia. Long surpassed by secular laws in most Muslim societies, *hudud* were reinstated in codified form in the late 1970s and early 1980s in Iran, Pakistan, and Sudan with the imposition of Islamist regimes.[18] The imposition of *hudud* elicited strong opposition among women both inside and outside these countries. Women as human rights activists and secular feminists in Pakistan through Shirgat Gah (which began as a women's resource center in 1975 with ties to WLUML) and through the Women's Action Forum (created in 1981) have fought the abuses perpetrated against women through aggressive campaigns of public protest and exposure, and letter-writing and petition campaigns – and continue to do so today, with a certain amount of success.[19] Meanwhile, Iranian women at home and in the disapora have mounted wide vigorous protests on behalf of women victimized under the *hudud* laws. The network called Nisa Meydaan (Women's Field), which includes long-term activists and lawyers including Shirin Ebadi and Mihrangaz Kar, as well as many scholars including Ziba Mir-Hosseini and Val Moghadam, is currently engaged in a vigorous (trans)national initiative called the "Stop Stoning Forever Campaign."[20] Pakistani and Iranian activists have made extensive use of the WLUML network in support of women condemned under the *hudud* laws, and to expose and discuss the laws *per se.*

When the *hudud* laws were proclaimed in Nigeria, local women activists, who had gained exposure to the workings of *hudud* laws in other countries and had supported the causes of women victimized under these laws were well-experienced, well-networked, and poised to act.

TWO *ZINA* CASES IN NIGERIA

Women-headed defense teams composed primarily of women lawyers along with specialists in jurisprudence and Arabists that were assembled by Baobab and WRAPA appealed the cases of Safiyatu Husseini and Amina Lawal in the higher *shari'a* courts. The *shari'a* court system (both the lower and higher courts) had only been accustomed to hearing personal status cases (or cases relating to family law and inheritance) since the early twentieth century when *hudud* (which previously had never been codified in Nigeria, although practiced in what were called "*qadis'* courts") had been outlawed under the British. With independence in the 1960s a national criminal code was enacted. Close and routine familiarity with Islamic jurisprudence concerning *hudud* was lacking, along with a recent history of precedents. In appealing the cases, the women-headed defense teams laid out details of *fiqh* demonstrating the stringent requirements of evidence and strict procedures that needed to be followed in *hudud* cases to protect the cause of justice. The cases, which resulted in acquittals, constituted an impressive public display of "learning through legal action," or "walking through *fiqh*." The acquittals were a triumph of the principles of Islamic equality and justice over patriarchal inequities. To date there have been no more convictions for *zina*, and accordingly no capital punishment carried out. While capital punishment is on the books in the Federation of Nigeria, its implementation has fallen into abeyance.[21]

While classical *fiqh* (consolidated during the formation of the major schools of jurisprudence in the ninth and tenth centuries) shored up a patriarchal model of the family, classical jurisprudence took a strikingly gender-egalitarian approach to crime and punishment. Requirements of evidence and procedures were to be strictly applied to both women and to men. It has been suggested that the penalty of death by stoning for those guilty of *zina*, prescribed for both sexes, was so onerous because it was meant to act as a deterrent, not a weapon to be easily wielded – especially against the vulnerable. It rankled when judges in the lower *shari'a* courts handed down quick verdicts of guilty to the two women accused of *zina* while the men involved were never brought before the courts, and that the convicted were poor women. It clearly did not signal the advent of social justice that the state-directed "return to the *shari'a*" had promised. People linked oppression against women and oppression of the poor. They began to insist that social and economic justice should prevail as part of living by the *shari'a* before *hudud* law might be introduced.

The cooperation between Muslim and Christian women in the *zina* cases occasioned a strengthening of transcommunal activism in support of justice and equality in Nigeria. Backing the cause of justice in the *shari'a* courts was not of necessity linked to a religious identity or faith position, as the support of Nigerian Christian activists acting on behalf of their endangered Nigerian and Muslim sisters illustrated. The activists shared common understandings of justice and equality, irrespective of their religious affiliations. This has seldom been noticed, as observers have been quick to circulate instances of interreligious strife rather than transreligious cooperation, especially around issues of women and gender.[22]

NIGERIAN MUSLIM WOMEN'S NARRATIVES

To understand the long-term impact of the activism around these two *zina* cases and the support initiated by women as part of the elaboration the project of Islamic feminism I spoke with women in the Muslim-majority states of the north, where *hudud* laws were in force, as well as with women in the Middle Belt, where Muslims were not in the majority and *hudud* laws were non-existent. I conducted a total of fifty interviews in February and March of 2004 in six of the twelve states in the north with *hudud* laws: Kano, Katsina, Sokoto, Kaduna, Niger State, and Zamfara, as well as women in Plateau State in the Middle Belt where Muslims and Christians are roughly equal in number, to get the views of those living in states without *hudud*.[23] The overall mix of persons I talked with included some men and a few Christians, whom I met more by chance than by design.

My interlocutors, as I prefer to call them, since the interviews resembled conversations, with a vibrant give-and-take, were middle-class women living and working in major cities. They included activists, academics, lawyers, journalists, writers, teachers, government employees, and some students. They represented mainly two generations: (1) those in their mid-forties and fifties, including, at the outer limit, some in their sixties who brought some historical depth to the current debates; and (2) those in or around their thirties. Their views inform the core of this chapter. A few encounters with students in their twenties pointed to the preoccupations of a third generation that would form an intriguing new project.

During the period of my research I participated in two conferences where I had interactions with Muslims and Christians, and with women and men: the Conference on Christian–Muslim Relations in Zamfara in March 2005 and the Conference on Promoting Women's Rights through Shari'ah in Northern Nigeria, sponsored by the Centre for Islamic Legal Studies at Ahmadu Bello University in Zaria.[24] On an earlier visit to Nigeria I had participated in the International Conference on the Implementation of Shari'ah in a Democracy: The Nigerian Experience, held in Abuja. My presentation, "Ongoing *Tafsir* on Men and Women in Islam: Constructions and Practices of Democracy and Social Justice" – in which I spoke about Islamic feminist discourse, mainly focusing on Amina Wadud and Asma Barlas – exposed me to the passions and perils the subject evokes.[25] These experiences in public forums were instructive and helpful in contextualizing my more private discussions with women.

In this chapter, as always, I am careful to make the distinction between Islamic feminism as a named discourse and Islamic feminist as an assumed identity. In my encounters in the north of Nigeria and the Middle Belt I did not find reference made to Islamic feminism as an explicit discourse, nor did I find persons who called themselves Islamic feminists. Moreover, I discovered that the terms "feminism" and "feminist" were not in general circulation, and that they were highly controversial, so to use such terms publicly would be provocative and counterproductive. I did, however, find what I recognized as Islamic feminist questions, concerns, ideas, and forms of activism.

In speaking of Islamic feminism or Islamic feminists in Nigeria I thus use the terms in a purely analytical sense, in order to be able to place the ideas and experience of Nigerians in the context of the global phenomenon of Islamic feminism and to discuss Nigerian expressions of Islamic feminism and their important (trans)national contributions. To protect their privacy, I will not identify women by name. I shall, however, quote some of their words to give readers direct access to their expressive voices. All the women whom I quote are activists, and thus I identify them further simply by profession.

WOMEN AND ("THE RETURN TO") THE *SHARI'A*

You have to know *shari'a* before you can implement it. We thought that because of the enormous protection that Islam gives women that this is what would obtain. Muslim women thought the *shari'a* states would give us this. [But] It was like we were at the receiving end. This issue of adultery and sentencing only women to death, even the manner in which it was done, made us feel that the *shari'a* was against women, which is not true. We feel maybe because it is a male-dominated society and because of selfish reasons that women only are at the receiving end. (professor)[26]

We are not quarreling with the *shari'a* as a concept, but we are quarreling with the implementation. Regarding our men: why is it for you *shari'a* implementation is about women being "proper"? If we are going to get what the *shari'a* stands for then we will be better off. We are going to hold you accountable. We are going to say the *shari'a* should be implemented with social justice. (professor)

Men hijack the *shari'a* to the detriment of women. (professor)

If the rich get off and the poor "get the *shari'a* on them" there will definitely be a problem. (student)

If we practice *shari'a* people will live in peace because some will not acquire too much wealth while others live in poverty. If the *shari'a* is practiced as it should be there will be more space for women in the society. (professor)

During the time of the two *zina* cases women's attention was riveted on *hudud*, but in the aftermath of the acquittals attention shifted to a broader discussion of the *shari'a* as a whole.[27] Some two years after the second acquittal the subject of the *shari'a* kept coming up in my conversations with women. Women, as the above quotations indicate, repeatedly spoke of how the male-defined (and/or the "state-defined") *shari'a* was constructed and deployed to the detriment of women and the poor. They expressed no doubt that this was a contradiction of the Qur'anic message. The *zina* cases were a wrenching example for women of the willingness to make scapegoats of women and the poor. Women pointed out publicly (as increasingly did men) that within the context of Islam *hudud* should only be put in force in a society where the social and economic well-being of all categories of people prevail; only then is it possible that justice might be served under *hudud*.

Concerning the state-announced "return to *shari'a*," women repeated that the *shari'a* had always been integral to Muslim life in Nigeria and important in their own lives. What was significant now was how the *shari'a* was understood by Muslims: to what were they "returning"? During conversations women showed that they had a firm idea of how patriarchal thinking had intruded into the egalitarian message of the Qur'an, thereby skewing understanding and practice of the *shari'a*. The women repeatedly insisted that access to formal training in religion should be widespread among women so they could understand the *shari'a* for themselves and be part of its broader articulation and practice.

Many women confided that they were not in favor of the *hudud*, and certainly not in conditions in which social and economic justice did not prevail; but in the face of a *fait accompli*, with *hudud* laws now in place, they would continue their vigilant struggle for justice within the existing legal framework. Women thus did not choose to contest the laws as such, but rather their applications. They also did not address head-on the question of the broader idea of a state-backed *shari'a*. This was a wise tactic – and probably their only real option, for women, as they told me, had far less public space to debate and dissent than men. In a conference on Comparative Perspectives on Shar'iah in Nigeria at the University of Jos in January of 2004, when Abdullahi an-Na'im, a renowned Sudanese scholar of law and Islamic jurisprudence, argued against the notion of a state-backed *shari'a*, he was met with an explosive outcry.[28]

Women found space – or more space – to confront discrimination and injustice to women in the context of the *shari'a* court than in the public societal arena at large. It was in the context of the courts that women brought different knowledge and understanding to bear. This was a stunning case of women's activism as Islamic knowledge production. It did not escape public attention that it was women who had taken the initiative in coming to the defense of the accused, who were also women. Women assembled the defense teams, which comprised mainly (but not only) women lawyers and specialists, who successfully took the cases of the condemned women to the higher *shari'a* courts, where men only presided. Thus, women's voices were heard through their legal defense teams in the context of the *shari'a* court system, where their solidly *fiqh*-backed arguments won the day. This underscored the notion of women as human beings (*insan*) capable of defending justice, and not simply a category in need of protection or as a group of weak, deficient, and vulnerable human beings.

This usurpation of the right within the Nigerian common law system for women to act as judges – and, indeed, within an Islamic system (for it is patriarchal convention rather than Islamic jurisprudence that prevents women from being judges) – leaves the adjudication of criminal cases in the *shari'a* courts solely in the hands of men. In certain other Muslim societies, such as Iran, Sudan, and Morocco, women have been able to act as judges, and, more recently, as a result of the persistence of Muslim women's feminist activist struggle, women in Egypt were allowed to be judges.[29]

The legal activism on the part of Nigerian women demonstrated that women were quicker than most men to support – and to rally support for – the vulnerable and victimized. Through their activism women not only saved other women from further victimization but served as examples of empowerment to their sisters.

It was also widely apparent that Muslim and Christian women as Nigerians worked together in the defense of their fellow citizens. One Muslim said: "I am a human rights activist. I believe in human rights because Islam has a charter. I am working with other human rights organizations because in the end we are all Nigerian. [I struggle] if my right is denied, the same with my Christian counterpart, so we are all working for human rights but I have guidance from my religion concerning what human rights is." Another Muslim activist woman said of the Christian supporters: "The Christians did not come out as Christians but as women." I have noted elsewhere that among the binaries Islamic feminism breaks down is opposition between Muslims and non-Muslims as well as between the secular and the religious.

NEED FOR NEW INTERPRETATION

We are looking beyond old interpretations and static ways of doing things, and at the need to engage with today. What will happen if Muslim women are not carried along as things are developing? The Qur'an gives women space, the right to participation, consultation. There is a tendency to use the cultural perspective to belittle women, to deny the consultation of women, making them irrelevant when it comes to decision-making, making them virtual minors who cannot take decisions, who need to have others take decisions for them. Are men addressing all the issues we want them to address? Aren't women best placed to examine things from a woman's perspective? (writer)

A problem with a lot of the *tafsir* is that it has been done centuries back. They were mainly made by scholars who had never encountered another culture so that they were operating with an understanding only of their own people. Because in Islam knowledge is a vibrant thing, ideally it should be a continuous looking at what others have done and adding to it not just closing down and saying that's it. (professor)

Until now the question of *ijtihad* [independent reasoning in approach to religious texts] has been kept silent. It has not been made public. (professor)

In conversations women repeatedly stressed the need for women themselves to conduct interpretation of the Qur'an and *fiqh*, the core project of Islamic feminism. The two *zina* cases made dramatically clear the need for gender-sensitive readings of religious sources.

Some women who had been university professors since the 1980s explained that two decades ago they had pointed to the need for women to engage in religious interpretation. They find themselves reiterating this today. The idea that women could read the Qur'an and other religious texts for themselves remains highly threatening to most people, especially as it could lead to the assumption of authority in religious matters on the part of women. A younger activist claimed that the trials of the two women "sensitized people to do research. The trials aroused their curiosity." She insisted that "the debates help in enlightening individuals and to push them to find out for themselves what *shari'a* entails."

A young woman professor declared quite simply: "Patriarchal ideas are presented as Islamic. You read the Qur'an and find most of what they are preaching is not in the Qur'an." She repeated a point that several other women made about the lack of public space in which they can debate issues of women and Islam. She confided: "You [women] risk being called Western, radical, or even having a *fatwa* put on you." Speaking not only of women she continued: "Our people are now beginning to perceive the heavy dose of religious prescription they are given and that at the same time [understand that] those dispensing it are not applying it to themselves." This is an example of the disenchantment I heard voiced a few years down the road from the state-heralded "return to the *shari'a*" in the wake of the *zina* cases. Women and the poor became the touchstone of society's protracted wait for justice.

How does one take the analysis into public space and make it operative? Repeatedly women spoke about the problem of being ostracized if they were too outspoken in public about their views on "sensitive issues" such as women and the *shari'a*. I heard the term "no-go area" often in relation to controversial subjects, and was plainly told that men have far more leeway to dissent in public than women. Although women have greater space to speak out in the contexts of universities and certain NGOs they are still more constrained than men are. One activist and former university professor said: "It is a social precept that Islam does not allow women to question, to condemn." Another professor and activist exclaimed: "Until now the question of *ijithad* or critical intellectual inquiry into religious sources has been kept silent. It has not been made public."

RECUPERATING A LOCAL FEMALE TRADITION OF SCHOLARSHIP AND AUTHORITY

Claiming a line of scholarly women within the Islamic tradition is important for contemporaries in establishing legitimacy and authority as females within the field of religious learning. Compiling histories of Muslim women of the past as models and inspiration for present-day women is integral to the project of Muslim women's feminisms. The genre of the biographical dictionary holds a central place in Islamic scholarship. Pakistani activists and Shirgat Gah members Farida Shaheed and Aisha Shaheed made a recent contribution to this genre when they published *Great Ancestors: Women Asserting their Rights in Muslim Contexts*,[30] which includes an essay on the illustrious Nigerian woman Nana Asma'u.[31]

Muslim women in Nigeria today who are not finding it easy to occupy a place within the ranks of *'ulama* (Islamic scholars) as Qur'anic interpreters or specialists in *fiqh* and other Islamic sciences can cite Nana Asma'u (1793–1864) as a revered female ancestor and renowned Islamic scholar and teacher to claim legitimacy for the work of contemporary women as religious scholars. Nana Asma'u, who came from a family of women and men who were religious scholars, was the daughter of Osman Dan Fodio, the leader of the religious revival and founder of the Sokoto caliphate.[32] She is well known for playing a key role in the spread of the Islamic revival, and especially in the education of women.

FOMWAN dedicated the cover story, "Muslim Women Scholars," in its journal *The Muslim Woman* in celebration of its twentieth anniversary in 2005 to promote the education, including religious education, of women.[33] FOMWAN member and director of the Center for Hausa Studies at Uthman Dan Fodio University in Sokoto, Sa'idiyya Umar, sees in the Yantaru movement that Nana Asma'u led, bringing schooling in religion and other subjects to women in villages far and wide, a model that FOMWAN continues today in its mission to provide religious formation and education for Muslim women throughout the country.[34] Laying claim to her past, Asma'u Joda, activist and member of Baobab, asserted: "In my Fulani community women have for centuries had a long tradition of being religious scholars. Asmau, daughter of Osman don Fodio was appointed in charge of religious affairs by her brother Muhammad Bello." She insisted: "We have to re-read our histories."[35]

CLAIMING A DEPATRIARCHALIZED ISLAM

It was evident in private conversations among women that the recent trials had triggered renewed debates about gender equality and social justice as principles found in the Qur'an but lacking in society, indicating an accelerated impatience with the lack of delivery of promises that the acclaimed "return to the *shari'a*" held out and the kind of oppression that can come with so-called law reform. The debates and activism around the *zina* cases produced a heightened Islamic feminist consciousness. They led to a clash of consciousnesses in Nigeria: an Islamic feminist consciousness and the Islamist or neo-fundamentalist consciousness. They represented very different approaches to the *shariʿa* and to the law. The challenge for women is how to move from analysis to action in the arena of the community and society at large, and not in the restricted atmosphere of the *shariʿa* courts. How can women construct a functioning, depatriarchalized Islam?

Islamic feminism, by whatever name, in Nigeria as elsewhere, is a work in progress. Nigerian Muslim women are aware of the dilemma and the challenge of moving themselves and the culture beyond a patriarchy claiming to be Islamic into the space where an egalitarian Islam is operative. From what I observed in Nigeria it seems that a process is now underway that cannot be reversed. It also appears that the road to a depatriachalized Islam there, as elsewhere, will be long and full of perils. However, the Nigerian success story in the *zina* cases and the debates about Islam and the *shariʿa*, and about equality and justice, is a salient chapter in the local and global Islamic feminist narrative.

*   *   *

Originally published in Carolyn Elliot (ed.), Global Empowerment of Women: Responses to Globalization and Politicized Religions (New York: Routledge, 2007).

NOTES

1. It is a pleasure for me to express my thanks at the outset for the various kinds of support that made this research both possible and enriching. I am grateful to the Fulbright New Century Scholars program for inviting me to be part of the cohort of scholars in 2003–2004 around the theme of global women's empowerment. I thank Aisha Imam for facilitating my affiliation with Baobab during the course of my project and members with whom I corresponded and met in person. I am grateful to Habu Muhammad, whom I met when he was a Fulbright scholar at the Program of African Studies in Northwestern University and who was very helpful in introducing me to people in Kano, where he teaches at Bayero University in the department of political science. I am grateful to Haruna Wakili, director of Mambaya House, and Ismaila Zango, deputy director, and professors at Bayero University for their warm welcome and help during my stay in Kano. I thank Hamidu Bobboyi, then director of Arewa House, for the hospitality he extended, and Aisha Lamu and her husband, Sheikh Lemu, for having me as their guest in Minna. I thank my colleague and friend Muhammad Sane Umar for our many conversations, both in Evanston and in Jos, where he was most helpful during my stay, as was Philip Ostien of the University of Jos. I thank all the women with whom I had extended interview-conversations for sharing their knowledge and for their candor and wit. They are at the center of this work. In this final moment as I write this note I wish to thank Carolyn Elliot, who was a

superb leader of the New Century Scholar group and who right up to the final editing of the volume in which this was first published was helpful to all of us. I appreciate the keen eye she brought to my chapter.

2. See Philip Ostien, Jamila M. Nasir, and Franz Kogelmann (eds.), *Comparative Perspectives on the Shari'ah in Nigeria* (Ibadan: Spectrum Books, 2005). This is a collection of papers from a conference on the *shari'a* held in Jos in 2004 as part of the year-long project undertaken by the University of Jos and the University of Bayreuth in Germany under the rubric: The Shar'iah Debate and the Shaping of Muslim and Christian Identities in Northern Nigeria.

3. For a stunning analysis of *zina* and contextualization of *hudud* see Charmaine Pereira, "Zina and Transgressive Heterosexuality in Northern Nigeria," www.feministafrica.org (May 2005).

4. The network Women Living under Muslim Laws has circulated a huge amount of information on women suffering under *hudud* laws, as have women's associations in different countries where *hudud* laws are in effect, such as Iran and Pakistan.

5. I wrote an article about my encounters entitled "Liberties of the Faithful" in *al-Ahram Weekly*, 19–25 May 2005, which has been republished in a slightly different form in Margot Badran, *Feminism beyond East and West: New Gender Talk and Practice in Global Islam* (New Delhi: Global Media Publications, 2006), pp. 67–76.

6. See, for example, Margot Badran, *Feminists, Islam, and Nation: Gender and the Making of Modern Egypt* (Princeton: Princeton University Press, 1995).

7. On WLUML see Farida Shaheed (one of the founding members), "Networking for Change: The Role of Women's Groups in Initiating Dialogue on Women's Issues," in Mahnaz Afkhami (ed.), *Faith and Freedom* (Syracuse: Syracuse University Press, 1995); and Valentine Moghadam, *Globalizing Women: Transnational Feminist Networks* (Baltimore and London: Johns Hopkins Press, 2005).

8. Sanusi Lamido Sanusi, "Fundamentalist Groups and the Nigerian Legal System: Some Reflections," www.whrnet.org provides telling insights into the movement and its implications. For a detailed study of the Izala movement see Ousmane Kane, *Muslim Modernity in Postcolonial Nigeria: The Society for the Removal of Innovation and Reinstatement of Tradition* (Leiden: Brill, 2003). The reader will note two different translations of this group; in the text I have preferred to use the one provided by Sanusi.

9. Muhammad Sane Umar discusses this young woman (preserving her anonymity) in "Mass Islamic Education and Emergence of Female 'Ulema' in Northern Nigeria: Background, Trends, and Consequences," in Scott S. Reese (ed.), *The Transmission of Learning in Islamic Africa* (Leiden: Brill, 2004).

10. For a self-profiled history of FOMWAN and its present structure and work see *FOMWAN: Twenty Years of Service to Islam* (Abuja: n.p., 2005). It is now under the leadership of its fifth head or *amira*, Bilkisu Yusuf.

11. *Baobab for Women's Human Rights and Sharia Implementation in Nigeria: The Journey So Far* (Lagos: Baobab, 2003).

12. I looked at Islamic feminism in two talks in Cairo, "Islamic Feminism: What's in a Name?" in 2002 and "Islamic Feminism Revisited" in 2006. Both can be found on the website of *al-Ahram Weekly* (www.ahram.org.eg/weekly), where they were originally published, and in Badran, *Feminism beyond East and West*, pp. 23–42.

13. I have discussed the confluences of Muslim women's secular feminisms in "Locating Feminisms: The Collapse of Secular and Religious Discourses in the Muslim Mashriq," *Agenda* (South African feminist journal), special 50th issue on African Feminisms, 59 (2001), pp. 41–57; and "Between Secular Feminism and Islamic Feminism: Reflections on the Middle East and Beyond," *Journal of Middle East Women's Studies*, inaugural issue (January 2005), pp. 6–28.

14. Ziba Mir-Hosseini, *The Religious Debate in Contemporary Iran* (Princeton: Princeton University Press, 1999); and Ziba Mir-Hosseini, *Marriage on Trial: A Study of Family Law, Iran and Morocco* (New York: I. B. Tauris, 2000).

15. The most recent example is the reform of the Moroccan Mudawwana in 2004, which is now the most progressive *shari'a*-backed Muslim family law. The earliest feminist efforts to reform Muslim personal status law go back to early twentieth-century Egypt, where the battle has been sustained but the gains minimal.

16. For a concise clarification of this see Ziba Mir-Hosseini, "Muslim Women's Quest for Equality: Between Islamic Law and Feminism," *Critical Inquiry* (Summer 2006), pp. 629–645.

17. On "the return to the *shari'a*" in Nigeria see Ostien, Nasir, and Kogelmann (eds.), *Comparative Perspectives on the Shari'ah in Nigeria*.

18. For a general exposition of *hudud* see Cherif Bassiouni (ed.), *The Islamic Criminal Justice System* (London and New York: Oceana, 1980).

19. See Khawar Mumtaz and Farida Shaheed, *Women of Pakistan: Two Steps Forward, One Step Backward?* (London and Karachi: Zed, 1987); Anita Weiss, "Implications of the Islamization Program for Women," in Anita Weiss (ed.), *Islamic Reassertion in Pakistan: The Application of Islamic Laws in a Modern State* (Syracuse: Syracuse University Press, 1986); and Anita Weiss, "Women's Action Forum," in *The Oxford Encyclopedia of the Modern Islamic World* (New York and Oxford: Oxford University Press, 1995), vol. 4, pp. 346–348. Shahla Haeri deals with the *hudud* and Islamization process initiated by the state in *No Shame for the Sun: Lives of Professional Pakistani Women* (Syracuse: Syracuse University Press, 2002).

20. See www.meydaan.org and Soheila Vahdati, "Stop Stonings in Iran, But Don't Confuse the Issue," *Women's eNews*, 4 January 2007.

21. I am grateful to Richard Joseph and Ndubisi Obiorah for confirmation of this.

22. On transcommunal cooperation see Ayesha Imam, "Fighting the Political (Ab)Use of Religion in Nigeria: BAOBAB for Women's Human Rights, Allies, and Others," in Ayesha Imam, Jenny Morgan, and Nira Yuval-Davis (eds.), *Fundamentalism: Warning Signs, Law, Media and Resistances*, on the WLUML website (www.wluml.org), December 2004.

23. I had originally wanted to speak with women of more modest backgrounds from villages as well as major cities, but for a number of reasons this proved totally beyond my reach.

24. In the Conference on Christian–Muslim Relations I was invited to give a presentation and encouraged to be an active participant. I received an invitation from the organizers to attend the Conference on Promoting Women's rights through Shari'ah in Northern Nigeria, where I was strictly an observer in the plenary sessions, although I contributed in the break-out session. In the first conference in Zamfara women and men intermixed in the sittings; in the Kaduna conference women and men were arranged in parallel groups in the hall.

25. This paper provoked both critical and favorable response, more the former than the latter.

26. From here forward I shall display quotations from Muslim women interviewed and simply designate their professions. All the activists I interviewed are women from various professions. I include quotations as the words of the women are pithy and powerful. Purely summarizing their thoughts and arguments does not convey the same force.

27. While my focus is on the debates as I gleaned them through interviews, conversations, group discussions, and at conferences, there has been much written in the press and learned publications. FOMWAN dedicated a special issue of *The Muslim Woman* to the theme: "Sharia Implementation in Nigeria," 8 (2003). In keeping with FOMWAN's education mission, stress is laid on the importance of education in understanding and living by the *shari'a*.

28. See his chapter, "The Future of Shari'ah and the Debate in Northern Nigeria," in Ostien, Nasir, and Kogelmann (eds.), *Comparative Perspectives on the Shari'ah in Nigeria*, pp. 327–357.

29. This adverse effect of the enactment of *hudud* has yet to be widely noticed. A woman lawyer, activist, and daughter of a former grand *qadi* said in an interview: "If a woman can adjudicate under common law I do not see any reason why she cannot do so as well under *shari'a* law."

30. Farida Shaheed and Aisha Shaheed, *Great Ancestors: Women Asserting their Rights in Muslim Contexts* (Lahore: Shirgat Gah, 2004).

31. "Nana Asma'u (1795–1865)," in ibid., chapter 4, "Women at the Cross-roads: The Nineteenth Century," pp. 51–54.

32. For an analysis of Asma'u's scholarly work, poetry, etc. within the context of Muslim intellectual and political life see Beverly Mack, "Muslim Women's Knowledge Production in the Greater Maghreb," in Margot Badran (ed.), *Gender and Islam in Africa* (forthcoming). For the first full-length biography see Jean Boyd, *The Caliph's Sister* (London: Frank Cass, 1989); and on her oeuvre Jean Boyd and Beverly Mack, *The Collected Works of Nana Asma'u bint Shehu Usman Dan Fodio 1793–1864* (East Lansing: Michigan University Press, 1997).

33. *The Muslim Woman*, 9 (2005).

34. "Nana Asma'u the Great Scholar," ibid.

35. Interview with Yoginder Sikand, www.islaminterfaith.org.

13

BETWEEN SECULAR AND ISLAMIC FEMINISM(S): REFLECTIONS ON THE MIDDLE EAST AND BEYOND

Feminism(s) in the Middle East are more than a century old.[1] There have been two major feminist paradigms, referred to as "secular feminism" and "Islamic feminism." The foundational moment of women's "secular feminism" may be traced to the late nineteenth century, while the emergence of "Islamic feminism" became evident in the late twentieth. These feminism(s) appeared mainly in Muslim-majority societies with plural religions and/or multiple ethnicities. They evolved in historical contexts in which new subjects and identities were being (re)fashioned out of shifting combinations of religious, class, ethnic, and national affiliation. The two *fin de siècle* feminisms surfaced as efforts to (re)construct states and vibrant social, economic, and technological transformations were underway. Secular feminism and Islamic feminism may be seen as two discursive modes. Secular feminism draws on and is constituted by multiple discourses, including secular nationalist, Islamic modernist, humanitarian/human rights, and democratic. Islamic feminism is expressed in a single, or paramount, religiously-grounded discourse taking the Qur'an as its central text. In this chapter I reflect on these two modes of feminism in the Middle East and consider what makes them distinct and how they intersect.

TWO ARRIVALS

When feminisms first arose in the Middle East in the late nineteenth and early twentieth centuries, its countries were variously confronting

Western imperialism and colonialism, declining Ottoman suzerainty, and decaying dynastic rule. The region was experiencing uneven socio-economic and technological transformation. Some segments of the population drew benefits from the swirl of change, while others faced setbacks as they were left out of the loop of modernity or access to new opportunity was slowed.

The Tanzimat reforms under way in Turkey from the middle of the nineteenth century and the constitutionalist movement in early twentieth-century Iran occasioned lively debate about religion and modernity. The Islamic reform movement, which began in late nineteenth-century Egypt under the leadership of Islamic modernist Muhammad 'Abduh, calling for a revival of *ijtihad,* or independent investigation of religious texts, and helping people face the challenge of how to be "modern and Muslim," was influential well beyond the borders of Egypt, and even the region.[2] Meanwhile, the Arab Nahda movement, led by Christians and Muslims from Greater Syria (many of whom had fled to Egypt to escape Ottoman control), generated a broad movement of Arab intellectual and cultural revival. The discourse of national liberation, calling for the creation of independent countries based on bonds of shared space and local culture, was the overriding discourse in Middle Eastern countries under expanding Western colonial rule and declining Ottoman control. The new national identities in the making were not coterminous with religious affiliation, as in the Ottoman *millet* system. Secular nationalism envisioned the construction of a new kind of collective identity bonded by people's historical roots in shared territory and a common, if variegated, cultural experience. Within the imagined secular nation, religion was taken for granted and citizens' plural religious identities accorded recognition and space.

From within this dynamic context, urban women of the middle and upper strata in various locations in the Middle East began to generate a "feminist discourse" that was both a critique of being held back from accessing the benefits of modernity as freely as their male counterparts because they were female, and a legitimization of their moves forward.[3] The rise of secular feminism coincided with two phenomena: the spread of new information technology in the form of the arrival of the printing-press; and the spread of literacy among women (of the middle and upper strata). Together these phenomena gave rise to a new female writing and reading public. Women transcended the bounds of religious community as they joined efforts in crafting a feminist discourse articulated in the new writings and fresh networks of women.[4] Women anchored this discourse firmly within that of religious reform, most notably Islamic modernist discourse, and at the same time within the new nationalist discourse, pairing their own liberation and advance with that of the nation, a trend in late nineteenth- and early twentieth-century women's struggle in parts of the Middle East that included other Asian societies, as Kumari Jayawardena noted.[5] Women, from the sites of their own experiences and observations as women, addressed the dimension of gender in more than the mainly rhetorical forms to which most men restricted themselves. During the twentieth century, feminist women as independent actors and leaders of their own social movements helped create and democratize new institutions of state and civil society. Turkey, where the state preempted feminism, was the exception. Women at diverse locations in the Middle East sustained their independent activist commitment to the dual liberation of the nation and women throughout the twentieth century, as their countries moved further away from foreign rule and its remnants.[6] At the end of the twentieth century, when the Cairo paper *al-Ahram Weekly* invited me to reflect on the past hundred years of feminism in Egypt, I recalled "Feminism in a Nationalist Century." I noted that before it ended, however, the old century had given birth to a new feminist paradigm for a new century.[7]

By the 1990s some observers detected the emergence of a new feminist discourse in parts of the Middle East that they began to call Islamic feminism.[8] The new feminism appeared at a moment of late postcoloniality and a time of deep disaffection over the inability of Middle Eastern nation-states to deliver democracy and foster broad economic prosperity. Islamic feminism surfaced earliest in parts of the Middle East where Islamism, or political Islam, had been longest in evidence – for example, in Egypt, where Islamist movements first emerged in the early 1970s and in Iran a decade after the installation of the Islamic Republic (and following the demise of Khomeini).

In the final third of the twentieth century, new groups and classes – mainly the recently urbanized entering the middle class – experiencing the pushes and pulls of modernity (expressed in uneven access to new opportunities and uncertain benefits) and an accompanying cultural *anomie*, were attracted to Islamism with its simultaneous critique of state and society and its recuperation of the comforts and assurances of "traditional" (patriarchal) culture. The disaffected in

different parts of the Middle East brought religion, in a newly ideolo-
gized and politicized form, to the rescue of their languishing nations.
The new Islamist discourse constituted a reappropriation of religion
in service of a restored nation that was both *umma* and *watan* – a people bonded by covenant and a people connected by attachment to a
land or country. It was a script in a gender-conservative voice.
Departing from both the earlier nationalist rhetoric, which had called
for the liberation of women, and the Islamic modernist rhetoric of
gender reform and innovation, the new Islamist rhetoric called for a
return of women to a "purer" and more "authentic" domestic life
away from the public scene. Before long, however, Islamist movements began to reverse this call as they expediently recruited women
in service of their goals, employing the rhetoric of shared participation of coreligionists as they held out the promise of a new Utopia.

Several elements catalyzed the rise of Islamic feminism. Women,
both secularists and the religiously oriented, grew increasingly concerned at the imposition and spread of a conservative reading of Islam
by Islamist movements, and found the need to respond in a progressive Islamic voice. Within Islamist movements women grew disaffected as they discovered their second-class status and dispensability
once certain goals were won (echoes of earlier secular nationalist
women).[9] For women in different parts of the Middle East who had
long enjoyed access to employment in the public sphere, and for their
families, who counted on their material contributions, the call for
retreat to the home in the name of Islam was decidedly disquieting.
Meanwhile, national discourses of the need for and significance of the
active participation and work of all citizens continued to resonate.
Moreover, by the latter decades of the twentieth century, education
had reached more women than ever before, extending across classes
and well into rural areas. In some parts of the Middle East, women
were also gaining access to education to the highest levels in the religious sciences. Women were thus well equipped by education and
experience to think for themselves and answer back. As with the earlier rise of secular feminism, the emergence of Islamic feminism coincided with the spread of a new form of information technology. This
time it was electronic technology that circulated information and
ideas freely and rapidly through cyberspace, creating an unprecedented simultaneity of local and global production.[10]

Once again, women shaped their own discourse as women from
their own perspective and experience.[11] By the start of the 1990s, it

was becoming increasingly apparent that women were (re)visioning a new feminism through their fresh readings of the Qur'an. The boldest and earliest initiatives occurred in post-Khomeini Iran, where women as public intellectuals (joined by some young male clerics) employed the language of the Qur'an, virtually the constitution of the Islamic Republic, to articulate a new feminism in an Islamic voice. This Islamic feminism did not whitewash the Islamic Republic of Iran, as some allege, but critiqued it and demanded a different reading of Islam – "stretching the limits," in Mir-Hosseini's apt phrase – in calling for gender justice.[12]

RELIGIOUS AND SECULAR

In our discussion of secular and Islamic feminisms it is important to unpack and historicize the terms "religious" and "secular." As a segue into this exploration, I note that secular feminism arose in a largely "religious era," while Islamic feminism surfaced in a "secular era." By this I mean to suggest that secular feminism emerged in a context in which religion, state, and society were highly enmeshed, while Islamic feminism appeared at a moment when the notion of secular state and society had taken hold.

The terms secular and religious need to be historicized, as their meanings and inflections change over time. The term secularism first came into circulation in parts of the Muslim world in the nineteenth century. The new Arabic coinage for secularism was *'almaniyya*, deriving from *'alam* (world). We have noted that the term "secular" used in relation to the nation or nationalism connoted a framing around the idea of shared territory, constituting a shift from "nation" understood as a religious community, while the secular nation was at the same time inclusive of all religions. Secular also connoted a certain separation or de-linkage between institutions of the state and religious institutions. In the Middle East, education and law – with the exception of family law – were removed from the jurisdiction of the religious authorities to that of the secular state (excluding countries of the Arabian Peninsula). Islam, however, lived on as a wellspring of law, and was enshrined in secular constitutions as the "state religion." In the Middle East, the striking exception to this incomplete separation of spheres was Turkey, with its rigid separation of state and religion, affirmed in its declaration of secularism as official state ideology. (The Turkish notion of secular resembles most closely the French notion, and indeed the Turkish word for secular, *lailik*, derives from the French *laïcité*.)[13] Generally, in the Middle East the term "secular" came to be associated with modernity, and often with the West, while "religious" came to be thought of by proponents of secularism as "traditional" and "backward," ultimately to the detriment of both.

Secular was given a new meaning in the 1970s by proponents of political Islam, who used it to signify un-Islamic, anti-Islamic, and non-Islamic. Islamists thus evacuated religion from the notion of secular, rigidly and dogmatically redefining and polarizing the terms, provoking Muslims to line up on one side or the other. The 1970s and 1980s was a time when secular feminism was pitted, and then pitted itself, against Islamists and their regressive, patriarchal definition of "religious." In this highly adversarial moment, secular feminists in the Middle East arrayed themselves against the gender-reactionary Islamists. This was a moment of fierce identity politics within Islam, when secular feminists reasserted their secularism and Islamists hurled the word "secular" as an epithet of condemnation.[14]

In the latter years of the twentieth century, when Islam as *din wa dunya* (religion and the world) had been so sundered that the religious and secular within Islam seemed at war with each other (and Muslims were pushed to choose between them), Abdullahi an-Na'im rightly felt it crucial to inject into the debates the by then all-but-forgotten notion of the enmeshment of the secular and the religious in Islam. He did so at the 1994 Conference on Religion, Culture, and Women's Human Rights in the Muslim World, which was notable for bringing women together across the "religious/secular divide".[15] Nearly a decade later, Talal Asad demonstrated how "religion" and "secularism" have mutually constructed each other, and recalled the trajectory of the narrowing of both constructs within the universe of Islam in modern times.[16] In short, Islam became reduced to "religion" and separated from the worldly (or the secular). Secularism itself had become sacrosanct, as John Esposito[17] and others began to point out, drawing attention to its excesses.

(RE)CONSIDERING FEMINISM(S)

Comparing the two feminisms in the Middle East, it can be observed that emergent secular feminism shared with secular nationalism a progressive narrative of gender and nation, although secular feminism developed the ideas of gender more fully and demanded that words be translated into actions in the present, not in some undefined future.[18] Nascent Islamic feminism, on the other hand, departed from the ascendant gender-conservative Islamist narrative, offering in its stead a progressive Islamic discourse. If Islamic feminism surfaced when Islamism was ascendant in the Middle East, this same Islamic feminism also sprang from the fertile home soil of a well-established tradition of Middle Eastern secular feminism.[19]

In discussing "secular feminism" and "Islamic feminism," it is important to consider the nomenclature, and what it reveals and what it conceals. While discourse and the names we give it help us frame and articulate, these labels also can limit, mislead, and obscure. At the beginning of this chapter I noted that secular feminism(s) as constructed in the Middle East is comprised of a cluster of discursive strands, including gendered secular nationalist and Islamic modernist (as well as more generic humanitarian/human rights and democratic) strands. The secular nationalist is an all-enveloping strand holding within it the other discursive strands. To say "secular feminism" is also to say Egyptian feminism, Iranian feminism, Turkish feminism, or any nation-based feminism – or, more broadly, Arab feminism (all of which may be pluralized to indicate variations within). I also observed that Islamic feminism is built upon a single, paramount, Qur'an-centered discourse. To distinguish by naming, however, is also to risk reifying difference and obscuring levels of likeness or what may be shared.

As my title announces, I am considering secular feminism and Islamic feminism as two named phenomena. While they are mainly seen as different, and often in tension with each other, they are seldom seen as flowing in and out of each other. I myself have written about the separate trajectories of these feminisms. In the late 1990s I began to note "the collapse of the religious and the secular" in feminist discourses when it seemed that the two discourses were being seen as too starkly different.[20] I use the word "between" in my title to indicate "from–to" as a historian looking diachronically, but also to indicate a "to and fro" within shared moments or across time. I argue that secular feminism is Islamic and Islamic feminism is secular, the way Islam as *din wa dunya*, to translate the phrase, joins "religion and the world."

Middle Eastern feminisms affect the world outside and exhibit connectivity with feminisms elsewhere, as the "beyond" in my title suggests. There are multiple points from which feminisms radiate outward. The West is not the patrimonial home of feminism, from which all feminisms derive and against which they must be measured. Indeed, Middle Eastern feminisms generated a critique of Western "imperial feminism(s)" as they brought the insights and activist modes of their own secular/national feminisms to the table of (Western-dominated) international feminism during the twentieth century. Islamic feminism arose simultaneously toward the end of the century in different parts of the Middle East (among the earliest locations, were Iran and Egypt), and in other regions such as Malaysia and South Africa, as well as in the West. The birthplace of Islamic feminism (or, a feminism in Islam, for those who shy away from the term) was not the liberal, democratic West, as Sofie Roald,[21] who has done important spade-work on Islam in Scandinavia, suggests. Islamic feminism(s), bursting on the scene in the midst of the cyber age, have exhibited from the start a special dynamic of "heres" and "beyonds." Zillah Eisenstein elucidates the multiple "elsewheres" (as she calls them) of feminisms as she de-centers feminisms, helping us see the complex choreography of feminism(s)' "heres" and "beyonds."[22]

Middle Eastern feminism(s) in the Middle East, whether secular or Islamic, it seems important to stress, originate in the Middle East. Like feminisms everywhere, they are born on and grow in home soil. They are not borrowed, derivative, or "secondhand." Yet feminism(s) in the Middle East, as in other places, may and do intersect with, amplify, and push in new directions elements of feminisms found elsewhere. Feminisms speak to each other in agreement and disagreement.[23] I make these assertive declarations in the context of perennial moves to discredit Middle Eastern feminisms, and feminisms more generally, among Muslims by de-legitimizing them as clones of "Western feminism" (whatever that is) and colonialist intrusions into "authentic" Middle Eastern and Islamic culture (whatever that is), which are more insidious than a computer virus.

Women's secular feminist movements in the Middle East for many decades in the twentieth century struggled with considerable success within the framework of the nation-state to make its institutions fully open and responsive to the needs of women and men alike as citizens. Employing Islamic modernist discourse, secular feminists tried with little success to reform Muslim personal status codes or family law. By the final years of the twentieth century, secular feminism, although doing good work and providing services especially within NGOs, seemed to have reached an impasse.[24] It had no new ideology or new tools, but this was what feminism needed. Interestingly, at this juncture, and I speak of the final decade of the twentieth century, in the arabophone Middle East an unambiguous term for feminism began to circulate, when feminists began to use *niswiyya* to signify feminist in place of *nisa'iyya*, which could mean either "feminist" or "women's." Feminists explained that they wished to distinguish themselves from conservative or conventional women's groups and projects.[25]

Feminism needed a new edge, and Islamic feminism provided it. Islamic feminism offered new thinking and new tools. Islamic feminism took from secular feminism its Islamic modernist strand and made progressive religious discourse its paramount discourse. And, in doing so, Islamic feminism extended secular feminism's Islamic modernist strand and made it more radical by affirming the unqualified equality of all human beings (*insan*). It affirmed the equality of women and men as *insan* across the public–private spectrum, and it grounded its assertions in new readings of the Qur'an. Secular feminism insisted on the full equality of women and men in the public sphere, but accepted a model of gender complementarity in the private or family sphere.[26] Interestingly, it accepted the model of different and complementary, but also hierarchical gender roles in the family, privileging male authority. Islamic feminism did not. Islamic feminism insists upon the practice of social justice, which cannot be achieved in the absence of full gender equality. It has yet to become a widely-based social movement, the way secular feminisms became organized movements (albeit with varying social bases and levels of outreach).[27] However, at various national locations in the Middle East, Islamic feminism is burrowing into sensitive places in the state, and women are attaining high positions through the force of Islamic feminist argumentation, as we shall see in a moment. Islamic feminism, meanwhile, is circulating globally with unprecedented speed, with the freedom that cyberspace offers.

INTERPRETING WOMEN AND GENDER JIHADISTS

At the outset I declared my intention both to examine secular feminism and Islamic feminism in the Middle East as two distinct modes of feminism and, at the same time, consider how they blend. I now move from observing what distinguishes each of these two modes of feminism to looking at how differences are obscured and how enmeshments occur. In doing so, I shift my focus from discourse to its producers, or to feminisms' agents. Through focusing on actors, the fluidity, dynamics, and dialogics of feminist thinking and practice become apparent. However, my intention in looking at the actors is not purely methodological but – in the best traditions of Middle Eastern (national) histories, Islamic *turath* (heritage) preservation, and women's histories in (re)claiming and naming women – is celebratory, which is both an epistemological and a political act.

Before naming and claiming, I would like to say a few words about identity, a subject I have expanded upon before. It is important to distinguish between secular and Islamic feminisms as analytical modes and descriptive categories and feminism(s) as an identity. Even the term "Islamic feminism" is often eschewed by its producers. The term, it should be noted, was invented by observers of the rise of a new feminist paradigm in the Middle East, who began to call it Islamic feminism.[28] Early twentieth-century feminist pioneers in the Middle East called their project secular feminism, or more often simply feminism, and publicly proclaimed themselves feminists. It was important at that moment to assert identities as part of the process of staking claims. Egyptians, Syrians, Algerians, Palestinians, etc. called themselves Egyptians, Syrians, Algerians, or Palestinians at a time when colonial rulers referred to them as "natives." Women struggling for women's rights in the contexts of nationalist struggles staked and announced their claims as feminists whose national(ist) credentials could scarcely be questioned. There was a moment in parts of the Middle East in the latter decades of the twentieth century when a new generation of women acting like feminists (in asserting themselves and their rights as women) shied away from the label – partly, it seems, out of expediency and partly perhaps as a kind of generational protest.

In the case of Islamic feminism, it has been noticeably different, starting with the naming of the project itself and particularly concerning issues of self-labeling or taking on an Islamic feminist identity. In part, there is considerable unease about "feminism," a lack of awareness of Middle Eastern (indigenous) feminist history(ies), and an inability to move beyond the notion that feminism is Western and a colonial imposition. The idea colonialists and Westerners circulated and that still resonates – that conceiving feminism was beyond the ability of Egyptians, Syrians, etc. – was a common refrain last century that lives on in the refrain that Muslims cannot possibly generate feminism. Such an arrogant and ignorant attitude is better rejected, it might be thought, than embraced. But seen from another angle, claiming an Islamic feminist project and identity seems, to committed Muslim gender-progressive intellectuals and gender activists, to be situating oneself outside Islamic parameters. Furthermore, a descriptive and analytical lexicon exists within Islam, an argument that Asma Barlas makes.[29] Throughout this chapter, as is my general practice, I use the terms "Islamic feminism" and "Islamic feminist" descriptively and analytically, not to impose a label of identity upon those who refuse it, but simply as a way of identifying what it appears particular actors think and do. In observing "women claiming Islam," miriam cooke talks of "speaking positions," which is helpful in capturing how women "claim," articulate, and practice feminism within Islam, getting beyond issues of identity.[30] Also, as she rightly underscores, we all have multiple identities; naming just one seems, to many, to threaten their other identities.

Feminisms in the Middle East were produced by women who had higher stakes than men in rethinking gender, religion, and culture. Women have both been expected to mark culture and be its faithful carriers as well as to scrupulously follow what is understood to be religiously-prescribed morality in their daily lives. (The tension between culture and religion is flattened out in favor of patriarchal culture and simplistic cultural readings of religions.) Women's honor and the honor of their men and their families have been connected with women's actual and perceived adherence to moral norms. Men may stray from adherence to moral norms without losing their own honor or that of their families. The tying of honor and morality to women's repetitious adherence to received cultural norms makes acts and projects of change highly fraught (and indeed, some women have literally paid with their lives).[31] The trump is religion re-read. Re-reading Islam from the late nineteenth century to this day is what women as secular and Islamic feminists in the Middle East have tried to do.

Interpreting women are "gender jihadists," or strugglers in the cause of gender justice, which includes promoting the practice of full equality. As Omid Safi puts it: "It is not sufficient to come up with a more luminous theology of Islam, but it is imperative for us to work on transforming the various societies around us."[32] If *jihad* (struggle) is a term deployed as a battle against "infidels" by Islamists (now this means the radical slice), it is also invoked by wider sections in the West in their own clarion call to do battle with Muslims. Muslim feminist women and men engaged in gender struggle, or what I have called gender activism, are (re)appropriating and rehabilitating the term in their internal struggles for gender justice.[33] The term "gender jihad" was first used by Omar Rashied, the South African struggler against multiple oppressions within the community and wider society, in the 1980s at the height of the anti-apartheid campaign that South Africans called the "Struggle."[34] Islamic feminists (still most often declining the label) are at once intellectuals and activists – indeed, many call themselves "scholar-activists" (the way secular feminists join thinking and activism or theory and practice) – engaging in (re)thinking or *ijtihad* (intellectual struggle to understand) and *jihad* (activist struggle). The connectedness of *ijtihad* and *jihad* is expressed in the fact that the two words come from the same Arabic root. Through its use by Middle Eastern and other Muslim feminists and progressives, and their observers, *ijtihad* is starting to gain circulation in Western societies as a positive enterprise. Perhaps, when others take note of the gender *jihad* of Middle Eastern and other Muslim feminists, they will gain another understanding of the term *jihad*, and will relinquish their essentializing negativity.

A CHAIN OF WOMEN

With these caveats and complexities in mind, I move from discussing discursive structures of the constructions of secular feminism and Islamic feminist to looking at feminism(s)' actors. I construct a *silsila* (chain) of "interpreting women" who have produced feminist discourse, including both those who might be seen as secular feminists and those who could be regarded as Islamic feminists. As might be presumed, the term "interpreting women" signals both "the interpreters" and "the interpreted." I use the word "interpret" to indicate the practice of conducting Qur'anic exegesis (*tafsir*) in the broader sense, approaching Islamic texts through independent reasoning (*ijtihad*), and cultural interpretation or cultural criticism. I suggest how "secular feminists" and "Islamic feminists" alike appropriate Islam in support of women to advocate and agitate (in the mode of the scholar- or intellectual-activist) for change and to eradicate negative thinking and behaviors. In my limited space I present a few examples of women in the much larger *silsila*.[35] I draw my sample from among women who "taught" me as I conducted my historical research and contemporary women from whom I also learned much. I offer but a few illustrative links in a much longer chain. Together we can offer strands in an intertwining garland.

Constructing *silsila*s is a time-honored practice in Islamic history. When Ruth Roded looked at women in Islamic biographical dictionaries and compendia from early to recent times, she found a rich harvest.[36] From the nineteenth century in the Middle East, as part of the rise of women's feminist awareness and new writing and publishing ventures, women created *silsila*s of women. Marilyn Booth has tracked biographical portraits of women in the women's Arabic press, in which some Western women are mingled with the majority, who are Middle Eastern.[37] She remarks on the power of naming and celebrating women, and the subversive work this act can do in transcending old boundaries and suggesting alternative models.[38] In 1944, the Arab Feminist Conference meeting in Egypt voted to create a women's encyclopedia. This dream is now coming into fruition within a broader context in the form of the *Encyclopedia of Women and Islamic Cultures*.[39] Two decades ago, Miriam Cooke and I began to weave women's writings into what we saw as distinctive, feminist threads. A few years later, we published a volume of selected writings of over fifty women organized within a feminist framework suggested by the pieces themselves.[40] In recent years, we began to see increasing explicit employment of Islam in women's writings as we reviewed additional pieces for the second edition of our anthology, which we published in 2004. When names and deeds are assembled and juxtaposed, larger pictures and patterns emerge.

My notion that lineages of secular feminists were clear was shaken when I observed in Egypt that secular feminists and Islamist women both claimed Nabawiyya Musa, a pioneering educator and essayist who was a founding member of the Egyptian Feminist Union (EFU) and a woman known for her fastidious attention to what might be called religious decorum.[41] Indeed, she is a good person with whom to begin the *silsila*. Musa can be called a spontaneous interpreter. Precocious and proficient in Arabic, she recounts how, as a girl around the beginning of the twentieth century, she challenged a cousin studying at al-Azhar with her reading of a Qur'anic verse, and how he admonished her for daring to interpret on her own.[42] Later, Musa attempted to enter the new Egyptian University but was refused, while the mere thought of studying at al-Azhar would have been beyond the wildest imagination of a woman in the first decade of the last century. Musa published a book called *al-Mar'a wa al-'amal* (Woman and work) in 1921, in which she advanced religious and nationalist arguments for women's education and new opportunities for work. She remained scrupulous in her defense of religion as endorsing women's rights and freedom from the oppressive constraints of patriarchal culture.

One of the Middle East's most remarkable interpreters of the Qur'an and other religious texts early last century was the Lebanese scholar Nazira Zain al-Din, who received a thorough training at home in the Islamic sciences at the hand of her father, a distinguished religious scholar. She published a book called *al-Sufur wa al-hijab* (Unveiling and veiling) in Beirut in 1928, making the underlying claim that all Muslims, and this included women, were free to engage in interpretation of religious texts. Zain al-Din argued that women, because of their experience as women, were better equipped to render women-sensitive exegesis, precisely as the African-American theologian Amina Wadud would at the other end of the century in her book *Qur'an and Woman: Rereading the Sacred Text from a Woman's Perspective.*[43] Writing at a time when covering the face was imposed on women and domestic seclusion was enforced among city women – except for the poor, whose labor outside the house was necessary for the material well-being of themselves and their families – Zain al-Din cited the Qur'an and other religious texts to debunk the assertions that these practices were religiously ordained. Applying the same methodology, she also attacked the allegedly Islamic notion of the inferiority of women, which is harder to extirpate from patriarchal cultures than veiling and cloistering practices. Zain al-Din was severely attacked and discredited as "an agent of Western imperialism" and as "spoiled by Christian missionary education:" perennial accusations. She published a second book, *al-Fatah wa 'l-shuyukh* (The young woman and the shaikhs) the following year to answer the hostile criticism that had been heaped upon her. She dedicated her book to "the woman ... because I believe that reform in the East is built upon the foundation of your freedom and struggle for right," and said poignantly: "I delivered my book straight from my room to the nation." Thereafter, Zain al-Din withdrew from public view, living into the final decade of the century that witnessed the rise of Islamic feminism but lost the sustained contribution of this remarkable interpreter.[44]

The Egyptian Zainab al-Ghazali illustrates the complexity of placing and defining interpreting women. In the mid-1930s she was briefly a member of the EFU, which she left after having attended a series of al-Azhar-initiated seminars for women at the Kulliyya Shar'iyya (the Islamic Law College) and going on to form the Muslim Women's Society. She was adamant about conducting her gender activism within the framework of Islamic discourse, assuming greater independence of movement for herself than for "ordinary" women. Al-Ghazali insists that women will find their full liberation in Islam and lauds the principle of "absolute equality" (*al-musawa al-mutlaqa*) of women and men in Islam. Nevertheless, she promotes adherence to conventional patriarchal gender roles and relations in the family for "ordinary" women – but not herself. Al-Ghazali, who clearly sees herself as exceptional, patterns herself after the early women warriors of Islam, whom, she says, "have given as much to Islam than men, even more."[45] Most secular and Islamic feminists take more sharply defined and consistent approaches, which does not mean there were no unaddressed complexities and contradictions.

From the middle decades of the twentieth century, a new set of interpreting women, educated in secular universities, began to appear on the scene. In Egypt, 'Aisha 'Abd al-Rahman (widely known by her pen name, Bint al-Shati') was the daughter of a religiously trained man who disdained his daughter's educational aspirations. She found her way nevertheless, becoming the second woman to earn a Ph.D. and become a professor in the department of Arabic literature at Ibrahim Pasha University (later called 'Ain Shams University). While a student, she contributed articles to the EFU's journal, *al-Misriyya*. Following the 1952 revolution in Egypt, when the socialist state was encouraging all citizens into the national workforce, Bint al-Shati' wrote a series of books on the lives of "women of the Prophet," presented as paragons of virtue and active involvement in the community.

A few decades later, the Moroccan sociologist Fatima Mernissi, a secular feminist, published a book that would be widely regarded as a pioneering text of Islamic feminism, called *Le harem politique*, translated into English (in the British edition) as *Women and Islam: An Historical and Theological Enquiry*. She turned her attention to a study of Hadith (sayings and deeds attributed to the Prophet Muhammad), employing classic Islamic analytical methods, exposing spurious, perennially circulating, female-hostile *hadith*s, and brilliantly deconstructing the misogyny masquerading as Islam that so blatantly "inferiorized" women. In Turkey, feeling the brunt of misogynist *hadith*s hurled at her, Hidayet Tuksal, a Ph.D. student in the faculty of religious studies at the University of Ankara on the eve of the twenty-first century, was also compelled to look more deeply, and went on to make the scrutiny of misogynist *hadith*s the subject of her dissertation, which she later published as a book called *The Traces of Misogynist Discourse in the Islamic Tradition.*[46] Her book attracted wide attention in both "secular" and "religious" circles, and was debated extensively on public television. Although Turkey is "officially secular," popular culture, and even deep-set notions among the élite, are influenced by invidious, patriarchal notions of Islam.

Women concerned with the ideals and practices of republican democracy in the Islamic Republic of Iran and the (officially secular) Turkish Republic became publicly vocal in the 1990s. In Iran, Shahla Sherkat, the founder of *Zanan*, and her colleagues, used the journal as a platform, and were among the first in the early 1990s to issue calls for gender equality and social justice as Muslims and as citizens from within the Islamic Republic.[47] In Turkey, Sibel Eraslan, a lawyer who, as head of the Istanbul women's section of the Refaat Partesi, had helped mobilize huge numbers in successful support of the party, became disaffected when women were subsequently shunted aside.[48] She told me the shallow promises of the Islamist men caused her politicization as a feminist and led to her eventual creation, with other Islamist women, of a legal office for women's human rights.[49] This is a story repeated among Islamist women elsewhere – and, indeed, echoes occasions earlier in the century when secular feminist nationalists were also disappointed by the empty promises made to them to help bring them into the life of the nation.

If in the early and middle decades of the twentieth century secular feminists fought, for the most part successfully, to gain admission for women to the modern secular professions in many countries, they were stymied in the drive to promote the appointment of women as judges, a position associated with religion, as judges serve in cases dealing with *shariʿa*-backed personal status or family law. In Egypt, Tahani al-Jibali, now serving on the High Constitutional Court, reveals that the combination of secular and religious argument in the final stage of the long battle for women to be judges finally won the day.[50] After obtaining her degree in law from Cairo University, al-Jibali secured an M.A. in religious studies at al-Azhar, which equipped her to solidly anchor arguments for gender justice in religious discourse. Suad Salih, professor of Islamic jurisprudence at al-Azhar University and dean of the Girls' College, also a daughter of a religious scholar, is leading a campaign for women to be appointed *mufti*s in Egypt. Her opportunity to become a specialist in Islamic sciences came at the beginning of the 1960s, when al-Azhar, under the direction of the socialist state, simultaneously opened its doors to women and began to offer secular subjects alongside the traditional religious sciences. Like those who taught her, Salih is aware that there are no gender qualifications for the position of *mufti*, but unlike them, she is broadcasting this, and making the call for women to fill this position the focus of the activist campaign she is leading. Along with other women interpreters, she also makes the convincing argument that women can bring their own experience to bear in providing sensitive religious readings to help people, especially women, live meaningful lives in times of change and uncertainty. As there are no religious justifications that can be made to prevent the appointment of women, the arguments of patriarchal culture are advanced to keep women back. At the intersection of the religious establishment and the people, the *mufti* is sensitively located, and enjoys considerable authority and, with it, power.[51]

In Yemen, a woman who uses a combined secular and religious discourse of feminism has made it to the center of the state establishment. Amat al-Aleem Alsoswa, the daughter of a religious judge and a woman who calls herself a feminist, tells how she figured out early in life that Islam held out rights to women that family and society prevented them from enjoying. Recently the first woman appointed as minister, holding the human rights portfolio, she firmly asserts that "women's rights are human rights are Islamic rights."[52] She does not operate with the notion of a split between the secular and the religious, which in Yemen has not been sundered as in so many other parts of the Middle East (beyond the Arabian Peninsula) as the result of a deeply penetrating colonial intrusion. She also understands the interface between the Islamic and universal constructions of human rights.

Early in the twentieth century, thinking/acting women wove a humanitarian discourse into their feminist articulation in demanding the practice of rights and enjoyment of justice by all, naming women among the "all." By the latter decades of the century, women were using the discourse of human rights, declaring its congruence with Islam, and demanding action. I end my *silsila* recitation with a woman vocal in the articulation of human rights, inclusive of women's human rights, the Iranian judge and activist Shirin Ebadi, who has taken the voice and the deeds of what we can recognize as Islamic feminism from within the Middle East, and specifically Iran, to the beyond. Ebadi iterates: "[The] divine book [the Qur'an] sees the mission of all prophets as that of inviting all human beings to uphold justice ... The discriminatory plight of women in Islamic societies, whether in the sphere of civil law or in the realm of social, political and cultural justice, has its roots in the male-dominated culture prevailing in these societies, not in Islam."[53] With the awarding of a Nobel Prize to one of them, in the person of Shirin Ebadi, the world, prodded by such accolades, was able to hear what interpreting women and gender jihadists have been saying. "Authority" is not just a problem within a culture that patriarchy upholds, but a problem of a hierarchical ranking and essentializing of culture/s themselves.

The thinking and actions of these interpreting women-cum-gender jihadists – who include those who self-identify as secular feminists and those who can be seen as Islamic feminists but may simply see themselves as committed, thinking Muslims – vividly indicate the enmeshments of secular and Islamic feminist discourses and projects. Islamic feminist thought is concerned with ideas of equality and justice and their application, while the ideals of secular feminist thought are in accord with the basic principles of religion. By now, halfway into the first decade of the twenty-first century, the gap between secular feminism and Islamic feminism is diminishing, the ability of the proponents of the two feminisms to come together in common cause is increasing, and together these (separate yet united) women face a common problem: it is not so much that the message is discredited (as it is becoming increasingly difficult to pretend that gender equality and social justice are alien to Islam) but the messenger(s). The women of the *silsila* are similarly placed by the seating chart of patriarchy away from the table of authority. But, as we see, the "seating chart" is being disturbed.

THE FUTURE OF FEMINISM(S) IN THE TWENTY-FIRST CENTURY

Islamic feminism, although it has large and ever-increasing numbers of women and more and more men producing and carrying its

message, does not, unlike secular feminism, have a large social movement behind it. This – to turn my historian's telescope forward – I see
as Islamic feminism's next stage. Secular feminists and Islamic feminists are now coming together more and more in the Middle East to
complete women's collective, unfinished business. Together they are
breaking down boundaries and binaries. Secular feminisms, rooted in
national soil and thus deeply local, and Islamic feminism's universal-
ism and global character together are recovering a holistic Islam in
which secular and religious dissolve back into each other. The two
feminisms are producing Islam's gender revolution – indeed, Islam's
revolution in the Middle East, and beyond.

*   *   *

Originally published in the *Journal of Middle East Women's Studies*,
inaugural issue (January 2005), pp. 6–28.

NOTES

1. This chapter represents a continuation of my thinking about the convergences
   and divergences of secular and Islamic feminist discourses in the Middle East
   and beyond. Most recently, I have given talks on the two discourses, with a focus
   on Egyptian experience, at Northwestern University, Loyola University, and the
   University of Wisconsin at Madison. I am grateful to audiences for their insightful questions and comments.
2. For example, 'Abduh's thinking was influential in Indonesia. See James
   Peacock's *Purifying the Faith: The Muhammadiyah Movement in Indonesia*
   (Menlo Park, Calif.: Benjamin/Cumming, 1978).
3. Huda Shaarawi, *Harem Years: The Memoirs of an Egyptian Feminist*, ed. and
   trans. Margot Badran (London: Virago Press, 1986 and New York: Feminist
   Press, 1987 [1986]).
4. Margot Badran and miriam cooke (eds.), *Opening the Gates: An Anthology of
   Arab Feminist Writing*, 2nd ed. (Bloomington: Indiana University Press, 2004
   [1990]); Beth Baron, *Woman's Awakening in Egypt: Culture, Society, and the Press*
   (New Haven: Yale University Press, 1994); Marilyn Booth, *May her Likes Be
   Multiplied: Biography and Gender Politics in Egypt* (Berkeley: University of
   California Press, 2002).
5. Kumari Jayawardena, *Feminism and Nationalism in the Third World* (London:
   Zed Books, 1986).
6. On women's secular feminism(s) and their contexts, there is now an abundant
   literature. On the rise of Arab women's feminist thought see Badran and Cooke
   (eds.), *Opening the Gates*, 1st and 2nd eds. On origins in Egypt see Margot
   Badran, *Feminists, Islam and Nation: Gender and the Making of Modern Egypt*
   (Princeton: Princeton University Press, 1995). On Egyptian feminism in late

twentieth-century Egypt see Nadje al-Ali, *Secularism, Gender and the State in the Middle East: The Egyptian Women's Movement* (Cambridge: Cambridge University Press, 2000). On feminism in Morocco see Fatima Sadiqi, *Women, Gender, and Language in Morocco* (Leiden: Brill, 2003). On women in Syria see Elizabeth Thompson, *Colonial Citizens, Republican Rights and Paternal Privilege and Gender in French Syria and Lebanon* (New York: Columbia University Press, 2000). On women in Palestine see Ellen Fleischmann, *The Nation and its "New" Women: The Palestinian Women's Movement: 1920–48* (Berkeley: University of California Press, 2003). On Iran see Eliz Sanasarian, *The Women's Rights Movement in Iran* (New York: Praeger, 1982). On Turkey see Nukhet Sirman, "Feminism in Turkey: A Short History," *New Perspectives on Turkey*, 3, 1 (Fall, 1989), pp. 1–35. On Sudan and gender discourses in secular and Islamic voices see Sondra Hale, *Gender Politics in Sudan: Islamism, Socialism, and the State* (Boulder: Westview Press, 1997).

7. Margot Badran, "Feminism in a Nationalist Century," *al-Ahram Weekly*, 30 December 1999–5 January 2000, p. 462.

8. I discuss this in Margot Badran, "Toward Islamic Feminisms: A Look at the Middle East," in Asma Afsarrudin (ed.), *Hermeneutics and Honor in Islamic/ate Societies* (Cambridge, Mass.: Harvard University Press, 1999), pp. 159–187, and chapter 9 in this volume, where I stress that Muslims themselves began to label the new gender-progressive discourse Islamic feminism because it is often alleged that this was the invention of Westerners.

9. On this in the case of Turkey, see Nilüfer Göle, *The Forbidden Modern: Civilization and Veiling* (Ann Arbor: University of Michigan Press, 1996) and Badran, "Toward Islamic Feminisms", chapter 9 in this volume.

10. There is an expanding literature on the rise and spread of Islamic feminism. See Hale, *Gender Politics in Sudan*. On the emergence of Islamic feminism in the Middle East, see Badran, "Toward Islamic Feminisms"; and Margot Badran, "Islamic Feminism: What's in a Name?," *al-Ahram Weekly*, 17–23 January– 2002), p. 609. In Iran see Ziba Mir-Hosseini, "Stretching the Limits: A Feminist Reading of the Sharia in Post-Khomeini Iran," in Mai Yamani (ed.), *Feminism and Islam: legal and Literary Perspecitves* (New York: New York University Press, 1996), pp. 285–319; Afsaneh Najmabadi, "Feminism in an Islamic Republic: Years of Hardship, Years of Growth," in John Esposito and Yvonne Haddad (eds.), *Gender, Islam, and Social Change* (New York: Oxford University Press, 1997), pp. 59–84; Valentine Moghadam, "The Emergence of Islamic Feminism," in Valentine Moghadam (ed.), *Modernizing Women: Gender and Social Change in the Middle East*, 2nd ed. (Boulder: L. Rienner, 2003), pp. 215–220. In Egypt see Azza Karam, *Women, Islamisms and the State: Contemporary Feminisms in the Middle East* (London: Macmillan, 1998). In Turkey see Göle, *The Forbidden Modern*.

11. Valentine Moghadam (ed.), *Identity Politics and Women: Cultural Reassertions and Feminisms in International Perspective* (Boulder: Westview Press, 1993).

12. Mir-Hosseini, "Stretching the Limits."

13. In the People's Democratic Republic of Yemen (PDRY, 1967–1990), the most secular state in the region after Turkey, while there was a separation of religion and state, it was less rigid, and indeed Islam was declared the state religion (art. 47 of the constitution). With the unification of North and South Yemen in 1990, the PDRY version of secularism vanished. See Margot Badran, "Unifying

Women: Feminist Pasts and Presents in Yemen," *Gender and History*, 10, 3 (1998), pp. 498–518, and chapter 11 in this volume.

14. Margot Badran, "Gender Activism: Feminists and Islamists in Egypt," in Moghadam (ed.), *Identity Politics and Women*, pp. 202–227, and chapter 6 in this volume.

15. Abdullahi an-Na'im, "The Dichotomy between Religious and Secular Discourse in Islamic Societies," in Mahnaz Afkhami (ed.), *Faith and Freedom: Women's Human Rights in the Muslim World* (Syracuse: Syracuse University Press, 1995), pp. 51–60.

16. Talal Asad, *Formations of the Secular* (Stanford: Stanford University Press, 2003), pp. 206–207.

17. John Esposito, "Islam and Secularism in the Twenty-First Century," in John L. Esposito and Azzam Tamimi (eds.), *Islam and Secularism in the Middle East* (New York: New York University Press, 2000), pp. 1–12.

18. Marie-Aimée Helie-Lucas, "Women, Nationalism and Religion in the Algerian Liberation Struggle," in Badran and Cooke (eds.), *Opening the Gates*, pp. 105–114.

19. I wrote about this in my D.Phil. thesis, "Huda Sha'rawi and the Liberation of the Egyptian Woman," Oxford University, 1977, which the Bodleian Library in Oxford made available for purchase. I published a reworked and expanded version of this as *Feminists, Islam, and Nation: Gender and the Making of Modern Egypt* in 1995. On the trajectory of Islamic thinking on gender over the *longue durée*, see Leila Ahmed, *Women and Gender in Islam: Historical Roots of a Modern Debate* (New Haven: Yale University Press, 1991).

20. Margot Badran, "Locating Feminisms: The Collapse of Secular and Religious Discourses in the Muslim Mashriq," *Agenda*, 59 (2001), pp. 41–57; Margot Badran, "Locating Feminisms: Secular and Religious Discourses, a Selective Look at the Middle East," in Fatima Sadiqi et al. (eds.), *al-Harakat al-nisa'iyyat: al-'asl wa al-tawjihat/Mouvements féministes: origines et orientations/Feminist Movements: Origins and Orientations* (Fes: Centre d'Etudes et de Recherches sur la Femme, Universite Sidi Mohamed ben Abdallah, 2000), pp. 73–88.

21. Anne-Sofie Roald, "The Mecca of Gender Equality: Muslim Women in Sweden," in Haifaa Jawad and Tansin Benn (eds.), *Muslim Women in the United Kingdom and Beyond: Experiences and Images* (Leiden: Brill, 2003).

22. Zillah Eisenstein, *Against Empire: Feminism, Racism, and the West* (London: Zed Books, 2004).

23. For examples concerning Iranian scholars' divergent views see Valentine Moghadam, "Islamic Feminism and its Discontents: Towards a Resolution of the Debate," *Signs*, 27, 4 (2002), pp. 1135–1171. Divergent views on feminism and Islam, occasioned by a piece by Bronwyn Winter on Algeria, were debated in a section on theoretical issues in the *Journal of Women's History*, 13, 1 (Spring 2001). Within the Middle East and Islamic world and between them and the West, see Margot Badran, "Who's Afraid of Islamic Feminism?," *al-Ahram Weekly*, 24–30 October 2001), p. 609.

24. Al-Ali, *Secularism, Gender and the State in the Middle East*.

25. This occurred in the period running up to the 1994 International Conference on Population and Development in Cairo and the 1995 UN International Women's Forum in Beijing, when it was explained that women whose organizations were feminist and not simple "women's organizations" wanted to make the distinction, as the Arabic term *al-nisa'iyya*, which was used for feminist, also signified

"of women." This was also the moment when Islamic feminism was on the rise, although its creators and proponents, as noted, eschewed the label "feminist" in any form.

26. This was the approach taken by the pioneering Egyptian feminist movement, which was influential in the Arab Fertile Crescent countries, and which remained paradigmatic throughout the twentieth century. Regarding Egypt and the Arab Feminist Union countries see Badran, *Feminists, Islam, and Nation*.

27. Jayawardena, *Feminism and Nationalism in the Third World*.

28. Badran, "Toward Islamic Feminisms."

29. Asma Barlas, "Toward a Theory of Gender Equality in Muslim Societies," paper presented at the Fifth Annual Conference of the Center for the Study of Islam and Democracy on Defining and Establishing Justice in Muslim Societies, Washington, DC, 2004.

30. miriam cooke, *Women Claim Islam: Creating Islamic Feminism through Literature* (London: Routledge, 2001).

31. There is a large literature on the subject of "honor and shame" in the Middle East and the wider Mediterranean world. For an early discussion of this in a Middle East and Muslim context see Fatima Mernissi, *Beyond the Veil: Male–Female Dynamics in a Modern Muslim Society* (Bloomington: Indiana University Press, 1987).

32. Omid Safi, "What Shirin Ebadi's Nobel means to Progressive Muslims," in MWU: Muslim Wakeup, online publication, at www.muslimwakeup.com (11 October 2003). On the necessary connection between thinking and action, see Omid Safi, *Progressive Muslims: On Justice, Gender, and Pluralism* (Oxford: Oneworld, 2003).

33. The term "struggle" was used earlier by nationalists fighting colonial hegemony and later by the left to signify the battle against class and imperialist oppression.

34. Farid Esack, *Qur'an, Liberation, and Pluralism: An Islamic Perspective of Interreligious Solidarity against Oppression* (Oxford: Oneworld, 1997); Farid Esack, *Being a Muslim: Finding a Religious Path in the World Today* (Oxford: Oneworld, 2000).

35. The small sample of women in my *silsila* includes those whom I know best through research or, in the case of contemporaries, through personal interactions.

36. Ruth Roded, *Women in Islamic Biographical Collections* (Boulder: L. Reinner, 1994).

37. Booth, *May her Likes Be Multiplied*.

38. In 1879, a Lebanese emigrant to Egypt, Maryam al-Nahhas, published a biographical dictionary of women, and in 1894 another Lebanese woman in Egypt, Zainab Fawwaz, published another compendium of notable women.

39. Published by Brill in Leiden under the general editorship of Suad Joseph, the first volume appeared in 2006.

40. Badran and Cooke (eds.), *Opening the Gates*.

41. Safinaz Kazim, "al-Ra'ida Nabawiyya Musa wa in'ash dhakirat al-umma," *Majallat al-Hilal* (1984).

42. She recounts this in a piece called "Tufulati" (My childhood) in her memoirs serialized under the rubric "Dhikriyyati" (My memories) from 5 May 1938 to 2 August 1942, in the magazine she founded, *Majallat al-Fatah*. I discuss the incident in Margot Badran, "Expressing Feminism and Nationalism in

Autobiography: The Memoirs of an Egyptian Educator," in Sidonie Smith and Julia Watson (eds.), *De/Colonizing the Subject: The Politics of Gender in Women's Autobiography* (Minneapolis: University of Minnesota Press, 1992), pp. 270–293.

43. First published in 1992 in Kuala Lumpur by Penerbit Fajar Bakati and re-published in 1999 by Oxford University Press, New York.

44. The EFU praised Zain al-Din in their journal, *l'Egyptienne*, not long after her book appeared. See Badran and Cooke (eds.), *Opening the Gates*, pp. 257–269; Bouthaina Shaaban, "The Muted Voices of Women Interpreters," in Afkhami (ed.), *Faith and Freedom*, pp. 61–77.

45. For a compelling analysis of al-Ghazali's words and deeds as an Islamic feminist, see cooke, *Women Claim Islam*. See also Valerie Hoffman, "An Islamic Activist: Zaynab al-Ghazali," in Elizabeth Fernea (ed.), *Women and the Family in the Middle East: New Voices of Change* (Austin: University of Texas Press, 1985), pp. 233–254. I discuss al-Ghazali in Margot Badran, "Competing Agenda: Feminists, Islam and the State in Nineteenth and Twentieth Century Egypt," in Deniz Kandiyoti (ed.), *Women, Islam, and the State*, (London: Macmillan and Philadelphia: Temple University Press, 1991), pp. 201–236, and chapter 1 in this volume. Al-Ghazali died in 2005 at the age of 91.

46. Tuksal recounted to me how deeply she was affected by the wanton use of misogynist *hadith*s as an intimidating device: interview with Hidayet Tuksal, Ankara, 28 June 2001.

47. Mir-Hosseini, "Stretching the Limits"; Najmabadi, "Feminism in an Islamic Republic"; Moghadam, "The Emergence of Islamic Feminism."

48. Göle, *The Forbidden Modern.*

49. Interview with Sibel Eraslan, Istanbul, 11 December 2001.

50. Göle, *The Forbidden Modern.*

51. Margot Badran, "Religion, Gender and Authority: The Power to Speak and Be Heard," *American Research Center in Egypt Bulletin*, 183 (Fall–Winter 2002–2003), pp. 20–22.

52. Amat al-Aleem Alsoswa, "Women's Rights are Human Rights are Islamic Rights," in Badran and cooke (eds.), *Opening the Gates*, 2nd ed., pp. 397–404.

53. Taken from her acceptance speech for the Nobel Peace Prize, Oslo: 10 December 2003.

14

ISLAMIC FEMINISM ON THE MOVE

I shall reflect on Islamic feminism, which now is nearly two decades old, and is resolutely on the move. Islamic feminism rearticulates a gender-egalitarian, socially-just Islam rooted in a Qur'anic ethos. It exposes the patriarchal thinking and practice (rampant in the society into which the Qur'anic message was revealed) that insinuated itself into Islam not long after the death of the Prophet Muhammad and that by the ninth century C.E. had been inscribed in books of jurisprudence with the consolidation of the major schools of *fiqh*. The key concepts of Islamic feminism are the Qur'anic principles of gender equality and social justice. Equality and justice cannot be fully actualized within a patriarchal system. Islamic feminism is trying to advance the Islamic message and to expel the traces of patriarchy from Islam.

Islamic feminism aims to recuperate the idea of the *umma* or Islamic community as shared space – shared by women and men equally – and as a pluralistic global community. Islamic feminism transcends dichotomies of East–West, public–private, and secular–religious. It is in opposition to divide and rule, divide and contain, or divide and discipline, which are hegemonic tactics and not an expression of the Qur'anic message.

Islam, uniquely among the three religions of the "people of the book," through its scripture – the Qur'an as the Word of God – introduced a message of the fundamental equality of women and men as human beings (*insan*), women's rights, and social justice, yet this message was subverted in the name of Islam itself. The patriarchal ideas and practices the Qur'an had come to temper and ultimately eradicate (in Arabia and other societies into which Islam was introduced over the centuries) proved highly resistant. Islam was embraced while patriarchy was retained. The hegemonic manipulation was such that the notion of a patriarchal Islam became naturalized, and the inherent contradiction between the revealed Word and patriarchy was obscured and Islam's call for gender equality and social justice was thwarted. It is a sad irony that the only religion that appeared with a message of gender equality embedded in its scripture, as the Word of God, is now considered to be the most patriarchal of all, with the myriad insults and injustices that accompany this. Muslim patriarchalists (in state, society, and family) and detractors of Islam, for their own very different reasons, have over the centuries had a vested interest in perpetuating the fiction of a patriarchal Islam.

In the beginning of Islam was the Word and the Qur'an as the Word of God was the starting point of Islamic feminism. *Ijtihad,* the exercise of rational thinking and independent investigation of religious sources, is the basic methodology of Islamic feminism. The starting point in the elaboration of what came to be called Islamic feminism is *tafsir,* or interpretation of the Qur'an. Two treatises that are considered seminal texts of Islamic feminism – based upon rereadings of the Qur'an – explicate the intersecting notions of gender equality and social justice and deconstruct patriarchy and disentangle it from Islam. They are well known: Amina Wadud's *Qur'an and Woman: Rereading the Sacred Text from a Woman's Perspective*[1] and Asma Barlas's *"Believing Women" in Islam: Unreading Patriarchal Interpretations of the Qur'an.*[2]

I have defined Islamic feminism as a feminist discourse and practice that derives its understanding and mandate from the Qur'an and seeks rights and justice within the framework of the equality of women and men in the totality of their existence as part and parcel of the Qur'anic notion of equality of all human beings (*insan*).[3] It calls for the implementation of gender equality in the state, civil institutions, and everyday life. Islamic feminism rejects the notion of a public–private dichotomy; it conceptualizes a holistic *umma* (Muslim community) in which Qur'anic ideals are operative in all space. It does not seek or endorse the idea of an Islamic state, even though in some places it, of necessity, works within Islamic states.

I see Islamic feminism at the center of a Transformation within Islam, struggling to make headway. I call this a Transformation rather than a Reformation. The Islamic Transformation is not about the reforming of patriarchal claims and practices insinuated into Islam; it is rather about the transforming of what has passed as "Islam" through a realignment of Islam with the Qur'anic message of human equality and social justice. I borrow the notion of "transformation" from the linguistic lexicon connoting the process by which "deep structures" are converted into "surface structures." The Transformation is about restoring the deep Qur'anic message to the surface of awareness and articulation. In this sense the Transformation, we might say, is returning Islam to itself (through the Book); it is not metamorphosing Islam into something else.

Islam is a world religion. The Islamic Transformation is a global phenomenon. Islamic feminism is a global movement. Islamic feminism, like Islam, is not about East and West, and North and South, as geographical locations (physical spaces) or ideological constructions (spaces of the mind). Feminism, as such, is seen by many Muslims as "Western," a code word for "alien to Islam." Such persons are uneasy, at the very least, about the juxtaposition of Islam and feminism. The term "Islamic feminism" is both contentious and tenacious. Terms can crystallize and provide frames for examination and debate. They can also draw fire and be demonized along with what they stand for.

In reflecting on the dynamics of Islamic feminist thinking and practice over the past two decades of its existence I shall look at: (1) the question of naming and claiming; (2) the contexts in which Islamic feminism emerged; and (3) Islamic feminist discourse and activism.

NAMING AND CLAIMING

Phenomena exist, of course, before they are named. To name is to recognize, to bring to attention, to stimulate engagement. Gesturings toward what soon became known as "Islamic feminism" were occurring in the 1980s. It was not, however, until the 1990s that the term Islamic feminism was coined. Some phenomena are named by their creators, while others are named by outsider observers. In the case of Islamic feminism as an emergent discourse, the name was bestowed not by its creators but by witnesses to something new underway. These were Muslim women public intellectuals, journalists, and scholars – who could be described as secularists and feminists – who were sympathetic observers of a turn in gender thinking and practice that they recognized as a new form of feminism: a feminism articulated in an Islamic paradigm. These women coined the term simultaneously in different parts of the globe. In the mid-1990s, I found Muslim women from Iran, Egypt, Turkey, and Saudi Arabia using the term Islamic feminism in print.[4] Their writing locations were to be found in both the East and the West. The term was also circulating orally. When I visited South Africa for the first time at the end of the 1990s I found progressive Muslims using the term Islamic feminism.

The creators of what came to be called Islamic feminist discourse, those who were conducting new *tafsir* or Qur'anic exegesis, were seeking answers in scripture to questions about women and gender, and about equality and justice. Although the Qur'anic message of gender equality and women's rights/human rights they articulated resonated for others as a "feminism within Islam" the pioneering exegetes themselves shied away from the word feminism. This was in part, as some have told me, because of feminism's "Western" associations. Instead they regarded what they were doing as giving voice to another reading of Islam. With time, however, some grew less resistant to the term when applied to them, especially when they saw it defined in a way that reflected their work. Yet the exegetes do not tend to proclaim an Islamic feminist identity. I think it is important to recognize these different approaches to naming and claiming.

The Internet quickly became a rapid transit lane for the flow of the new Islamic feminist discourse and a locus for wide interaction and ongoing debate. By the beginning of the twenty-first century, newer producers of Islamic feminist discourse and expanding numbers of activists, especially the younger generation, were embracing the term Islamic feminism and claiming the identity.

East–West dichotomy

The controversy surrounding the term "Islamic feminism" is connected to the notion that "feminism" is Western and as such alien, if not anathema, to Islam. This idea may arise out of real ignorance or be enlisted as a tool to delegitimize any kind of feminism. The Islamic feminist project itself, whatever it is called, is deeply threatening for many. A focus on terminology conveniently distracts attention from the project itself.

Attention to history demonstrates that feminism has been neither an exclusively Western construct nor monolithic. Feminist ideas and movements originated simultaneously in parts of the East and West. At its most basic, or generic, feminism is a critique of women's subordination and a challenge to male domination (in various contexts in time and space) and includes efforts to rectify women's situation. History shows that multiple expressions of feminism, or multiple feminisms, have been generated over time in diverse locations around the globe.

Muslim women in Egypt, for example, who, together with Christians, embarked on an organized, collective movement for women's rights and liberation in the early 1920s, employed the term "feminism" (precisely in French and more equivocally in Arabic) around the time it first began to be used in the United States, which was not long after it had come to Britain from France, where it had been originally coined. Egyptians and women from various other countries in Asia and Africa in the first half of the twentieth century, as the historical record attests, did not import feminism from the "West." They constructed their own feminisms from an amalgam of nationalist, religious reform and humanitarian discourses, as Kumari Jayawardena shows in her 1986 book examining feminist movements in several Eastern countries from the late nineteenth through the first half of the twentieth centuries.[5]

Not only did Eastern Muslims not borrow from the West, but as feminist nationalists they countered Western colonialism, including the imposition of colonial patriarchal policy and practices, while concurrently as nationalist feminists they struggled against the indigenous patriarchy that was embedded in the state, which had intruded into ideas of Islam and into law enacted in the name of Islam in various national locations, and which was simultaneously rife in the everyday life of family and society. The feminism that Muslim women, together with their compatriots of other religions, created last century was called "secular feminism" to connote a feminism that, like the secular nation, was organized around a nationalist discourse of equality of all citizens irrespective of religion, race, and gender and that recognized and protected religions and the religious affiliations of citizens. Secular feminism was another way of saying national feminism or Egyptian feminism, Syrian feminism, etc.

To allege that feminism is Western not only advertises ignorance of historical experience but serves to perpetuate the notion that has widely circulated in the West that Muslims and Easterners are incapable of generating critiques of patriarchy and female subordination, and incapable of organizing movements to put things right, that is, to produce feminism. As we know all too well, this allegation has been widely used to denigrate Islam and Muslims – and is today the trump card in the hand of Islam-bashing, trotted out to "justify" of all sorts incursions and invasions. Islamic feminism lays claim to its own territory, upholds its own understanding of Islam derived from its own rigorous *ijtihad*, and employs its own language, moving beyond the ideological categories of East and West and related claims of knowledge production, ownership, and authenticity.

Secular–religious dichotomy

While tension has arisen from Western connotations of feminism there has also been tension connected with the terms "secular" and "secularist" and an imposed polarization between secular and religious. Words have histories, and there are moments when meanings are radically altered. The original meaning of the term secular within a Muslim or mixed religion context, as seen in the Egyptian example just cited, did not connote an absence of religion, but an equal embrace of and freedom for all religions within a collective national space. Secular implied a separation of state and religion. However, there were varying degrees of separation. In formerly-colonized Arab countries, for example, there were within the corpus of laws of secular states state-promulgated religious laws in the form of Muslim personal law or family law, as well as state-enacted religion-based family laws for Christians, in countries where they existed.

With the rise of political Islam in the 1970s and 1980s, Islamists (as its protagonists are called) in different parts of Africa and Asia began to re-cast the words "secular" and "secularist" as un-Islamic, anti-Islamic, and even non-Muslim. Meanwhile, the notion of a secular–religious dichotomy became exaggerated. In the context of Islamic revival, Muslim women who began to observe religion with a renewed scrupulosity were referred to as "religious women." These religious women, whether or not they were associated with Islamist groups, were pitted by Islamist forces against secular Muslim women – and especially feminists. Clichés abounded and feminism was recklessly demonized.

The deeper tension, however, was between Muslims as gender-progressives and Muslims as gender-reactionaries. It was a tension between ways of thinking and being Muslim, and between competing definitions of Islam. It was not a simple secular–religious tension, but rather an acrimonious polarization induced and fanned by political Islam (or Islamism). Islamist women and men let it be known through their words and actions that "secular" Muslim women and "religiously defined" Muslim women must be kept apart and in a state of mutual antagonism.

Along with being tarred by the "Western brush," Muslims' feminisms – painted in grotesque and stereotyped ways as a Western aberration – were also tarred by the "secularist brush" as religiously deviant Muslims or anti-Muslim. Women associated with or sympathetic to Islamists claimed that their take on issues of women and gender was the authentic interpretation. Islamist women, along with Islamist men, were instrumental in keeping the tension focused on religion versus secularism, Islam versus the West. They were not interested in free debate on women and gender. Meanwhile, some secular feminists for their part displayed simplistic notions of "religious women," and sometimes conflated patriarchal practices imposed in the name of Islam with the religion itself – precisely the tangled skein Islamic feminism undertook to unravel.

These days there is increasing interaction between secular and Islamic feminists, as well as with women religious scholars (the *'alimat*, who have joined the ranks of the *'ulama*), who possess a vital stock of knowledge. Notwithstanding what some would have us believe, Islamic feminism and Muslims' secular feminism are not in opposition to each other; rather, they are mutually reinforcing. Liberal and progressive women in Muslim societies in the East are increasingly using both the arguments of Islamic feminism and secular feminism. They are also pooling organizational, communications, and academic disciplinary skills to advance the cause of all women. In the complex worlds in which we are variously positioned we all engage multiple discourses and we all possess plural identities, whether or not we publicly assert them.

Islamic feminism is an important chapter in global feminist history, and is making its own unique contributions. Naming helps us to recognize and locate this.

CONTEXTS IN WHICH ISLAMIC FEMINISM EMERGED

If Muslims' secular feminisms burst on the scene as social movements rooted in national space within an overarching nationalist discursive frame in various countries in the East under colonial domination (as well as in Turkey during the decline of empire or Iran under dynastic decline), Islamic feminism surfaced as a new global discourse in different locations in the East and West. By now, however, Islamic feminism's universalist discourse is catalyzing the formation of a broad transnational social movement.

Islamic feminism first appeared in places in the East where movements of political Islam had been around longest and had tried with different degrees of success to roll back earlier feminist gains which often took the form of attempts either to evacuate women from the public sphere (as in Egypt, although this was soon abandoned for strategic reasons) or to control women's appearance and movements in public (such as in Iran, where women were needed in the workforce, especially with the eruption of the Iran–Iraq war). Islamic feminism not only arose among Muslim women from outside movements of political Islam but also among disaffected women inside Islamist groups and parties, as happened in Turkey. Islamic feminism emerged in South Africa following the end of the anti-apartheid struggle, much as secular feminist movements had appeared in the wake of anti-colonial struggles in Muslim societies earlier in the twentieth century.

In various parts of the East Islamic feminism appeared at a time when Muslim women in unprecedented numbers had achieved access to the highest levels of education in all fields and disciplines, including the religious sciences. Islamic feminism emerged as new groups and classes (including recently urbanizing citizens) were confronting the challenges of modernity, and new opportunities and use of space.

Islamic feminism appeared in the West in the context of rapidly growing permanent Muslim populations comprising immigrants, new and second-generation citizens, and growing numbers of converts, of whom the majority are women. Muslim women in Western countries originating from Muslim societies in Africa and Asia were confronted with social practices imposed in the name of Islam that many found difficult to accept, and sought answers through their own investigation of the Islamic religion on issues of gender, equality, and justice. Muslim women converts, many of whom were uneasy with what they saw as conservative cultural norms imposed in the name of Islam, were also impelled to examine the religion for themselves.[6]

ISLAMIC FEMINIST DISCOURSE AND ACTIVISM

Tafsir

The development of Islamic feminist theory is an ongoing process and, as noted, Qur'anic interpretation is at the center of this process. Women as exegetes, whose work is considered foundational to Islamic feminist theory, ask questions of scripture as a timeless text, approaching their quest from the vantage point of their own experience, knowledge, and observation, as all Qur'anic interpreters before them have done and, like them, are rooted in their own time and place. When Islamic feminism articulates a Qur'an-based idea of equality of all human beings irrespective of sex, race, or ethnicity (or tribe) it stresses that scripture makes clear that different attributes – or differences – do not modify human equality. Any modification or qualification would constitute a negation of the basic principle of equality. Islamic feminism also insists that equality is not simply an abstract notion, but must be applied.

Males and females are equal and biologically different. The Qur'an addresses this biological difference where it is significant – that is, in the domain of procreation. Related to equality is the principle of balancing (*tawwazun*). In the context of the conjugal relationship when a woman is involved in childbearing and nursing (which only women can do), the husband is given responsibility to provide material support, which is seen as a balancing of labor. The Qur'an does not lay out specific roles, but instead affirms the notion of the mutuality of the conjugal relationship: that spouses are protectors of each other, or mutual helpers. It is patriarchal thinking that specifies and imposes roles, and does so in a social order that places males above females in a complex hierarchical power grid, justifying this in the name of Islam. The designation of specific roles in the family and society is simply the product of social or cultural construction.

To use biology as a pivot for human inequality in family and society is as absurd as it is un-Qur'anic. To draw lines in space and designate one space private and the other public, or one female and the other male, and to patrol the borders between them is nothing more than social construction and a product of time, place, class, etc. It certainly is not Qur'anically inspired. When confusion sets in, and Islam is used to shore up un-Islamic notions and practices, there is a need to re-articulate the Qur'anic principles, which is exactly what Islamic feminism has set out to do.

Islamic feminism's articulation of gender equality is more radical than Muslims' earlier secular feminist discourse, which articulated the notion of full gender equality in the public sphere but accepted the notion of gender complementarity (rather than gender equality) in the private sphere, and with this accepted the idea of separately ordained roles for women and men and the notion of a male-headed family. This idea reflects patriarchal thinking rather than Qur'anic thinking. The Islamic feminist articulation of gender equality, as integral to full human equality without spatial or contextual limitations, dismantles the notion of an artificial public–private divide, and the idea and practice of gender equality stopping at the border of the private or the family sphere.

If inspiration is drawn from a fresh look at the Qur'an, Islamic feminism is meanwhile applying its renewed understanding of Qur'anic equality and justice to scrutinizing *hadith*s (the sayings and deeds of the Prophet Muhammad) and *fiqh* (Islamic jurisprudence), as important to righting wrongs.

Hadiths

Examination of *hadith*s, or the sayings and deeds of the Prophet Muhammad, using investigative procedures developed within the Islamic sciences, contributes to the elaboration of the Islamic feminist project by rejecting anti-woman elements in what purports to be Islamic concerning women and gender. The words and acts of the Prophet Muhammad, encapsulated and preserved as Hadith, provide guidance in translating the scripture's message into practice, and serve as the highest exemplar of lived Islam. When people use *hadith*s to denigrate women, and to keep them, or put them, in "their place," claiming that they constitute the authentic words and deeds of the Prophet Muhammad, this is tantamount to saying that the Prophet himself was misogynist. Misogynist *hadith*s which fly in the face of Qur'anic principles, and which within the realm of Islamic logic could not possibly be associated with the Prophet Muhammad, have circulated over the centuries as "true," to undermine women. Moroccan sociologist Fatima Mernissi[7] and Turkish religious studies scholar and specialist in Hadith Hidayet Tuksal have both used classic Islamic investigative methodologies to expose misogynist *hadith*s as spurious.[8] Mernissi belongs to the secular feminist tradition. Tuksal is an Islamic feminist, now working with the Dinayet or Department of Religious Affairs in Turkey on a project to remove misogynist *hadiths* from collections that the Dinayet, which oversees 76,000 mosques, publishes, along with other religious books, for broad circulation.

Fiqh

Islamic feminism also investigates *fiqh*, or Islamic jurisprudence. Gender-sensitive critics have found *fiqh* to be markedly patriarchal, reflecting the society in which the foundational schools of jurisprudence were consolidated by the end of the ninth century.[9] The attempt to stop *ijtihad*, or independent rational investigation of religious sources, following the consolidation of the four major schools of jurisprudence, reveals efforts to monopolize thought thenceforth. As two major sources of *fiqh* are the Qur'an and Sunna (encapsulated in the *hadiths*), the new gender-sensitive *tafsir* and deconstruction and exposure of misogynist *hadiths* are crucial to rethinking Islamic jurisprudence. While works of classical *fiqh* reflect patriarchal thinking, *fiqh* is a complex corpus that puts checks and balances on patriarchal thought and contains tools for the implementation of equality and justice. The creators of the classic schools of jurisprudence, it is important to point out, were more cautious than their followers, who have translated this caution into doctrine.

Nowhere has *fiqh* been more pervasively used to disrupt the Qur'anic notion of equality and gender balance than in modern *shari'a*-backed Muslim personal status laws or Muslim family laws enacted as state law.[10] The dual weight of the religious establishment and the state together created the legal scaffolding of the patriarchal family in many Muslim-majority countries in Africa and Asia. From the start Muslim women's secular feminism(s) included demands supported by religious arguments for changes in Muslim personal codes in various Muslim-majority states that would help restore to women their Qur'an-based rights. Generally, they met with very limited success because of the hold of patriarchal politics and its manipulation of religious thought.

Iranian anthropologist Ziba Mir-Hosseini, in her extensive writing on *fiqh*, reemphasizes the distinction (all too often willfully or otherwise overlooked) between jurisprudence deriving from human interpretation and *shari'a* or "the path" as revelation embodied in the

Qur'an. The collapsing of *fiqh* and *shari'a* has created a *cordon sanitaire* around patriarchal constructions of jurisprudence, effectively locking out the ideas and practices of egalitarian readings and practices of Islam.[11]

After the beginning of the twenty-first century there was a signal victory for Islamic feminism and demonstration of how fresh interpretations of *fiqh* can be marshaled to amend Muslim personal laws, bringing them into greater conformity with egalitarian principles. I speak of the Muslim family law in Morocco, the *Mudawwana*, which was overhauled to express and safeguard an egalitarian model of the family. The revised Muslim family law makes wife and husband equal heads of family, virtually eliminates polygamy, and makes it possible for women, along with men, to effect divorce, etc. The legal revisions were made after a long and concerted struggle on the part of feminists, human rights activists, lawyers, scholars, religious specialists, etc. This could be seen as a joint victory for Muslim women's secular feminism(s) and Islamic feminism.

In *fiqh* the patriarchal model does not predominate in the domain of crime and punishment. In Islam it is so onerous to accuse, condemn, and carry out a death sentence for "the crime of adultery" as a departure from what is deemed licit sex in Islam that stringent conditions have been elaborated in *fiqh*, rendering conviction and implementation of death sentences for both sexes virtually impossible. Within Islamic jurisprudence the severe punishment for adultery, it is argued, serves as a strong deterrent rather than a sentence to be meted out. Yet in practice, in countries where *hudud* laws exist, women are often summarily condemned to death, and sentences have been carried out (for example, in Iran, Pakistan, and Saudi Arabia), while the men involved routinely go free. An important exception is the case of Nigeria, where *hudud* or Islamic penal laws were created in the last few years in several northern states. So far there has been no stoning to death of women for adultery. But there might have been had it not been for the rigorous appeals made in higher *shari'a* courts in two high-profile cases involving poor women convicted of adultery and sentenced to death by stoning in the lower *shari'a* courts in states in northern Nigeria. Feminists, NGO activists, lawyers, and Islamic scholars banded together, under the leadership of Baobab for Women's Human Rights and Women's Rights Advancement, and another team was formed by the Women's Rights and Protection Association (WRAPA) to provide a legal defense for two women condemned to death for adultery. Their partners, meanwhile, got off scot-free. The defense culled arguments from *fiqh* that led to acquittals of the two women that now serve as powerful precedents. The cases were won within the framework of Islamic jurisprudence. It may also be noted that Muslim and Christian activists worked together in their NGOs in joint defense of justice for two of their sister Nigerians (in a country where Muslims and Christians are roughly equal in number).

Religious professions

Islamic feminists promote equality for women in the religious public sphere, demanding access to religious professions. It is striking how women have attained remarkable equality in secular professions while they continue to be kept out of most religious professions. The Qur'anic principle of human equality, ironically, does not apply to the domain of the religious public sphere.

Women specialists in Islamic jurisprudence are using their knowledge and training acquired in higher institutions of Islamic learning such as al-Azhar (where they have obtained the same credentials as male scholars, or *'ulama*) to demonstrate that Islamic jurisprudence does not preclude women from entering religious professions such that of mufti, or the dispenser of religious readings called *fatwas*, or judges in religious courts. Suad Salih, a scholar of comparative *fiqh* and professor at al-Azhar, has been leading a campaign for women to be officially appointed to the position of mufti in Egypt. However, in many other Muslim-majority countries, women are appointed as muftis, such as, for example, in Indonesia.

The mosque

Gender equality within the context of the mosque is a contentious issue today. The mosque is the site of public communal worship, weekly congregational prayer on Yaum al-Jum'a (day of gathering), and feast prayers and rituals. When Muslims make the pilgrimage (one of the five pillars of Islam) they find that women and men pray together in the Grand Mosque and appear together in the *mataf* (the circumambulation area) as they circulate around the Ka'ba. This holy site has been place of deeply meaningful ritual practice for Muslims and a powerful symbol of equality (of gender, race, ethnicity, class) where women and men have historically gathered together in prayer in shared space. It has been an exemplar of the ideal and practice of Qur'anic equality – at the site of revelation – while practice in the surrounding country reflects the patriarchal inequalities and injustices that Islam came to redress.

For Muslims in old Muslim-majority countries in Africa and Asia the sense of communal space is broader than the terrain of the mosque. For Muslims living in new communities in the West, as well as for older minority communities in Africa and Asia, the mosque is the physical and symbolical site and center of the Islamic community.

Mosque space and practice in new Muslim communities in the West have reproduced patriarchal templates from the older Muslim societies in Africa and Asia from which Muslim immigrants to the West have come. The mosque has been a spatial expression of a patriarchal ethos: men are accorded the main or central space in the mosque, which they enter directly by a main door, and assume the role of *imam*, leading the communal prayer and giving the sermon, or *khutba*. Women typically enter the mosque through a separate door, and are usually relegated to upstairs, downstairs, or adjacent facilities that are often inferior, cramped, and out of sight or hearing of the *imam* or, if allowed access to the main prayer space, are typically positioned behind rather than alongside men.

Growing numbers of women are now demanding equal access to main mosque space. In 1994 South African women in a mosque in Cape Town (the Claremont Main Road Mosque) pioneered in entering the main mosque space for congregational prayer, sitting in parallel rows with men. The Cape Town mosque, on that occasion, was the site of the first pre-sermon talk to be given by a woman, the visiting American theologian Amina Wadud. In North America women have also claimed equal use of main mosque space for congregational prayer and equal access through the front door. In Morgantown, West Virginia, a few years later, Asrar Nomani led other women in entering the local mosque through the front door and taking their place in the main hall.

In North America women have also paved the way in assuming the role of *imam*, leading women and men in congregational prayer. When Amina Wadud led a group of women and men in prayer in New York in 2004 it attracted a great outcry, but also occasioned discussions in the print and electronic media on the subject. Islamic feminists and women religious scholars referenced the Qur'an and *hadiths* in support of women's equal use of the mosque and of women acting as *imams*. Male religious scholars cited the Qur'an, Hadith, and other religious sources, advancing arguments pro and con.

In arguing for equal access to main mosque space for communal prayer, Islamic feminists have pointed to experience during the pilgrimage to Makka where in proximity to the Ka'ba, the holiest site of Islam, women and men pray together and make the *tawwaf*, or circumambulations in unison. This has been a powerful source of inspiration for women and a sign of their equal place in Islam, and is said to be a continuation of practice since the beginning of Islam. Practice at Makka has been a beacon for women who are reclaiming mosque space and resuming their place in the religious community.

Saudi Arabia recently announced a plan to remove women from the area near the Ka'ba (the *mataf*) and relocate them further away because of lack of space. There was a huge global outcry from women, including women inside Saudi Arabia, protesting, via the media and in a petition campaign (a thousand signatures), their removal as gender discrimination that makes a mockery of the Islamic principle of human equality. They also objected that the decision was taken for women without their participation. Saudi historian Hatoon al-Fassi was vocal in the press, saying the proposal to remove women contradicted women's right "to pray at the holiest place on earth, near the Holy Kaaba" and contravened historical practice from the earliest days of Islam. She also noted that women face constraints at the Prophet's mosque in Madina, where women "unlike men are not allowed to face the grave of the Prophet and can only pass by the side of it."

Less than a month after the plan was announced, the deputy chief of the Presidency of the Two Holy Mosques declared that the move to relocate women had been dropped. In conveying the news, Nasir al-Khuzayyam stressed that "women and men stand on an equal footing in Islam." The announcement came after a strong and concerted global outcry from Muslim women and worldwide attention.

* * *

There is a wide cyber-network of Islamic feminists who share news of local issues and events, and who from near and far support each other as needed – as shown in the case, above, of the *mataf* in Makka. Islamic feminists act both in local and global space as they

demonstrate how discourse and activism continues to feed the elaboration of Islamic feminism.

*　*　*

This chapter originated as a paper presented to a wide audience representing a range of views, as evidenced in the discussion, at the
Conference on Islamic Feminism in Paris (organized by Islam &
Laicité and UNESCO, September 2006). An abbreviated version
under the title "Itlaq al-haraka al-niswiyya al-islamiyya" was published in *Le Monde diplomatique*, editions arabes, November 2006,
and in French, "Le féminism islamique en mouvement," in *Existe-t-il
un féminism islamiquemusulman?* (Paris: l'Harmattan, 2007).

NOTES

1. New York: Oxford University Press, 1999.
2. Austin: University of Texas Press, 2002.
3. Margot Badran, "Islamic Feminism:What's in a Name?," *al-Ahram Weekly*, 17–23 January 2002.
4. Ibid.
5. Margot Badran, *Feminists, Islam and Nation: Gender and the Making of Modern Egypt* (Princeton: Princeton University Press, 1995); Kumari Jayawardena, *Feminism and Nationalism in the Third World* (London: Zed, 1986).
6. Karin Van Nieuwkerk, *Women Embracing Islam: Gender and Conversion in the West* (Austin: University of Texas Press, 2006).
7. Fatima Mernissi, *Women and Islam: An Historical and Theological Enquiry* (Oxford: Basil Blackwell, 1991), trans.Mary Jo Lakeland from the French origi-nal, *Le harem politique* (Paris: Michel Albin, 1987).
8. Hidayet Tuksal, *Kadin Karşiti Söylemin İslam Geleneğindeki İzdüsümleri* (Traces of misogynist discourse in the Islamic tradition, 1st ed., Istanbul: Kitâbiyât, 2000).
9. Barbara Stowasser, *Women in the Qur'an, Traditions, and Interpretation* (New York: Oxford University Press, 1994).
10. John Esposito and Natana J. Delong-Bas, *Women in Muslim Family Law*, 2nd ed. (Syracuse: Syracuse University Press, 2002).
11. See, for example, Ziba Mir-Hosseini, "How the door of Ijtihad was Opened and Closed: A Comparative Analysis of Recent Family Law Reform in Iran and Morocco," *Washington & Lee Law Review*, 64, 4 (Fall 2007), pp. 1499–1511; "Muslim Women's Quest for Equality: Between Islamic Law and Feminism," *Critical Inquiry*, 32 (Summer 2006), pp. 629–645; *Islam and Gender: The Religious Debate in Contemporary Iran* (Princeton: Princeton University Press, 1999). In the realm of personal status or family law based on intepretations of the *shari'a* of the kind that Mir-Hosseini, Aziza al-Hibri, and Farida al-Banani have made, coupled with strategic activism and favorable political circumstances, some victories for gender justice within family law are now being won.

INDEX